Spatial Disparities and Development Policy

Spatial Disparities and Development Policy

Edited by
Gudrun Kochendörfer-Lucius
and Boris Pleskovic

in\Went

Internationale Weiterbildung   Capacity Building
und Entwicklung gGmbH   International, Germany

THE WORLD BANK
Washington, D.C.

ISBN: 978-0-8213-7723-9
eISBN: 978-0-8213-7798-7
DOI: 10.1596/978-0-8213-7723-9

ISSN: 1813-9442

Contents

Part VII: Spatial Policy for Growth and Equity

Part VIII: Wrap-Up Discussion and Closing Remarks

Appendix 1: Program

Appendix 2: Participants

About This Book

The World Bank and InWEnt (Capacity Building International, Germany) hold a Development Policy Forum every fall in Berlin. This meeting, known as the "Berlin Workshop," provides a forum for the European research community to contribute its perspectives to early discussions in preparation of the World Bank's annual *World Development Report*. The Workshop offers new ideas and distinctive perspectives from outside the World Bank. Participants in the Workshop come from a range of academic, governmental, think-tank, and policy-making institutions in Europe, the United States, and the Russian Federation, as well as from the World Bank and the German development institutions. Conference papers are written by the participants and are reviewed by the editors. Participants' affiliations identified in this volume are as of the time of the conference, September 30–October 2, 2007.

The planning and organization for the Workshop involved a joint effort. We extend our special thanks to Indermit Gill, Director of the World Bank's *World Development Report 2009*. We wish to thank Aehyung Kim and Marisela Monoliu Munoz for their advice and suggestions. We also would like to thank the conference coordinators, Marianne Donda, Klaus Krüger, Joachim Müller, and Claudia Schäfer at InWent, and Theresa Bampoe at the World Bank, whose excellent organizational skills kept the workshop on track. Finally, we would like to thank the editorial staff, especially Stuart Tucker and Rick Ludwick, from the Office of the Publisher, and Grit Schmalisch, of InWent for all of their work on this volume.

Introduction

GUDRUN KOCHENDÖRFER-LUCIUS AND BORIS PLESKOVIC

The Berlin Workshop Series 2009 presents a selection of papers from meetings held on September 30–October 2, 2007, at the tenth annual Berlin workshop, jointly organized by InWent–Capacity Building International, Germany, and the World Bank in preparation for the World Bank's *World Development Report* (WDR) 2009. The workshop brings diverse perspectives from outside the World Bank, providing a forum in which to exchange ideas and engage in debate relevant to development of the WDR.

Participants at the workshop discussed challenges and successes pertaining to spatial disparities and development policy. As a country develops, economies of scale tend to result in increasing spatial concentration of industry and services. Agglomeration of economic activities widens the income gap between "leading" and "lagging" subregions within a country and creates a disparity in access to basic public services. Over the course of seven sessions, the workshop explored the interactions of government policies and economic geography in addressing spatial disparities and development.

Macro Trends: Spatial Patterns of Economic Activity, Income, and Poverty

Session I highlights questions regarding typical patterns of income disparities within countries and regions. *Steven Haggblade* describes two parallel movements in economic growth: a spatial shift of population from predominantly rural to predominantly urban settlements and a sectoral shift from agriculture to manufacturing and services. Historically, humans have inhabited rural areas because of

Gudrun Kochendörfer-Lucius is Managing Director of InWEnt – Capacity Building International, Germany.

Boris Pleskovic is Research Manager, The World Bank, Washington, D.C.

Berlin Workshop Series 2009

their agricultural or natural resource-based potential, and agriculture requires physically dispersed production. Thus the spatial distribution of rural population corresponds tightly to agroecological potential. During structural transformation, as productivity gains in the economy drive households to diversify consumption into nonfoods, agriculture's share of total production falls. Because nonfarm production normally benefits from economies of scale, the sectoral shift from agriculture to manufacturing and services drives the spatial movement of population from rural to urban areas. Given the strong economic links between rural areas and the towns that serve them, rural towns frequently grow quite rapidly in prosperous agricultural zones, while they atrophy in stagnant rural economies. As a result, both the pace and the structure of urbanization depend, in part, on the dynamics under way in agriculture and the rural economy.

Peter Lanjouw examines spatial patterns of rural poverty in the developing world using detailed estimates of rural poverty at a spatially disaggregated level—derived from an ongoing program of research on small-area estimation of poverty and inequality—with geographically referenced information on agricultural potential and proximity to urban centers. Lanjouw examines the association between rural poverty and "marginality," focusing on the five developing countries of Brazil, Cambodia, Ecuador, Kenya, and Thailand. "Marginal areas" are defined as arising through a combination of low agricultural potential and remoteness. The paper brings together a set of tentative stylized facts about rural poverty and location to pose a question for policy concerning the desirability of crafting an explicit strategy of urban development that focuses on small towns.

New Economic Geography and the Dynamics of Technological Change: Implications for Less Developed Countries

Session II debates the pattern of urbanization and economic activity between and within countries and its implications for development policy. *Eduardo Haddad* presents experimental results derived from a spatial computable general equilibrium model for the Brazilian economy. In the Brazilian case, firms can exploit increasing returns to scale without serving a national market due to market imperfections associated with transportation costs that essentially serve to segment markets. Furthermore, the asymmetries in the distribution network due to the primacy of São Paulo serve to strengthen existing competitive advantages. Haddad argues that research on the new economic geography in recent years has identified some important theoretical inconsistencies between competitive regimes, conceptualized by space-less and spatial economies. The challenges to competitive equilibrium in the spatial economy presented by the new economic geography remain largely untested. He offers one approach to narrow the gap between theory and empirical application. The Brazilian economy, sharing features of both developed and developing countries, presents a further challenge: the lack of uniformity of the spatial distribution of resources and population, the glaring disparities in welfare across states and regions, and the presence of a hegemonic economy, in São Paulo, that renders traditional computable general equilibrium modeling of limited value.

Ingo Liefner argues that the diffusion of technology has never leveled the spatial concentration of knowledge and that applying complex technologies requires a profound and often subject-related knowledge. The cumulative character of certain technologies fosters spatial differentiation between leading and lagging regions with respect to technology. Knowledge disparities and related economic disparities widen most quickly in developing countries that open up for trade, foreign direct investment (FDI), and related technology transfer. During phases of fast technological catch-up, the absorption of technology in the technologically leading regions within newly industrialized countries is more powerful and faster than the trickle down of technology into lagging regions. For example, China's spatial economy illustrates that fast technological catch-up depends on and produces spatial concentration of human capital, technology, and FDI. If developing countries wish to benefit from technology that is accessible through inward FDI, it is crucial to help the leading urban regions to create an economic environment suitable for learning. As a complement, developing countries have to accept that many other urban areas will have to concentrate on less technology-oriented industries, such as labor-intensive manufacturing.

Perspectives: Rural-Urban Transformation: Leading, Lagging, and Interlinking Places

Session III covers urbanization processes and resulting challenges for lagging regions. *Mantang Cai* presents China's success in its economic reform over the last 30 years, starting with reforming the agricultural sector and then opening up coastal areas. He argues that agricultural reform contributed a great deal to improving the general livelihood of the rural population despite its marginal contribution to gross domestic product (GDP) growth. However, under the GDP-focused development process, China's economic reform policy quickly shifted its focus to urban-based industrial development, particularly in the coastal areas. This development process has resulted in an increasing disparity in multiple dimensions, particularly between urban and rural areas and between the east and the west. At the same time, farmers' income growth slowed down after the 1990s, with a widening income gap between rural and urban areas. In recent years, the Chinese government has recognized the disparities and initiated several new development policies, including new development plans for the western, northeast, and middle regions. At the same time, rural development has again become a focus of the government's development policy, generally understood as the *San Nong* issues (three rural development issues, that is, agriculture, countryside, and farmers). Under the new development policy, a great deal of government investment has been directed to support rural development through various programs, and development policy in general has shifted from "GDP-illustrated" development to the "construction of a harmonious society." In this context, Cai lays out key issues facing rural development policy.

Frank van Oort and *Philip McCann* view urbanization as being influenced predominantly by regional disparities in potential economic growth. In explaining this, they note an increase in the use of geographic models in economic analyses, given the failure of orthodox economics to explain adequately the variation in the wealth and poverty of areas. However, questions remain concerning why firms decide to locate in particular areas and which kind of agglomeration is needed to foster localized growth. Rooted in the new growth theory, this "rediscovery" of space in economics has led to an extensive empirical literature on which spatial circumstances give rise to agglomeration externalities that *endogenously induce economic growth*. Van Oort and McCann emphasize the importance of economic complementarities, as these can stimulate growth in a system (network) of cities—that is, the sum is more than its parts. Local specializations in urban networks might help cities in developing countries to integrate functionally with their regions.

Spatial Disparity and Labor Mobility

Session IV focuses on migration processes and their consequences for regional development. *Ángel de la Fuente Moreno* examines the case for using education as a regional policy tool in Spain. Drawing on the results of some recent work in collaboration with Rafael Doménech, de la Fuente Moreno examines the evolution of regional educational disparities in Spain during the last four decades and the prospects for further educational convergence in the future. He also analyzes the determinants of regional productivity in Spain, paying special attention to the role of human capital. He finds that education is an important source of regional income disparities. He estimates the social return to investment in different types of productive assets in each territory and draws some tentative conclusions regarding the changes in our pattern of investment that may help to speed up the growth of the country as a whole and to reduce internal inequality.

Adama Konseiga argues that parental migration is often found to be negatively correlated with child health in Africa, although the causal mechanisms are poorly understood as a result of limited data. Konseiga uses a data set that provides information from the respondent parent on child morbidity in both rural and urban settings and addresses the analytical weakness of previous studies assuming that the health environment is exogenous. He finds that households first endogenously determine whether they will gain from participating in migration and, if they will, decide whether to leave the children behind or not. The final choice is made to ensure the optimal survival chances for the child. Konseiga highlights the importance of understanding the health consequences of raising children in the context of slums and increasing urban poverty in Nairobi, Kenya. His findings indicate that households in the slums of Nairobi who migrated together with their children experienced higher child morbidity than households who adopted the split-migration strategy, leaving children in their up-country home. Even though children of migrants are safer up-country, not all households can afford this strategy. Households are able to choose this strategy only if they have a strong social support network in their community of origin or a large number of household members. This is an important finding in targeting the Millennium Development Goals (MDGs) because the split strategy involves policies that facilitate the costly monitoring of family members left up-country.

Roman Mogilevsky and *Aziz Atamanov* present the framework of the Asian Development Bank study on remittances and poverty in Central Asia and the South Caucasus, which analyzes the impact of remittances on the macroeconomic situation and financial sector development in the Kyrgyz Republic. The analysis is based on surveys of representative households and remittance recipients as well as on a database of international monetary transfers created by the National Bank of the Kyrgyz Republic. Analysis of the data reveals methodological problems with measuring remittances in the Kyrgyz Republic and allows the identification of remittance-sending patterns, including the countries of origin for remittances and the typology of senders and recipients, among others. The results of the analysis indicate that Kyrgyz migrants' remittances become an increasingly important force driving development of the country's economy and, in particular, its financial sector.

Africa: Rethinking Growth and Regional Integration

Session V refers to the distinct patterns of spatial development in select African countries, combining agglomeration without noticeable economic growth. The session discusses which elements of economic development strategies could be implemented. *Hassen Mohamed* explains that South Africa's spatial economy is characterized by social and economic disparities that have evolved historically over a long period of time. The unevenness in spatial development is unique, however, in that it is the product of both established patterns of growth that have persisted since the early twentieth century as well as the oppressive system of apartheid. In 2003 the South African government adopted the National Spatial Development Perspective (NSDP). The NSDP was updated in 2006 and serves as an overarching framework in which to coordinate infrastructure investment across government. It provides guidelines to enable government to ensure that the infrastructure investment and development programs achieve spatial outcomes consistent with the objectives of fostering economic growth, addressing poverty, and promoting social cohesion. Mohamed reviews the purpose and rationale of the NSDP as a distinctive policy response of government to the stark social and economic dualism evident in South Africa's spatial landscape.

Wim Naudé argues that, to overcome disadvantages due to unfavorable geography, four issues need to be prioritized in regional cooperation in Africa: transport infrastructure, trade facilitation, decentralization and local economic development, and migration. Efforts to improve the credibility of regional agreements on transport infrastructure could be included in World Trade Organization (WTO) binding rules on trade facilitation, and attention could be given to the development of transport corridors. In support, the international community could focus on linked aid, ensuring adherence to the international rights of landlocked countries, provide trade preferences to Africa, and align those trade preferences with current African regional integration initiatives.

Learning from Europe's Efforts at Integration and Convergence

Session VI is devoted to lessons learned from European experiences with special reference to select instruments of the European Union's regional policy. *Nicola de Michelis* examines the role and objectives of European cohesion policy. He argues that the policy has accompanied the construction of the single market and has functioned as a regulatory mechanism to accompany the structural adjustment of weaker economies. He explains that European cohesion policy has multiple objectives linked to redistribution, allocation of resources, and political legitimacy. However, debate tends to concentrate on the first of these objectives, although the others are equally important. Paradoxically, de Michelis observes, cohesion policy is receiving more interest outside the European Union than within. Indeed, as recent formal agreements with many third countries suggest, European cohesion policy is perceived as a unique experiment in governing a regional integration zone. Despite its successes, the policy needs to evolve, and many difficult questions remain, in particular related to the issue raised by the recent Organisation for Economic Co-operation and Development (OECD) report on the European Union: how can the policy become more performance based?

Rolf J. Langhammer summarizes the experiences with European convergence funds and examines whether lessons can be drawn for similar endeavors in African integration schemes. Empirical evidence on the European Union (EU) experience shows a large variance with respect to the effects of funds on economic growth in Europe. Side conditions such as "good policy conditions" are found to be necessary, but not sufficient, for success. Similarities to the debate on aid effectiveness are striking, pointing to the importance of diminishing returns to scale, endogeneity, and reverse causality. EU experiences are not easily transferred to African integration schemes because the uniqueness of "deep integration" and a strong regulatory framework in Europe prevents easy copying or even adaptation. Rather than redistributing African taxes between the members of integration schemes that, in most cases, did not work well in the past, Langhammer suggests considering financing convergence funds from the EU side in the European Partnership Agreements as a way to balance efficiency and equity, the latter being so important for African integration to succeed.

Philippe Martin analyzes some of the theoretical and empirical arguments that serve to legitimate regional policies in Europe. He reviews the existing evidence that European integration has led to a process of convergence between countries but not between regions within countries and suggests mechanisms through which this may have occurred. Taking the example of France, Martin shows that, in the past 20 years, regional divergence in production has indeed increased. However, the geography of incomes has, during the same period, become more equal, producing a "scissors effect" between the geographies of production and income. This suggests that transfers, which have nothing to do with regional policies, have, at least in France, more than compensated the increase in production inequality. Hence, "regional convergence" is not a synonym of "regional cohesion," at least at the national level. Martin also reviews evidence on a possible trade-off between growth and regional inequalities to suggest that regional policies are difficult to defend on grounds of efficiency. Both evidence and theory suggest that regional concentration leads to efficiency gains. This also implies that the EU is faced with a choice it has tried to avoid until now. Either it puts its effort in slowing or even reversing the process of spatial economic concentration at the national level, or it concentrates on policies to speed up the convergence between poor and rich countries. Finally, Martin analyzes the relation between spatial and social inequalities. He reports empirical evidence for Europe that suggests a strong empirical relation between the two: even after controlling for transfers and other possible determinants of individual inequalities, he finds that countries with more regional inequalities also have more individual inequalities.

Spatial Policy for Growth and Equity

Session VII explores regional policy options from the perspective of economic and social development and addresses current development challenges and issues of multicountry strategies for regional cooperation. *Grzegorz Gorzelak* explains that the meaning of cohesion—a term crucial for the policies of the European Union—has recently been broadened to embrace its territorial dimension, supplementing the two traditional ones: economic and social. This creates grounds for discussing the meaning of territorial cohesion.

Traditionally, territorial cohesion has been attached to convergence—that is, to equalization of the levels of development of the territorial systems. However, that convergence is very difficult to achieve in practice. In the EU there has been convergence between the member states, but more divergence between regions. Gorzelak asks whether policy should aim to reach a goal of regional convergence that is not achievable. Moreover, directing limited resources to a convergence-driven cohesion policy may weaken the global competitiveness of the EU. Gorzelak contemplates disconnecting cohesion from convergence and suggests attaching convergence to a functional meaning of cohesion. Territorial cohesion would then mean an arrangement of the EU space that would allow for more economic and social cohesion that relies on cooperation and linkages among firms, institutions, territorial communities, and individuals across the EU territory.

Peter Nijkamp argues that spatial disparities reflect differences in regional growth and productivity and calls for a profound analysis of their driving forces. He offers a concise and selective overview of various elements of regional development theories. Starting from traditional regional growth theory, Nijkamp introduces findings from location and agglomeration theory, including infrastructure and network modeling, with a particular emphasis on spatial accessibility. Next, innovation, entrepreneurship, and knowledge are addressed and interpreted as critical conditions for successful regional development. Elements from endogenous growth theory and the new economic geography are introduced as well. Nijkamp highlights significant contributions from the social capital school, as they may be particularly relevant for enhancing regional productivity. Finally, he pays attention to the regional convergence debate, concluding with some prospective views on spatial disparity analysis.

Federico Bonaglia, Nicolas Pinaud, and *Lucia Wegner* note that strong commodity prices are driving Africa's growth, which should be about 6 percent in 2007 and 2008. Nevertheless, commodities are only part of the story, and oil-importing countries have registered record growth thanks to better macroeconomic policies, improved political stability, and favorable harvests. The challenge for oil-exporting countries will be to ensure that a large proportion of the proceeds from the minerals sector is invested in infrastructure and human capital development in order to support medium- and long-term needs for diversification. Oil-importing countries will need to contain inflationary pressures now running into double digits as a result of oil price increases and to finance or contain increases in their current account deficits. Globalization—the deepening of financial and trade integration associated with technological progress and multilateral liberalization—is creating unprecedented opportunities for developing countries to accelerate growth and lift millions of people out of poverty. African countries need to be among the beneficiaries. The rapid growth of the Asian emerging economies can offer this opportunity, as it is creating demand for Africa's commodities (oil, metals, and precious stones) and resulting in improved terms of trade. There are still risks and uncertainties, but they can be reduced by strengthening the internal capacities of African countries and nurturing the private sector in order to realize fully the opportunities that globalization creates, while adequately coping with the risks.

Keynote Address

INDERMIT GILL

The organizers of this workshop plan to serve up a feast of ideas over the next two days. I provide just a small appetizer. First I summarize the motivation for the *World Development Report* (WDR) and its likely messages, and then I briefly discuss the contents and structure for the report.

The motivation for the report comes from two stylized facts:

- As countries develop, economic activities become more spatially concentrated. That is, economic activity is packed geographically more tightly in developed than in developing countries. Coastal regions account for 20 percent of China's land mass, but 50 percent of its economic output. Tokyo has 4 percent of Japan's land area but generates 40 percent of its output. The area around Paris constitutes only about 2 percent of France's land mass but accounts for 30 percent of its economic output.

- Spatial disparities in welfare levels, such as household income, consumption, and poverty, and in standards of education and health are much smaller in developed than in developing countries. For example, while otherwise similar households have consumption levels that are, on average, more than 75 percent higher in leading than in lagging regions in developing countries, this ratio falls to less than 25 percent in developed countries such as Canada, Japan, and the United States.

The main point is that spatial concentration of economic activities and spatial disparities in welfare levels are not the same thing: one goes up with development, while the other goes down. These two stylized facts raise several questions:

- The first is whether, as countries grow, market forces automatically bring about *both* of these changes: rising concentration of economic mass and falling spatial disparities in living standards.

Indermit Gill is Director, World Development Report 2009. The World Bank, Washington D.C.

Berlin Workshop Series 2009
© 2009 The International Bank for Reconstruction and Development/The World Bank

- A related question is whether these patterns are linear or not linear, monotonic or not monotonic. That is, do spatial disparities first rise and then fall, or do they fall monotonically? Does concentration keep rising monotonically, or does it first rise and then fall?

- A third question is whether governments have helped or hindered these spatial transformations. More positively, what should governments in developing countries do to shape them?

Let me tell you what might be the overall message of the WDR, although we are still at an early stage in our work, and we still have lots to do. At this point, the main message of the report could be something like this:

- First, economic concentration is generally good for development and should not be resisted by governments; in some cases, it should even be encouraged.

- Second, large, growing, or persistent spatial disparities in economic well-being are not good for development and should not be ignored by policy makers.

- Third, the general principle for getting both the economic benefits of concentration and the social benefits of equity is integration: integration of urban and rural areas within countries, integration of leading and lagging regions within countries, and integration of well-connected and isolated countries within world regions.

Just as researchers often start with working hypotheses and then refine or change them as the research results come in, at the World Bank we often start with "tentative overall messages" and then refine or change them as the work progresses. Think of this as the policy equivalent of a working hypothesis. Workshops like this one are critical in getting the focus right.

Presuming for now that this message is indeed the one that we would like to convey to readers of the WDR, how do we propose to convey these messages in the report? Essentially, we aim to do three things:

- Characterize in a simple, easily remembered way the spatial transformations that come with development and that are necessary for economies to develop. We intend to do this by examining changes in three spatial dimensions: rising density, falling distance, and persisting division.

- Identify the main drivers of these spatial transformations. We intend to do this by looking at the interplay of economies of scale, mobility of productive factors, and costs of transport and trade. This interplay has been identified in the academic and policy work as key for understanding both spatial concentration and equalization.

- Assess whether and how governments have exploited these insights, or how they can exploit them to better integrate markets, taking into account the role of natural endowments, social and cultural factors, and political structures. Here we intend to address three policy debates: the debate on the role of urban versus rural development in speeding growth and poverty reduction, the debate on how best to help lagging regions within countries, and the debate on regional versus global integration.

The report will accordingly have three parts, each describing, explaining, or drawing lessons from the spatial transformations that have been observed in both developed and developing countries.

The first section of the report will be factual and present the stylized facts on economic concentration and welfare disparities, for both developing and developed countries, over the last two centuries. It will have three chapters. The first chapter will document the increase in density through the rising concentration of economic activities in cities. It will survey the evolution of disparities between rural and urban areas and within urban areas. The second chapter will document the decline of distance as firms and people move closer to domestic and international markets. In particular, it will examine the evolution of lagging and leading regions within countries, both in terms of concentration and in terms of differentials in living standards. The third chapter will document the persistence of division between countries, which can hinder increased concentration and the movement of labor, capital, goods, and services. In particular, it will document the concentration of economic activities in some regions of the world and assess whether these regions have seen greater international convergence in living standards than other world regions.

The second part of the report will identify the main drivers of these changes, distilling the insights provided by the advances in economic thought over the last two decades. In essence, the objective is to exploit these insights to identify the sharpest instruments for getting both good concentration and sustainable differences in living standards. It will have three chapters, one on each of the factors identified as critical in analyses that formally recognize the importance of increasing returns: economies of scale that are associated with people and places, mobility of capital and labor, and costs of transporting goods and services. Put another way, these chapters will each focus on a facet in the interactions between the forces of agglomeration, migration, and specialization.

The first chapter will exploit the insight that comes from the new economic geography literature: for scale economies, it is not the size of the city that matters, but the composition of activities that are located in the city. It will provide evidence on the size and sources of these scale economies, for both developing and developed countries, and try to identify the policy implications of these findings. The second will exploit the insight that comes from the new economic growth, which highlights another aspect of scale economies: other factors move to where they are scarce, while human capital moves to where it is plentiful. That is, unlike other factors, human capital reaps a higher reward in places where it is abundant. The third chapter will exploit the fundamental insight that comes from the new international trade literature: a decline in transport costs increases trade with neighboring countries more than it increases trade with distant countries.

The third section of the report will discuss the policy implications, in essence identifying the public policy priorities that help countries to realize the immediate economic benefits of greater concentration and the social and long-term economic benefits of moderate spatial disparities. These chapters will emphasize the importance of integrating places where economic mass is concentrated with places where it is not. All three of the policy chapters will be "two-handed chapters."

The first will look at the urban and rural prerequisites for sound urbanization strategies. In terms of factors of production, *land* will figure prominently, as the rural-urban transformation depends critically on land improvements, land use regulations, and property rights. The second will examine the priorities for both lagging and leading regions for achieving successful territorial development. In terms of factors of production, *labor* will figure prominently. Policies to increase the mobility of labor, or second-best policies for regions where labor is not mobile, should figure prominently in this chapter. The third will identify the priorities for connected and isolated countries to achieve successful facilitation of regional trade, so that even small, poor countries can exploit the benefits of concentration and share the gains from trade. In terms of factors of production, *intermediate inputs* should figure prominently in this chapter.

Put another way, the first part of the report will examine and contrast the experience of developed and developing countries. For example, let us say that, based on a cross-sectional comparison of countries at different stages of development, the report shows a rising spatial concentration of economic activities, but a convergence in living standards between places where economic activity is concentrated and places where it is not. That is, it may find that living standards are not as different between the northeastern and southern parts of the United States as they are between the northeastern and southern parts of Brazil or between the coastal and interior regions of China. Or it may find that differences in living standards between Delhi and rural northwestern India are much greater than those between Paris and its surrounding rural areas.

Let us also say that the report finds that concentration is increasing in China or in India, but that rural-urban or regional disparities are also increasing. That is, a time-series analysis yields concentration and divergence, while a cross-sectional analysis shows concentration and convergence. This contrast should lead to three questions:

- Is this a normal phase that developed countries also experienced?

- Is the phase occurring because this is a different era than the one during which today's industrial countries developed?

- Is the phase occurring because today's developing countries are missing policies that are present in today's developed countries?

The structure of the report is well suited for answering these three questions:

- Part I should help to answer the first question; that is, did spatial disparities first rise and then fall in today's developed countries?

- Part II should help to answer the second: can theory developed over the last two decades help us to understand how things are different now? Technological advances have made it possible to exploit scale economies more today than earlier. Capital is more mobile today, and so is human capital, but the potential for international migration is much lower today for unskilled workers than it was when today's developed countries were poorer. And the costs of communication and transport have fallen, more for the former than for the latter. Not coincidentally, these are the "second-nature geography" factors that the theory identifies as important for understanding the spatial transformation of economies.

- Part III should ideally answer the third question: if this is not a normal phase, are today's developing countries not doing something that developed countries did? Or, if it is a normal phase, but it is also a different era, do today's developing countries have to do less or more or something different?

In essence, the report will emphasize that neighborhoods are important for development. This is true for cities, for regions, and for countries: it is difficult for a city to prosper in the middle of a squalid countryside, it is difficult for a province to prosper rapidly when other provinces in the country are squalid, and it is difficult for a country to prosper for long when the countries around it are mired in squalor.

The report will propose that the solution for cities, regions, and countries is to invest in neighborhoods. The principle is to deepen integration and not to attempt isolation.

Keynote Address
Rethinking Economic Growth
in a Globalizing World:
An Economic Geography Lens

ANTHONY J. VENABLES

Recent work in trade and economic geography provides a lens through which to assess trade, globalization, and economic growth. This strand of research investigates the way in which globalization shapes countries' growth prospects and draws out policy implications. Analysis is based on three facts about the technology of trade and modern sector production. The first is that modern sector activity is surrounded by increasing returns to scale deriving from many sources, including social, political, and economic. The second is that space still matters, both in defining the geographic scope of these increasing returns and in shaping economic relationships more broadly. The third is that globalization is changing the nature of international trade, in particular, by facilitating the fragmentation of production.

These facts support a view of the world different from that offered by standard trade or growth theory, although consistent with the evidence. In particular, there are equilibrium disparities between regions of the world and between subregions within countries. Rapid economic growth can occur and is likely to be associated with growth in the modern export sector. It will typically be "lumpy" in three senses. First, in geographic space growth will be uneven, being concentrated in some countries, regions, or cities. Second, in product space these regions are likely to be narrowly specialized, perhaps even specializing in a few tasks rather than in the production of integrated products. Third, temporally, growth will be rapid, but only once some threshold level of capabilities has been reached. Growth will tend to be sequential rather than parallel, with certain regions growing very fast, while others lag behind. Both middle-income and very low-income regions will tend to be left behind in this process.

This is a world in which there are many market failures and associated policy questions. Given the importance of increasing returns to scale, how can countries or regions reach the threshold at which they become attractive as export bases for

Anthony Venables is Professor of Economics at the University of Oxford and Chief Economist in the Department for International Development (DFID) in the United Kingdom.

Berlin Workshop Series 2009

manufacturing and at which they start to benefit from increasing returns? How should we understand the economic relationship between regions or countries? Do developments in one region complement or compete with developments in another?

The discussion of these issues starts by laying out the facts and then draws out implications and some policy messages.

Modern Trade and Production

Three facts about the technology of modern trade underlie our thinking.

Increasing Returns

Increasing returns are inherent to much modern sector activity.[1] They arise through a wide variety of mechanisms, some narrowly technical and others to do with wider socioeconomic feedbacks. Increasing returns may be internal to the firm—average costs fall with the length of the production run—but their implications for the performance of the economy are greatest if they are external, between rather than within economic units. What are the sources of such external economies of scale?

One category is technological externalities, such as knowledge spillovers when one firm benefits from the knowledge capital of another. The mechanism through which knowledge transfer occurs may be labor mobility, face-to-face social contact between workers, or observation of the practices of other firms. Such effects are particularly important in innovation-intensive activities, and a large literature points to the spatial concentration of innovative activities (for example, Audretsch and Feldman 2004). Location-specific knowledge spillovers also arise if firms learn about the characteristics (such as the productivity) of the location and are unable to keep their knowledge private, as in the "self-discovery" story of Hausmann and Rodrik (2003). This may be a story of learning about the real characteristics of locations or simply a story of "herding," as firms choose to copy the location decisions of other (successful) firms.

Possibly more important than technological externalities are pecuniary externalities. In an imperfectly competitive market there are allocative inefficiencies, and these inefficiencies may depend on the size of the market. Increasing returns arise if increasing the size of the market brings about a reduction in these inefficiencies. For example, in goods markets, there is a trade-off between having firms large enough to achieve internal economies of scale without becoming monopolists. Increasing market size shifts this trade-off, allowing the benefits of both large scale and more intense competition; as a consequence, firms will be larger, operating at lower unit costs and setting lower prices. If firms have different levels of productivity, then a larger market and the associated increase in competition will cause firms with high productivity to grow and firms with low productivity to exit. This argument supports the empirical finding that much of the gain from trade liberalization is due to a change in the mix of firms within each sector, favoring high-productivity firms at the expense of low-productivity firms. A larger market will also support a greater variety of products. These price and variety effects benefit consumers and also, if the goods are intermediates, benefit firms in downstream sectors. For example, a larger market will support a greater variety of specialized input producers, tailoring their products to the needs of other firms. Downstream firms benefit from this variety, while upstream firms benefit from the large number of downstream firms. This is simply a modern restatement of old ideas of forward and backward linkages— that is, firms benefit from the proximity of both suppliers and customers (see Fujita, Krugman, and Venables 1999).

In addition to efficiency gains deriving from the size of the goods market, there are also gains from operating in a large labor market. The larger the pool of workers that a firm can access, the more likely it is that the firm will find the exact skills that suit its needs (see Amiti and Pissarides 2005). If firms are subject to idiosyncratic shocks, then a larger labor market will expose workers to less risk, increasing the probability of reemployment if they are made redundant. A large labor market will increase the incentives for workers to undertake training. This argument, like some of those in the product market, turns on increased intensity of competition. In a small market, workers who acquire specialist skills may be "held up" by monopsonistic employers, so there is no incentive for them to invest in skills. The presence of a large number of potential employers removes this threat of opportunistic behavior and thereby increases the incentives to undertake training (Matouschek and Robert-Nicoud 2005).

A further set of arguments, relating to density of activity as much as to scale of activity, has to do with communication between workers. In many activities, face-to-face communication is important (Storper and Venables 2004). Face-to-face contact enables higher-frequency interchange of ideas than is possible by e-mail, phone, or video conference. Brainstorming is hard to do without the ability to interrupt and use parallel means of communication—oral, visual, and body language. Face-to-face communication is also important for building trust, once again by enabling one to observe the body language and a wide range of other characteristics of one's interlocutor. By breaking down anonymity, face-to-face contact enables networks of the most productive workers to develop and promotes partnerships and joint projects between these workers. All of these considerations enhance productivity.

Increasing returns are also common in the provision of public sector goods and services, and again there are several mechanisms. The simple one is technological: many publicly provided services are also public goods and so (by definition) have declining average cost. An important twist on this is that many inputs, including public services and utilities, have a complementary relationship when used in production (see Kremer 1993). Efficiency in the production of goods requires a continuous supply of electricity *and* water *and* roads *and* security. If any (or all) of these inputs is subject to increasing returns, then returns to scale for the package as a whole are amplified.

Increasing returns in the provision of public sector goods, services, and institutions are also based on a much broader argument. There is often suboptimal provision of fundamental governance services, such as the protection of property rights and the maintenance of economic and personal security and the rule of law. One factor determining the quality of the institutional environment for doing business is the firm-level demand for a high-quality environment, which creates a positive feedback. The larger is the business sector, the greater is the demand for a good business environment, the greater is the political payoff from providing these governance services, and the better is the ensuing business environment. If the initial position was suboptimal, then this feedback is a source of increasing returns: the larger the sector, the closer provision will be to the optimal level.

Spatial Frictions and Economic Geography

The second fact about modern trade and globalization is that distance still matters. This can be seen most clearly by thinking through the externalities discussed in the previous subsection, almost all of which are spatially limited. Knowledge spillovers occur within very concentrated economic regions: clusters and districts within cities. "Self-discovery" is, by definition, discovery of the characteristics of a particular location. Labor market effects operate within a travel-to-work area. Public goods and utilities (such as water supply and security) are hard to trade across space. Institutional effects may be national or subnational, operating at the level of provinces, cities, or just within special economic zones. The key element of "distance" is slightly different in each of these and other contexts. Distance matters, as it raises the monetary and time cost of trading goods, of moving workers, or of spreading ideas. It also underlies jurisdictions and hence man-made barriers to mobility.

Globalization has had its greatest impact in the product market, although even here distance matters. Firms can use small trade frictions as a way to soften competition, as witnessed by the long-running struggle to turn the European Union (EU) into a truly integrated market. Distance has a large effect in choking off trade flows, and gravity models of trade suggest that the full costs of trade are far higher than suggested by simply looking at tariffs or transport costs (see Anderson and van Wincoop 2004). Part of the cost is associated with time-in-transit, and "just-in-time" management techniques have increased the cost of slow or uncertain delivery times. Hummels (2001) estimates the cost of time-in-transit for manufactures to be nearly 1 percent of the value of goods shipped *per day*.

The spatial dimension provides a way of estimating the quantitative importance of increasing returns, and a well-established literature measures the productivity advantages of large-scale urban centers. A recent survey of the literature reports a consensus view that, over a wide range of sizes, doubling city size is associated with a productivity increase of some 3–8 percent (Rosenthal and Strange 2004). This is a large effect—moving from a city of 50,000 inhabitants to one of 5 million is predicted to increase productivity by more than 50 percent. Analysis of the spatial scale of these effects indicates that they are quite concentrated. Work on the United

Kingdom suggests that they attenuate rapidly beyond 45 minutes of driving time (Rice, Venables, and Pattachini 2006). Effects also vary across sectors, generally being larger in higher-technology sectors of activity.

Fragmentation

The third characteristic of globalized trade is fragmentation—otherwise known as unbundling or splitting the value chain. It refers to the fact that different stages involved in producing a particular final good are often performed in different countries. Particular "tasks" may be outsourced (or offshored) and can be undertaken in different places. This occurs in response to productivity or factor price differences and may take place within a single multinational firm or through production networks of supplier firms.[2] Although widely reported, solid evidence on the extent of fragmentation is quite hard to obtain. It is estimated that just 37 percent of the production value of a typical U.S. car is generated in the United States. Grossman and Rossi-Hansberg (2006) report that the share of imports in inputs to U.S. goods manufacturing has doubled to 18 percent over a 20-year period. In China, it is estimated that domestic value added amounts to around 60 percent of the value of goods exported, falling to less than 30 percent in equipment—electrical, communications, and transport—sectors (see Cuihong and Jianuo 2007). Up to 78 percent of East Asian trade is in intermediate goods.

Fragmentation means that comparative advantage now resides in quite narrowly defined tasks. This is highly beneficial for developing countries, particularly when accompanied by learning effects and increasing returns to scale. It means that countries do not have to acquire capability in all stages of an integrated production process; instead they can specialize in a narrow range of tasks, which entails a much easier learning process.

Implications for Growth and Development

What are the implications of these facts for the world economy and for growth? There are several important points.

Equilibrium Disparities

Diminishing returns to scale are a force for convergence. A city or country that offers high returns to firms or workers will attract inflows of these factors, thus reducing their returns and giving convergence to equilibrium. A consequence of this is that an economic model dominated by diminishing returns offers no theory of international or spatial inequality. Regions may differ because of exogenous factors, but economic processes tend to reduce these differences.

Spatially concentrated increasing returns offer a very different view. If a city or country offers high returns to firms or workers, then they are attracted to the area, which increases their returns further and amplifies any initial differences. The process may be unbounded: some regions may empty out, or all of world production of some good may occur in a single place. Or the process may be bounded, as when, beyond some point, diminishing returns come to dominate scale effects. Thus cities eventually run into diminishing returns because of congestion costs. Production of a good occurs in several places because of transport costs (or time differences) in supplying world demand from one location. The most important source of diminishing returns to concentration of activity is that the prices of immobile factors are bid up, which reduces the return to mobile factors. In the urban context, land prices increase, making the city less attractive to mobile workers. In the international context, wages rise, making a country less attractive to mobile firms.

But whether bounded or unbounded, the point is that increasing returns create a force for divergence. Locations may be identical in their underlying characteristics, but economic forces make them different as the economy "self organizes" into clusters. Differences in the prices of immobile factors and in income levels are then an equilibrium outcome, not a transient consequence of some initial difference.

Wage Gradients

The fact that the benefits of increasing returns to scale and access to large markets depend on proximity to centers of activity means that we should expect to observe wage or income gradients as we move from central to peripheral locations. Redding and Venables (2004) investigate this at the international level. They use international trade data and a gravity model to get a measure of each country's access to foreign markets and then investigate the relationship between per capita income and this measure of market access. The work shows strong evidence of a "wage gradient," where countries with good market access have, conditional on other factors, significantly higher wages. The finding that proximity to foreign markets is a statistically significant and quantitatively important determinant of income levels is consistent with the work of Frankel and Romer (1999), who use geography as an instrument for the effect of trade on income.

Lumpy Growth

What does economic growth look like in this world? It has three characteristics, each of which is a sort of "lumpiness."

The first aspect is that growth is lumpy or uneven across *space*. Instead of all regions growing in parallel, they have a tendency to grow in sequence. Some countries or regions grow rapidly as increasing returns cut in, and they transit from one "convergence club" to another. Other countries are left out of the process. To see the logic behind this, suppose that the world is divided between high-income countries that have manufacturing activity and low-income countries that do not. This is an equilibrium, as wages in the former group are matched by the high productivity associated with scale, so there is no incentive for any firm to relocate. Now suppose that some growth process occurring in the world economy as a whole—such as technical progress—is raising income and hence demand for manufactures. This increases employment and raises wages in the manufacturing regions until a point is reached at which the productivity advantage of being in an existing cluster is outweighed by the higher wages in the cluster. It then becomes profitable for some firms to relocate, but where do they go? Spatially concentrated increasing returns mean that firms tend to cluster in a single newly emergent manufacturing location. A situation in which all countries gain a little manufacturing is unstable; a country that gets ahead even slightly has the advantage, attracting further firms. As this process runs through time, countries join the group of high-income nations in sequence. Each country grows quickly, as it joins the club, and is then followed by another country, and so on.

Of course, the strict sequence of countries should not be taken literally. The key insight is that the growth mechanism does not imply more-or-less-uniform convergence of countries, as some economic growth theorists argue (see, for example, Lucas 2000). Instead, growth is sequential, not parallel, as manufacturing spreads across countries and regions. Which countries go first, and the order in which countries join the high-income club, is determined by a range of factors to do with endowments, institutions, and geography. Proximity to existing centers may be an important positive factor, as with development in Eastern Europe and regions of Mexico, East Asia, and China.[3] Institutional failure, bad macroeconomic policy, and conflict are powerful negative factors.

The second aspect of lumpiness is that growth is uneven in *time*. Small initial differences between countries may mean that some countries get ahead, while others are left behind for a long period of time. Countries that fall below some threshold—in terms of investment climate and institutional quality—do not participate in the process.

The third feature is that growth may be lumpy across *products*, as it is likely to be concentrated in particular sectors. This occurs as many of the sources of increasing returns are sector specific—that is, the acquisition of skills and capacity occurs in quite narrowly defined sets of products or tasks. A corollary of narrow specialization is, of course, that growth is highly export dependent. This is consistent with the Asian experience and with empirical work on growth accelerations (see, for example, Hausmann, Pritchett, and Rodrik 2005). Direct measures of the sectoral concentration of exports are given by Hausmann and Rodrik (2003), who conclude that "for all economies except possibly the most sophisticated, industrial success entails concentration in a relatively narrow range of high-productivity activities."[4]

Initial Difference: Who Gains and Who Is Left Behind?

In the preceding argument we emphasize that inequalities could emerge even between similar (or ex ante identical) countries. But given that there are underlying differences between countries, what sort of countries might expect to do well, and what countries might expect to do badly as a result of globalization? We make just two points.

The first is that some countries have failed to meet the necessary conditions to achieve full integration in the global economy and inclusion in production networks. The obvious comparison is between the performance of much of Asia and of Africa. Asian manufacturing has crossed the threshold, and diversification into exports of manufactures has raised wages and been contagious across the region. In Africa this process has yet to start. Africa has lagged behind partly because its economic reforms have lagged those of Asia: in the 1980s when Asia first broke into global markets, no mainland African country provided a comparable investment climate. "Lumpiness" in the development process means that these initial differences translate into very large differences in outcomes and may create long lags before Africa can attract modern sector activity. Several African cities now offer investment climates as good as those offered earlier in Asia. However, these cities now face the obstacle that Asia has a head start and is benefiting from clusters of shared knowledge, availability of specialist inputs, and pools of experienced labor. Africa's potential export locations do not have these advantages and so face an entry threshold or "chicken-and-egg" problem. Until clusters are established, costs will be above those of Asian competitors, but *because* costs are currently higher, individual firms have no incentive to relocate.

A second point is that globalization tends to benefit the extremes and squeeze the middle. It permits a finer division of labor, enabling the highest-skilled countries to concentrate on skill-intensive tasks and the lowest-skilled countries to concentrate on low-skill tasks, subject to crossing a capability threshold. What happens to middle-income countries during this process? They do not have an "extreme" comparative advantage to exploit and, at the same time, are faced with changing terms of trade, due largely to increased supply from Asia. Price changes of this magnitude have brought gains to consumers worldwide, but they also have placed producers under pressure. The pressure has not fallen primarily on producers in high-income countries but instead has been felt in middle-income countries, which are producing goods that are technologically relatively unsophisticated. This is one of the reasons why globalization appears not to have benefited many middle-income countries (see also Summers 2006).

Policy Issues: Threshold Effects and Coordination Failures

What are the policy implications of the economic environment we have described? There are multiple market failures and plenty of arguments for policy intervention, yet at the same time spatial policy—regional policy in particular—has generally been a failure. Researchers in new economic geography have been hesitant to make policy recommendations.

In thinking about policy, there are (at least) two difficult sets of issues that need to be understood. The first set concerns the threshold effects and coordination failures that arise in the presence of external economies of scale, and we discuss them in this section. The second set concerns linkages and spillover effects: how do changes in one country or region have an impact on other countries and neighboring regions? We discuss this issue later.

The world we have described is one of lumpiness and extreme specialization. A corollary is that it is difficult to get started in a new industry or location, although the activity is viable once scale economies have been attained. There are several policy responses. The first is to increase the confidence with which investors see future benefits and also increase the ability to borrow against future returns. The second is to internalize any external benefits that new entrants create. The third is to offer temporary support through some form of industrial policy. We discuss these options through two examples: the growth of new cities and the prospects for African export diversification.

Threshold Effects: Creating an Urban Structure

Cities are areas of high productivity and, in many developing countries, rapid economic growth. But economies of scale are balanced against diseconomies of urban congestion and pollution, suggesting that there is an optimal urban size. We know little about what this size is; it will vary according to the geography, industrial structure, and governance of each city (see Au and Henderson 2004). Threshold effects do, however, suggest that there may be a tendency for cities to become larger than is optimal. The reason is that external economies of scale make it hard to start new cities. Small cities do not benefit from urban-scale economies and so are unattractive to firms; as a consequence, they fail to grow into large cities. Since new urban centers are hard to establish, existing cities grow well beyond their optimum scale, possibly to the point where, at the margin, diseconomies such as congestion outweigh positive economies of scale. Such an outcome is clearly inefficient, and the policy challenge is to determine how to promote the growth of new cities or the deconcentration of existing ones.

There are likely to be two distinct market failures. One is that increasing returns to scale give rise to externalities, so that the benefits *created* by a single economic agent (a migrant to the city or a relocating firm) are not internalized. The other is that the benefits *received* by a single economic agent (reciprocal externalities, so firms and migrants receive as well as transmit benefits) accrue over time, and their future development will be highly uncertain. These two issues require different policy responses. We address the second one first.

When does it become worthwhile for a single "small" firm or individual to decide to invest in a new city? (This section draws on Henderson and Venables 2008.) It will be sooner the more confident the investor is in the future development of the city and the greater is his or her ability to capture the future economic benefits, most obviously by having secure property rights to the land on which the investment takes place. It will also be sooner the easier it is for the individual to borrow against these future benefits. Policy can have a direct and important impact in all of these areas. The first may require government investment, playing the dual role of constructing the new urban infrastructure and also signaling to investors that this particular city (as compared to the numerous other potential city sites) is one in which there is commitment to growth. Given this, long-term property rights in urban land and access to credit are then standard prescriptions for making markets work.

Adopting these measures increases the incentives to be an early mover from an existing mega city to a new secondary city, but it does not move the economy to a "first-best optimum." Investors are investing in the expectation of receiving the external benefits of a dynamic growing city, but they are not capturing the benefits of the externalities that they are themselves creating. There are two textbook solutions to this problem. One is to internalize these benefits, by having "large developers" buy up land in the city, attract firms and immigrants, and then take all the land rents. The other is for the public sector to subsidize the creation of external benefits. In practice, neither of these solutions is likely to be satisfactory. Developers play this role in shopping malls and office developments, but they are unlikely to be large enough to capture more than a fraction of the benefits of a city. Public subsidies to the myriad externalities created by urban activity are expensive, difficult to target, subject to abuse, and consequently difficult to recommend.

The important point to take away from this discussion is that, even without compensating for the externalities, policy can move a large part of the way toward efficiency just by the first set of policy measures. Creating confidence that a particular urban site will develop and having property rights such that forward-looking individuals will be induced to invest in the site solve the coordination failure, even if doing so does not internalize the externality.

Threshold Effects: Can Africa Export Manufactures?

Threshold effects matter for countries as well as for cities. As we argue above, Africa has, at least until recently, been below the threshold required to be an attractive location from which to source imports.

What is the role for policy? Several observations follow by analogy with this discussion of cities. Provision of a good business environment and appropriate infrastructure has direct benefits and may also signal the government's commitment to development. Government may reinforce its commitment by high-level engagement—the idea of a "developmental state." Delivering these things in a particular location—perhaps a special economic zone—has two advantages. The first is that provision of a full set of high-quality complementary inputs and utilities is relatively cost-effective; complementarity means, roughly put, that it is better to provide inputs well in one place than half as well in two places. The second advantage of a special economic zone relates to our discussion of urbanization. In the long run, there are efficiency gains from clustering activity, and in the short run it is important to signal this by committing to a particular location.

Active industrial policy going beyond these measures is controversial. There are multiple market failures in the environment we have described and hence a case for intervention to reduce coordination failure and internalize externalities. But direct interventions are hard to target, difficult to withdraw, and subject to political economy manipulation. Trade preferences are an alternative policy instrument that merits consideration (see Collier and Venables 2007). Unlike other forms of industrial policy, trade preferences in Organisation for Economic Co-operation and Development (OECD) markets are under the control of OECD governments. This gives them major advantages over the policies that are available to African governments to provide the (temporary) advantage needed to form clusters. First, they are relatively immune from recipient-country political economy problems, because they are set by foreign, not domestic, government. Thus there is no way the level of trade preferences can be escalated in support of failing firms. Second, because trade preferences support exports, they offer a performance-based incentive: firms benefit only if they export. Firms therefore face the discipline—on quality as well as on price—imposed by international competition. Rodrik (2004) argues that this discipline was an important positive factor underlying the success of export-oriented strategies, as compared to import substitution. Finally, they are fiscally costless to African governments and virtually costless to OECD governments and so compete with neither government spending on social needs nor aid.

Current practice with trade preferences is not particularly successful in promoting the growth of manufacturing export clusters. However, current practices typically set conditions at variance with some of the characteristics of modern international trade that we noted above. As we saw, much world trade now takes the form of trade in tasks, with production fragmented between many countries and high levels of intermediate trade. This fragmentation is potentially beneficial for Sub-Saharan Africa because it is much easier to develop capabilities and grow economies of scale in a narrow range of tasks than in integrated production of an entire product. However, most preferential trading schemes have rules of origin that prohibit this sort of trade, insisting that a high proportion of value added (or transformation) is performed within the country or region and ruling out sourcing intermediate inputs from the lowest-cost source (often China). The implication for preferential trading schemes is that rules of origin must be liberal enough not to exclude countries from participating in such production networks.

The second point is that preferences should be open to countries that are close to the threshold of developing globally competitive clusters of activity. Preference schemes that favor only the least-developed countries have the effect of excluding countries such as Kenya and Ghana, which have just arrived at the threshold and are manifestly more likely to develop manufacturing exports than are Liberia and Somalia. The effect of concentrating on the least-developed countries is therefore to exclude precisely those African countries best placed to take advantage of preferences for export diversification.

In practice, if preferences are offered with rules of origin allowing specialization in tasks and open to members beyond the least-developed countries, will export diversification occur in response? These conditions are offered by one policy regime—the special rule for apparel contained in the U.S. African Growth and Opportunity Act— and the evidence is of a strong export response, with apparel exports from Kenya, Lesotho, Madagascar, and other areas of Southern Africa soaring from around US$300 million to US$1.5 billion a year (Collier and Venables 2007).

Policy Issues: Spatial Linkages and Spillovers

Some countries stand little chance of breaking directly into world manufacturing export markets, perhaps because of very low starting positions or perhaps because of natural geography, such as being landlocked. These economies are relatively dependent on the performance of their neighbors. This is an aspect of a larger question: what are the economic linkages between spatially proximate cities, regions, or countries? At one level this is a straightforward question of comparative statics. How do the effects of some exogenous or policy change spread out across regions? Yet it is a question about which we do not yet have all the answers. This is partly because the specification of the policy shock often needs clearer thinking. Is it contained within one region, does it affect many, or is it an "integrative shock," affecting regions only via its effect on the links between them? But even given the specification of the policy shock, the presence of increasing returns means that comparative statics is difficult, and effects can be qualitatively ambiguous depending in a delicate way on characteristics of the regions and the linkages between them.

Spatial Linkages: Complementary or Competing Regions?

How does change in one region affect neighboring regions? Overman, Rice, and Venables (2008) develop a simple diagrammatic structure to address this question. The structure is based on three key relationships that shape interregional linkages. The first is the relationship between employment and earnings, a within-region relationship relating earnings in a region to the size of its labor force; the relationship may be increasing or decreasing, depending on returns to scale. The second is the relationship between employment and cost of living; within a region, how does additional population change the cost of living? Some factors make this relationship negative (more intense competition and more varieties of nontraded goods meaning an economically large region has a lower cost of living), and others make it positive (commuting costs and the price of land and houses). The third relationship is migration: an interregional relationship measuring the responsiveness of population to differences in real earnings.

Depending on the shape of these relationships, equilibrium could be stable or unstable. Concentrating, for obvious reasons, on stable equilibria, regions may be in either a "complementary" or a "competing" relationship with each other. When regions are complementary, the effects of a positive shock that originates in one region are spread across other regions. Thus an increase in productivity in one region will trigger in-migration, which tends to dampen the productivity increase in this region, while increasing productivity in others. But when regions are competing, economic adjustment has the opposite effect, amplifying the impact of a productivity shock in one region, while causing productivity in other regions to fall. This might arise because increasing returns mean that an increase in the labor force is associated with *higher* productivity, and equilibrium is restored only by large changes in population and regional living costs. Understanding whether parameters are such that regions are "complementary" or "competing" is fundamental for evaluating policy. For example, the U.K. government has launched debate on whether to relax planning regulations to allow more houses to be built in the booming southeast of England. If regions are in a competing relationship, the effect of this will be to *increase* house prices in the region and amplify regional differentials. The mechanism is population inflow combined with increasing returns to scale to generate higher earnings, which induces further inflow of population until it is choked off by higher house prices.

While this example may not be directly relevant to developing countries, it contains several lessons. First, it is possible to synthesize key relationships from many theoretical models in a simple "reduced-form" manner and to study the interaction between these relationships in a straightforward way. Second, these relationships are amenable to empirical investigation: by looking at both the separate relationships and the behavior of the system as a whole, it is possible to determine whether regions are competing or complementary. And third, doing this is a necessary input for undertaking regional policy; without it, even the sign of response to policy change is unknown. These approaches need to be applied to developing countries, for example, to analyze the problem of lagging regions in a fast-growing economy. To do this requires both analytical work on the main channels through which regions are interlinked and empirical work establishing whether regions are complementary or competing.

Integrative Shocks: A Force for Convergence or Divergence?

Much spatial policy deals not with shocks within a region, but with shocks aimed at changing the relationship between regions—for example, trade policy or road and communications improvements. What do we know about the effects of such integrative shocks?

Here too there are ambiguities. Under some circumstances a reduction in trade costs between two regions will reduce disparities, while under other circumstances it may increase them. The mechanisms essentially derive from the interplay between product markets and factor markets. The product market mechanism is that firms want to locate where there is good market access. If one region is slightly larger than the other, then reducing trade costs will cause firms to move to the larger location and export to the smaller one, amplifying differences between regions. The factor market mechanism is that firms relocate in response to wage differences and are more likely to relocate to a low-wage region the lower are trade costs. Putting these effects together in a general equilibrium framework (in which both the location of demand and wage rates may be endogenous) typically yields an inverse U–shaped relationship between trade costs and regional disparities. Reducing trade costs from a high to an intermediate level tends to increase dispersion. But reducing them from an intermediate to a low level will reverse this, leading to convergence.

What is the evidence? Some work on this has been done in the European Union. There has been a continuing worry that the centripetal forces will dominate, drawing activity into the center of the EU at the expense of peripheral regions. However, most recent research suggests that trade costs are low enough for further reductions to have the effect of reducing rather than increasing disparities. This EU-based work leaves issues open for developing countries. Once again these are perfectly researchable issues that need to be studied as input to policy formation.

Conclusions

There are many reasons for variation in the prosperity of countries and regions. Some factors are truly exogenous—such as first-nature geography—and others are a function of political and institutional history. On top of these exogenous factors, we need to place a theory of the location of economic activity. International trade theory gets us part of the way, and the new economic geography approach broadens this out to capture (in a micro-founded and evidence-based way) endogenous variations in productivity. The approach offers an explanation for the emergence of disparities between countries and regions and their persistence. It suggests that even as globalization causes dispersion of activity, so economic development will be in sequence, not in parallel; some countries will experience rapid growth, while others will be left behind. At the micro level, it points to the importance of overcoming coordination failures and threshold effects in building new cities and establishing new industries in developing economies.

This literature provides a basis for new and innovative thinking about policy, but a note of caution is essential. Policy is difficult because there are multiple market failures. Even in the simple world of theory, policy does not map continuously (and perhaps not even uniquely) into outcomes, because there is rapid change and there may also be multiple equilibria. Comparative statics may depend in a delicate way on characteristics of the economy. But the fact that policy is not straightforward is not surprising to researchers on growth and development, and the lens of economic geography provides further insights for grappling with these problems.

Bibliography

Amiti, Mary, and Christopher A. Pissarides. 2005. "Trade and Industrial Location with Heterogeneous Labor." *Journal of International Economics* 67 (2): 392–412.

Anderson, James, and Eric van Wincoop. 2004. "Trade Costs." *Journal of Economic Literature* 42 (3): 691–751.

Arndt, Sven W., and Henryk Kierzkowski, eds. 2001. *Fragmentation: New Production Patterns in the World Economy*. Oxford: Oxford University Press.

Au, Chun-Chung, and J. Vernon Henderson. 2004. "Are Chinese Cities Too Small?" Unpublished paper, Brown University, Providence, RI.

Audretsch, David, and Maryann Feldman. 2004. "The Geography of Innovation." In *Handbook of Regional and Urban Economics*, ed. Jacques-François Thisse and J. Vernon Henderson, vol. 4. Amsterdam: North Holland.

Collier, Paul, and Anthony J. Venables. 2007. "Rethinking Trade Preferences: How Africa Can Diversify Its Exports" *World Economy* 30 (8): 1326–45.

Cuihong, Y., and P. Jianuo. 2007. "Input Dependence of Foreign Trade." Chinese Academy of Sciences.

Duranton, Gilles, and Diego Puga. 2004 "Micro-Foundations of Urban Agglomeration Economies." In *Handbook of Regional and Urban Economics*, ed. Jacques-François Thisse and J. Vernon Henderson, vol. 4. Amsterdam: North Holland.

Frankel, Jeffrey A., and David Romer. 1999. "Does Trade Cause Growth?" *American Economic Review* 89 (3): 379–99.

Fujita, Masahisa, Paul R. Krugman, and Anthony J. Venables. 1999. *The Spatial Economy: Cities, Regions, and International Trade*. Cambridge, MA: MIT Press.

Gallup, John L., and Jeffrey Sachs. 1999. "Geography and Economic Development." In *Annual World Bank Conference on Development Economics: 1998*, ed. Boris Pleskovic and Joseph E. Stiglitz. Washington, DC: World Bank.

Grossman, Gene M., and Esteban Rossi-Hansberg. 2006. "The Rise of Offshoring: It's Not Cloth for Wine Any More." Unpublished paper, Princeton University, Princeton, NJ.

Hausmann, Ricardo, Lant Pritchett, and Dani Rodrik. 2005. "Growth Accelerations." *Journal of Economic Growth* 10 (4): 303–29.

Hausmann, Ricardo, and Dani Rodrik. 2003. "Economic Development as Self-Discovery." *Journal of Economic Growth* 72 (2): 603–33.

Henderson, J. Vernon, and Anthony J. Venables. 2008. "The Dynamics of City Formation." NBER Working Paper 13769, National Bureau of Economic Research, Cambridge, MA.

Hummels, David. 2001. "Time as a Trade Barrier." Unpublished paper, Purdue University, West Lafayette, IN.

Imbs, Jean, and Romain Wacziarg. 2003. "Stages of Diversification." *American Economic Review* 93 (1): 63–86.

Kremer, Michael. 1993. "The O-Ring Theory of Economic Development." *Quarterly Journal of Economics* 108 (3): 551–75.

Kremer, Michael, and Marcos de Carvalho Chamon. 2006. "Asian Growth and African Development." *American Economic Review Papers and Proceedings* 96 (2): 400–04.

Krugman, Paul R. 1995. *Development, Geography, and Economic Theory*. Cambridge, MA: MIT Press.

Krugman, Paul R., and Anthony J. Venables. 1995. "Globalization and the Inequality of Nations." *Quarterly Journal of Economics* 110 (4): 857–80.

Leamer, Edward E. 2007. "A Flat World, a Level Playing Field, a Small World after All, or None of the Above? Review of Friedman." *Journal of Economic Literature* 45 (March): 83–126.

Lucas, Robert E. 2000. "Some Macroeconomics for the Twenty-First Century." *Journal of Economic Perspectives* 14 (1): 159–68.

Markusen, James, and Anthony J. Venables. 2007. "Interacting Factor Endowments and Trade Costs: A Multi-Country, Multi-Good Approach to Trade Theory." *Journal of International Economics* 73 (2): 333–54.

Marshall, Alfred. 1890. *Principles of Economics*. London: Macmillan [8th ed., 1920].

Matouschek, Niko, and Frederic Robert-Nicoud. 2005. "The Role of Human Capital Investments in the Location Decisions of Firms." *Regional Science and Urban Economics* 35 (5): 570–83.

Overman, Henry G., Patricia G. Rice, and Anthony J. Venables. 2008. "Economic Linkages across Space." Forthcoming in *Regional Studies*.

Puga, Diego, and Anthony J. Venables. 1999. "Agglomeration and Economic Development: Import Substitution versus Trade Liberalisation." *Economic Journal* 109 (455): 292–311.

Redding, Stephen, and Anthony J. Venables. 2004. "Economic Geography and International Inequality." *Journal of International Economics* 62 (1): 53–82.

Rice, Patricia G., Anthony J. Venables, and Eleonara Pattachini. 2006. "Spatial Determinants of Productivity: Analysis for the U.K. Regions." *Regional Science and Urban Economics* 36 (6): 727–52.

Rodrik, Dani. 2004. "Industrial Policy for the Twenty-First Century." Unpublished paper, Kennedy School, Harvard University, Cambridge, MA.

Rosenthal, Stuart S., and William C. Strange. 2004. "Evidence on the Nature and Sources of Agglomeration Economies." In *Handbook of Regional and Urban Economics,* ed. Jacques-François Thisse and J. Vernon Henderson, vol. 4. Amsterdam: North Holland.

Storper, Michael, and Anthony J. Venables. 2004. "Buzz: Face-to-Face Contact and the Urban Economy." *Journal of Economic Geography* 4 (4): 351–70.

Summers, Lawrence. 2006. "The Global Middle Cries Out for Reassurance." *Financial Times*, October 29.

Venables, Anthony J. 2006. "Shifts in Economic Geography and Their Causes." *Federal Reserve Bank of Kansas City Economic Review* (fourth quarter): 61–85.

Young, Allyn A. 1928. "Increasing Returns and Economic Progress." *Economic Journal* 38 (152): 527–42.

Notes

1. Of course, there is an enormous body of work looking at increasing returns, from (at least) the work of Young (1928) onward.

2. See Arndt and Kierzkowski (2001) for discussion of fragmentation; for more recent treatments, see Grossman and Rossi-Hansberg (2006); Markusen and Venables (2007).

3. The implications of market size and trade barriers are investigated by Puga and Venables (1999), who assess the alternatives of export-oriented versus import-substituting manufacturing development. See also Kremer and de Carvalho Chamon (2006) for a model of a "development queue."

4. Imbs and Wacziarg (2003) point to the fact that the degree of diversification increases in the earlier stages of diversification before declining.

Keynote Address
Africa: Rethinking Growth and Regional Integration

PAUL COLLIER

Geography is an enormously important lens through which to see Africa. As a prelude, one can first think of Jared Diamond's east-west and north-south continental axes, which give you some insight on why Africa was so much slower to take off agriculturally than other continents (Diamond 1997). Second, one can think of Jeffrey Sachs's work on health and William Masters's work on frosts (see Gallup and Sachs 2000; Masters and Sachs 2001; Masters and Weibe 2000). The importance of frosts is not widely recognized, yet frosts are nature's disinfectant. Third, one can think of security. For example, Azar Gat's book, *War in Human Civilisation*, is an economic geography of warfare going back about 40,000 years (Gat 2006). Gat's analysis shows that, at an early stage of development, Africa was not able to form political units capable of defending territory, which explains why it has had so much more slavery than anywhere else and suffered so much more from it. Because security is one of the scale-economy activities, it is a recurring theme.

The typology I use for Africa is a geographic typology. On the one hand, it is a physical geography typology, and, on the other, it is a human geography typology. The physical geography typology is fairly well known. In this context, the key cleavage is between resource-rich countries and resource-scarce countries, and there are two reasons why the cleavage is so important. The first one is economic and related to the so-called Dutch disease, which I think is overplayed. The second is related to the political economy: where there are resource rents, a large flow of money comes to the government without a tax base, that is, without the government having to tax citizens. This offers an enormously powerful opportunity to distort the political process. It also means that countries with a lot of resource rents almost inevitably have a large state, meaning large public revenues relative to gross domestic product (GDP), and so the key economic challenge is to run a big state

Paul Collier is Professor of Economics in the Department of Economics at Oxford University, and Director, Centre for the Study of African Economies in the United Kingdom.

Berlin Workshop Series 2009
© 2009 The International Bank for Reconstruction and Development/The World Bank

effectively. The growth story in those countries revolves around whether governments can spend public money effectively. This creates a paradox because, in all
these countries, the first-order issue is spending money effectively, but, because the
governments do not tax citizens (and should not tax them given that government
already has a lot of revenue), they have low accountability, which implies that large
volumes of public spending meet low accountability of public spending. There are
radical solutions, such as the Rajan and Subramanian (2007) approach, which is to
give the money to citizens and then tax it back. However, this is possible in theory,
but not in reality.

Among the resource-scarce countries, the next fundamental cleavage is whether
the country is coastal or landlocked. A well-known statistic says that, outside of
Africa, resource-scarce, landlocked areas account for only 1 percent of a developing
country's population; in Africa, they account for about a third of the population.
Another way of stating this is that, outside of Africa, landlocked and resource
scarce countries have not become countries, but rather parts of more fortunately
endowed countries. This is very sensible, but, unfortunately, in Africa they are
countries. From a historical point of view, there has not been a plan to take the
resource-scarce, landlocked countries even to the middling level, other than by piggy-backing on the opportunities of their more fortunately endowed neighbors. Yet
such piggy-backing depends on two things. First, the more fortunately endowed
neighbors have to take advantage of their opportunities, which in Africa has not
happened, and, second, they have to run the regional economy in such a way as to
maximize spillovers, which means good transport, low transport costs, and open
trade policies regarding your neighbors, none of which has occurred in Africa. So
far, that has not mattered because there has been little growth to spill over. As it
were, the sequence for growth in resource-scarce, landlocked countries is, first, to
fix the more fortunate neighbors and, second, to integrate with the more fortunate
neighbors. In brutally concrete terms, the only hope for Niger is growth in Nigeria.

This leaves us with the coastal, resource-scarce countries, which economists
understand because their models are all about integrating and harnessing labor
abundance in the global economy, which is what Asia has done with success. We
understand this kind of economic model in theory, and it works in practice, because
it takes countries rapidly to middle-income levels. However, this has not occurred
in Africa, a subject to which we return later.

The human geography typology has two considerations. First, Africa is much
more ethnically diverse than any other region on earth. Ethnic diversity has various
implications, of which the most important one—probably the empirically best
established one—is that ethnic diversity reduces the capacity to cooperate. It
reduces the level of communal trust and makes cooperation in the public sphere
harder, thus reducing the capacity to supply public goods. There may well be offset-
ting advantages to ethnic diversity, such as the creation of networks of information
(and trust) used by ethnically integrated entrepreneurs: ethnically diverse societies
have an absolute disadvantage in public goods, but an absolute advantage in private activities. In this case, one would expect an ethnically diverse society to have a

smaller public sphere and a larger private sphere. Ethnically diverse societies would look like America, and ethnically more integrated societies would look like Europe. Bearing this in mind and the fact that Africa is even more ethnically diverse than the United States, one could argue that part of Africa's disastrous history is that, after becoming free of Europe in the 1950s, Africa has spent five decades trying to look like Europe in the 1950s, which implies an intensive effort to build public goods. Africa did not model itself on America.

The second consideration is that, despite having a lot of ethnic diversity, Africa has an enormous number of countries. For instance, while Africa has got fewer people than India by far, it is split up into 53 countries. Small country size has many consequences. One of these is what I refer to as scale economies in security. Building on my own model of civil war, I show that there are powerful scale economies in security, more precisely, in internal security. If one were to split India up into 53 countries, one would enormously increase the incidence of civil war within the territory of India. Another consequence that is revealed in my empirical work is that being small slows the pace of reform out of very bad economic policies and governance. Since reform is about a society's capacity to generate a public critique of what has gone wrong, devise a strategy for change, and implement it, one can argue that reform is about knowledge. However, just as securities are a scale-economies activity, knowledge is also a scale-economies activity. Thus if knowledge has these scale economies, then very small societies will be slower to reform, which is what I find globally. Related to the scale-economies argument, it is significant that nearly all of our evidence on scale economies comes from developed countries, and yet we are dealing with what in economic terms can be referred to as micro states. Thus there are potentially powerful economies of scale in many other activities, which implies that more research is needed using data from economic micro states.

These two typologies—(a) the physical geography split between the resource-rich countries and (b) the landlocked and the coastal countries and the human geography features of Africa (that is, ethnic diversity and very small country size)—then come together in three interactions. The interaction of resource-rich countries with a lot of ethnic diversity produces a dismal conundrum, which is that the resource-rich societies almost inevitably need to have big states. Resource-rich societies have big governments, because they have a lot of revenue to spend. These societies have the normal problems of low accountability because of low taxation, but also the problems of ethnic diversity, which make cooperation politically difficult. This explains why a big state is inefficient: low accountability plus inability to cooperate. This is the heart of the dilemma facing the third of Africa that is defined by resource riches: how to get around the very high costs of cooperation and the very low impetus for scrutiny. A political technology is needed to overcome those impediments, and it is not clear what it would be, yet there are no alternatives to developing it.

The second dilemma is that resource richness interacts with ethnic diversity and small states to produce a high incidence of violence. Ethnic diversity tends to foment rebellion, which, when combined with small states that do not reach economies of scale in security and with resource riches that increase the propensity to internal violence, produces a high risk of civil war. This, of course, has been seen.

The final interaction is between resource scarce and small coastal countries, which leads to slow reform. Thus one can argue that it is due to their small size that Africa's coastal resource-scarce countries have missed the boat vis-à-vis Asia in breaking into global markets. At the time when Asia had just got some of its economies sufficiently together to be able to break into global markets and manufacturing, coastal Africa was still mired in various policy impediments. Although those policy impediments have been resolved, Africa is stuck because Asia got into that activity first. A depressing thesis, which could be possible, is that the world may have enough manufacturing sites given the share of manufacturing consumption in global consumption. This would exclude Africa from the production of these goods. It would also mean that trying to push Africa in this direction might not work anymore. However, even though there are no guarantees for success, trying to push Africa in this direction and failing have virtually no costs, because there is a huge asymmetry in the costs of failure relative to the payoff to success. If Africa is given trade preferences, builds export platforms, and yet does not break into global markets and manufacturing production, nothing happens because the costs incurred are minimal. However, if the effort does succeed and some countries take off, they will enter a phase of falling costs and long-term expansion. Thus a cost-benefit analysis of the distribution of risk would show that what is called for is not further research, but action. By the time we have nailed the research, the window of opportunity will be over, because the world is moving away from trade protectionism and, in 10 years time, there will be no scope for letting Africa into global markets.

Another important point when discussing resource-scarce coastal economies is that these countries desperately need well-functioning ports. Ports are the key transport infrastructure if a country is located on the coast. However, ports supply a public good, and thus we return to the point that, because Africa is ethnically diverse, it is particularly inefficient at supplying public goods. More generally, if transport costs matter, as they unfortunately do, a key determinant of transport costs is public spending—that is, public spending on the capital cost of ports, the capital cost of roads, and the maintenance and management of this infrastructure. One reason Africa faces high transport costs is a corollary of the fact that it is inefficient at supplying public goods. In other words, while we usually work from the cost of transport to the need for public policy, we might work the other way around and argue that the political economy is such that the provision of public goods is going to be deficient and, therefore, Africa is going to have geographic problems because transport is going to be poor in these various dimensions.

I now turn to a few additional points regarding landlocked countries. Just as ports are key for resource-scarce coastal countries, for resource-scarce landlocked countries, the key is to create transport corridors to the coast. These are, in some sense, regional public goods, which, in my opinion, is a misleading way of describing them. The key feature of these transport corridors to the coast is an asymmetry of power between the landlocked and the coastal neighbors. The coastal neighbor does not internalize the benefits, because the benefits accrue to the landlocked neighbor. Thus the coastal neighbor systematically underinvests in transport, even if it does not actively use poor transport as a control device and an arm of foreign policy against its neighbor, although this has happened in a lot of Africa. The reason this power asymmetry is important is because it matters for donors. Over the last 10 years there has been a massive move among the donor community toward this so-called "country ownership," which means decentralizing aid budgets and giving governments of countries the right to determine how their own aid budget is spent. However, in this sphere, this is a big mistake. If so much aid goes to Uganda, which Uganda controls, and so much aid goes to Kenya, which Kenya controls, then Kenya will underspend on the transport that Uganda needs. The donor community—in particular, the World Bank—has tried to address this problem ineffectively by defining transport corridors as regional public goods and by creating a pan-Africa regional public goods fund. This is inefficient because, for example, a transport corridor between Uganda and Kenya is not a public good for the whole of Africa, which leads to a free-rider problem. What is needed instead is to take a slice of aid to Uganda and Kenya before the governments of Uganda and Kenya get any of it and assign that to a transport corridor. In other words, there needs to be conditionality for those transport corridors. One can appreciate the benefits of this approach intellectually, but this has not happened over the last 40 years, which is why there are no transport corridors worth mentioning.

What also matters for the landlocked, resource-scarce countries is air transport and e-transport, but they are still somewhat underplayed. The sheer organization of air transport, which is about a quarter of African exports by value, is a very important matter for Africa. On the other hand, e-transport is a matter of telecommunications regulation and pricing, which, again, is a rather neglected area. One of the enormously important questions to research for the landlocked countries is why landlocked Africa has not established call centers, when these are being shifted from India to the Philippines. A huge opportunity is being missed, and the explanation probably has to do with telecommunications regulation. More research is clearly necessary.

A final suggestion regarding the resource-rich countries is that an element of economic geography is missing, which is the economic geography of natural resource extraction. In Africa, there is a whole crescent of massively valuable minerals around the sort of arc on the northern fringes of the Democratic Republic of the Congo. Different minerals are available, and new refining technology means that it is economic, in principle, to extract ores, even if the amount of mineral in the ore is very low. However, since these minerals are a long way from the coast and very heavy, there potentially is an economics of finding a local source of energy, refining the mineral locally, and transporting the refined, lighter mineral to the coast. So far, there is only one player thinking of combining energy and mineral extraction, refining the mineral locally, and creating a transport corridor to take the refined material to the coast. That player is China. If China is the only player thinking in those terms, it will realize the enormous rents. Ideally, it would be better for these things to become public knowledge and then auctioned as packages, so that the rents accrue to the national governments rather than to China.

Finally, something more controversial is the fact that more than half of the costs related to adverse spillovers coming from civil war and badly managed states accrue to neighbors. This, in my opinion, calls into question the whole basis of national sovereignty. What is more desirable is a political economy that maps Africa's economic problems more properly, for instance, with some degree of neighborhood sharing of sovereignty. We do not observe this, but rather the attempt to create an African Union, which, because Africa has got so many countries, has overwhelming free-rider problems. Instead, the right political geography for Africa would be sub-regional groupings.

References

Diamond, Jared. 1997. *Guns, Germs, and Steel: The Fates of Human Societies*. New York: W. W. Norton.

Gallup, John L., and Jeffrey D. Sachs. 2000. "The Economic Burden of Malaria." CID Working Paper 52, Center for International Development, Harvard University, Cambridge, MA.

Gat, Azar. 2006. *War in Human Civilisation*. New York: Oxford University Press.

Masters, William, and Jeffrey D. Sachs. 2001. "Climate and Development." Department of Agricultural Economics, Purdue University.

Masters, William, and K. D. Weibe. 2000. "Climate and Agricultural Productivity." Department of Agricultural Economics, Purdue University.

Rajan, Raghuram, and Arvind Subramanian. 2007. "Does Aid Affect Governance?" *American Economic Review* 97 (2): 322–27.

Part I: Macro Trends: Spatial Patterns of Economic Activity, Income, and Poverty

Spatial Patterns of Population and Economic Activity in the Developing World

STEVEN HAGGBLADE

Human population is becoming increasingly concentrated in cities. Worldwide over the past 200 years, the urban share of population has increased from 11 percent to roughly 50 percent today (Bairoch 1988; United Nations 2007). In developing countries over that same interval, the urban share of population grew from 9 to 44 percent (see figure 1).

FIGURE 1. Spatial Concentration of Population in Developing Countries, 1800–2005

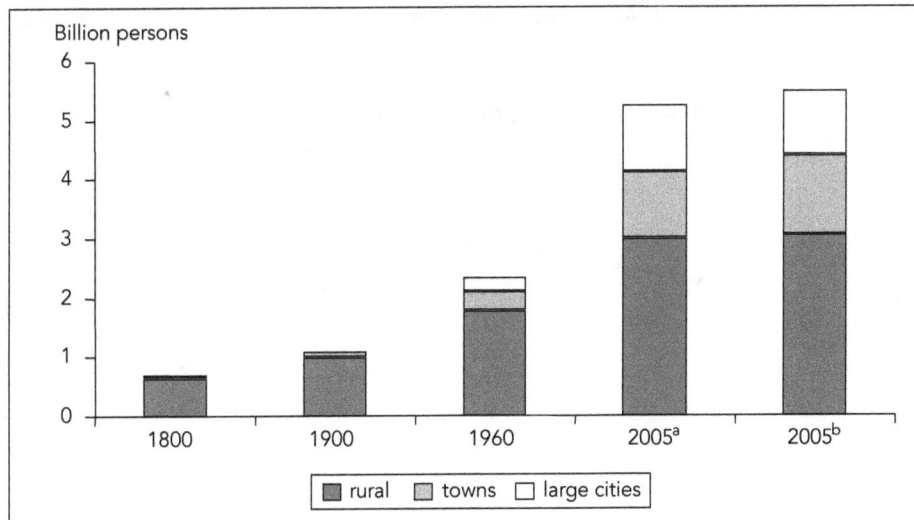

Source: Bairoch 1988; United Nations 2007; World Bank 2008.
[a] United Nations.
[b] WDR (World Development Report).

Steve Haggblade is Professor of International Development in the Department of Agricultural Economics at Michigan State University in the United States.

Berlin Workshop Series 2009

In parallel with this growing concentration of human population, economic activity has undergone a structural shift, as the share of agriculture in national income has fallen, while that of services and manufacturing has risen. This structural transformation is a widely observed process in which broad-based productivity growth drives a shift in the sectoral composition of economic activity (see figure 2). Productivity gains—whatever their source—raise incomes. As incomes rise, Engel's Law observes that people spend a decreasing proportion of their income on food. Because of the finite capacity of the human stomach, consumer spending increasingly shifts from food to manufactured goods and services. This shift in demand triggers a corresponding shift in the sectoral structure of economic production. Agriculture's share of total production falls, and transfers of labor and capital out of agriculture help to fuel a corresponding rise in manufacturing and services.

Thus economic growth typically involves two parallel movements: a spatial shift of population from predominantly rural to predominantly urban settlements and a sectoral shift out of agriculture and into manufacturing and services. These two transitions are tightly linked. Because agriculture involves spatially dispersed production, the initial settlement of rural areas typically depends on the dispersion of agricultural land or other natural resource potential. Yet manufacturing and services benefit from spatial concentration and the resulting economies of scale and agglomeration. Hence industrial and service enterprises tend to be most competitive when clustered together, usually near transport and energy sources. During structural transformation, as agriculture's share of total production falls, so too does the rural share of total population. As a result, the sectoral shift from

FIGURE 2. Structural Transformation of Economic Activity, 1986

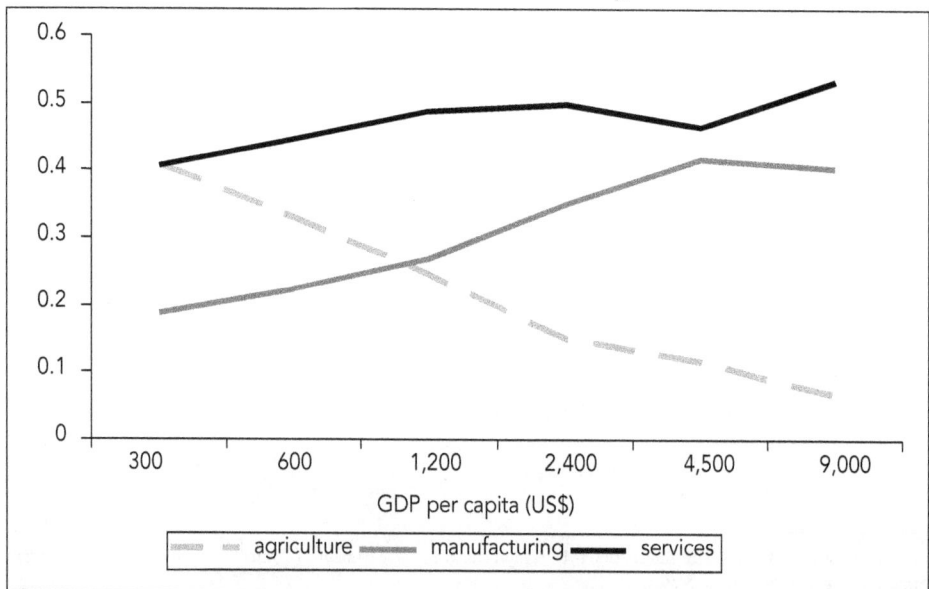

Source: Chenery and Syrquin 1986.

agriculture to manufacturing and services drives the spatial movement of population from rural areas to cities.

Cross-sectional data suggest a strong correlation between urbanization and economic growth (see table 1). In part, urbanization is a consequence of economic growth and structural transformation. In turn, the increasing concentration of economic activity in intermediate towns and large cities serves as an accelerator, contributing to faster rates of economic growth through economies of agglomeration and lower transaction costs.

Today in the developing world, more than 50 percent of the population and 75 percent of the poor live in rural areas (United Nations 2007; World Bank 2007). Therefore, efforts to eradicate poverty will need to pay careful attention to spatial processes under way in rural areas.

Historically, humans have inhabited rural areas because of their agricultural or natural resource-based potential. Indeed, spatial patterns of rural population correspond tightly to agroecological potential. In Africa, the Sahara and Namib deserts remain largely uninhabited, while the well-watered and fertile East African highlands, the Niger and Nile river deltas, and the North African coast are densely populated agricultural zones. Similarly, South Asia's most fertile agricultural areas—the Punjab and the Ganges River valley and delta—remain the most densely populated rural areas in the subcontinent.

Although rural populations typically follow agriculture, rural economies are not solely agricultural. Considerable nonfarm activity takes place, even in rural areas. Cross-sectional data from a wide array of developing countries suggest that nonfarm earnings typically account for one-third to half of total rural income (see table 2).

Reviews of the rural nonfarm economy suggest that, in the early stages of economic development, agriculture drives growth and development of the rural nonfarm economy, through a variety of economic linkages (Haggblade, Hazell, and Dorosh 2007). Demand from rural farm households for consumer goods and for personal, processing, and transport services drives growth of a large rural nonfarm economy. Growth linkage studies suggest that every dollar of agricultural income

TABLE 1. Spatial Distribution of Population, by Region, 2005 (by percentage)

Region	Rural	Urban	
		Intermediate	Large[a]
World	51	25	24
Developed countries	26	40	35
Developing countries	57	22	21
Least developed countries	73	16	11
Latin America and the Caribbean	23	37	40
Southeastern Asia	56	29	15
Sub-Saharan Africa	65	20	15

Source: United Nations 2007.
[a] Cities with population of 500,000 or more.

TABLE 2. Nonfarm Share of Rural Income, by Region (by percentage)

Region	Nonfarm share
Africa	38
Asia	51
Latin America	47

Source: Haggblade, Hazell, and Reardon 2007: table 1.1. Figures represent the average of available rural income studies for the 1990s and 2000s: 23 studies from Africa, 14 from Asia, and 17 from Latin America.

increases demand for rural nonfarm goods and services by an additional US$0.25 to US$0.64 (see table 3). Because demand for services—construction, health care, education, transport, prepared foods, milling, agricultural equipment repair, and personal services—dominates incremental consumer spending, services typically dominate the rural nonfarm economy (see table 4).

Agricultural wage rates and work calendars likewise influence the opportunity cost of rural labor as well as the opportunities for seasonal migration. In agriculturally prosperous regions, where agricultural wage rates rise, so too does the opportunity cost of labor in rural nonfarm pursuits. Through these labor market linkages, rising agricultural productivity stimulates rising rural wage rates and triggers a clear shift out of low-return, last-resort nonfarm activities and into increasingly remunerative nonfarm businesses (see table 5). In contrast, where

TABLE 3. Agricultural Demand Linkages, by Region (by percentage)

Linkage	Asia	Africa	Latin America
Initial agricultural income growth	1.00	1.00	1.00
Additional income growth			
Other agricultural	0.06	0.17	0.05
Nonfarm	0.58	0.30	0.21
Total	0.64	0.47	0.26
Source of linkages			
Consumption	81	87	42
Production	19	13	58

Source: Haggblade and Hazell 1989.

TABLE 4. Sectoral Share of Rural Nonfarm Employment, by Region (by percentage)

Sector	Africa	Asia	Latin America
Manufacturing	21	22	23
Trade	31	29	22
Services	36	34	35
Construction	12	15	20
Total	100	100	100

Source: Haggblade, Hazell, and Reardon 2007: table 1.2.

agricultural productivity remains stagnant in the face of demographic pressure, per capita incomes and agricultural wage rates fall, inducing a corresponding fall in the volume and productivity of nonfarm activity. Agriculture thus influences both the scale and the composition of rural nonfarm activity.

Many of these nonfarm services cluster in rural towns where businesses enjoy access to power, communications, and transport links. Even in rural areas, nonfarm businesses benefit from economies of agglomeration. As a result, empirical studies observe frequent clustering of nonfarm businesses, in both rural areas and rural towns. Silk-weaving factories in Thailand have concentrated in northeastern Thailand, particularly around the town of Pak Ton Chai, while many villages in the region specialize in silk yarn production (Haggblade and Ritchie 1992). In Indonesia, rural production of textiles and roofing tiles tends to cluster geographically (Weijland 1999). Some towns in Pakistan specialize in the production of soccer balls, while some towns in India specialize in the production of plastic jewelry (Papola 1987), and still others concentrate on more specialized services such as snake charming (International Herald Tribune 1989). Tanning, shoe production, sawmilling, and metal working likewise often cluster together in specific locations (Burger, Kameo, and Sandee 2001; Freeman and Norcliffe 1985; Kennedy 1999; Schmitz 1999; Schmitz and Nadvi 1999).

In later stages of economic growth, as urbanization proceeds and the costs of urban labor and land rise, many countries witness a phase of urban-led urban-to-rural subcontracting that becomes increasingly important in driving rural nonfarm

TABLE 5. Labor Market Linkages between Agriculture and the Rural Nonfarm Economy in Bangladesh

Sector	Income per hour in agriculturally underdeveloped regions (taka per hour)	Percent by which agriculturally developed regions exceed underdeveloped areas[a]		
		Income per hour[b]	Employment (hours per week)	Income per household
Agriculture	5.1	29	8	40
Nonagriculture				
Services	11.4	4	30	35
Cottage industry	4.4	90	−81	−63
Wage labor[c]	2.8	6	−41	−38
Trade	2.3	195	−28	113
Total	4.4	59	−29	12

Source: Hossain 1988: 95, 120.

[a] Hossain distinguishes agriculturally "developed" and "underdeveloped" regions by various criteria: access to irrigation, use of modern rice varieties, and fertilizer consumption, among others. In the agriculturally developed regions, modern varieties cover 60 percent of cropped area compared with only 5 percent in the underdeveloped areas.

[b] Calculated from Hossain (1988: tables 48, 64).

[c] Nonfarm wage labor includes earth-hauling, construction, transport, and "other" employment.

growth, particularly in close proximity to urban centers and along transport corridors (Otsuka 2007).

Rural towns stimulate nonfarm activity as well as agricultural activity in surrounding areas. They provide key productive infrastructure for nonfarm businesses, while at the same time creating new markets for agricultural producers. Recent decades have seen an explosion in urban demand for high-value agricultural products such as milk, meat, vegetables, and fruits. Rural towns further stimulate agricultural productivity by improving the range, quality, and availability of farm inputs, financial services, agricultural markets, and processing services (Evans 1992; Rondinelli 1986; Tacoli 1998, 2003; Tacoli and Satterthwaite 2003). As a result, intermediate cities constitute key elements of the spatial hierarchy, linking rural producers with large cities and export markets (see tables 6 and 7).

Because of the strong links between rural areas and the towns that serve them, rural towns frequently grow quite rapidly in prosperous agricultural zones (Hardoy and Satterthwaite 1986; Rondinelli 1987a, 1987b; Tacoli and Satterthwaite 2003). Rising rural wage rates in these areas favor the emergence of mechanization and other investments in worker productivity. Conversely, stagnant rural economies give rise to feeble demand linkages, limited commercial exchange, and stagnant rural

TABLE 6. Share of Employment, by Activity and Size of Locality
(% unless otherwise noted)

Country and year	Total labor	Agriculture	Total nonfarm	Manufacturing	Commerce and transport	Personal, financial, and community services	Construction, utilities, and mining
ISIC code		1	2–9	3	6, 7	8, 9	2, 4, 5
Bangladesh							
Rural	100	58	42	10	17	12	3
Intermediate							
Urban	100	16	84	27	28	23	6
Chittagong and							
Dhak	100	8	92	26	29	32	5
Chile, 1984							
Rural	100	65	35	5	9	17	4
Intermediate							
Urban	100	7	98	14	29	41	9
Santiago	100	1	99	20	26	46	7
Zambia, 2000							
Rural	100	90	10	1	2	7	1
Intermediate							
Urban	100	22	78	7	31	30	10
Lusaka	100	0	100	14	22	54	10

Source: Haggblade, Hazell, and Reardon 2007: table 1.6.

TABLE 7. Spatial Distribution of Population and Economic Activity in the Developing World, 2005 (% unless otherwise noted)

Indicator	Rural	Urban Intermediate	Large[a]	Total
Population share				
UN definition	57	22	21	100
WDR definition	56	24	20	100
Relative income				
Estimated ratio	1.0	1.5	2.0	0.0
Per capita income (US$)	448	671	895	592
Income share				
Agriculture	91	6	3	100
Manufacturing	27	35	39	100
Services	27	33	40	100

Source: Population share is from United Nations 2007; World Bank 2008. Per capita income is from World Bank, World Development Indicators. Income share by locality size is estimated from Haggblade, Hazell, and Reardon 2007.
[a] Cities with populations 500,000 and above.

wage rates, triggering an exodus of unskilled rural workers seeking employment in other agricultural zones or in cities and towns.

These differences suggest that the health of the rural economy influences the vibrancy of the intermediate cities that serve them. As a result, both the pace and the structure of urbanization will depend, at least in part, on the dynamics under way in agriculture and in the rural economy.

References

Bairoch, Paul. 1988. *Cities and Economic Development from the Dawn of History to the Present*. Chicago: University of Chicago Press.

Burger, Kees, Daniel Kameo, and Henry Sandee. 2001. "Clustering of Small Agro-Processing Firms in Indonesia." *International Food and Agribusiness Management Review* 2 (3-4): 289–99.

Chenery, Hollis, and Moshe Syrquin. 1986. "Typical Patterns of Transformation." In *Industrialization and Growth*, ed. Hollis Chenery, Sherman Robinson, and Moshe Syrquin. New York: Oxford University Press.

Evans, Hugh E. 1992. "A Virtuous Circle Model of Rural-Urban Development: Evidence from Kenya." *Journal of Development Studies* 28 (4): 640–67.

Freeman, Donald B., and Glen B. Norcliffe. 1985. "Rural Enterprise in Kenya: Development and Spatial Organization of the Nonfarm Sector." Research Paper 214, Department of Geography, University of Chicago.

Haggblade, Steven, and Peter Hazell. 1989. "Agricultural Technology and Farm-Nonfarm Growth Linkages." *Agricultural Economics* 3 (4): 345–64.

Haggblade, Steven, Peter Hazell, and Paul A. Dorosh. 2007. "Sectoral Growth Linkages between Agriculture and the Rural Nonfarm Economy." In *Transforming the Rural Nonfarm Economy,* ed. Steven Haggblade, Peter Hazell, and Thomas Reardon, ch. 7. Baltimore, MD: Johns Hopkins University Press.

Haggblade, Steven, Peter Hazell, and Thomas Reardon, eds. 2007. *Transforming the Rural Nonfarm Economy: Opportunities and Threats in the Developing World.* Baltimore, MD: Johns Hopkins University Press.

Haggblade, Steven, and Nick Ritchie. 1992. "Opportunities for Intervention in Thailand's Silk Subsector." GEMINI Working Paper 27, Development Alternatives, Bethesda, MD.

Hardoy, Jorge E., and David Satterthwaite. 1986. *Small and Intermediate Urban Centres: Their Role in National and Regional Development in the Third World.* Boulder, CO: Westview.

Hossain, Mahabub. 1988. Nature and Impact of the Green Revolution in Bangladesh. Research Report 67. Washington, DC: International Food Policy Research Institute.

International Herald Tribune. 1989. "In India, Hard Times Beset a Charming Village." *International Herald Tribune,* December 28, p. 3.

Kennedy, Loraine. 1999. "Cooperating for Survival: Tannery Pollution and Joint Action in the Palar Valley (India)." *World Development* 27 (9): 1673–92.

Otsuka, Keijiro. 2007. "The Rural Industrial Transition in East Asia: Influences and Implications." In *Transforming the Rural Nonfarm Economy,* ed. Steven Haggblade, Peter Hazell, and Thomas Reardon, ch. 10. Baltimore, MD: Johns Hopkins University Press.

Papola, T. S. 1987. "Rural Industrialization and Agricultural Growth: A Case Study on India." In *Off-Farm Employment in the Development of Rural Asia,* ed. R. T. Shand, vol. 1. Canberra: Australian National University.

Rondinelli, Dennis. 1986. "The Urban Transition and Agricultural Development: Implications for International Assistance Policy." *Development and Change* 17 (2): 231–63.

———. 1987a. "Cities as Agricultural Markets." *Geographical Review* 77 (4): 408–20.

———. 1987b. "Roles of Towns and Cities in the Development of Rural Regions." In *Patterns of Change in Developing Rural Regions, ed.* Raphael Bar-El, Avrom Bendavid-Val, and Gerald J. Karaska. Boulder, CO: Westview.

Schmitz, Hubert. 1999. "Global Competition and Local Cooperation: Success and Failure in the Sinos Valley, Brazil." *World Development* 27 (2): 1627–50.

Schmitz, Hubert, and Khalid Nadvi. 1999. "Industrial Clusters in Developing Countries." *World Development* 27 (9): 1503–14.

Tacoli, Cecilia. 1998. "Rural-Urban Interactions: A Guide to the Literature." *Environment and Urbanization* 10 (1): 147–66.

———. 2003. "The Links between Urban and Rural Development." *Environment and Urbanization* 15 (1): 3–12.

Tacoli, Cecilia, and David Satterthwaite. 2003. "The Urban Part of Rural Development: The Role of Small and Intermediate Urban Centres in Rural and Regional Development and Poverty Reduction." Rural-Urban Interactions and Livelihood Strategies Working Paper 9, International Institute for Environment and Development, London.

United Nations. 2007. *World Population Prospects: The 2004 Revision and World Urbanization Prospects: The 2005 Revision.* New York: Population Division, Department of Economic and Social Affairs, United Nations Secretariat. http://esa.un.org/unup.

Weijland, Hermine. 1999. "Microenterprise Clusters in Rural Indonesia: Industrial Seedbed and Policy Target." *World Development* 27 (9): 1515–30.

World Bank. 2007. *World Development Report 2007: Development and the Next Generation.* New York: Oxford University Press.

———. 2008. *World Development Report 2008: Agriculture for Development.* New York: Oxford University Press.

Notes

1. Definitions of "rural" vary widely across countries. The United Nations data collection system, which reports data for individual countries according to their own specific rural cutoffs, projects a rural population of 57 percent in the developing world in 2005. The World Bank's *World Development Report* (WDR) team has developed a more standardized cutoff to aid in cross-country comparisons. Under the WDR definition, rural areas accounted for 56 percent of total population in the developing world in 2005.

Some Stylized Facts about Rural Poverty and Geography and a Question for Policy

PETER LANJOUW

This paper summarizes the findings emerging from an ongoing research project on the spatial patterns of rural poverty in the developing world (Buys and others 2007 provide an early summary). The project is assembling data from a group of countries in order to explore the extent to which rural poverty is concentrated in marginal areas. Detailed estimates of rural poverty at a spatially disaggregated level, coming from an ongoing program of research on small-area estimation of poverty and inequality, are combined with geographically referenced information on agricultural potential and proximity to urban centers. Attention is initially focused on five developing countries: Brazil, Cambodia, Ecuador, Kenya, and Thailand. "Marginal areas" are defined as arising through a combination of low agricultural potential and remoteness.

The analysis points tentatively to six stylized facts.

First, *extreme rural poverty and vulnerability are generally most evident in marginal areas, but these patterns are observed most clearly in countries that are urbanizing more rapidly and transitioning out of agriculture.* In the five countries considered here, there is some evidence that the headcount rate is higher in those areas that can be considered as "unfavorable" in terms of agricultural productivity and, particularly, in terms of accessibility (see figure 1). However, this pattern is most evident in the three countries (Brazil, Ecuador, and Thailand) that are transitioning out of agriculture. In Cambodia and Kenya, where traditional agriculture is still the dominant economic sector, the evidence of higher poverty in areas with low agricultural potential and low access is weaker. Poverty rates are very high throughout those two countries, and the poor seem to be spread evenly around rural areas.

Second, *the spatial distribution of poor people is also of policy interest. The general pattern is that the bulk of the rural poor are located in readily accessible and more productive localities.* The geographic distribution of population in most

Peter Lanjouw is Lead Economist of the Development Research Group (DECRG) at The World Bank in Washington, D.C.

Berlin Workshop Series 2009
© 2009 The International Bank for Reconstruction and Development/The World Bank

FIGURE 1. Incidence of Poverty and Geographic Characteristics in Select Countries

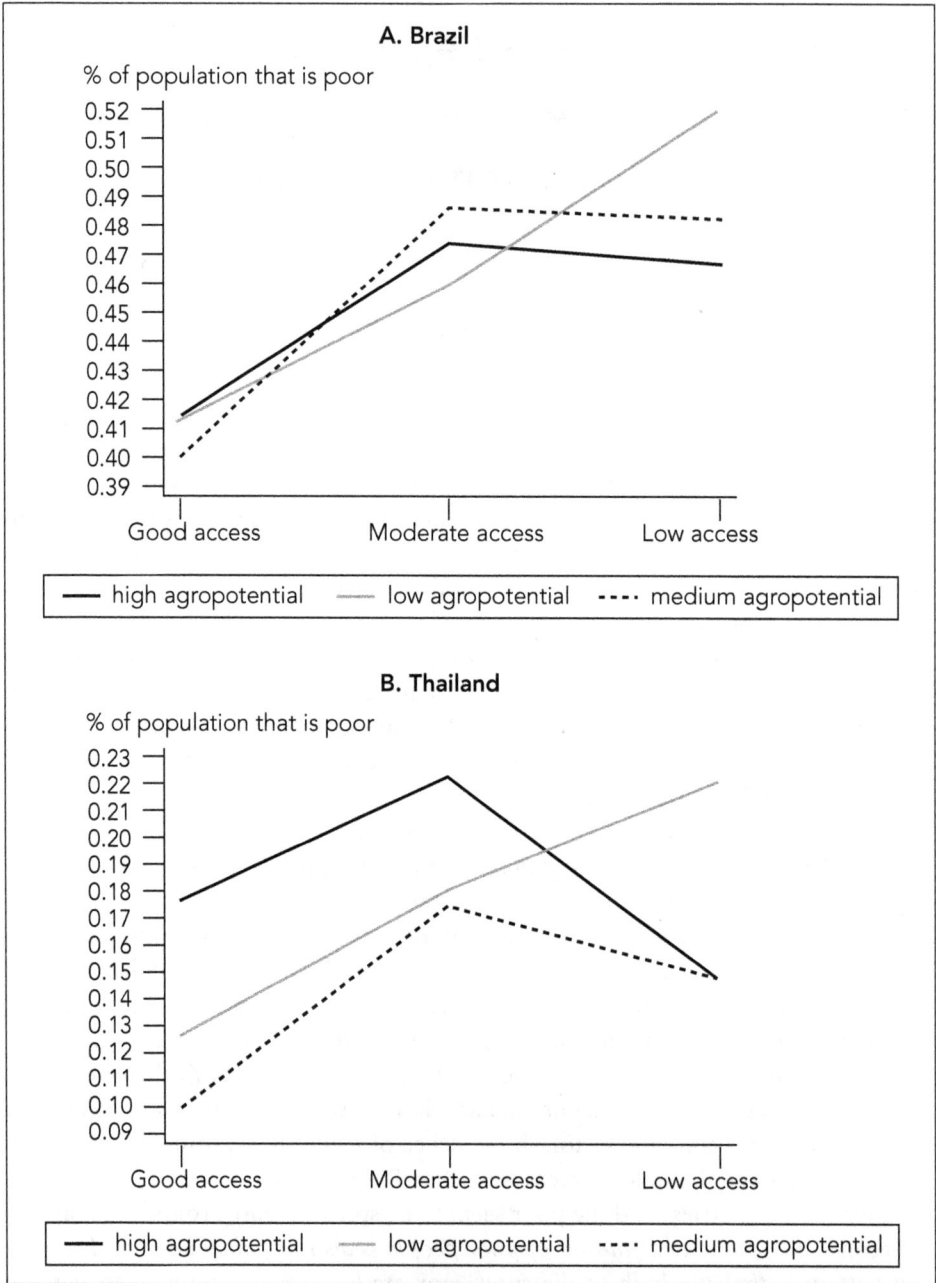

A. Brazil

% of population that is poor

— high agropotential   — low agropotential   ---- medium agropotential

B. Thailand

% of population that is poor

— high agropotential   — low agropotential   ---- medium agropotential

FIGURE 1. *(continued)*

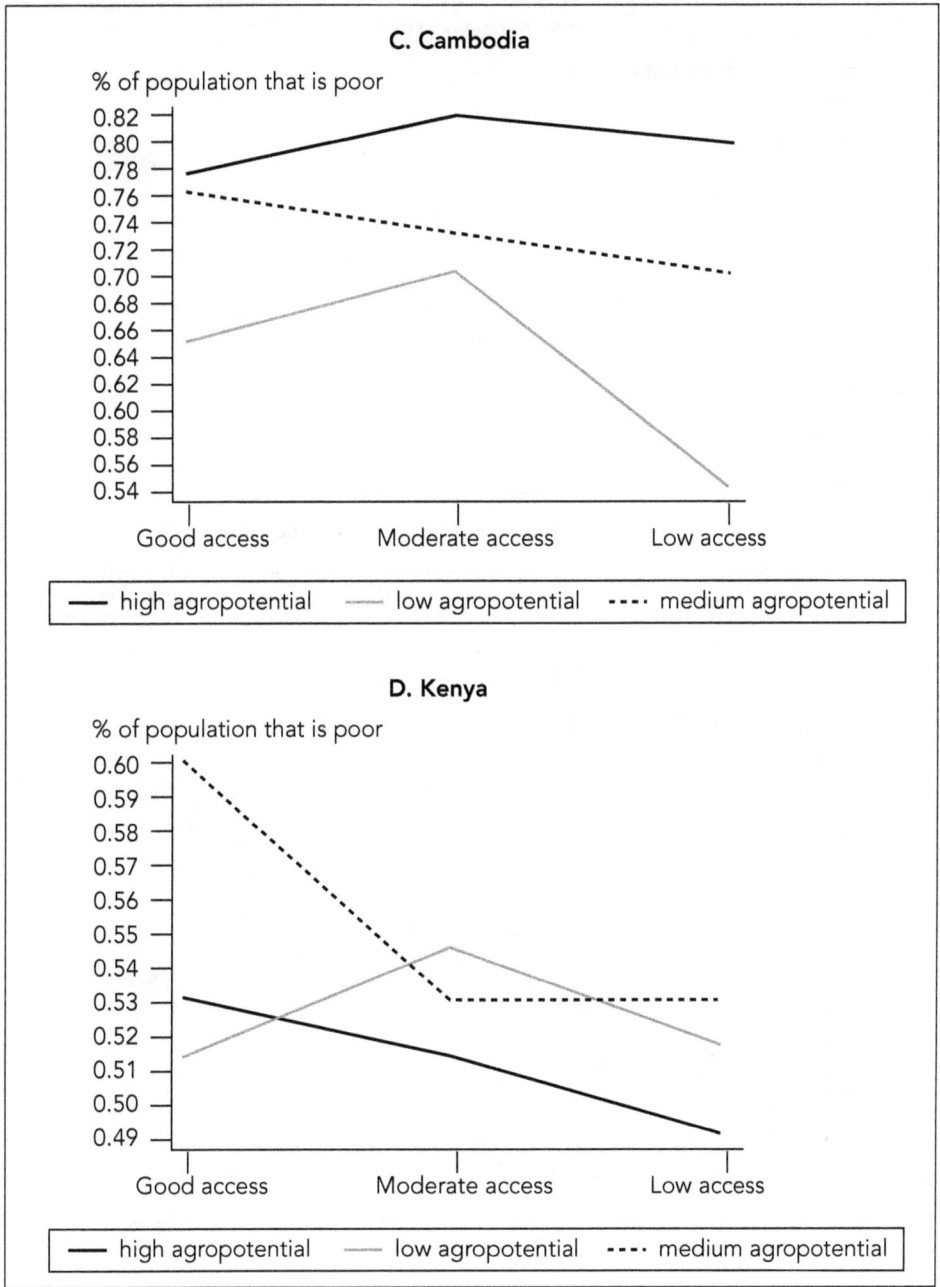

C. Cambodia

% of population that is poor

Good access — Moderate access — Low access

— high agropotential   — low agropotential   ···· medium agropotential

D. Kenya

% of population that is poor

Good access — Moderate access — Low access

— high agropotential   — low agropotential   ···· medium agropotential

FIGURE 1. *(continued)*

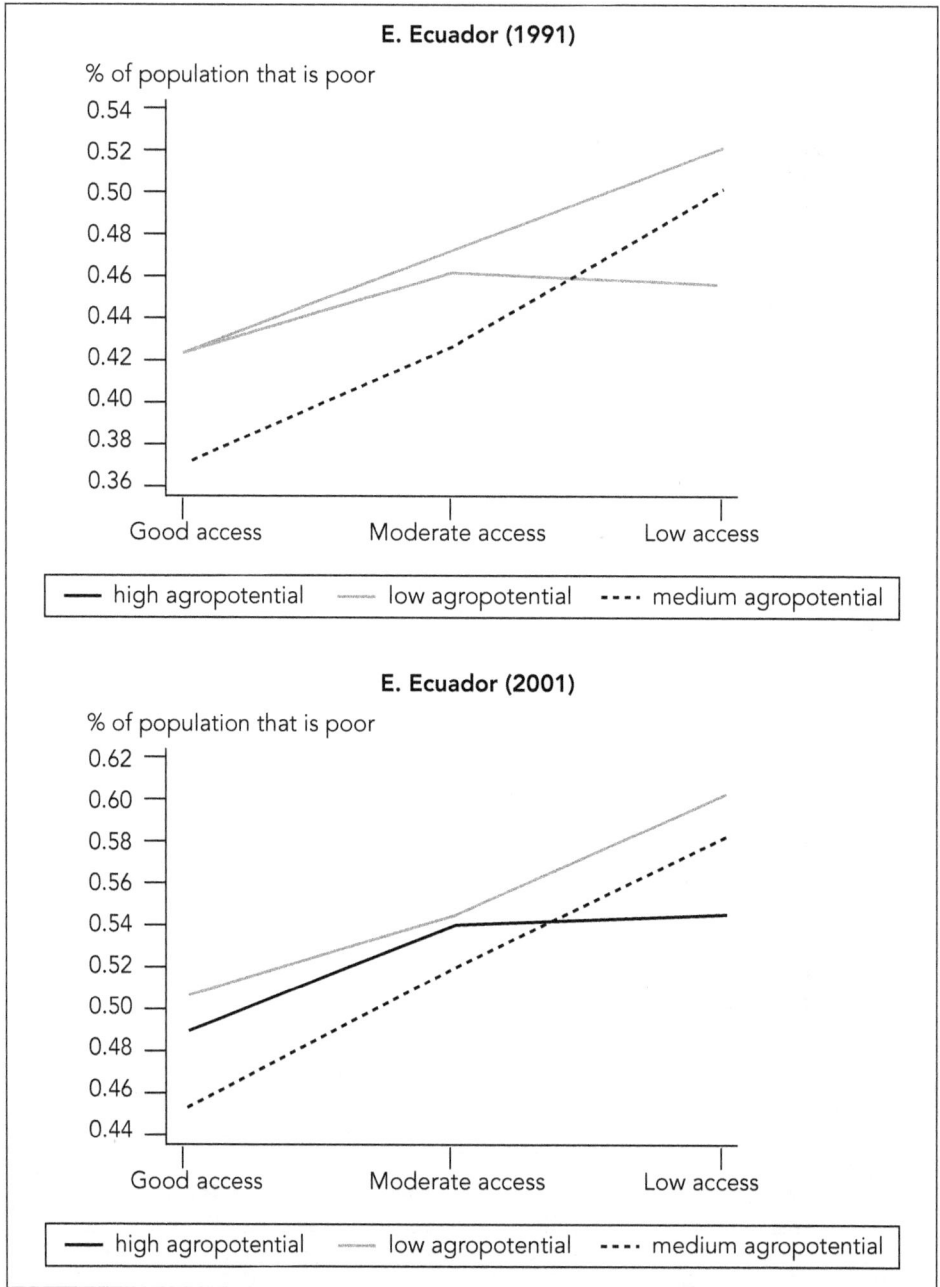

E. Ecuador (1991)

% of population that is poor

high agropotential ─── low agropotential ╌╌ medium agropotential

E. Ecuador (2001)

% of population that is poor

high agropotential ─── low agropotential ╌╌ medium agropotential

countries is far from uniform. Even though population density is particularly high in areas with low poverty rates, the absolute number of poor people in those localities may still be very high. Indeed, in the five countries considered by Buys and his coauthors, the bulk of the rural poor generally are located in readily accessible and more productive localities.

Third, *national patterns often obscure more clearly discernible patterns at the subnational level.* In the center-west, north, and northeast of Brazil, poverty is associated much more clearly with remoteness and low agricultural potential than is observed at the national level. In the wealthier southeastern and southern regions, the association between rural poverty and geography is less marked. In Thailand, too, the association is particularly strong in the north. Even in Kenya, where there seems to be little association between poverty and geography at the national level, the link between poverty, on the one hand, and remoteness and agricultural potential, on the other, is readily discernable in the western region of the country (see figure 2).

Fourth, *internal migration accounts, at least in part, for the observation that poverty rates and poverty densities do not coincide.* The paper by Buys and his coauthors examines rural poverty maps for Ecuador in 1990 and 2001. Between these two years, the economy experienced major macroeconomic upheaval and crisis. In both years, the estimated incidence of poverty in a locality was significantly higher in localities that were remote and also had low agricultural potential. Analysis of *changes* in poverty between 1990 and 2001, however, reveals that the incidence of poverty increased sharply in those localities that also saw the sharpest rise in their population. Rural areas with positive population growth were located close to urban centers, while population declined in remote and low-productivity areas. Indeed, poverty rates actually *declined* in those localities with a high share of land designated as of moderate accessibility and low agricultural potential. These patterns are consistent with a process of distress-induced migration of poor people to those areas that, in each year, were less poor (see figures 3 and 4).

Fifth, *the pattern of greater rural poverty in areas that are remote from urban centers is not necessarily confined to large urban centers.* In Brazil, 60 percent of the urban population resides in towns and cities with populations of 500,000 or less, while 30 percent of the urban population resides in centers with 100,000 people or less. Small towns and cities thus account for a very large fraction of the urban population. Analysis that distinguishes between urban areas in terms of population in Brazil finds the same pattern: rural poverty is generally lower in localities closer to urban centers, even when those centers are small (see table 1).

Sixth, *there is an association between urban poverty and both rural poverty and rural nonfarm diversification.* A study by Ferré, Ferreira, and Lanjouw (2008) indicates that, while 30 percent of the urban population in Brazil resides in towns of 100,000 or less, these centers account for as many as 40 percent of the urban poor. (Nearly 60 percent of the urban poor reside in cities of 500,000 inhabitants or less.) Similar patterns are observed in several other developing countries (Ferré, Ferreira, and Lanjouw 2008). Buys and others (2007) indicate that, in Brazil, the gradient

FIGURE 2. Poverty Incidence and Geographic Characteristics in Select Regions

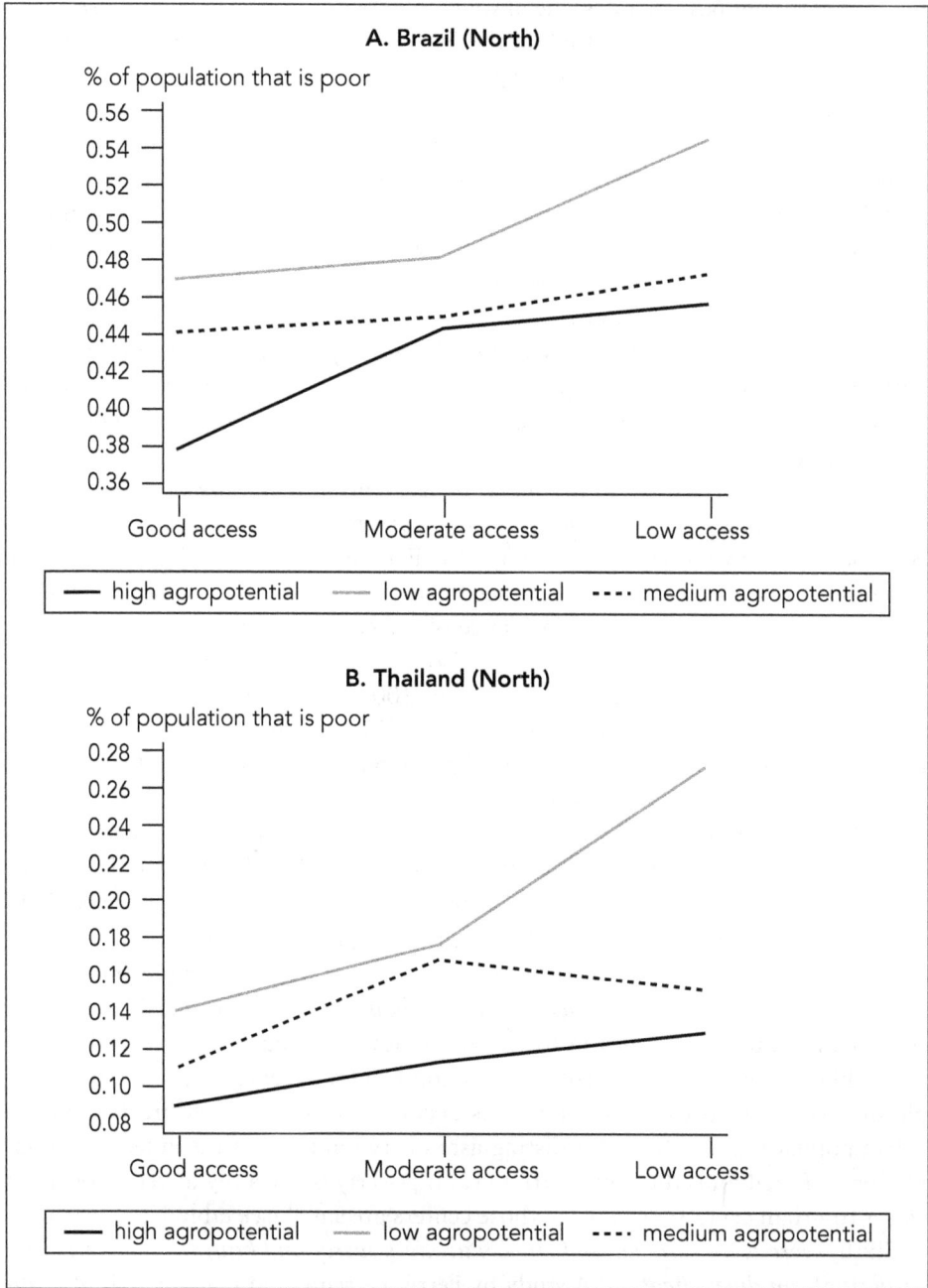

A. Brazil (North)

% of population that is poor

— high agropotential   — low agropotential   ···· medium agropotential

B. Thailand (North)

% of population that is poor

— high agropotential   — low agropotential   ···· medium agropotential

Source: Buys and others (2007).

FIGURE 2. *(continued)*

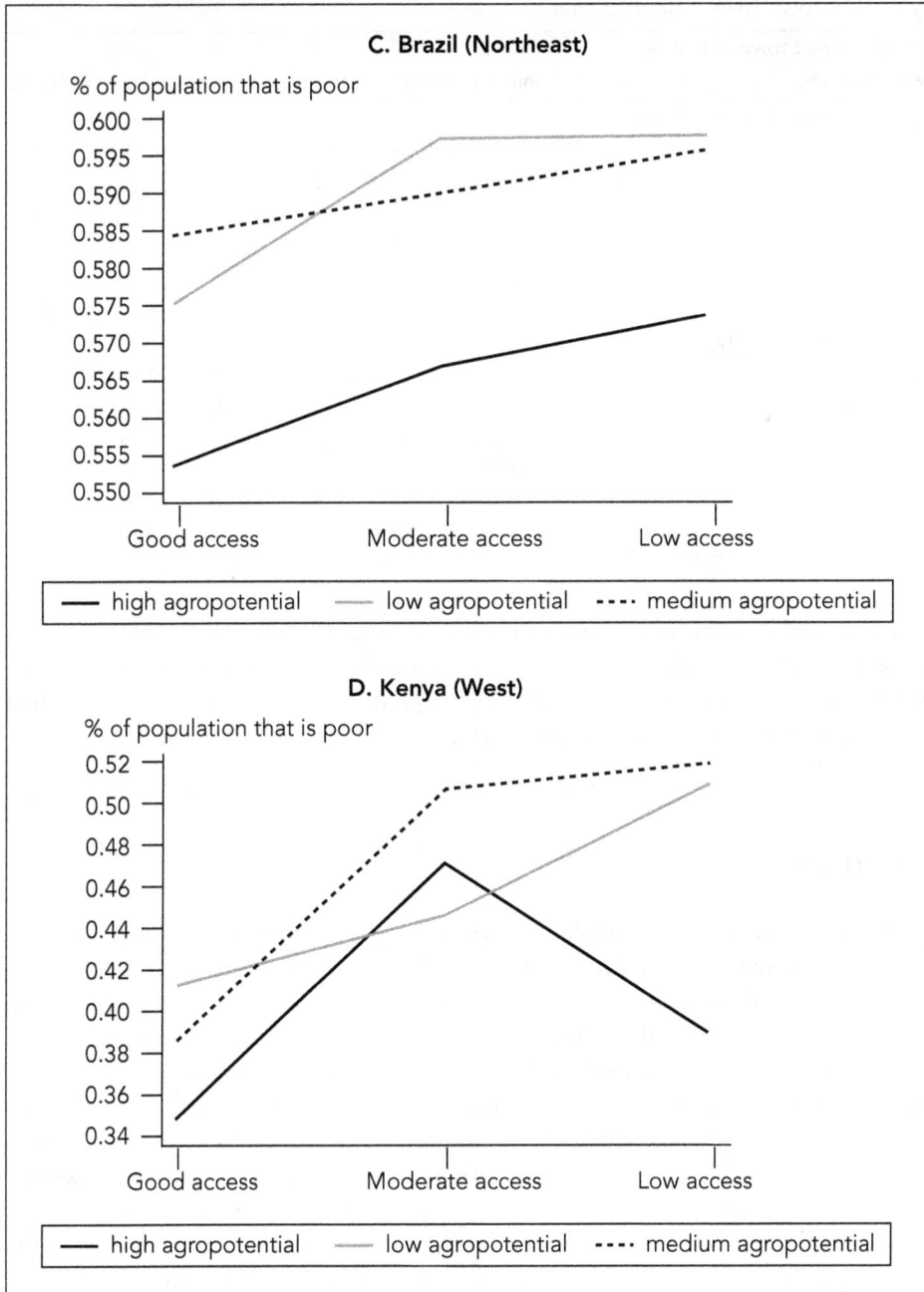

C. Brazil (Northeast)

% of population that is poor

legend: high agropotential · low agropotential · · · · medium agropotential

D. Kenya (West)

% of population that is poor

legend: high agropotential · low agropotential · · · · medium agropotential

Source: Buys and others (2007).

TABLE 1. Rural Poverty in Brazil and Proximity to, and Poverty in, Nearest Town, by Size of Town (travel time to nearest town)

Size of nearest town and urban headcount (%)	<= 6 minutes	15 minutes	30 minutes	1 hour	1.5 hours	2+hours
Nearest town of 25,000–100,000						
0–5	0.02	0.06	0.09	0.13	0.15	0.16
5–10	0.14	0.17	0.21	0.24	0.26	0.27
10–20	0.33	0.36	0.39	0.42	0.43	0.44
20–30	0.47	0.49	0.52	0.54	0.55	0.55
30–40	0.54	0.57	0.58	0.59	0.60	0.60
45+	0.56	0.58	0.59	0.60	0.60	0.60
Nearest town of 100,000–500,000						
–5	0.08	0.13	0.15	0.16	0.16	0.17
5–10	0.21	0.26	0.28	0.29	0.29	0.30
10–20	0.40	0.46	0.48	0.48	0.49	0.49
20–30	0.52	0.57	0.59	0.59	0.58	0.58
30–40	0.56	0.61	0.61	0.60	0.59	0.57
45+	0.55	0.58	0.58	0.57	0.56	0.53

Source: Buys and others 2007.

between rural poverty and distance from an urban center is much sharper the lower is the poverty rate within that urban center. Similarly, the lower poverty is in the urban center, the greater is the amount of nonfarm diversification in surrounding rural areas. These patterns hold irrespective of city size (table 1).

Discussion

Spatial variation in rural population densities and in rural poverty levels can be understood in light of urbanization patterns. Rural poverty is generally more accentuated where urban areas are distant. At the same time, rural populations (and therefore rural poverty densities) are generally located closer to urban centers. Population movements are likely to account for these patterns: in times of economic stress, remote areas with low agricultural potential see outmigration either as outright rural-urban migration or as migration toward rural areas surrounding cities. It is important to recognize that urban areas are heterogeneous—in size and in poverty levels. Emerging evidence suggests that a sizable majority of the developing world's urban population resides in small towns and cities, as opposed to the mega cities and large metropolitan areas that receive so much popular attention. The correlation between rural well-being and proximity to urban centers is not necessarily weaker for small towns, but the correlation is attenuated when poverty in those towns is high. The evidence shows, for example, that rural nonfarm diversification is positively associated with proximity to small urban centers, but negatively associated with poverty in those centers. Ferré, Ferreira, and Lanjouw (2008)

FIGURE 3. Change in Share of Rural Population in Ecuador, by Access to City and Agricultural Potential, 1991–2001

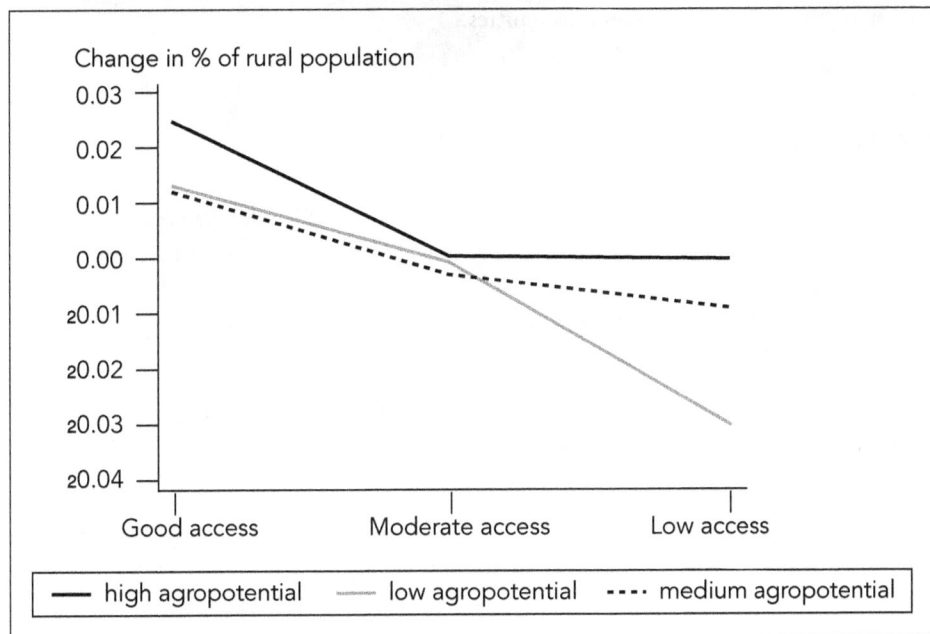

Source: Buys and others (2007).

FIGURE 4. Change in Share of Poor Population in Ecuador, by Access to City and Agricultural Potential, 1991–2001

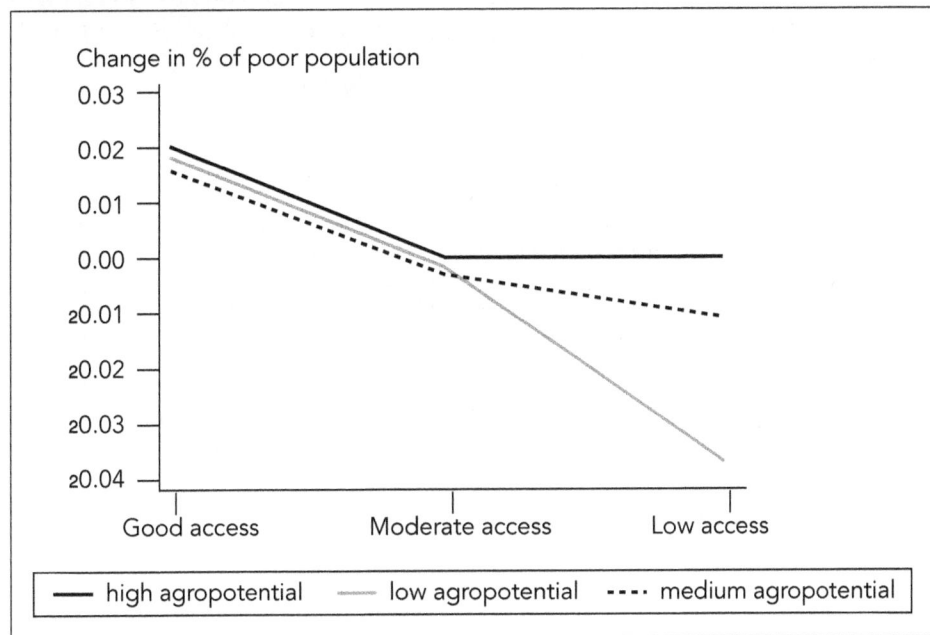

Source: Buys and others (2007).

find that poverty rates in small towns are generally higher than in large cities and indicate that, relative to large cities, small towns are generally poorly served by infrastructure services and other amenities.

A Policy Question

This discussion prompts the following question. Would stimulating economic development in small urban areas via, for example, local infrastructure provision (electricity, telecommunications) or improved connectivity to the national economy via transport infrastructure investments, help not only to address an important urban poverty concern but also to dampen *rural* poverty?

- To what extent can greater infrastructure provisioning (or other policy interventions) galvanize activity levels in small towns and reduce poverty rates in such areas?

- To what extent will increased economic activity in small urban areas translate to greater nonfarm diversification (or rising agricultural productivity) in surrounding rural areas?

Answers to these policy questions are not presently available. It is not even clear, for example, whether the transmission path that connects rural welfare with proximity and incomes in small urban centers flows from towns to rural areas. One cannot rule out the opposite direction of causality: perhaps small towns emerge and grow as a response to growth and diversification in the rural economy. A great deal of additional analysis is needed. This paper is intended to stimulate such efforts.

References

Buys, Piet, Celine Ferré, Peter Lanjouw, and Timothy Thomas. 2007. "Rural Poverty and Geography: Towards Some Stylized Facts in the Developing World." Unpublished paper, Development Economics Research Group, World Bank, Washington, DC.

Ferré, Celine, Francisco Ferreira, and Peter Lanjouw. 2008. "Is There a Metropolitan Bias? Urban Poverty and Access to Services by City Size in Six Developing Countries." Unpublished paper, Development Economics Research Group, World Bank, Washington, DC.

Part II: New Economic Geography and the Dynamics of Technological Change—Implications for Less-Developed Countries

New Economic Geography and Transportation Policies: The Case of Brazil

EDUARDO HADDAD

This paper reports on some experimental results derived from a spatial computable general equilibrium (SCGE) model for the Brazilian economy. While it addresses some of the theoretical developments derived from the new economic geography, it provides some intermediate perspectives between a core-periphery model, on the one hand, and a perfectly competitive, homogeneous space model, on the other. In the Brazilian case, firms can exploit increasing returns to scale without serving a national market; in large part, market imperfections derive from transportation costs that essentially serve to segment markets. Further, asymmetries in the distribution of productive activity, with the primacy of São Paulo, serve to strengthen existing competitive advantages.

The new economic geography has revisited the issues associated with the application of various competitive market structures to the spatial economy. Research in the last decade has identified some important theoretical inconsistencies between competitive regimes conceptualized in space-less and spatial economies (see Fujita, Krugman, and Venables 1999; Fujita and Thisse 2002). However, even the new economic geography theory does not seem able to cover the notion of some intermediate form of space between homogeneous and not homogeneous that would essentially give rise to the Brazilian case.

Domingues and Ruiz (2005: 11–12) identify spatial industrial agglomerations (SIAs) in Brazil.[1] According to the study, there are 15 SIAs in Brazil, in a restricted group of 254 out of 5,507 Brazilian municipalities, accounting for 75 percent of the industrial production of companies operating in the country. The spatial distribution of SIAs is notably concentrated in Brazil, particularly in clearly delimited industrial corridors across the south and southeast regions. The northeast region has SIAs that are confined within metropolitan areas of major state capitals, and no

Eduardo Haddad is Associate Professor of the Faculty of Economics Administration and Accounting at the University of São Paulo in Brazil.

Berlin Workshop Series 2009
© 2009 The International Bank for Reconstruction and Development/The World Bank

The ideas presented in this article draw on Haddad and Hewings (2005) and Haddad and others (2007).

SIA was identified in the northern region, despite the significant contribution of the Manaus Free Trade Zone to national industrial production. In turn, the absence of SIAs in the central region reveals that intense expansion of agribusiness over the last two decades has not been sufficient to build the industrial density needed to produce spillover and industrial effects over the space.

While appeal to core-periphery outcomes could be made, it seems that, with high transportation costs, firms can exploit increasing returns to scale within less-than-complete national markets. The very size of São Paulo provides opportunities that could not be realized by similar firms located within the northeast of Brazil; further, certain asymmetries exist in competitive advantage. With improvements in transportation, the São Paulo firms, already further down the range of increasing returns to scale, possess a competitive advantage to exploit scale economies further by reducing transportation costs, thereby exacerbating the welfare differentials between regions. One of the main reasons for their competitive advantage is their central position, not geographically central, but central in terms of the locus of productive activity or purchasing power (see Haddad and Azzoni 2001). However, the presence of other relevant industrial areas outside São Paulo provides some intermediate perspectives with a core-periphery model.

The Brazilian case has been complicated further by a transportation infrastructure that until recently was regulated and biased toward investment in highways to the exclusion of water and railroad modes of transportation. Efficiency gains from investments apparently have not been considered from a broader perspective, such as enhancing interregional cohesion, but instead have been oriented toward supporting increased exports. How are these investments to be estimated, and can some method be found to simulate the effects of transportation policies, through a process of increased competition that reduces the costs of spatial transfer?

In what follows, we explore results from the use of computable general equilibrium models applied to multiregional configurations of the Brazilian economy in a way that reflects some of the current market imperfections. Some of these imperfections arise from historical investment decisions, some from Brazil's geography, and some from a combination of many factors, including Brazil's recent decision to open its markets.

Moreover, the models used adopt an explicit specification of transportation costs, avoiding some of the difficulties of iceberg formulations ably discussed by McCann (2005). The objective is to identify the efficiency gains from investments in a broader perspective, such as enhancing interregional cohesion, as well as to explore possible asymmetries in the welfare effects as transportation costs between pairs of regions are reduced.

Modeling issues associated with the treatment of nonconstant returns and transportation costs are discussed. As mentioned, recent theoretical developments in new economic geography bring new challenges to regional scientists and spatial economists, in general, and to interregional CGE modelers, in particular. Experimentation with the introduction of scale economies, market imperfections, and transportation costs should provide innovative ways of dealing explicitly with theoretical issues related to integrated regional systems. An attempt to address these issues is also discussed.

Transportation Infrastructure in Brazil

Brazilian transport infrastructure is deteriorating rapidly from lack of investment and maintenance, showing a larger number of critical points, or bottlenecks, in most of the corridors. Decay in the transportation system curtails economic growth, hampering competitiveness in both the internal and external markets. Deterioration of Brazil's transportation network has contributed to high operational costs, obstructing the competitive integration of the country.

The lack of well-developed multimodal transport in Brazil, in addition to the low quality of road infrastructure, has had negative effects on the competitiveness of the country. A summary breakdown of soybean production and export costs shows that Brazil loses its production cost advantage over U.S. production due to higher transport and export costs (including customs administration).

As shown in table 1, while U.S. costs of transporting soybeans from the place of production to export ports represent about 7.7 to 12.8 percent of final costs, the comparative figure for Brazil is 15.5 and 30.1 percent, respectively. As a result, Brazil loses its cost advantage, mostly due to domestic transport costs. Put another way, Brazilian domestic transport costs from the farm gate to port are 122–274 percent of the same costs in the United States, while freight costs are 140–197 percent of U.S. costs.

TABLE 1. Estimated Export Costs of Soybeans, by Destination and Origin, First Quarter 2006 (US$ per metric ton)

Destination	From Brazil[a]	From United States[b]	Brazil to U.S. cost ratio
Germany (Hamburg)			
Production cost	157.86	204.78	0.77
Transport cost to export port	84.65	30.84	2.74
Freight cost to Hamburg	38.51	19.53	1.97
Final cost in Hamburg	281.02	255.15	1.10
China (Shanghai)			
Production cost	180.71	202.34	0.89
Transport cost to export port	42.49	34.80	1.22
Freight cost to Shanghai	50.13	35.71	1.40
Final cost in Shanghai	273.33	272.85	1.002

Source: U.S. Department of Agriculture, Brazil Soybean Transportation, August 2006 (World Bank 2008).
[a] From Mato Grosso to Hamburg and from Goias to Shanghai.
[b] From Iowa to Hamburg and from Minneapolis to Shanghai.

Recent government initiatives in Brazil to promote investments in infrastructure include the Programa de Aceleração do Crescimento (PAC, the Growth Acceleration Program), unveiled at the end of January 2007.[2] Investments in logistic infrastructure are an estimated US$58.3 billion in the four-year period from 2007 to 2010, US$33.4 billion (57.3 percent of the total) in road infrastructure alone.[3]

Concomitant with the four-year program (PAC), the federal government has also signaled its intention to revive long-term planning in transportation in the country. The design of an ambitious Plano Nacional de Logística e Transportes (PNLT, National Plan of Logistics and Transportation) has been initiated, involving different stakeholders. It aims to support decision makers in attaining economic objectives through policy initiatives related to both public and private infrastructure and organization of the transportation sector.[4]

At the state level, few initiatives have taken place in the realm of transport planning. States such as Bahia, Minas Gerais, and Rio Grande do Sul have all developed thorough diagnostics of the sector, including forward-looking exercises with a long-term view of the possible policy interventions within the respective state borders.[5]

In the next two sections, we present results from simulations using a fully operational SCGE model implemented for the Brazilian economy, based on previous work by Haddad and Hewings (2005), in order to assess the likely economic effects of recent changes in road transportation policy in Brazil.[6]

Among the features embedded in this framework, modeling of external scale economies and transportation costs provides an innovative way of dealing explicitly with theoretical issues related to integrated regional systems. The explicit modeling of transportation costs is built into the interregional CGE model, based on origin-destination flows, which takes into account the spatial structure of the Brazilian economy. This creates the capability of integrating the interstate CGE model with a geographically coded transportation network model, enhancing the potential of the framework to aid in understanding the role of infrastructure in regional development. The transportation model used is the so-called Highway Development and Management Model, developed by the World Bank and implemented using the software TransCAD. Further extensions of the current model should be considered that integrate other features of transport planning in a continental industrializing country like Brazil, with the goal of building a bridge between conventional transport planning practices and the innovative use of CGE models.

In order to illustrate the analytical power of the integrated system, I present a set of simulations, which evaluate the economic impacts of physical and qualitative changes in the Brazilian road network (such as a highway improvement), in accordance with recent policy developments in Brazil. Rather than providing a critical evaluation of this debate, I emphasize the likely structural impacts of such policies. I expect that the results will reinforce the need to specify spatial interactions in SCGE models better. I look first at two projects that have a key role in the national integration of markets and then revisit the efficiency-equity issue, from a spatial perspective, to look at 75 transportation infrastructure projects.

Case Study 1: Integration Axes

This section illustrates the analytical capability of the unified framework in the evaluation of specific transportation projects contemplated in the PAC program. The case study under consideration refers to two projects to improve federal highways—BR-262 and BR-381—in the state of Minas Gerais.

The guidelines that have been used to justify the choice of the specific tracks of the BR-262 and BR-381 highways to be improved are based on the strategic location of these network links in the national transportation system, which constitute two of the main corridors related to the more dynamic regions of the country. Moreover, it is hoped that such improvements will foster regional development in Minas Gerais, one of the leading economies of the country.

With a total length of 441 kilometers between Betim and Uberaba, the BR-262 project is duplicating the existing road link between Betim and Nova Serrana and constructing climbing and passing lanes between Nova Serrana and Araxá. The project will cost an estimated BRL 554 million.[7]

The BR-381 project is duplicating the track between Belo Horizonte and Governador Valadares, a total length of 304 kilometers. The total cost of implementation is an estimated BRL 1.395 billion.

The distinction between the two projects lies in the role they play in the integration of Brazilian regions. While the BR-262 project constitutes a major improvement on the east-west integration of the country, linking the coast of the southeast to the more agricultural areas of the midwest, the BR-381 has a strategic role in integrating the northeast with the southeast and south of the country. These distinct axes of integration play different roles in the interregional Brazilian system, as spatial competition occurs to a lesser degree in the case of the BR-262 than in the case of the BR-381 link. In the latter case, denser economic spaces are involved directly in the spatial process, while in the former, more specialized spaces have more prominent roles.

The spatial effects on gross domestic product (GDP) reveal, both in the short run and in the long run, positive impacts in regions influenced directly by the BR-262 as well as in the country as a whole. Noteworthy is that these positive impacts are spread over space in the long run. Moreover, relocation effects tend to be directed to the agriculture-producing regions in the west as well as to the areas linked directly to the project itself, within the borders of Minas Gerais.

In the case of the BR-381, spatial competition clearly plays a prominent role. Given the favorable scenario for relative costs of production in the northeast, in a context of systemic low quality of transport infrastructure, the northeast increases its spatial market area, while the richer southeast suffers from the network (congestion) effects. Lower growth with decreasing regional inequality is the main long-run macro result (see localized spillover models—Baldwin and others 2003—for a theoretical view).

Case Study 2: Efficiency versus Equity

This section takes a closer look at a portfolio of multimodal infrastructure projects within the borders of the Brazilian state of Minas Gerais. Following work by Almeida and others (forthcoming), the objective is to reveal that, methodological differences aside, the evidence about the nature of the relationship between the provision of transport infrastructure and regional equity is controversial, due to a fundamental characteristic associated with this issue. In other words, even with the same theory or model, method, and its specification, one may continue to obtain different results about this relationship. This outcome arises because this relationship crucially depends on where the transport infrastructure is located. In addition to methodological considerations, there seem to exist authentic spatial reasons that might yield controversial results. Indeed, transport infrastructure is strongly region-dependent. The spatial structure of the provision of transport infrastructure matters in this question, playing a fundamental role in determining its effects on the economic system (Almeida and others forthcoming: 2–3).

According to Almeida and others (forthcoming), demonstrating empirically the relationship between transport and regional equity is very difficult. In the literature, the evidence about this relationship is often contradictory, although most of the problems seem to stem from methodological discrepancies. In what follows, an alternative approach was followed, by adopting an SCGE model with new economic geography features. The theoretical model, the method of investigation, as well as its specification were kept constant; only the spatial structure of the provision of transport infrastructure (captured through reductions in transportation costs) was changed. Seventy-five projects (simulations), considered in the recently concluded Plano Estadual de Logística e Transportes (PELT Minas), were analyzed with a view to the efficiency-equity trade-off associated with investments in transportation infrastructure. Among the 75 projects, 3 are investments in waterways, 5 in railways, 3 in pipelines, and 64 in roads.

Figure 1 summarizes the results for the effects on efficiency (measured in terms of real gross regional product growth) and regional disparity (measured in terms of the relative growth of the poor regions in the north of the state and the state as a whole; a negative value indicates that the poor region is growing at a slower pace). The results reflect a long-run environment, in the new economic geography tradition, in which the equilibrating mechanisms draw heavily on the balance of real wage differentials through labor mobility. There is a clear trade-off between efficiency and regional equity. Projects that produce higher impacts on GDP growth also contribute more to regional concentration.

FIGURE 1. Regional Equity-Efficiency Trade-off of Transportation Infrastructure Investments in Minas Gerais, Brazil

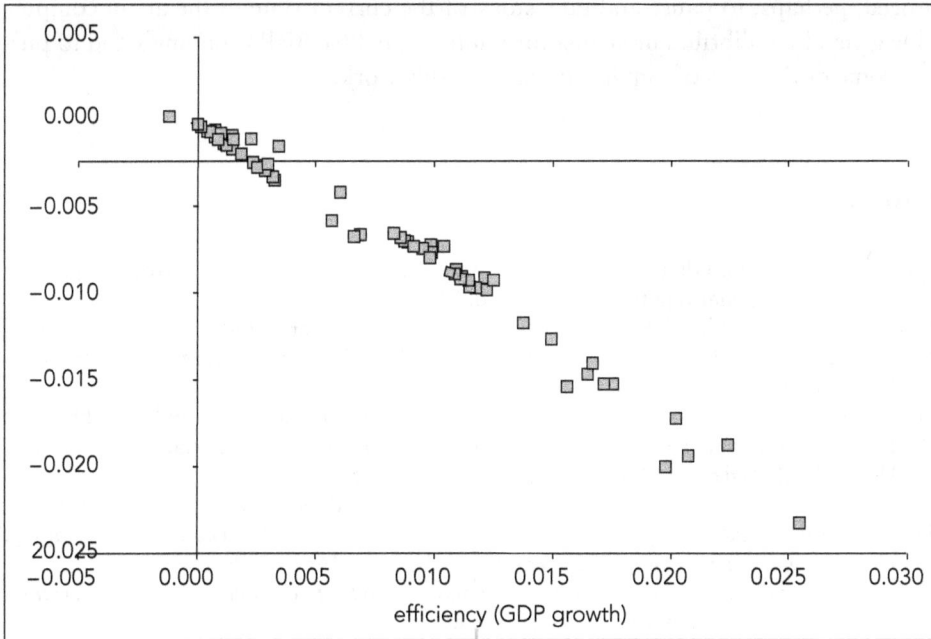

Source: Elaborated by the author.

Final Remarks

Appropriate tools are needed to assess the economic impacts of transportation infrastructure policies. This paper has attempted to tackle this issue. It has been suggested that SCGE models can potentially be used to analyze transport planning policies. This paper has illustrated ways in which this potential has been implemented. However, this tool is not yet a recurrent part of the transport planning process. To do so, further amendments are needed, in order to cope with methodological advances both in economic and in transport modeling.

However, the results provided are encouraging in the sense that the issues, while difficult, are not insurmountable. The challenges to competitive equilibrium in the spatial economy presented by the new economic geography remain largely untested. This paper offers one approach to narrowing the gap between theory and empirical application. The Brazilian economy, sharing features of both developed and developing countries, presents a further challenge: the lack of uniformity of the spatial distribution of resources and population, the glaring disparities in welfare across states and regions, and the presence of a hegemonic economy, in São Paulo, that renders traditional computable general equilibrium modeling of limited value.

The results reveal that it is possible to handle increasing returns to scale, to address issues of asymmetric impacts of transportation investment, and to approach the problems of more flexible functional forms, uncertainties about data, and parameter estimates in ways that are tractable and theoretically defensible. There is a need, perhaps, to pause and take stock of the current state of the art in computable general equilibrium modeling for multiregional (spatial) economies and to pursue some of the lines of inquiry initiated by this work.

References

Almeida, Eduardo S., Eduardo A. Haddad, and Geoffrey J. D. Hewings. Forthcoming. "The Transport-Regional Equity Issue Revisited." *Regional Studies.*

Baldwin, Richard, Rikard Forslid, Philippe Martin, Gianmarco Ottaviano, and Frédéric Robert-Nicoud. 2003. *Economic Geography and Public Policy.* Princeton, NJ: Princeton University Press.

Domingues, Edson P., and Ricardo M. Ruiz. 2005. "Industrial Cores and Peripheries in Brazil." Discussion Paper 261, Centro de Desenvolvimento e Planejamento Regional, Universidade Federal de Minais Gerais, Belo Horizonte.

EIU (Economist Intelligence Unit). 2007. "Brazil: Country Report." EIU, London, February.

Fujita, Masahisa, Paul Krugman, and Anthony J. Venables. 1999. *The Spatial Economy: Cities, Regions, and International Trade.* Cambridge, MA: MIT Press.

Fujita, Masahisa, and Jacques-François Thisse. 2002. *Economics of Agglomeration.* Cambridge, U.K.: Cambridge University Press.

Haddad, Eduardo A., and C. R. Azzoni. 2001. "Trade Liberalization and Location: Geographical Shifts in the Brazilian Economic Structure." In *Structure and Structural Change in the Brazilian Economy,* ed. Joaquim J. M. Guilhoto and Geoffrey J. D. Hewings. London: Ashgate.

Haddad, Eduardo A., and Geoffrey J. D. Hewings. 2005. "Market Imperfections in a Spatial Economy: Some Experimental Results." *Quarterly Review of Economics and Finance* 45 (2): 476–96.

Haddad, Eduardo A., Fernando S. Perobelli, Edson P. Domingues, and Mauricio Aguiar. 2007. "Assessing the Economic Impacts of Transportation Infrastructure Policies in Brazil." Unpublished paper, University of São Paulo.

McCann, Philip. 2005. "Transport Costs and the New Economic Geography." *Journal of Economic Geography* 5 (3): 305–18.

World Bank. 2008. "Brazil: Evaluating the Macroeconomic and Distributional Impacts of Lowering Transportation Costs." Report 40020-BR. World Bank, Washington, DC, July.

Notes

1. Domingues and Ruiz (2005: 11) estimate the correlation of the industrial value added of each Brazilian municipality in relation to that of its $m - 1$ neighbors, in a given set of m contiguous municipalities, allowing the identification of industrial agglomerations in Brazil without necessarily taking into account its political and administrative division. The incidence of these agglomerations depends first on the statistical significance of the spatial autocorrelation test (set at 10 percent), as it may limit the number of agglomerations within the territory and exclude existing agglomerations that are not statistically significant. For this reason, they name the existing significant agglomerations as spatial industrial agglomerations, which are more restricted than those industrial agglomerations identified in other studies in Brazil.
2. The PAC will aim to raise average annual GDP growth to 5 percent a year (almost double the country's long-term average), principally through increased investment in infrastructure, which will be fostered in part through targeted tax breaks (EIU 2007).
3. www.brasil.gov.br (Programa de Aceleração do Crescimento 2007–10).
4. www.centran.eb.br (Programa Nacional de Logística e Transportes).
5. In the Minas Gerais case, the PELT Minas was based on the use of state-of-the-art methodological approaches to deal explicitly with the interface between transport and economy, from diagnostics to evaluation of transport projects.
6. The simulations were carried out for supporting the government of Minas Gerais to prepare the PELT Minas.
7. Values as of December 2006.

Spatial Disparities of Knowledge Absorption, Technological Change, and Prosperity: Theoretical Considerations and Empirical Evidence from China

INGO LIEFNER

This paper aims to highlight some basic connections between technological change and the emergence and development of spatial disparities in developing and newly industrializing countries. It uses the example of China to illustrate key arguments. The first section refers to a number of well-established theoretical concepts focusing on the implications of these theories for spatial developments. Empirical evidence of the spatial economic effects of technological change is abundant when it comes to analyzing disparities between countries using secondary data. The connections between technological change and spatial developments on a subnational scale are much harder to depict because of missing data. Thus the paper draws on both secondary and primary data, acknowledging the difficulties regarding generalizability. Still, some cautious conclusions can be derived concerning the relation between spatial structures and technological change in developing countries. This leads to policy recommendations that allow exploiting the technology-related growth opportunities brought about by globalization and international knowledge flows.

Technology and Spatial Disparities on the Subnational Level

New technology (or technological knowledge) is and always has been spatially concentrated, mirroring the location of higher education institutions, research and development (R&D) potential, and technology-intensive industries. This holds true on all spatial scales, from the global pattern down to the subnational level. In contrast to this, market forces, private returns to technology investment, and

Ingo Liefner is Professor of Economic Geography at the University of Giessen in Germany.

Berlin Workshop Series 2009
© 2009 The International Bank for Reconstruction and Development/The World Bank

The author would like to thank the German Research Foundation (DFG) and the Volkswagen Foundation for sponsoring the research referred to in the third section of this paper. He would also like to thank the many colleagues in China, notably Gang Zeng (Shanghai) and Jie Fan (Beijing), for their cooperation.

consumer preferences in particular lead to spatial diffusion of technology. Technology diffusion has been greatly enabled by the rise of digital information and communication technologies and the decline in transport costs. Such technology diffusion, however, has never leveled the spatial concentration of knowledge. There are various reasons for this (for example, Bell and Pavitt 1997; Howells 2002; Meusburger 2001; Oinas 1999). First, understanding and applying complex technologies requires a profound and often subject-related knowledge. Thus only people, firms, or regions that possess the relevant stock of knowledge can generate or acquire new knowledge in that particular field. The cumulative character of certain technologies fosters the spatial differentiation between leading and lagging regions with respect to technology. Second, the speed of technology transfer and diffusion depends on the character of the underlying knowledge. The diffusion of knowledge that is so immature that it cannot be expressed verbally, mathematically, or graphically (tacit knowledge) depends on face-to-face contacts. Thus the pace of its diffusion is very slow.

The counteracting forces that favor either the concentration of knowledge or its diffusion lead to a complex and dynamic spatial pattern of rising and falling technology-intensive regions complemented by a knowledge periphery (for a sector model, see, for example, Gomulka 1990). These technology-intensive regions comprise companies, universities, and R&D organizations related to one another in a regionally confined setting (for a synopsis of concepts, see Moulaert and Sekia 2003). They represent regional clusters. In times of fast technological progress, which involves specialized and tacit knowledge, the cumulative process of learning seems to dominate and outpace the diffusion of technology. Thus knowledge disparities increase.

As soon as new technology is turned into products, it creates temporary monopolies on the new commodities or services and fosters profits and economic development. Thus spatial disparities in technology affect spatial disparities in growth rates and wealth. Economic disparities, however, are not as marked as technological disparities, because counterbalancing forces, such as the relocation of labor-intensive industries away from technology-intensive regions, limit spatial-economic divergence.

In industrial countries these effects can be viewed on the subnational scale, for example, when comparing high-tech regions with lagging regions. But in developing and newly industrializing countries, the processes leading to spatial concentration of technology are magnified by additional forces. Developing countries that open their economies to international trade and factor mobility benefit from inward foreign direct investment (FDI) and other forms of cooperation, such as technology transfer under the original equipment manufacturer system (Ernst 2002; Hobday 2000; Lall 2002; Mowery and Oxley 1995). These forms of cooperation—and inward FDI in particular—induce an enormous inflow of technology. This technology may be regarded as mature from the angle of industrial countries, but it is new for developing countries. The availability of new technology relative to the existing stock of knowledge is thus much higher in developing than in industrial countries. The absorption of technologies of ever higher standards accelerates cumulative learning processes (Mathews 2001; Viotti 2002). But this absorption takes place only in a few regions with the largest existing stock of knowledge (Asheim and Vang 2006). Hence the process of technology-induced spatial differentiation is very pronounced in developing countries. Knowledge and related economic disparities widen most quickly in developing countries that open up for trade relations and FDI.

During phases of fast technological catch-up, the process of technology absorption in the technologically leading regions within the newly industrializing countries is more powerful and faster than the trickle down of technology into lagging regions. In other words, technology diffusion is rapid on the global scale, but slow at the subnational level.

To allow some regions within developing countries to develop the preconditions for cumulative learning and quick absorption of knowledge (these are a relatively strong base of human capital, investment in education and in science and technology infrastructure, and the basic conditions for attracting FDI) is essential for fast technological catch-up, economic restructuring, and sustained growth. Thus increasing spatial disparities are both an outcome of technological progress and a precondition for knowledge absorption and future technology-oriented growth.

Spatial disparities in developing countries are not only rural-urban disparities. Economic differences between (city) regions, reflecting differences in the ability to generate and absorb technology, add up to a pattern of rural-urban disparities.

Technology and Urban Economies in China

This section discusses empirical evidence from China, the single most important developing country regarding technology absorption following a huge inflow of FDI and related technology. Moreover, the country has made public and private efforts to boost the level of education as well as the quality and quantity of domestic R&D (Schwaag Serger and Breidne 2007). These efforts create conditions favorable for technology absorption and learning. Table 1 is based on data published by the National Bureau of Statistics, Beijing. All other tables and figures are based on surveys and research projects carried out by the Department of Economic Geography, University of Hannover, and various Chinese partners (Beijing ZGC Innovation Survey, Shanghai ZJ Innovation Survey). The projects were sponsored by the German Research Association (DFG) and the Volkswagen Foundation and were carried out between 2003 and 2005.

China's spatial economy is characterized by the dominant position of leading agglomerations in coastal provinces (Beijing, Guangzhou, Shanghai). These provinces are the hub of investment in education and R&D in terms of quality and quantity. For example, they host the country's leading universities and research institutes and attract the most talented students. They host the most skilled workforce and the most technology-intensive domestic companies. They also attract the bulk of FDI and related technology (Grewal and Sun 2002; Taubmann 2001;

TABLE 1. Spatial Disparities in China

Location	Number of postgraduate students in higher education institutions per 1,000 inhabitants, 2002[a]	Total R&D expenditures per capita, 2005 (yuan)	FDI stock per capita, 2005 (US$)	GDP per capita, 2005 (yuan)	Annual GDP growth, 2001–05 (%)[b]
Coast					
Shanghai (City)	0.62	1,172	4,805	51,486	15.13
Beijing (City)	1.54	2,484	1,549	44,774	16.72
Tianjin (City)	0.32	696	2,575	35,452	17.82
Zhejiang	0.08	333	846	27,435	18.14
Jiangsu	0.12	361	1,504	24,489	17.95
Guangdong	0.06	265	1,487	24,327	16.75
Shandong	0.04	211	366	20,023	19.13
Liaoning	0.13	295	857	18,947	12.31
Fujian	0.05	152	1,069	18,583	12.69
Hebei	0.03	86	120	14,737	16.31
Hainan	0.01	19	547	10,804	12.50
Guangxi	0.02	31	131	8,746	15.64
Central					
Nei Mengu	0.03	49	171	16,327	22.79
Heilongjiang	0.10	128	117	14,428	12.92
Jilin	0.16	145	174	13,329	14.31
Shanxi	0.04	78	69	12,458	19.79
Hubei	0.15	131	175	11,419	13.85
Henan	0.02	59	80	11,287	17.61
Hunan	0.05	70	112	10,293	14.17
Jiangxi	0.02	66	215	9,410	16.85
Anhui	0.03	75	97	8,783	13.43
West					
Xinjiang	0.03	32	37	12,956	14.95
Chongqing	0.09	114	102	10,974	14.83
Ningxia	0.02	53	258	10,169	15.77
Qinghai	0.01	54	50	10,006	15.99
Shaanxi	0.18	249	150	9,881	16.28
Tibet	0.01	13	72	9,069	14.52
Sichuan	0.06	118	81	8,993	14.52
Yunnan	0.03	48	65	7,804	12.89
Gansu	0.05	76	53	7,456	14.50
Guizhou	0.01	30	28	5,306	14.96
China average	0.09	192	495	15,511	16.18
Gini	0.546	0.510	0.629	0.271	
Correlation coefficient (Pearson) with GDP per capita	0.744	0.827	0.897	1.000	0.247

Source: NBS 2002a, 2002b, 2004, 2006.

[a] Excluding students at specialized colleges and research institutes.

[b] Nominal data, not controlled for inflation.

Zhao and Tong 2000; see also Sun and Parikh 2001). The economic success of these provinces is evident despite the weaknesses of official data. The Gini coefficient for interprovincial disparities of per capita income seems to have grown during the last two decades, from 0.222 in 1985 to 0.253 in 1995 and to 0.271 in 2005. This increase in spatial disparities has been accepted by the Chinese government as an integral part of and a precondition for the chosen reform process under the label "Let some get rich first." From the late 1970s onward, the Chinese way of technological change and economic development sought to attract FDI to the coastal provinces. Differing levels of wealth were seen as unavoidable (Long and Ng 2001; Wei 1999). After nearly 30 years of promoting the coastal regions, official documents and speeches have begun to acknowledge the arguments for a more spatially balanced growth.

Data from the segment of high-tech companies of two of the country's most technologically successful regions—Zhongguancun Science Park (Beijing) and Zhangjiang Hightech-Park (Shanghai)—give insight into the fundamental processes underlying these developments. Knowledge absorption affects product innovation and productivity and thus fosters economic success.

Taking the introduction of new products as an indicator of successful absorption (or generation) of knowledge allows us to depict the rates of technology acquisition (see table 2). The comparison of high-tech companies in Beijing and Shanghai with firms from other successful Asian metropolises (Bangkok, Penang, Singapore), which were surveyed with a comparable method, shows the tremendous speed of technological development in China's technologically leading regions (Revilla Diez and Berger 2005; Revilla Diez and Kiese 2006).

TABLE 2. Indicators of Innovation in Asia (% of firms)

Region	R&D[a]	Patents[b]	Innovating[c]			Innovative[d]		
			Total	Product	Process	Total	Product	Process
Beijing, China	55.5	48.3	64.3	60.8	47.6	44.0	38.0	29.4
Shanghai, China	56.3	47.6	89.7	82.9	74.6	69.0	58.3	51.0
Singapore	29.7	7.8	39.0	30.2	29.4	19.5	12.3	15.7
Penang, Malaysia	26.6	5.8	42.4	34.6	38.7	20.9	12.6	16.2
Bangkok, Thailand	15.1	—	17.8	13.9	12.8	7.5	4.7	5.6

Sources: Beijing ZGC Innovation Survey 2003; Shanghai ZJ Innovation Survey 2003; EDB/NUS-CMIT National Innovation Survey Singapore 2000; Penang State Innovation Survey 2000; Thailand R&D/Innovation Survey 2000; see Hennemann and Liefner 2006.

— Not available.

[a] Share of companies carrying out R&D.

[b] Share of companies holding patents.

[c] Share of companies introducing new products or processes within the last three years.

[d] Share of companies making more than 25 percent of their turnover with new products or processes.

On the level of individual companies, the key factors of technical progress and innovation become clear. Within the segments of Beijing's and Shanghai's high-tech industries, innovation depends on the absorption of knowledge from universities and public research organizations, from foreign-invested companies, or—the most promising constellation—from both sources (Liefner and Hennemann 2008; Liefner, Hennemann, and Lu 2006). Absorption itself is enabled by the companies' base of human capital, internal R&D activities, and managerial capacity to build up strong connections with knowledge sources (Cohen and Levinthal 1989). Close cooperation with technology-providing partners abroad drives product innovation and productivity (Blomström and Kokko 2001).

Moreover, cooperation with foreign partners affects the efficiency of internal R&D efforts (see table 3). The impact of foreign technology absorption is significant even within the quite homogeneous segment of high-tech companies. For cooperating firms, the share of internal R&D expenses correlates significantly with the share of new products (r_{xy}: 0,335; $p < 0.01$). Correlations between other indicators—for example, the share of R&D personnel and the introduction of new processes—are significant, too. However, for firms that do not cooperate with foreign companies, these correlations are all weak and insignificant (Liefner 2006: 149). Thus foreign knowledge is the main driver behind successful innovation in Chinese high-tech companies, and successful innovation (learning) depends on initial investment in absorptive capacity and absorption. It is a cumulative process.

It is very difficult to trace the path of technology diffusion. However, analyzing the spatial scope of the innovation-related linkages of technology-absorbing companies in Shanghai and Beijing and companies in neighboring provinces offers some insight. Less than 20 percent of the innovating companies surveyed reported that they closely cooperate with firms in neighboring provinces. Most of the innovation-related contacts are within the two agglomerations or are directed toward distant agglomerations in China or other countries. Technology stays largely within urban settings. This spatial pattern is similar to that of supplier-customer linkages (Liefner 2006: 186–91; Young and Lan 1997).

Structural differences regarding knowledge between urban regions of comparable size have been shown to turn into economic differences. The cases of Beijing and Wuhan are illustrative. Both cities are comparably large and have a profound base of human capital as well as an established industrial core. But clear differences exist regarding FDI inflow, the technological level of the economy, the flexibility of the political-institutional system, and location. These differences affect, for example, the commercialization of university-generated knowledge. Beijing is the core of the northern coastal region, whereas Wuhan is located in central China. The urban region of Wuhan—lacking a sufficient stock of administrative and techno-economic knowledge—seems unable to turn new knowledge generated in the university system into commercial success. For Beijing the opposite holds true: the formation of university spin-offs—the main way to commercialize technology in China throughout the 1990s and early 2000s—expanded much more rapidly in Beijing and was apparently hampered by an inflexible political system in Wuhan (Kroll and Liefner 2008). Other forms of knowledge, such as administrative flexibility and innovativeness, openness to FDI, and new, market-oriented policies, add up to the technologi-

TABLE 3. Effects of Cooperation with Foreign Companies

Indicators	Cooperating firms	Noncooperating firms
Share of new products (percent)	41.3	26.3
Productivity (turnover per employee, yuan)	945,798	526,689

Source: Shanghai ZJ Innovation Survey.

cal differences between city regions. The outcome, again, is increasing disparities between leading and lagging urban agglomerations.

These findings illustrate the statements based on theoretical considerations in the last section. Fast technological catch-up depends on and produces spatial concentration of human capital, technology, and FDI. Under circumstances of rapid technological development, for developing countries this means rapid inflow of technology and spatial-economic concentration that increases and fuels both economic growth and spatial disparities, both urban-rural and urban-urban.

Policy Options

These findings can be turned into development strategies. If developing countries wish to benefit from technology that is accessible through inward FDI and use that technology for accelerated economic development, it is crucial to help those urban regions that seem to attract FDI and related technology inflow to create an economic environment suitable for learning. Higher education institutions as well as R&D organizations should be set up, in-migration of talented students and skilled personnel from lagging areas should be promoted, and public policy should encourage inward FDI, including offshore innovation. All policies designed to achieve this kind of spatial concentration or clustering are favorable.

As a strategic complement, developing countries have to accept that many other urban areas will have to concentrate on less technology-oriented industries, such as tourism, the exploitation and processing of natural resources, and labor-intensive manufacturing. Only in the long run will rural areas benefit from overall economic growth, remittances, and trickle-down effects.

Conclusions

This paper has emphasized the role of knowledge in the globalizing world, stressing the hypothesis that, in order to reap the benefits of globalization, developing countries have to accept and sometimes foster spatial disparities. And that goes beyond the rural-urban dichotomy: the cumulative nature of learning leads to a differentiation between technology-oriented and less technology-oriented cities. The former ones absorb and integrate knowledge for the national economy.

Of course, this view may be challenged from different perspectives. Some developing countries still have restrictive trade policies. Others are dominated by elites that distract foreign investors. Still others cannot secure fundamental preconditions for investment and growth, such as a stable, functioning legal system. These countries will not be able to follow the path outlined here. Not all countries may be ready to accept increasing spatial disparities for various reasons. Important considerations in this respect may be escalating social tensions between the residents of prosperous and less prosperous regions, tensions created through migration, and environmental problems stemming from economic concentration. Not all countries may be able to concentrate spatially enough human capital and attract enough foreign investment to stimulate cumulative learning and self-sustaining growth (attain critical mass). This ability clearly depends on the size of the country, its initial income level, the general level of education, and its attractiveness for foreign investors.

The latter point needs to be considered in the context of efforts to replicate the Chinese success in other developing countries. Large African countries may be big enough to create sufficient spatial concentration on their own, but many African countries lack other preconditions for attracting inward FDI. Smaller countries, moreover, might have to rely on cross-national migration and cooperation if they want to establish visible technology-absorbing agglomerations. In turn, other countries may have to function mainly as peripheries for a few growing agglomerations in certain countries. Few agglomerations seem to have such growth potential (Cape Town, Johannesburg, or other South African cities, Cairo, maybe Nairobi, Lagos, or Accra). Obviously, some of these cities still lack basic institutional factors allowing for massive inflow of FDI. Many countries and agglomerations in Latin America, South Asia, and Southeast Asia seem to be in a much more advantageous position. Still, it seems worthwhile to try to use the forces of global capital and technology flows as China did.

References

Asheim, Bjørn, and Jan Vang. 2006. "Regions, Absorptive Capacity, and Strategic Coupling with High-Tech TNCs: Lessons from India and China." *Science, Technology, and Society* 11 (1): 39–66.

Bell, Martin, and Keith Pavitt. 1997. "Technological Accumulation and Industrial Growth: Contrasts between Developed and Developing Countries." In *Technology, Globalisation, and Economic Performance,* ed. Daniele Archibugi and Jonathan Michie, 83–137. Cambridge, U.K.: Cambridge University Press.

Blomström, Magnus, and Ari Kokko. 2001. "Foreign Direct Investment and Spillovers of Technology." *International Journal of Technology Management* 22 (5-6): 435–53.

Cohen, Wesley M., and Daniel A. Levinthal. 1989. "Innovation and Learning: The Two Faces of R&D." *Economic Journal* 99 (September): 569–96.

Ernst, Dieter. 2002. "Global Production Networks and the Changing Geography of Innovation Systems: Implications for Developing Countries." *Economics of Innovation and New Technology* 11 (6): 497–523.

Grewal, Bhajan, and Fiona Sun. 2002. "Foreign Markets and Foreign Capital: The Role of Trade in China's Economic Transformation." In *China's Future in the Knowledge Economy: Engaging the New World,* ed. Bhajan Grewal, Lan Xue, Peter Sheehan, and Fiona Sun, 194–211. Melbourne: New Zealand International Review.

Gomulka, Stanislaw. 1990. *The Theory of Technological Change and Economic Growth.* London: Routledge.

Hennemann, Stefan. 2006. "Technologischer Wandel und wissensbasierte Regionalentwicklung in China." Wirtschaftsgeographie 35, Kooperationen im Innovationsprozess zwischen Hightech-Unternehmen und Forschungseinrichtungen/Universitäten, Münster.

Hennemann, Stefan, and Ingo Liefner. 2006. "Kooperations- und Innovationsverhalten von chinesischen Hochtechnologieunternehmen: Empirische Ergebnisse aus Beijing und Shanghai." *Zeitschrift für Wirtschaftsgeographie* 50: 58–71.

Hobday, Mike. 2000. "East versus Southeast Asian Innovation Systems: Comparing OEM- and TNC-led Growth in Electronics." In *Technology, Learning, and Innovation: Experiences of Newly Industrializing Economies,* ed. Linsu Kim and Richard Nelson, 129–69. Cambridge, U.K.: Cambridge University Press.

Howells, Jeremy R. L. 2002. "Tacit Knowledge, Innovation, and Economic Geography." *Urban Studies* 39 (5-6): 871–84.

Kroll, Henning, and Ingo Liefner. 2008. "Spin-off Enterprises as a Means of Technology Commercialisation in a Transforming Economy: Evidence from Three Universities in China." *Technovation* 28 (5): 298–313.

Lall, Sanjaya. 2002. "FDI and Development: Research Issues in the Emerging Context." In *Foreign Direct Investment: Research Issues,* ed. Bijit Bora. Routledge Studies in the Modern World Economy. London: Routledge.

Liefner, Ingo. 2006. "Ausländische Direktinvestitionen und internationaler Wissenstransfer nach China: Untersucht am Beispiel von Hightech-Unternehmen in Shanghai und Beijing." Wirtschaftsgeographie 34, Kooperationen im Innovationsprozess zwischen Hightech-Unternehmen und Forschungseinrichtungen/Universitäten, Münster.

Liefner, Ingo, and Stefan Hennemann. 2008. "Cooperation in Chinese Innovation Systems: Key Determinants and Outcomes." In *Greater China's Quest for Innovation,* ed. Henry S. Rowen, Marguerite G. Hancock, and William F. Miller, 157–68. Stanford Project on Regions of Innovation and Entrepreneurship (SPRIE). Palo Alto, CA: Stanford University.

Liefner, Ingo, Stefan Hennemann, and Xin Lu. 2006. "Cooperation in the Innovation Process in Developing Countries: Empirical Evidence from Beijing Zhongguancun." *Environment and Planning A* 38 (1): 111–30.

Long, Guoying Y., and Mee Kam Ng. 2001. "The Political Economy of Intra-provincial Disparities in Post-Reform China: A Case Study of Jiangsu Province." *Geoforum* 32 (2): 215–34.

Mathews, John A. 2001. "National Systems of Economic Learning: The Case of Technology Diffusion Management in East Asia." *International Journal of Technology Management* 22 (5-6): 455–79.

Meusburger, Peter. 2001. "Geography of Knowledge, Education, and Skills." In *International Encyclopedia of the Social and Behavioral Sciences,* ed. Neil J. Smelser and Paul B. Baltes, 8120–26. Amsterdam: Pergamon.

Moulaert, Frank, and Farid Sekia. 2003. "Territorial Innovation Models: A Critical Survey." *Regional Studies* 37 (3): 289–302.

Mowery, David C., and Joanne E. Oxley. 1995. "Inward Technology Transfer and Competitiveness: The Role of National Innovation Systems." *Cambridge Journal of Economics* 19 (1): 67–93.

NBS (National Bureau of Statistics of China). 2002a. *China Statistics Yearbook on High-Technology Industry 2002.* Beijing: NBS.

———. 2002b. *China Statistical Yearbook on Science and Technology 2002.* Beijing: NBS.

———. 2004. *Educational Statistics Yearbook of China 2003.* Beijing: NBS.

———. 2006. *China Statistical Yearbook 2006.* Beijing: NBS.

Oinas, Päivi. 1999. "Activity-Specificity in Organizational Learning: Implications for Analysing the Role of Proximity." *GeoJournal* 49 (4): 363–72.

Revilla Diez, Javier, and Martin Berger. 2005. "The Role of Multinational Corporations in Metropolitan Innovation Systems: Empirical Evidence from Europe and Southeast Asia." *Environment and Planning A* 37 (10): 1813–35.

Revilla Diez, Javier, and Matthias Kiese. 2006. "Scaling Innovation in South East Asia: Empirical Evidence from Singapore, Penang (Malaysia), and Bangkok." *Regional Studies* 40 (9): 1005–23.

Schwaag Serger, Sylvia, and Magnus Breidne. 2007. "China's Fifteen-Year Plan for Science and Technology: An Assessment." *Asia Policy* 4 (July): 135–64.

Sun, Haishun, and Ashok Parikh. 2001. "Exports, Inward Foreign Direct Investment (FDI), and Regional Economic Growth in China." *Regional Studies* 35 (3): 187–96.

Taubmann, Wolfgang. 2001. "Wirtschaftliches Wachstum und räumliche Disparitäten in der VR China." *Geographische Rundschau* 53: 10–17.

Viotti, E. B. 2002. "National Learning Systems: A New Approach on Technical Change in Late Industrializing Economies and Evidences from the Cases of Brazil and South Korea." *Technological Forecasting and Social Change* 69 (7): 653–80.

Wei, Yehua H. D. 1999. "Regional Inequality in China." *Progress in Human Geography* 23 (1): 49–59.

Young, Stephen, and Ping Lan. 1997. "Technology Transfer to China through Foreign Direct Investment." *Regional Studies* 31 (7): 669–79.

Zhao, X. B., and S. P. Tong. 2000. "Unequal Economic Development in China: Spatial Disparities and Regional Policy, 1985–1995." *Regional Studies* 34 (6): 549–61.

Part III: Perspectives: Rural-Urban Transformation— Leading, Lagging, and Interlinking Places

Comparative Competitiveness of Agriculture under a Multidimensional Disparity Development Process: A Narrative Analysis of Rural Development Issues in China

MANTANG CAI

China achieved great success in its economic reform over the last 30 years. The reform started with successful reform of the agricultural sector, followed by opening up of the coastal area. The agricultural reform contributed a great deal toward improving the general livelihood of the rural population but little toward stimulating gross domestic product (GDP) growth, which was the main goal of the economic reform for a long period of time. Under the so-called GDP-illustrated development process, China's economic reform policy quickly shifted its focus to urban-based industrial development, particularly in the coastal areas. This shift resulted in increasing disparity, particularly between urban and rural areas and between the east and the west. Furthermore, farmers' income growth slowed during the 1990s, and the gap between urban and rural areas widened quickly. After entering the twenty-first century, the Chinese government recognized the growing disparities and initiated several new development policies, including new development plans for the western, northeast, and middle regions. At the same time, rural development once again became a focus of the government's development policy, generally understood as the *San Nong* issues (meaning three rural development issues, that is, agriculture, countryside, and farmers). Under the new development policy, government is directing a great deal of investment to rural development through various programs and is shifting general development policy from GDP-illustrated development to the "construction of a harmonious society." This paper reviews the rural development process in China over the last 30 years in an effort to improve our understanding of the key issues facing rural development policy.

Mantang Cai is Deputy Director and Associate Professor of Beijing Development Institute at Peking University in the People's Republic of China.

Berlin Workshop Series 2009
© 2009 The International Bank for Reconstruction and Development/The World Bank

Review of China's Rural Development Process

China launched its economic reform in the late 1970s, and agricultural reform played an important role in the overall economic reform process, particularly in the early stages. These 30 years of agricultural development can be divided into three periods: 1978–88, 1988–98, and 1998 to the present.

1978–88

In the first 10 years, agricultural development played an important role in the overall economic reform of China. Up to 1983, more than 99 percent of rural China completed the transition from the commune system to the household responsibility system. This was a critical step in China's agricultural reform and increased the productivity of farm work and improved farmers' living conditions. From 1982 to 1987, the Chinese government launched reform of the governing system in rural China, transforming it from the commune system to township government. The government also encouraged the transformation of agricultural production from a more subsistence to a more market-oriented system. From 1978 to 1984, production increased from 300 million tons of grain to 400 million tons, the total value of production output increased 68 percent, and farmers' income increased 166 percent. At the same time, the newly developed township industries also created a total output value of Y200 billion and provided opportunities for 60 million rural laborers to earn off-farm income. However, the economic reform only addressed the microeconomic issues affecting rural China, not the macroeconomic issues. In particular, the government did not allow full ownership of the land that farmers were initially allocated during the land reform of the 1950s. In fact, the new household responsibility system had limited impact. Total agricultural production increased 42.2 percent from 1978 to 1984; of this, the new tenure system contributed 46.9 percent, the increased application of chemical fertilizers contributed 32.2 percent, higher prices for agricultural products contributed 16 percent, and other reform policies contributed the remainder. The limited impact of the new land tenure system gradually disappeared. In fact, from 1984 to 1988, the per capita production of grain declined from 400 to 364 kilograms. At the same time, due to lack of full ownership, land was converted to urban purposes quickly at very low cost. More than 250,000 hectares of arable land were converted for urban purposes every year, making a total loss of 6.6 million hectares of arable land for the first 25 years after reform. The farmers received only about Y500 billion from the land conversion allowance, but the government and commercial entities generated capital resources up to Y9 trillion. As a result, more than 45 million farmers were without land.

1988–98

Agricultural development slowed down, following the rapid growth of the first 10 years. The main reason was that the macroenvironment for development was "reassessed" and partially influenced by the increased "collective components" in the rural production system. For example, Henan Province launched 59,342 collective projects in its 47,678 villages, with an official production value of Y13.7 billion and 1.63 million jobs for farmers. However, most of these projects failed. The economic reform policy was "resumed" after 1992, when Deng Xiaoping visited the coastal areas and called for a more open policy.

However, new obstacles arose in agricultural development: (a) the economic burden of farmers increased; (b) the grain production–dominated agricultural development policy created a situation of "cannot be consumed, cannot be stored, and cannot be sold"; and (c) financial support from the central government declined as development priority was shifted to urban areas. From 1985 to 2000, centrally financed agricultural investment declined from 18 to 8 percent, and total investment in rural infrastructure was Y170.4 billion, accounting for just 2 percent of the country's total infrastructure investment. The income of the rural population declined steadily: 4.6, 4.3, 3.8, and 2.1 percent each year from 1997 to 2000.

1998–Present

After placing so much emphasis on urban and industrial development, the government reassessed the development process and reaffirmed that the three rural issues—agriculture, countryside, and farmers—are key issues influencing the overall process of economic reform and modernization. A new round of discussions on agricultural development was held, including policies related to improving the coordination between urban and rural areas and between industries and agriculture. The government also launched various taxation reform and financial support policies for the rural areas, including a pilot taxation reform starting in 2003 and a people-centered development model in 2004, among others. The total agricultural investment from the central government reached Y262.6 billion in 2004, three times that in 1977, and Y300 billion in 2005. Starting in 2006, all agricultural taxes were waived, reducing farmers' agricultural taxes Y120 billion a year.

Agricultural Competitiveness and Disparities

In reviewing China's rural reform process and policy, the government made great efforts to help the rural population to improve their livelihood. As a national social development policy, the reform was a success. However, the context has been changing over the last 15 years, particularly after China became a member of the World Trade Organization (WTO). China's agriculture is not a simple issue of "producing enough food to feed the nation," and China's agricultural sector faces new challenges.

As indicated, China's agricultural development was largely the result of two factors: (a) the new land tenure system and (b) the application of new technologies (particularly increased application of fertilizers). However, the impacts of both factors are limited.

The new land tenure system has been constraining commercial production that is globally competitive due largely to the small scale of production. The application of chemical fertilizers has caused severe land degradation and become an obstacle to further development of agriculture.

As a result, under China's rapid urbanization and industrialization, agriculture is lagging far behind other sectors. Figure 1 demonstrates income per capita of the urban and rural populations. The gap between them is expanding very quickly, and the ratio of urban to rural income has increased from about 2:1 at the beginning of the economic reform to the current 3:1.

Agriculture relies largely on natural resources. For this reason, there is also a large disparity in income among regions, as shown in figure 2. The regional disparity is a function of both natural conditions and distance, or accessibility, to market. The eastern part of China is located along the coast; it was the first focus of economic reform, and the economic system is relatively advanced. The west is far behind the coast in this respect.

In order to improve the competitiveness of agriculture, it is important to consider the following factors in an integrated way: division of labor, economy of scale, investment, and regional disparity.

FIGURE 1. Income per Capita in Rural and Urban Areas of China, 1983–2004

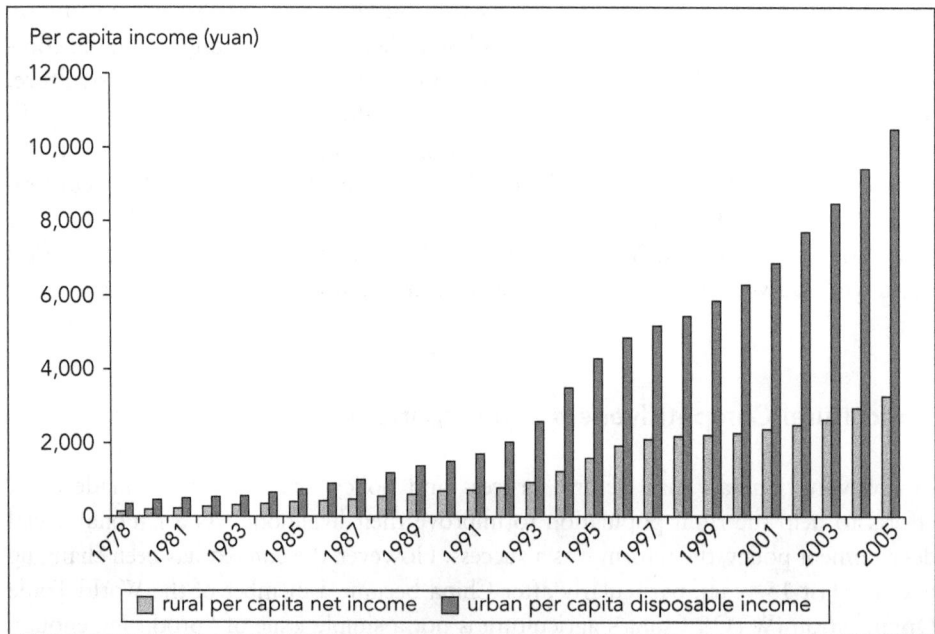

Division of Labor

China is a big country with a large surplus of rural laborers. There is only about 0.28 (1983) to 0.24 (2005) hectare of arable land per laborer. At the beginning of the economic reform, more than 90 percent of rural workers generated their income from agricultural production; in 2005 the figure was only about 60 percent. The labor productivity of China's agricultural production is about three to four times lower than that in developed countries. As the principal rural development policy still focuses on a land-bound approach, it limits the mobility of labor and the division of labor. In reality, at least half of rural workers seek off-farm income. Younger male workers usually spend all or part of their time in off-farm work, but they cannot leave the land because of the *hukou* system, which prohibits them from leaving their place of registration, in this case the rural community. The real farmers in rural communities are disadvantaged groups such as elders, women, and the disabled, who have difficulty bringing the land into full production.

Economy of Scale

At present, China's rural lands are managed by households, who operate on a very small scale, in most cases too small for commercial production. The government has not been inclined to change its land policy, which is a hallmark of the current regime. However, government is encouraging the "industrialization of agriculture" or the "integration of agriculture." Among central financial support to agriculture, a large proportion of the investment is being allocated to agro-processing industries, so-called "development of dragon head agro-processing industries." This

FIGURE 2. Income per Capita in Different Regions of China, 2005

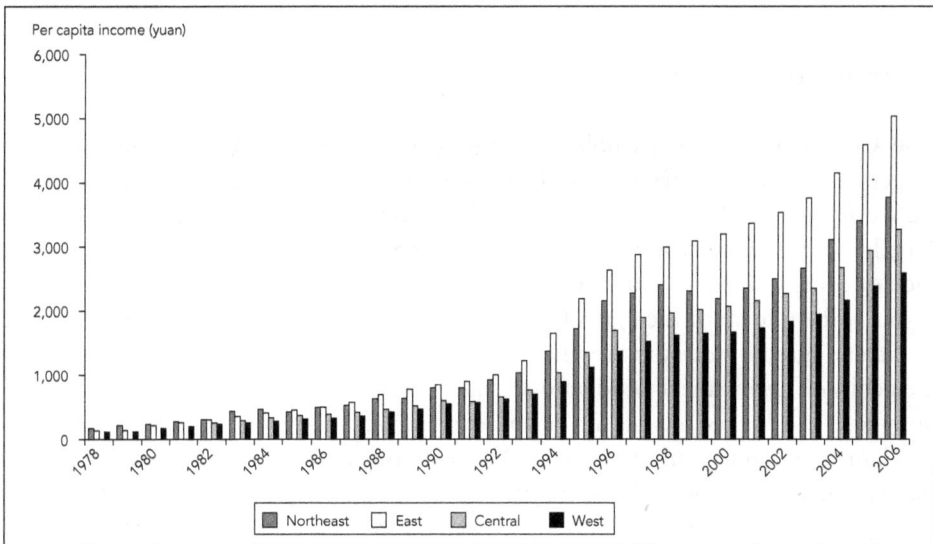

approach has not shortened the distance between rural and urban areas because most of the processing industries are based in urban areas. Measures are also taken to build up farmers' cooperatives, and a national law for farmers' economic cooperatives was issued two years ago. But the current situation is still at an early stage. In a project funded by the World Bank in central China's Hunan Province, 20 "farmers' associations" applied for support, and less than 30 percent of those that applied were really farmers' associations.

Investment

Another obstacle in rural areas is investment, or agricultural, credit. Due to low economic return and management difficulties, financing institutions are normally not interested in providing credit for agricultural projects, including both short- and long-term loans and agricultural insurance.

Regional Disparity

Agriculture is relatively weak because of poor accessibility to market, which is a result of both distance to market and difficulty accessing information, supplies, and technologies. In addition, accessibility varies from region to region as a result of weak transportation and communication infrastructure. Therefore, different strategies should be applied in different regions to take advantage of the conditions of a particular region.

It is critical for government policies to address these factors in an integrated way. However, the current centralized and sector-divided operational system of the Chinese government faces a big challenge in coming up with a comprehensive solution.

Concluding Remarks

The Chinese government's policy on agriculture is based on social development targets—that is, an effective rural administrative system, expanded coverage of public finance, and a solid rural education system. Achieving these goals will rely largely on government investment. This approach will not be able to address the lack of competitiveness of agriculture in the global market.

First, the reform of the agricultural economic system has not been completed. A complete agricultural system will need the support of markets for all the major elements of agricultural production, that is, land, credit, labor, technology, and supplies. The biggest constraint is the current land use policy. Land is the most fundamental element in rural people's livelihood, and it is very sensitive to any adjustments. The possible solution is to build up innovative institutional arrangements, such as economic cooperatives for farmers who work the land. Under the new institutional arrangement of various types of farmers' organizations, economy of scale can be established and provide a basis for the rational allocation of productive resources such as investment and labor.

Second, further administrative reform is needed. The current centralized, sector-divided system does not make effective use of resources. Various experiments have been conducted to initiate such reform at the county level of government. Integrated planning and use of resources at the county level have been approved, and an effective mechanism has been devised to build up regional advantages and improve overall competitiveness at the grassroots level.

Economic Growth in Cities and Urban Networks

FRANK VAN OORT AND PHILIP MCCANN

What explains the pace and pattern of urbanization in developed and developing countries? A general notion in the literature is that urbanization is predominantly influenced by regional disparities in economic growth potentials and that, although in different time regimes, mechanisms of economic growth are more or less the same in different macro geographic settings, such as Europe, the United States, and currently also Asian countries (Cheshire and Duranton 2004; Enright, Scott, and Chang 2005; Van Dijk 2006). The case of China shows that challenges exist for currently lagging regions.

But can we determine what matters for urban economic growth? From the 1980s onward, there has been an increase in the use of geographic models in economic analyses. This development can mainly be ascribed to the failure of orthodox economics to provide appropriate explanations for the variation in the wealth and poverty of areas. Inspired by the success of Silicon Valley, Cambridge (United Kingdom), and the Third Italy compared to the decline of other regions in the West (in particular, the old industrial areas), pressing issues are to understand why firms decide to locate in particular areas, which kind of agglomeration is needed to foster localized growth, and how geographic location affects the performance of firms. Rooted in new growth theory, this "rediscovery" of space in economics has led to an extensive empirical literature examining which spatial circumstances give rise to spatial externalities (or "agglomeration externalities") that endogenously induce economic growth. This paper reviews the state-of-the-art literature on economic agglomeration, urbanization, and economic growth in cities and urban networks. We pay special attention to economic complementarities, as these can stimulate growth in a system (network) of cities in which the sum is more than its parts. Local specializations in urban networks might help cities in developing countries to integrate functionally in their regions.

Frank van Oort is Professor of Urban Economics and Spatial Planning at Utrecht University in The Netherlands.

Berlin Workshop Series 2009

Classical and Neoclassical Insights into Urban Economic Growth: Specialization, Diversity, and Technology

The major developments in spatial economics and economic geography from the late nineteenth century up until the 1960s came from a variety of traditions and a variety of analysts. In terms of the location of economic activities, major insights were provided by, among others, Weber (1909) and Isard (1956). At the same time, related work on the causes of and consequences for regional growth of the spatial clustering of economic activities was also being undertaken by Vernon (1960) and Chinitz (1961), whose work focused specifically on issues relating to growth and agglomeration. In particular, their work focused on the features of different types of agglomeration economies, and their analyses were undertaken within the traditional analytical framework of agglomeration phenomena, which had emerged as a fusion of the insights of Marshall (1890) and Hoover (1948). Marshall (1890) focused on the role of local knowledge spillovers and the existence of nontraded local inputs and a local pool of specialist labor, while Hoover (1948) allocated the sources of agglomeration advantages into internal and external economies of scale in the form of localization and urbanization economies. On the one hand, internal increasing returns to scale may occur to a single firm due to production cost efficiencies realized by serving large markets, and as such there is nothing inherently spatial in this concept other than that the existence of a single large firm in space implies a large local concentration of factor employment. On the other hand, external economies are qualitatively very different.

Whether due to firm size or a large initial number of local firms, a high level of local factor employment may allow the development of external economies within the group of local firms in a sector. These are termed localization economies. The strength of these local externalities is assumed to vary, so that these are stronger in some sectors and weaker in others (Duranton and Puga 2000). The associated economies of scale comprise factors that reduce the average cost of producing outputs in that locality. The theories on localization economies can be enhanced further by explicitly taking market form into consideration (Gordon and McCann 2000). Externalities characterized by knowledge spillovers between firms in a spatially concentrated industry are generally known as Marshall-Arrow-Romer (MAR) externalities. The MAR theory in a dynamic context (Glaeser and others 1992; Henderson, Kuncoro, and Turner 1995) predicts that local monopoly is better for growth than local competition, because local monopoly restricts the flow of ideas to others and allows optimal profiting from internal scale economies. Porter (1990) agrees with the importance of localization economies, also arguing that knowledge spillovers in specialized, geographically concentrated industries stimulate growth. However, urbanization economies reflect external economies passed to enterprises as a result of savings from the large-scale operation of the agglomeration or city as a whole, which are therefore independent from industry structure. Relatively more populous localities, or places more easily accessible to metropolitan areas, are also more likely to house universities, industry research laboratories, trade associations, and other knowledge-generating institutions. It is the dense presence of these institutions, which are not solely economic in character, but also social, political, and cultural in nature, that supports the production and absorption of know-how, stimulating innovative behavior and differential rates of interregional growth (Harrison, Kelley, and Gant 1997). The diverse industry mix in an urbanized locality therefore improves the opportunities to interact, copy, and modify practices and innovative behavior in the same or related industries. In her well-known theory on urban growth, Jane Jacobs (1969) defines diversity as a key source of agglomeration economies and, unlike the MAR theory, believes that the most important knowledge transfers come from outside the own industry.

Quigley (1998) describes four features of agglomeration economies. The first feature concerns scale economies or indivisibilities within a firm that are the historical rationale for the existence of productivity growth in agglomerated industries in the first place (Brakman, Garretsen, and Van Marrewijk 2001). Without the existence of scale economies in production, economic activities would be dispersed so as to save transportation costs (Fujita, Krugman, and Venables 1999). In consumption terms, the existence of public goods leads to urban amenities. Cities function as ideal institutions for the development of social contacts corresponding to various kinds of social and cultural externalities (Florida 2002).

The second factor—namely, shared inputs in production and consumption—encompasses the economies of localized industry described by Marshall. The use of shared inputs to produce more differentiated consumption goods in agglomerations associated with variety, fashion, culture, and style is well known (Katz and Shapiro 1985).

A third possible reason why agglomeration economies may provide greater economic efficiency arises from potential reductions in transaction costs (Martin and Ottaviano 1999). The Western economies in general have developed primarily into services-based economies. Business and consumer services now make up most of urban employment, and most of these urban activities are characterized in terms of a knowledge-based information society. A logical outcome of the interaction between urban economies and knowledge-based service industries is the growing importance of transactions-based explanations of growth in local economic productivity (Castells 1989; Gottmann 1983). The so-called California school of economic geography emphasizes transactional costs in explaining agglomeration economies (Scott 1988) and the survival of local firms and the lower search costs of workers (Acemoglu 1996; Helsey and Strange 1990) and demonstrates that, in a matching context, returns to human capital accumulation can be shown to exist, even when all output in a city is produced with constant returns to scale and no technological externalities. Again analogous to production, better matching may occur in consumer functions (shopping).

The fourth set of potential economies identified by Quigley (1998) relates to the application of the law of large numbers to the possibility of fluctuations in the economy. Fluctuations in purchases of inputs are usually as imperfectly correlated across firms as are the sales of outputs across buyers. As such, firms are required to hold less inventory due to the greater possibilities for pooling supplies.

Each of these aspects of agglomeration economies provides a possible rationale for why cities and regions characterized by agglomeration generally exhibit higher growth than those without such features. In addition to these features of agglomeration economies, two additional features of cities contribute to the growth potential of a city region. First, the structure of a regional or urban economy can be considered in a manner analogous to corporate diversification in product portfolios. Regional variety can be considered a portfolio strategy to protect regional income from sudden asymmetric sector-specific shocks in demand (Attaran 1986; Dissart 2003). This will especially protect labor markets and thus prevent the occurrence of sticky unemployment. Even if interregional labor mobility is high, asymmetric shocks reduce economic growth as agglomeration economies and the tax base deteriorate (Krugman 1993). Following this reasoning, industrial variety at the regional level would reduce regional unemployment and promote regional economic growth, while specialization would increase the risk of a rise in unemployment and a slowdown in growth. As for firms, a central question is whether related or unrelated diversification is most rewarding for stability and growth (Baldwin and Brown 2004). One can expect that related industries more often (though, again, not as a rule) have correlated demand shocks. Therefore, spreading risk over unrelated sectors is likely to be preferred from the viewpoint of a portfolio strategy. However, one should take into account the possible benefits from related diversification as well. Analogous to economies of scope at the firm level, one expects knowledge spillovers within the region to occur primarily among related sectors and only to a limited extent among unrelated sectors. In terms of agglomeration theory, Jacobs's externalities are expected to be higher in regions with a related variety of sectors than in regions with an unrelated variety of sectors (Frenken, Van Oort, and Verburg 2007).

Second, technological development and the diffusion of knowledge and innovation are central to the modern concept of regional growth. However, the concept of knowledge diffusion across space in the economic geographic literature dates back some 60 years, beginning with the growth pole theory of Perroux (1950), which was subsequently embedded in geographic space by Boudeville (1966). Its main assumption is that economic growth, manifested in the form of innovations, is spread throughout a growth center's hinterland to lower-order cities and localities nearby. Innovations and knowledge once generated in a certain central location are expected to spread among regions from one locality to its neighbors (Parr 1999; Richardson 1978). Hirschman (1958) distinguished two types of spillover effects associated with growth pole theory: backward linkages and forward linkages. The former effects are associated with activities that provide inputs to economic activities, drawing toward the location of the clients. The latter concern activities that use outputs by creating new activities or by expanding existing activities that draw them toward locations where these existing activities are already (over) represented. This can turn into backwash effects that are usually unanticipated, occurring when the growth pole attracts so much attention and cumulative growth that it drains the surrounding areas. Migration of workers toward the pole and the concentration of investment capital in the initial center of innovation initiate the emergence of high-level urban services in the growth pole. This can then lead to a further polarization of economic growth, restricting growth elsewhere (Richardson 1978). The existence of spread effects is based on the belief that the ongoing growth of the core location (the growth pole) will lead eventually to diseconomies of scale due to congestion and the appreciation of factor costs. A parallel stream of work also emerged from Vernon (1960) and Chinitz (1961), in which the role of cities as incubators of new firms and new ideas was regarded as critical. More recently, this theoretical framework has been applied in agglomeration studies of Henderson (1997) and Rosenthal and Strange (2001). The central argument concerns an urban product cycle notion that new products are more easily developed in large diverse metro areas with a diversified industrial structure and skill base, particularly those with many corporate headquarters (Pred 1977), whereas mature products eventually are decentralized to hinterland or peripheral areas.

After the period of rapid analytical developments up to the late 1960s that were associated with the quantitative revolution in economic geography and the microeconomic breakthroughs in regional science (Isard 1956), outside of the specialist research field, widespread interest in spatial economic issues largely waned in both economics and geography for a period of two decades. As such, another 20 years passed before a major resurgence of interest was witnessed in spatial and regional economic issues. This resurgence of interest was associated with the work of Paul Krugman (1991) and Michael Porter (1990), and both of these commentators not only borrowed from the existing insights but also added new insights.

The 1990s Revolution: New Economic Geography and New Growth Theory

Prior to the development of new trade theory, traditional international trade theory was largely unable to explain intra-industry, intra-national, or intra-regional trade. At the same time, gravity models suggested that most trade tended to be localized. The development of new trade theory based on the Dixit and Stiglitz (1977) modeling framework subsequently led to renewed interest in both localized and intra-industry trade. These developments in international trade theory, in turn, led to a renewed interest in modeling spatial economics in the form of new economic geography, and regional economics as a whole subsequently experienced a resurgence via a combination of developments in both new economic geography and new growth theories.

New economic geography is based on the insights and analytical approaches that are common to new growth theory and new trade theory. As both new growth theory and new trade theory predate new economic geography, it is worthwhile to recap the basic features and insights of new economic geography's two antecedent literatures. In both of these strands of literature, the dominant analytical approach is the modeling of imperfect competition and increasing returns to scale within the monopolistic competition framework of Dixit and Stiglitz (1977), in which utility is a function of variety. New theories now allow for the modeling of inter- as well as intra-industry trade flows within a general equilibrium framework in which the structure of demand and supply is endogenously determined.

Krugman (1991) first applied this modeling framework to the question of geography under conditions of economies of scale and labor mobility and reinterpreted Marshall's principles of externalities as stemming from the benefits of the pooling of the local labor supply and the demand for specialized nontradable inputs. In these models, spatial concentration and dispersion were seen to emerge as a natural consequence of market interactions involving economies of scale at the level of the individual firm, with many of the results generated by these models being reminiscent of the results of central place theory and the rank-size rule (Fujita, Krugman, and Venables 1999). Indeed, the cumulative causation characteristics of these models is in many ways akin to the processes described by Pred (1977), among others; in this respect, the work by Fujita, Krugman, and Venables builds on most of the standard location theory (Dymski 1996; Krugman 1993).

This spatial version of the Dixit-Stiglitz monopolistic competition theory has since become a crucial element of all spatial economic models on the location of economic activities (Abdel-Rahman 1988; Fujita, Krugman, and Venables 1999), and several key insights have emerged from this literature. First, if internal economies of scale are strong and transportation costs are low, this induces a circularity that tends to keep geographic concentration in existence once established (compare Pred 1977 and Myrdal 1957 on their notions of cumulative causation). The reason is that manufacturers in the larger economic agglomerations have an advantage, because the size of local demand allows them to profit more from internal economies of scale, and hence they can afford higher nominal wages. A higher local demand for goods induces a greater variety of goods, which induces real income effects, which attract new workers, consumers, and firms. These developments are manifested in a greater range of local forward linkages (the supply of a greater variety of goods increases the worker's real income) and local backward linkages (as greater numbers of consumers attract more firms), as pecuniary externalities create scale economies at the individual firm level that are transformed in increasing returns at the level of a location as a whole. In general, this effect will be stronger as local demand is greater and internal economies of scale are higher.

Meanwhile, this observation of spatial industrial concentration is consistent with the observation that some producers survive in peripheral locations. One reason is that peripheral producers exhibit local advantages outside the large agglomeration due to higher transportation costs, which mean that they face less competition for their local demand. A second reason is that negative externalities such as congestion and high land rents in the larger agglomerations (Quigley 1998) may eventually lead to decreasing returns to scale in cities (Glaeser, Scheinkman, and Schleifer

1995; Moomaw 1985). If the industrial sector itself constitutes a principal source of demand for industrial products, and if transportation costs increase with distance, then firms will cluster because they produce under increasing returns. The existence of sufficiently high transportation costs therefore ensures that multiple clusters will exist instead of one monocentric city. As such, the pull of Krugman's pecuniary externalities balances the push of transportation costs. The ultimate equilibrium depends on the initial point of departure, the extent of economies of scale, and the level and structure of transportation costs (McCann 2005). Equilibrium no longer automatically means that spatial units of observation converge in terms of regional growth (Kubo 1995).

A second and related body of literature related to geography and space has been developed on the basis of the new or endogenous growth theories. These theories themselves are built on foundations similar to those of new trade theory and new economic geography (Barro and Sala-i-Martin 1995), although they are different in that they do not treat time in a comparative static manner, but take growth over time and its determinants as the principal subjects of the analysis. According to this view, when individuals or firms accumulate new capital, they inadvertently contribute to the productivity of capital held by others. Such spillovers may occur in the course of investment in physical capital or human capital (Lucas 1988). As Romer (1990, 1994) demonstrates, if the spillovers are strong enough, the private marginal product of physical or human capital can remain permanently above the discount rate, even if individual investments would face diminishing returns in the absence of external boosts to productivity. These model approaches became widely known as "endogenous growth" theory, because technological change is also seen to be endogenously determined in these models.

When applied to regions and geography, these models all assume that the notion of increasing returns is spatially embodied in agglomeration economies. Endogenous regional growth models are similar to new economic geography models in that such effects can only operate within an environment of imperfectly competitive monopolistic competition. However, these regional growth models are different from mainstream new economic geography models in that, in the endogenous growth framework, local external economies not only may be associated with market size or pecuniary external economies but also can be related to information or technological externalities and spillovers. However, whereas agglomeration in new trade theory and new economic geography is the geographic outcome of modeling, in new growth theory it forms an endogenously determined explanation of growth. These types of arguments therefore provide additional possible explanations for systematic variations in competitive advantage (Porter 1990) across regions and why certain regions are able to maintain and even reinforce their advantages over other regions, once certain locations have taken a lead in a particular activity (Arthur 1994; Krugman 1991).

Economic-Geographic Criticism and Common Ground

Several criticisms of the monopolistic modeling logic underpinning new economic geography have come from economic geography schools of thought (Martin 1999; Martin and Sunley 1996) as well as both orthodox (Neary 2001) and heterodox schools of economics (Peneder 2001). These critiques focus variously on the immeasurability of some of the notions of increasing returns inherent in these frameworks, the static nature of some of the assumptions, the specific focus on the representative firm, the presence of pecuniary economies and the absence of either human capital or technological spillovers as externalities, and the problems associated with the iceberg transport costs assumption (McCann 2005). Other evolutionary critiques (Martin and Sunley 2003) also question the originality and validity of the Porter (1990) concept of clusters. However, many of these criticisms relate to specific models and specific papers rather than to the whole field. Yet the most fundamental critique of these fields in general relates to the question of institutions and the relationship between knowledge and institutions. Within economics, institutions are regarded as being important in explaining economic growth (Aghion and Howitt 1998; Helpman 2004; North 1990). However, for economic geographers and heterodox economists working within the arenas of evolutionary and institutional economics, the role played by institutions in economic development is paramount. In this intuitional-evolutionary schema, cities, regions, and countries that have more efficient institutions are superior in both the generation and diffusion of knowledge and consequently have better prospects for economic growth. As such, while new economic geography and new growth theories are mathematically complex, these analysts regard them as being philosophically too simplistic. This is because they aim to produce generalizable predictions based on a representative model, whereas the counterargument implies that the appropriate investments, favorable institutional arrangements, and entrepreneurial dynamics that allow regions to grow are features of regions that have emerged for historically and spatially contingent reasons rather than generalizable reasons. For economic geographers, as well as institutional and evolutionary economists working in this tradition, cultural and cognitive proximity are therefore deemed to be just as important as geographic proximity in the transmission of ideas and knowledge. Boschma and Lambooy (1999) further argue that the generation of local externalities is crucially linked to the importance of selection in terms of "fitness" of a local milieu, the sociological dimensions of which can be institutional, cultural, legal, and historical. According to these perspectives, these specific historically contingent and geographically contingent features of space, rather than simply space as a dimension, are crucial in determining the geography of entrepreneurship and growth (Audretsch, Keilbach, and Lehmann 2006).

The original behavioral geographic literature (Pred 1966; Webber 1964) focused on incomplete information, the limited cognitive capacities of entrepreneurs, and the differences in the ability of firms to absorb information at different stages in their life cycle (Alchian 1950). However, institutional structures are now regarded as being much more than simply the aggregation of individual choices: rather they are seen as the result of many interactive processes. Economic geography research has always emphasized the untraded interdependencies that function as externalities and spillovers (Storper 1997), and this has led to calls for research to focus on institutional issues (Amin and Thrift 2002). As such, evolutionary economic geography theory focuses primarily on the creation of new spatial structures, rather than on explaining equilibrium states. Within the same spatial and institutional context, firms and entrepreneurs may arrive at different location behavior by means of either chance occurrences or by fundamental processes of neo-Schumpeterian, creative destruction. Alternatively, different spatial and institutional contexts will mean that firms and entrepreneurs may arrive at either different or similar locational outcomes, but for a variety of reasons. As such, the initial states that determine allocations may vary significantly, although the future trajectories of these initial outcomes are determined primarily by path-dependency phenomena, which themselves are underpinned by local externalities and spillovers. In turn, these path-dependent phenomena subsequently give rise to localized regional clustering.

Although the differences between the formal modeling approaches of new economic geography, new growth theory, and the evolutionary-institutional approaches to regional growth at first appear to be irreconcilable, common ground between these competing theories can be found on several key points. First, in each of these strands of literature, as we have seen, the role of agglomerations is regarded as being a crucial element of regional performance, and the common element is the issue of local knowledge generation, accumulation, and spillovers. Second, and related to the first point, is the issue of the level of connectivity: specifically, all of these theories regard the number of connections between local regional nodes and other key international nodal points in the global economy as being important (Saviotti 1996). Recent work on global cities suggests that particular cities that are well connected via international hub airports, in particular, are consistently at an advantage with regard to other locations in their ability to acquire relevant knowledge spillovers. Third, the geographic scale over which knowledge spillovers operate is regarded as critical, and once again, most of the apparently competing theories are largely in agreement.

Regarding this third point, one of the features that neither the new economic geography nor the new growth theory explicitly models is the actual geographic scale over which any mechanisms of knowledge spillover operate. As Jaffe, Trajtenberg, and Henderson (1993) conclude, we know very little about where such spillovers actually go, although we can acquire some information regarding this point by studying the geographic location of patent citations. Jaffe, Trajtenberg, and Henderson (1993) therefore test the extent to which knowledge spillovers are geographically localized. Their measured effects were particularly significant at the local level, indicating that localization fades over time, but very slowly. Further research by Acs (2002), Audretsch and Feldman (1996), and Feldman (1994), among others, provides corroborating evidence that knowledge spillovers tend to be geographically bounded within the location where the new economic knowledge was created.

Lucas (1993) emphasizes that the most natural context in which to understand the mechanics of dynamic knowledge externalities and economic growth is in metropolitan areas where the compact nature of the geographic unit facilitates communication and human capital accumulation. He argues that the only compelling reason for the existence of cities would be the presence of increasing returns to agglomerations of resources, which make these locations more productive. This view of human capital as social input that induces productivity gains in cities has been further explored by others (Bostic, Gans, and Stern 1997; Cheshire and Duranton 2004; Rosenthal and Strange 2004), who all argue that the microeconomic foundation of the external effect of human capital is the sharing of knowledge and skills among workers that occurs through both formal and informal interactions. The distinction between tacit and implicit knowledge, as against explicit knowledge, is deemed to be crucial here in terms of how those knowledge externalities are embodied in growth (implicit) and innovation (explicit) externalities. Intuitively, it seems clear that the higher is the average level of human capital (knowledge) or the more spatially concentrated is the number of agents, the more "luck" these agents will have with their meetings and the more rapid will be the diffusion and growth of knowledge (Rauch 1993: 381).

These observations, which emphasize the role played by the city as a knowledge and information environment, largely accord with many of explanations employed by the economic geography, institutional, and evolutionary approaches. The original behavioral arguments generally pointed to large urban agglomerations as being superior incubator locations to other places (Chinitz 1961). This thinking has heavily influenced contemporary thinking on economic geography. The difference, however, is in the emphases. The evolutionary-institutional approaches stress institutions and policy makers (Amin and Thrift 2002) on the assumption that, in each observed case, the actual impact of these externalities on productivity remains heavily dependent on the historical economic context (Bostic, Gans, and Stern 1997), the industrial structure (Moomaw 1985; Glaeser and others 1992), and the specific role played by face-to-face contact in local production processes (McCann 2007). Therefore, when behavioral and evolutionary explanations for interregional economic development are taken seriously, primary attention is paid to the behavioral and entrepreneurial causes of agglomeration. The concept of externalities in this schema is therefore also related to the nature of mechanisms that transmit information among actors in firms and the cognitive and interactive characteristics that determine the construction of locational preferences.

Cities and Urban Systems in the Network Society

Steadily, cities shifted their functional borders when mobility steadily increased and communication technology further developed. These developments led to the rise of larger metropolitan areas. Local economic growth and prosperity were not only contingent on the urban core, but also on the economic development in the suburbs.

Nevertheless, the relationship between the urban core and its suburbs at first instance remained hierarchical-nodal. Most of the economic activities were based in the urban core, commuting flows were directed toward the central cities, and suburbs only fulfilled a residential function. In other words, one center was responsible for the labor demand, while the surrounding areas took care of the labor supply. Nowadays, such straightforward city-hinterland separation is supposed to be nonexistent in Western societies. Legal status has become uniform, at least in each national area, the functional borders of cities reach far beyond the (former) city walls, and social and economic processes are taking place at an ever larger geographic scale. At the same time, suburban areas increasingly emerge into local centers that develop their own economic activities and, because of this, start competing with the original urban core. It is generally argued that these changes in contemporary urban systems are fueled by the rise of the network economy (Castells 1996), which is exemplified by recent advances in transport and communication technology, the ongoing globalization, the rise of the service economy, and the individualization of production (Anas, Arnott, and Small 1998; Batten 1995; Graham and Marvin 2001). Due to these developments, the role of physical proximity in shaping inter-firm relations is losing ground, resulting in greater spatial flexibility for economic actors. Moreover, to compete in the network economy, firms have to make production processes more flexible with respect to time, place, contracts, and job content. This need for flexibility is increased by growing international competition and product differentiation. It is not only the price of a product that influences the purchasing behavior of consumers, but also quality, brand preferences, and market trends. This has led to increasing uncertainty in markets. To deal with this uncertainty, the outsourcing of economic activities that do not belong to the core activities of the company, as well as cooperation with firms active within the same sector, have become more important.

This process of making economic processes more flexible, and the functional division of tasks between companies, create opportunities for a spatial division of labor: different spatial settings or locations become suitable for different economic functions. The result is often argued to be of polycentric and multinodal structures, in which flows of goods, services, and people are not one-sided, but rather two-sided and crisscrossed. This leads to the emergence of systems of economically complementary urban regions. The notion of a central city on which the population of the surrounding towns is heavily dependent for amenities and employment becomes obsolescent in this view. One location may be regarded as "central" in terms of one particular function, while other places may be central in terms of another function. As a result, the cities' catchment areas will overlap. The greater urban conurbation then loses significance as an independently functioning daily urban system, instead forming part of an urban network. These urban networks are regarded as the cities of the future, both in Western countries and in developing countries (Van Oort, Burger, and Raspe 2007).

Cities are agglomerations, characterized by a high degree of human interaction. Originally cities were the outcome of economic agents seeking physical proximity to one another. In the network economy, it is not only physical proximity to other firms that determines the pattern of interaction among companies, but also techno-economic and sociocultural proximity (Boschma 2005). One can think of similarities in the organization of production, similarities in strategies, similarities in technologies employed by firms, and firms having a joint history or common background. It is argued that these new types of proximity require less physical proximity. Cooperative relationships between companies and individuals need not be predominantly local in nature anymore; instead they can manifest themselves at any spatial scale (Lambooy 1998). As a result, the functional boundaries of cities are moving, the catchment areas of cities will overlap, and metropolitan areas will stop functioning as a daily urban system, instead forming part of an urban network. However, what the original cities and the contemporary urban networks have in common is that they are both characterized by a high degree of interaction between economic agents. In other words, both cities and urban networks can be characterized by a high degree of spatial integration. The Greater Pearl River delta in China is a good example of an urban regional network outside Europe and the United States (Enright, Scott, and Chang 2005).

According to Quigley (1998), the degree of economic diversification explicitly separates a city from an agglomeration, which can be regarded as a concentration of similar agents. Accordingly, in order to label urban networks as the cities of the future, the cities in this network should be specialized in different sectors, thereby fulfilling different economic roles. This touches on the earlier-mentioned spatial division of labor, which means that cities in a network will specialize in those activities that arise from their comparative advantages. Specialization offers a more productive (integrated) whole than each individual town or city would be able to offer in isolation. In other words, cities in an urban network complement each other. Policies directed toward specialization and integration of economic activities in systems of cities not only reflect Western urban developments, but also might help cities in developing countries to integrate functionally in their regions.

References

Abdel-Rahman, Hesham. 1988. "Product Differentiation, Monopolistic Competition, and City Size." *Journal of Urban Economics* 18 (1): 69–86.

Acemoglu, Daron. 1996. "A Microfoundation for Social Increasing Returns in Human Capital Accumulation." *Quarterly Journal of Economics* 111 (3): 779–804.

Acs, Zoltan J. 2002. *Innovation and the Growth of Cities.* Cheltenham: Edward Elgar.

Aghion, Philippe, and Peter Howitt. 1998. *Endogenous Growth Theory.* Cambridge, MA: MIT Press.

Alchian, Armen A. 1950. "Uncertainty, Evolution, and Economic Theory." *Journal of Political Economy* 58 (3): 211–21.

Amin, Ash, and Nigel Thrift. 2002. *Cities: Reimagining the Urban.* Cambridge, MA: Polity Press.

Anas, Alex, Richard Arnott, and Kenneth Small. 1998. "Urban Spatial Structure." *Journal of Economic Literature* 36 (3): 1426–64.

Arthur, W. Brian. 1994. *Increasing Returns and Path Dependence in the Economy.* Ann Arbor: University of Michigan Press.

Attaran, Mohsen. 1986. "Industrial Diversity and Economic Performance in U.S. Areas." *Annals of Regional Science* 20 (2): 44–54.

Audretsch, David B., and Maryann P. Feldman. 1996. "R&D Spillovers and the Geography of Innovation and Production." *American Economic Review* 86 (3): 630–40.

Audretsch, David B., Max C. Keilbach, and Erik E. Lehmann. 2006. *Entrepreneurship and Economic Growth.* New York: Oxford University Press.

Baldwin, John T., and W. M. Brown. 2004. "Regional Manufacturing Employment Volatility in Canada: The Effects of Specialisation and Trade." *Papers in Regional Science* 83 (3): 519–41.

Barro, Robert J., and Xavier Sala-i-Martin. 1995. *Economic Growth.* Cambridge, MA: MIT Press.

Batten, David F. 1995. "Network Cities: Creative Urban Agglomerations for the 21st Century." *Urban Studies* 32 (2): 313–27.

Boschma, Ron A. 2005. "Proximity and Innovation: A Critical Assessment." *Regional Studies* 39 (1): 61–74.

Boschma, Ron A., and Jan G. Lambooy. 1999. "Evolutionary Economics and Economic Geography." *Journal of Evolutionary Economics* 9 (4): 411–29.

Bostic, Raphael W., Joshua S. Gans, and Scott Stern. 1997. "Urban Productivity and Factor Growth in the Late Nineteenth Century." *Journal of Urban Economics* 41 (1): 38–55.

Boudeville, J. R. 1966. *Problems of Regional Economic Planning.* Edinburgh: Edinburgh University Press.

Brakman, Steven, Harry Garretsen, and Charles Van Marrewijk. 2001. *An Introduction to Geographical Economics.* Cambridge, U.K.: Cambridge University Press.

Castells, Manuel. 1989. *The Informational City: Information Technology, Economic Restructuring, and the Urban-Regional Process.* Oxford: Blackwell.

———. 1996. *The Rise of the Network Society.* Oxford: Blackwell Publishers.

Cheshire, Paul C., and Gilles Duranton. 2004. *Recent Developments in Urban and Regional Economics.* Cheltenham: Edward Elgar.

Chinitz, Benjamin J. 1961. "Contrasts in Agglomeration: New York and Pittsburgh." *American Economic Review* 51 (2): 279–89.

Dissart, Jean Christophe. 2003. "Regional Economic Diversity and Regional Economic Stability: Research Results and Agenda." *International Regional Science Review* 26 (4): 423–46.

Dixit, Avinash K., and Joseph E. Stiglitz. 1977. "Monopolistic Competition and Optimum Product Diversity." *American Economic Review* 67 (3): 297–308.

Duranton, Gilles, and Diego Puga. 2000. "Diversity and Specialisation in Cities: Why, Where, and When Does It Matter?" *Urban Studies* 37 (3): 533–55.

Dymski, G. A. 1996. "On Krugman's Model of Economic Geography." *Geoforum* 27 (4): 439–52.

Enright, Michael J., Edith E. Scott, and Ka-Mun Chang. 2005. *Regional Powerhouse: The Greater Pearl River Delta and the Rise of China.* Singapore: John Wiley and Sons.

Feldman, Maryann P. 1994. *The Geography of Innovation.* Boston: Kluwer Academic Publishers.

Florida, Richard. 2002. *The Rise of the Creative Class.* New York: Basic Books.

Frenken, Koen, Frank G. Van Oort, and Thijs Verburg. 2007. "Related Variety, Unrelated Variety, and Regional Economic Growth." *Regional Studies* 41 (5): 685–97.

Fujita, Masahisa, Paul Krugman, and Anthony Venables. 1999. *The Spatial Economy: Cities, Regions, and International Trade.* Cambridge, MA: MIT Press.

Glaeser, Edward L., Heidi D. Kallal, Jose A. Scheinkman, and Andrei Schleifer. 1992. "Growth in Cities." *Journal of Political Economy* 100 (6): 1126–52.

Glaeser, Edward L., Jose A. Scheinkman, and Andrei Schleifer. 1995. "Economic Growth in a Cross-Section of Cities." *Journal of Monetary Economics* 36 (1): 117–43.

Gordon, Ian R., and Philip McCann. 2000. "Industrial Clusters: Complexes, Agglomeration, and/or Social Networks?" *Urban Studies* 37 (3): 513–32.

Gottmann, Jean. 1983. *The Coming of the Transactional City.* College Park, MD: University of Maryland.

Graham, Stephen, and Simon Marvin. 2001. *Splintering Urbanism, Networked Infrastructures, Technological Mobilities, and the Urban Condition.* London: Routledge.

Harrison, B., M. K. Kelley, and J. Gant. 1997. "Innovative Firm Behavior and Local Milieu: Exploring the Intersection of Agglomeration, Firm Effects, and Technological Change." *Economic Geography* 72 (3): 233–58.

Helpman, Elhanan. 2004. *The Mystery of Economic Growth.* Cambridge, MA: Harvard University Press.

Helsey, Robert W., and William C. Strange. 1990. "Matching and Agglomeration Economies in a System of Cities." *Regional Science and Urban Economics* 20 (2): 189–212.

Henderson, J. Vernon. 1997. "Externalities and Industrial Development." *Journal of Urban Economics* 42 (3): 449–70.

Henderson, J. Vernon, Ari Kuncoro, and Matt Turner. 1995. "Industrial Development in Cities." *Journal of Political Economy* 103 (5): 1067–85.

Hirschman, Albert O. 1958. *The Strategy of Economic Development.* New Haven, CT: Yale University Press.

Hoover, Edgar M. 1948. *The Location of Economic Activity.* New York: McGraw-Hill.

Isard, Walter. 1956. *Location and Space-Economy: A General Theory Relating to Industrial Location, Market Areas, Land Use, Trade, and Urban Structure.* Cambridge, MA: MIT Press.

Jacobs, Jane. 1969. *The Economy of Cities.* New York: Vintage.

Jaffe, Adam B., Manuel Trajtenberg, and Rebecca Henderson. 1993. "Geographic Localization of Knowledge Spillovers as Evidenced by Patent Citations." *Quarterly Journal of Economics* 108 (3): 577–98.

Katz, Michael, and Carl Shapiro. 1985. "Network Externalities, Competition, and Compatibility." *American Economic Review* 75 (3): 424–40.

Krugman, Paul R. 1991. "Increasing Returns and Economic Geography." *Journal of Political Economy* 99 (3): 483–99.

———. 1993. "On the Relationship between Trade Theory and Location Theory." *Review of International Economics* 1 (2): 110–22.

Kubo, Yuji. 1995. "Scale Economies, Regional Externalities, and the Possibility of Uneven Regional Development." *Journal of Regional Science* 35 (1): 29–42.

Lambooy, J. G. 1998. "Polynucleation and Urban Development." *European Planning Studies* 6 (4): 457–67.

Lucas, Robert E. 1988. "On the Mechanics of Economic Development." *Journal of Monetary Economics* 22 (1): 3–42.

———. 1993. "Making a Miracle." *Econometrica* 61 (2): 251–72.

Marshall, Alfred. 1890. *Principles of Economics.* New York: Prometheus Books.

Martin, Philippe, and J. P. Ottaviano. 1999. "Growing Locations: Industry Location in a Model of Endogenous Growth." *European Economic Review* 43 (2): 281–302.

Martin, Ron. 1999. "The New 'Geographical Turn' in Economics: Some Critical Reflections." *Cambridge Journal of Economics* 23 (1): 65–91.

Martin, Ron, and Peter Sunley. 1996. "Paul Krugman's Geographical Economics and Its Implications for Regional Development Theory: A Critical Assessment." *Economic Geography* 72 (3): 259–92.

———. 2003. "Deconstructing Clusters: Chaotic Concept or Policy Panacea?" *Journal of Economic Geography* 3 (1): 5–35.

McCann, Philip. 2005. "Transport Costs and New Economic Geography." *Journal of Economic Geography* 5 (3): 305–18.

———. 2007. "Sketching out a Model of Innovation, Face-to-Face Interaction, and Economic Geography." *Spatial Economic Analysis* 2 (2): 117–34.

Moomaw, Ronald L. 1985. "Firm Location and City Size: Reduced Productivity Advantages as a Factor in the Decline of Manufacturing in Urban Areas." *Journal of Urban Economics* 17 (1): 73–89.

Myrdal, Gunnar. 1957. *Economic Theory and Under-developed Regions*. London: Duckworth.

Neary, J. Peter. 2001. "Of Hype and Hyperbolas: Introducing the New Economic Geography." *Journal of Economic Literature* 39 (2): 536–61.

North, Douglass C. 1990. *Institutions, Institutional Change, and Economic Performance*. Cambridge, U.K.: Cambridge University Press.

Parr, John B. 1999. "Growth-Pole Strategies in Regional Economic Planning: A Retrospective View. Part 1: Origins and Advocacy." *Urban Studies* 36 (7): 1195–216.

Peneder, Michael. 2001. *Entrepreneurial Competition and Industrial Location: Investigating the Structural Patterns and Intangible Sources of Competitive Performance*. Cheltenham: Edward Elgar.

Perroux, François. 1950. "Economic Space: Theory and Applications." *Quarterly Journal of Economics* 64 (February): 89–104.

Porter, Michael. 1990. *The Competitive Advantage of Nations*. New York: Free Press.

Pred, A. R. 1966. *The Spatial Dynamics of U.S. Urban-Industrial Growth 1800–1914: Interspective and Theoretical Essays*. Cambridge, MA: MIT Press.

———. 1977. *City-Systems in Advanced Economies: Past Growth, Present Processes, and Future Development Options*. London: Hutchinson.

Quigley, John M. 1998. "Urban Diversity and Economic Growth." *Journal of Economic Perspectives* 12 (2): 127–38.

Rauch, James E. 1993. "Does History Matter Only When It Matters Little? The Case of City-Industry Location." *Quarterly Journal of Economics* 108 (3): 843–67.

Richardson, Harry W. 1978. *Regional and Urban Economics*. Hindsdale: Dryden Press.

Romer, Paul M. 1990. "Endogenous Technological Change." *Journal of Political Economy* 98 (5): S71–102.

———. 1994. "The Origins of Endogenous Growth." *Journal of Economic Perspectives* 8 (1): 3–22.

Rosenthal, Stuart S., and William C. Strange. 2001. "The Determinants of Agglomeration." *Journal of Urban Economics* 50 (2): 191–29.

———. 2004. "Evidence on the Nature and Sources of Agglomeration Economics." In *Handbook of Regional and Urban Economics: Cities and Geography*, ed. J. V. Henderson and J. F. Thisse, 2119–72. Amsterdam: North Holland.

Saviotti, Pier P. 1996. *Technological Evolution, Variety, and the Economy*. Cheltenham: Edward Elgar.

Scott, Allen J. 1988. *New Industrial Spaces: Flexible Production Organization and Regional Development in North America and Western Europe*. London: Pion.

Storper, Michael. 1997. *The Regional World: Territorial Development in a Global Economy*. New York: Guildford Press.

Van Dijk, Meine-Pieter. 2006. *Managing Cities in Developing Countries: The Theory and Practice of Urban Management*. Cheltenham: Edward Elgar.

Van Oort, Frank G., Martijn J. Burger, and Otto Raspe. 2007. "Economic Networks and Urban Complementarities: The Spatial and Functional Integration of Randstad Holland." GaWC Research Bulletin 243, Globalization and World Cities Research Network, Geography Department, Loughborough University.

Vernon, Raymond. 1960. *Metropolis 1985*. Cambridge, MA: Harvard University Press.

Webber, M. M. 1964. "The Urban Place and the Nonplace Urban Realm." In *Explorations into Urban Structure*, ed. M. M. Webber, 79–153. Philadelphia, PA: University of Pennsylvania Press.

Weber, Alfred. 1909. *Theory of the Location of Industries*. Chicago: University of Chicago Press.

Part IV: Spatial Disparity and Labor Mobility

Can Investment in Human Capital Reduce Regional Disparities? Some Evidence for Spain

ÁNGEL DE LA FUENTE MORENO

Can educational policies be used to reduce regional income disparities? In principle, the answer should be a clear "yes." If educational attainment is an important determinant of productivity—and the available evidence suggests that this is indeed the case[1]—raising average schooling in backward regions should help to bring their income levels closer to the national average. A possible complication is that skilled youngsters may choose to migrate to other regions, thereby mitigating the expected contribution of educational investment to income convergence. If we are worried about regions as such, this possibility may be a cause for some concern. But if we worry about individuals, as we should, the case for increased educational investment in low-income regions does not depend on the degree of mobility of their population.

This paper examines the case for using education as a regional policy tool in Spain. Drawing on the results of some recent work in collaboration with Rafael Doménech, I examine the evolution of regional educational disparities in Spain during the last four decades and the prospects for further educational convergence in the future. I also analyze the determinants of regional productivity in Spain, paying special attention to the role of human capital. I use the results to quantify the importance of education as a source of regional income disparities, to estimate the social return to investment in different types of productive assets in each territory, and to extract some tentative conclusions regarding the changes in our pattern of investment that may help to speed up the growth of the country as a whole and to reduce internal inequality.

Angel de la Fuente Moreno is Associate Professor at Universitat Autònoma de Barcelona in Spain.

Berlin Workshop Series 2009
© 2009 The International Bank for Reconstruction and Development/The World Bank

This note summarizes some of the main results of de la Fuente and Doménech (2006a) and de la Fuente (2006a). Financial support from the European Regional Development Fund (ERDF) and from the Spanish Ministry of Education (through project ECO2008-04837/ECON) is gratefully acknowledged.

The Evolution of Regional Schooling Levels and Perspectives for Future Educational Convergence

In de la Fuente Moreno and Doménech (2006a) we use data from the national census and the municipal registers to construct new regional series of educational attainment covering the period 1960–2000. Figure 1 summarizes some of the key features of these data. Educational attainment in Spain, measured by average years of schooling of the adult population, rose more than 60 percent between 1960 and 2000, while the dispersion of attainment levels across regions fell 28 percent. Progress on both fronts was considerably faster during the second half of the sample period. Following some oscillations in the first two decades of the sample, regional disparities in attainment decreased steadily after 1980, and the growth rate of years of attainment roughly doubled relative to the first half of the sample.

Using data for 1995, figure 2 shows that educational attainment is closely related to income per capita. The correlation between relative income per capita and relative attainment (both measured in percentage deviations from the national mean) is 0.773, and the majority of regions concentrate on the northeastern and southwestern quadrants of figure 2, indicating that below-average income goes hand in hand with below-average attainment. In particular, all Objective 1 regions but two (Asturias and Cantabria) have attainment levels below the national mean.[2]

Using data from the 2001 census in de la Fuente Moreno (2006a), I construct measures of educational attainment by cohort for the different regions and explore their implications for the likely future evolution of regional educational disparities. In particular, I construct indicators of educational convergence across regions as we move to younger and younger cohorts and interpret them as pre-

FIGURE 1. Average Years of Schooling in Spain and Coefficient of Variation of Regional Attainment Levels, 1960–2000

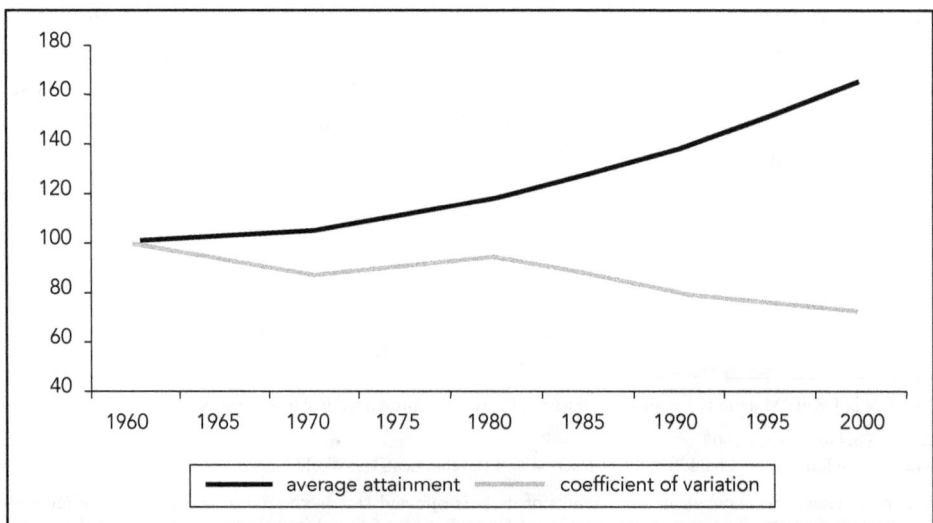

Source: Author's calculations

FIGURE 2. Relative Attainment versus Relative GDP per Capita in Spain, 1995

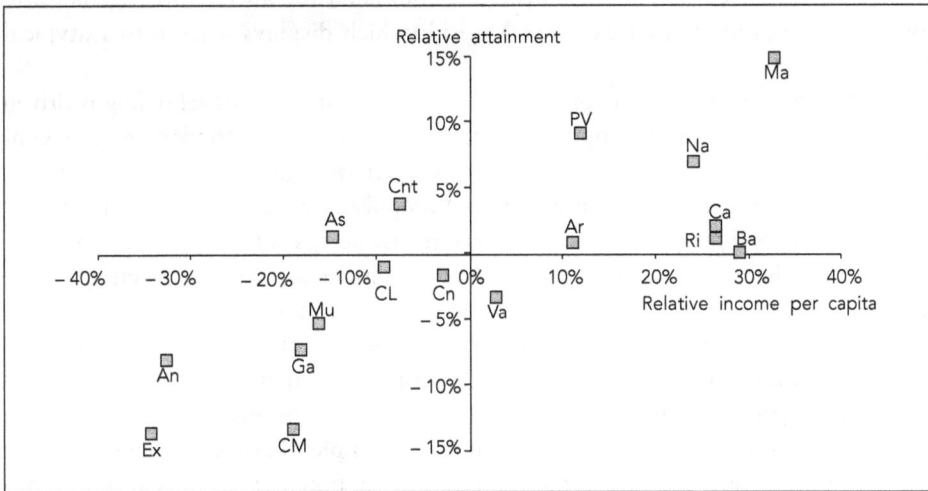

Source: Author's calculations.

Note: Relative income per capita is GDP per capita in percentage deviations from the national average in 1995. The data used to calculate it are taken from Fundación BBV (2000). An = Andalucía; Ar = Aragón; As = Asturias; Ba = Baleares; Cn = Canarias; Cnt = Cantabria; CL = Castilla y León; CM = Castilla la Mancha; Cat = Cataluña; Va = Valencia; Ex = Extremadura; Ga = Galicia; Ma = Madrid; Mu = Murcia; Na = Navarra; PV = País Vasco; Ri = Rioja.

dictors of future trends in educational convergence. Although the dispersion of schooling levels across regions is significantly smaller for younger cohorts than for the overall population, I conclude that sizable disparities are likely to persist in the future. At higher levels of attainment, differences across regions may actually be expected to increase over time.

As expected, attainment rises sharply and its dispersion across regions falls as we move from older to younger cohorts. A comparison between the entire adult population and its youngest cohort can be especially informative, as it tells us how the existing situation is likely to change in the future, assuming that current patterns of enrollment remain unchanged and that there are no significant migration flows. Under these assumptions, regional disparities in attainment can be expected to fall 26.3 percent in the future (that is, the coefficient of variation of relative attainment would drop from 9.2 to 6.8 percent). This is a rather significant change, but it would still leave a substantial amount of regional inequality and a difference in relative attainment of more than 20 points between the top and the bottom regions.

To see what is driving the process of regional convergence in years of schooling across cohorts, it is useful to examine how regional disparities vary across age groups for different educational levels. Figure 3 shows the degree of convergence across cohorts for four educational indicators: average number of years of schooling and the fraction of the population that has completed at least each of three successively higher levels of education (lower secondary, upper secondary including vocational training, and the first cycle of university). Convergence is measured by the percentage reduction in the coefficient of variation across regions of the relevant measure of attainment that we observe as we go from the entire population to the youngest relevant cohort. This indicator is computed for all regions together and for a restricted sample that excludes Madrid (which displays some rather atypical behavior).[3]

The figure suggests that the process of convergence in years of schooling is driven mainly by the extension of compulsory schooling to the lower secondary level. Attainment rates at this level are uniformly very high across regions for younger cohorts. Things are rather different, however, for postcompulsory cycles. If we exclude Madrid from the sample, there is absolutely no convergence across cohorts in terms of upper-secondary (or better) attainment, and regional disparities in terms of university attainment can actually be expected to increase by 30 percent in the future.

Figure 4 shows what is behind this last finding. It plots the increase in relative university attainment as we go from the entire adult population (25+) to the 25–34 age group against the relative attainment of the 25+ population. Madrid is an extreme outlier in this figure. If we keep it in the sample, there is a broadly negative relationship between the two variables that may be taken as an indication of convergence (that is, that initially less educated regions are making faster progress). In the absence of Madrid, however, this is no longer the case. Moreover, more than half the regions display divergent behavior, meaning that university attainment tends to rise further in regions that are already above the national average (Castilla and León, Aragón, Navarra, and País Vasco) and to fall in regions that are below the Spanish mean (Baleares, Murcia, Andalucía, Canarias, and Cantabria).

These findings are clearly not good news from the point of view of the future prospects for increased internal cohesion and suggest that a more activist

FIGURE 3. Regional Convergence of Attainment Levels across Cohorts in Spain (in percentage)

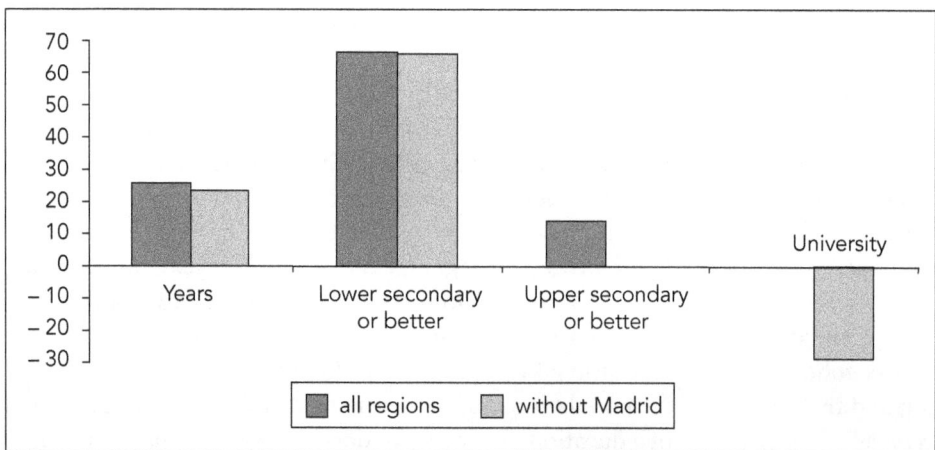

Source: Author's calculations.

Note: Percentage decrease in the coefficient of variation across regions as we go from the entire adult population (25+) to the youngest cohort (20–24 for lower and upper secondary or better and 25–34 for university).

FIGURE 4. Regional Convergence in University Attainment across Cohorts in Spain

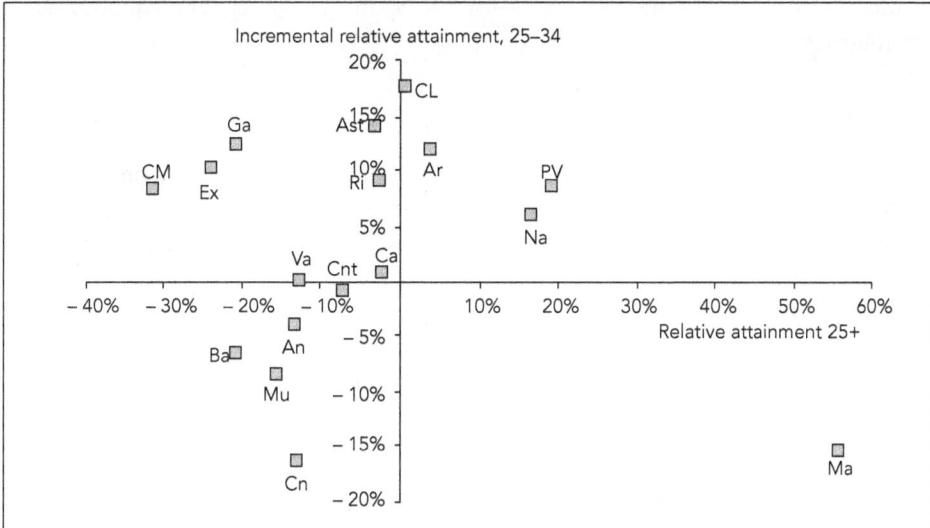

Source: Author's calculations.
Note: For abbreviations, see note to figure 2.

educational policy in favor of disadvantaged groups may be required to reduce the educational gap of the more backward regions.

As noted in the introduction, labor mobility may reduce the effectiveness of such policies when measured in terms of their effects on regional income levels. In the case of Spain, however, this potential "problem" would seem to be relatively unimportant due to low mobility. This is illustrated in figure 5, which plots the relative attainment of the 25–34 age group against the relative university graduation rate by region of origin.[4] The correlation between these two variables is clearly positive, indicating that most graduates tend to remain in their home region.

Large deviations from the fitted regression line in figure 5 alert us to regions where migration flows are important determinants of university attainment rates for young cohorts. As expected, Madrid shows a large positive deviation that signals a large inflow of young university graduates from other regions (or an inflow of university students who remain in the region after graduation). At the other extreme, the migration of highly qualified young people appears to be an important problem in Murcia, Castilla la Mancha, Canarias, and Andalucía. In all these regions, however, gross graduation rates are well below the national average, indicating that migration is not the only cause of the problem.

Educational Attainment and Regional Productivity

In the remainder of the paper, I attempt to quantify the impact of schooling on regional income and estimate the social return to investment in education and in other assets. In de la Fuente Moreno and Doménech (2006a), we estimate a regional production function using panel data for the Spanish regions. The equation is of the following form:

$$\Delta q_{it} = c + \mu_i + \eta_t + \lambda b_{it} + \alpha_k \Delta k_{it} + \alpha_k \Delta x_{it} + \beta \Delta s_{it} + \varepsilon_{it} \tag{1}$$

where Δ denotes annual growth rates (over the subperiod starting at time t), q_{it} is the log of output per employed worker in region i at time t, k and x are the logs of the stocks of (noninfrastructure) physical capital and infrastructure per employed worker, s is the log of the average number of years of schooling of the adult population, and b_{it} is a measure of technological gap that enters the equation as a determinant of the rate of technical progress in order to allow for a catch-up effect. This term is the Hicks-neutral total factor productivity (TFP) gap between each region and Madrid *(M)* at the beginning of each subperiod, given by

$$b_{it} = (q_{Mt} - \alpha_k k_{Mt} - \alpha_x x_{Mt} - \beta s_{Mt}) - (q_{it} - \alpha_k k_{it} - \alpha_x x_{it} - \beta s_{it}) \tag{2}$$

To estimate this specification, I substitute equation 2 into equation 1 and use nonlinear least squares with data on both factor stocks and their growth rates. In this specification the parameter measures the rate of (conditional) convergence in relative TFP levels. If this parameter is positive, relative TFP levels eventually stabilize, signaling a common asymptotic rate of technical progress for all territories,

FIGURE 5. Relative University Attainment of Individuals 25–34 Years of Age versus Relative Graduation Rate, by Region of Origin in Spain

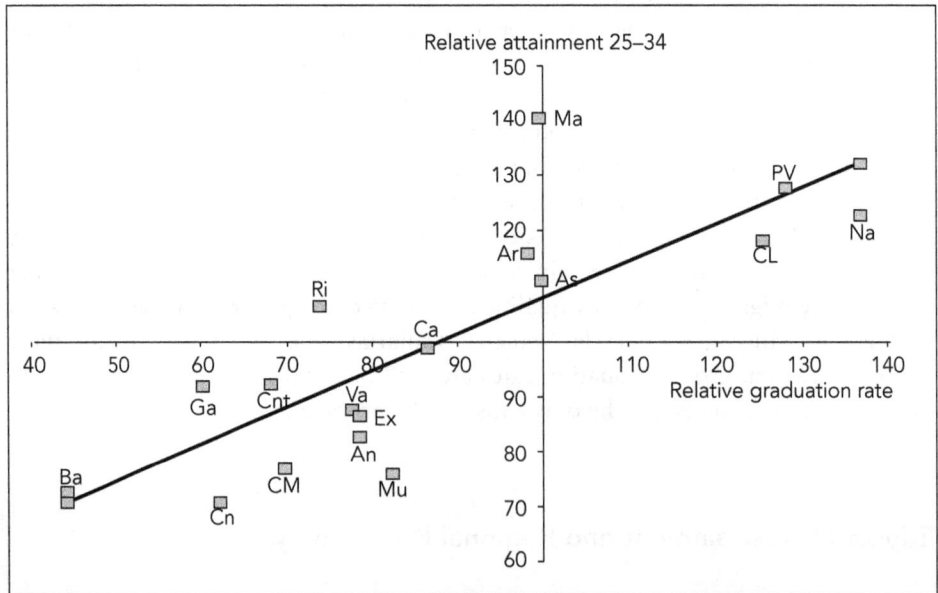

Source: Author's calculations.

Note: For abbreviations, see note to figure 2.

and the regional fixed effects capture permanent differences in relative total factor productivity that will presumably reflect differences in research and development (R&D) investment and other omitted variables.

The data on regional employment (number of jobs) and output (gross value added, at factor cost) are taken from Fundación BBV (1999, 2000). Gross value added is measured in pesetas of 1986 and excludes the value added of the building rental sector, which includes imputed rents on owner-occupied buildings. Employment in this sector, which is very small, is also deducted from overall employment. The series of infrastructure and noninfrastructure capital stocks have been constructed by Mas, Pérez, and Uriel (2002). The (net) stock of physical capital, which is also measured in 1986 pesetas, is broken down into two components. The infrastructure component (x) includes publicly financed transportation networks (roads and highways, ports, airports, and railways), water works, sewage, urban structures, and privately financed toll highways. The stock of noninfrastructure capital (k) includes private capital, net of the stock of residential housing, and the stock of public capital associated with the provision of education, health, and general administrative services. These last three items are aggregated with the capital stock of the private sector because our output measure includes government-provided services. As a proxy for the stock of human capital, we use our own series of average years of schooling.

The results are reported in table 1. Inspection of the table and a comparison with other studies reveal a number of interesting results. First, the coefficient of human capital (β) displays a large and significant positive value that is roughly consistent with our estimates of the same parameter using cross-country data for a sample of Organisation for Economic Co-operation and Development (OECD) countries (de la Fuente Moreno and Doménech 2006b).

TABLE 1. Estimation Results

Variable	Coefficient
α_k	0.171
	(3.50)
α_x	0.0560
	(3.88)
β	0.835
	(4.13)
λ	0.045
	(6.36)
Adjusted R^2	0.763
Standard error regression	0.0094
Number of observations	255

Source: Author's calculations.

Note: The equation includes a full set of period dummies and those regional dummies that were significant in the first iteration. White's heteroskedasticity-consistent t ratios are in parentheses below each coefficient.

Second, our estimate of β implies that human capital accounts for a substantial fraction of cross-regional disparities in productivity. Figure 6 shows the contribution of schooling to the relative productivity of the Spanish regions. Relative productivity is defined as log real output per job measured in deviations from the (unweighted) sample average of the same variable. Using regression weights to average the different regions, we find that the share of schooling in average productivity was 39.86 percent in 1995—that is, for the typical Spanish region, schooling accounts for four-tenths of the productivity gap with the sample average.[5]

FIGURE 6. Contribution of Schooling to Relative Regional Productivity in Spain, 1995 (in percentage)

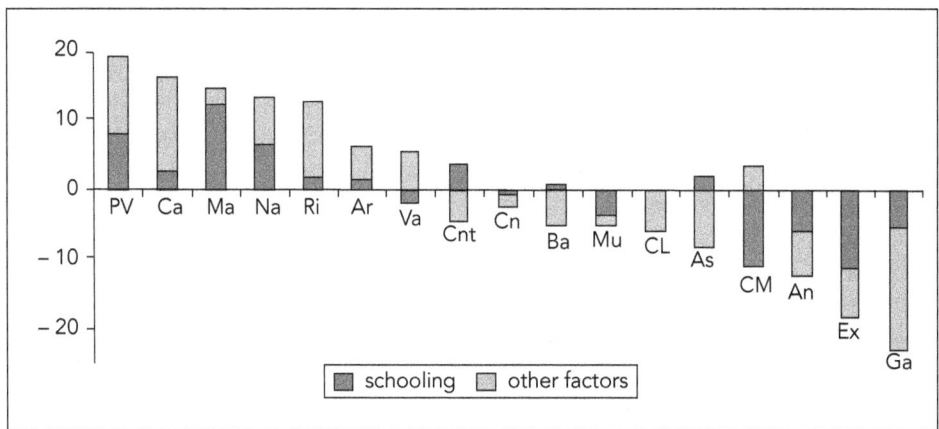

Source: Author's calculations.

Note: For abbreviations, see note to figure 2.

Third, our results also imply private returns to education (measured by the wage increase induced by an additional year of schooling) that are well above those obtained through the estimation of wage equations with individual-level data. That is, the estimated value of β is too high to be capturing only the direct level effects of human capital that should translate into higher wages. This discrepancy can be interpreted as evidence of the existence of externalities linked to the accumulation of human capital.

Turning to the remaining coefficients of the model, finally, we find that both the stock of private capital and the stock of infrastructure enter the equation with positive and significant coefficients. However, both of these coefficients are smaller than those obtained in previous studies that have made use of similar regional data, including in some cases older schooling series constructed using Labour Force Survey data.[6] The sum of these two coefficients is about 25 percent below capital's share of national income, whose average value over the last decade in our sample was 31.4 percent. To be on the safe side when comparing the social returns to different assets, I scale up the coefficient of private capital (α_k) so that the sum $\alpha_k + \alpha_k$ is equal to the share of capital in national income. This ad hoc correction yields a baseline value of α_k of 0.258.

Using our corrected estimates of the parameters of the production function, figure 7 shows the shares of schooling and private and public capital in the relative productivity of a typical Spanish region in 1965 and 1995. The figure shows that differences in schooling have become relatively more important over time as a source of (shrinking) disparities in productivity across regions, making this variable a potentially very powerful instrument of regional redistribution. By contrast, remaining differences in the stock of private capital account for only 10 percent of observed disparities in productivity in the last year of our sample, and infrastructure stocks display a slightly negative correlation with relative productivity.

The Social Return to Schooling and the Optimal Pattern of Investment

In de la Fuente Moreno and Doménech (2006a), we construct estimates of the social rate of return to schooling and to other assets in each of the Spanish regions. Our findings suggest that, at the national level, the economic returns to human capital are at least comparable to, and probably slightly higher than, those to noninfrastructure physical capital. However, the estimated return to infrastructure investment appears to be significantly higher than the return to private and human capital. The situation, however, varies greatly across regions, particularly in terms of the relative returns to education and infrastructure.

Figure 8 plots the *social premium on human capital* relative to infrastructure (defined as the difference between the social rate of return to schooling and the expected return to infrastructure) against regional income per capita in 1995. According to our estimates, the return to public capital exceeds that to human capital in 10 out of 17 regions. Education, however, continues to yield the highest return in most of the poorer territories. For the richest Spanish regions (Madrid,

FIGURE 7. Shares of Different Factors in Relative Productivity in Spain, 1965 and 1995

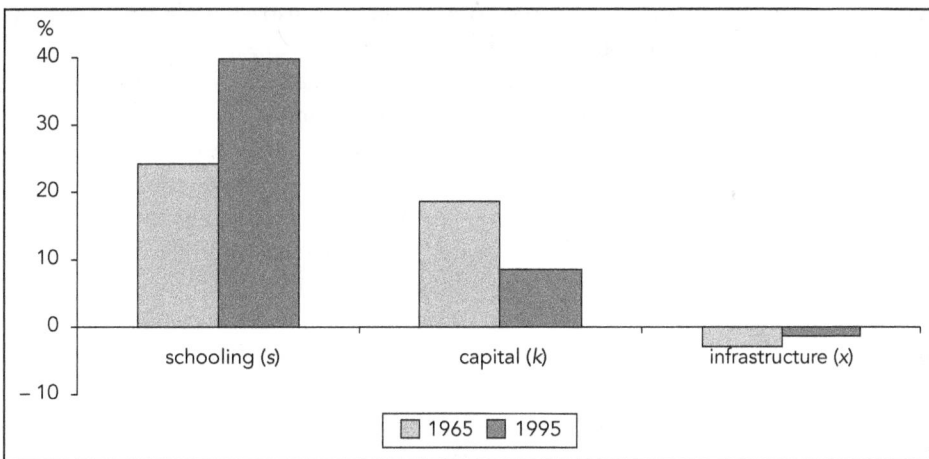

Source: Author's calculations.

Baleares, and Cataluña), the expected returns to infrastructure investment are extremely high and exceed those to education by more than 10 percentage points. For the rest of the regions, the differences in estimated returns are much lower, and the human capital premium is generally positive in the poorer regions and tends to decline with income per capita. This suggests that public investment strategies should differ across regions. Infrastructure stocks appear to be the critical bottleneck at the top of the income distribution, while increasing educational attainment seems to be crucial for low-income regions.

Conclusions

Infrastructure investment and training schemes, together with location incentives for private investment, have traditionally been the main instruments of regional policy and have played a key role in European Union (EU) efforts to increase internal cohesion. Our results indicate that both schooling levels and infrastructure endowments are significant and quantitatively important determinants of income. One direct implication is that investment in both education and infrastructure can be effective in reducing internal disequilibria within Spain and in promoting the country's convergence toward average EU income levels.

The results summarized in this paper also suggest that there are important differences in the role that these two types of investment can and should play in achieving these two objectives. First, there seems to be more room for reducing internal inequality through investment in human capital than in infrastructure. Differences in schooling levels account for around 40 percent of productivity differentials across regions, while the distribution of infrastructure stocks contributes very little to such differences and actually reduces them marginally. Second, the pattern of returns across regions is very different for the two factors. While the expected returns to infrastructure are generally higher in the richer regions and reach extremely high levels in Madrid, Baleares, and Cataluña, the return to education tends to be higher in the poorest territories, where it also exceeds that to infrastructure. Hence, a conflict between the two goals of cohesion policy—national convergence to EU income levels and the reduction of internal disparities—arises in relation to infrastructure, but not with regard to education.

These considerations suggest that it may be possible to increase the effectiveness of both national and EU cohesion and growth policies by devoting greater resources to investment in human capital in poorer regions and by redirecting part of EU and national financing for infrastructure toward richer regions. As I have argued elsewhere (de la Fuente Moreno 2004), a shift in the pattern of infrastructure investment in this direction, by itself, is likely to generate a net welfare gain because the operation of the standard mechanisms for personal redistribution within Spain will channel a substantial part of the resulting output gains back to the poorer regions and to the needier segments of the population. If part of the reduction in infrastructure investment in Objective 1 regions is compensated by an increase in educational funding, the net welfare gains are likely to be considerably larger, for aggregate output will rise faster without a substantial increase in internal inequality.

FIGURE 8. Human Capital Premium Relative to Infrastructure versus Relative Income per Capita in Spain, 1995

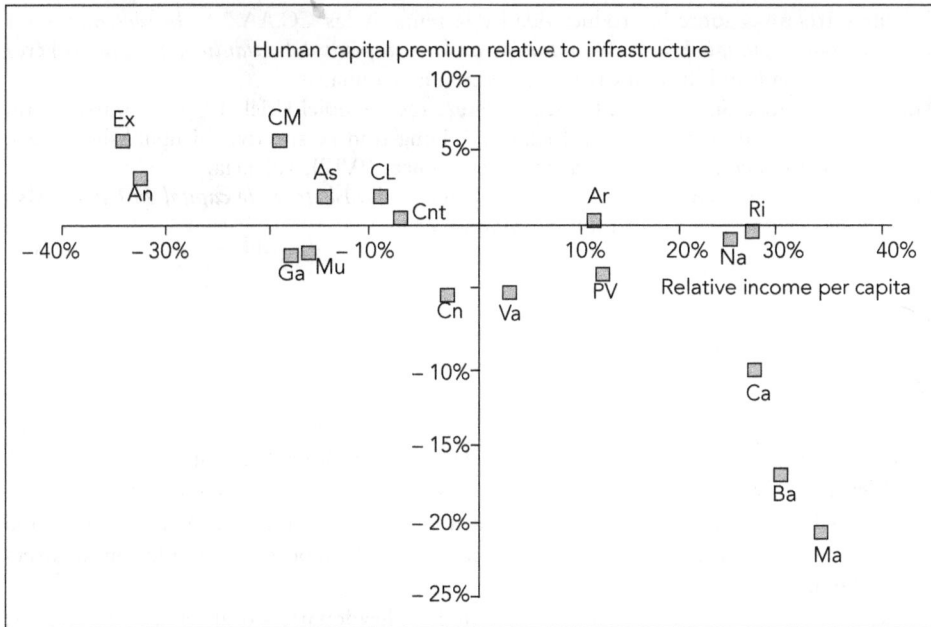

Source: Author's calculations.
Note: For abbreviations, see note to figure 2.

References

Dabán, Teresa, and Ana Lamo. 1999. "Convergence and Public Investment Allocation, Spain 1980–93." Documento de Trabajo D-99001, Dirección General de Análisis y Programación Presupuestaria, Ministerio de Economía y Hacienda, Madrid.

de la Fuente Moreno, Ángel. 2002. "The Effect of Structural Fund Spending on the Spanish Regions: An Assessment of the 1994–99 Objective 1 CSF." CEPR Discussion Paper 3673, Centre for Economic Policy Research, London.

———. 2004. "Second-Best Redistribution through Public Investment: A Characterization, an Empirical Test, and an Application to the Case of Spain." Regional Science and Urban Economics 34 (5): 489–503.

———. 2006a. "La educación en las regiones españolas: Algunas cifras preocupantes." Presupuesto y Gasto Público 44 (3): 7–49.

———. 2006b. "Human Capital and Growth: A Survey." Unpublished paper, Instituto de Análisis Económico.

de la Fuente Moreno, Ángel, and Rafael Doménech. 2006a. "Capital humano, crecimiento, y desigualdad en las regiones españolas." Moneda y Crédito 222: 13–56.

———. 2006b. "Human Capital in Growth Regressions: How Much Difference Does Data Quality Make?" Journal of the European Economic Association 4 (1): 1–36.

de la Fuente Moreno, Ángel, and Xavier Vives. 1995. "Infrastructure and Education as Instruments of Regional Policy: Evidence from Spain." Economic Policy 20 (April): 11–54.

Fundación BBV. 1999. Renta nacional de España y su distribución provincial: Serie homogénea; Años 1955 a 1993 y avances 1994 a 1997, vol. 1. Bilbao: Fundación BBV.

———. 2000. *Renta nacional de España y su distribución provincial: Año 1995 y avances 1996–1999*. Bilbao: Fundación BBV.

González-Páramo, José Manuel, and Isabel Argimón. 1997. "Efectos de la inversión en infraestructuras sobre la productividad y la renta de las CC.AA." In *Infraestructuras y desarrollo regional: Efectos económicos de la Autopista del Atlántico,* ed. Emilio Pérez Touriño. Madrid: Editorial Civitas, Colección Economía.

Mas, Matilde, Joaquín Maudos, Francisco Pérez, and Ezequiel Uriel. 1995. "Infrastructures and Productivity in the Spanish Regions: A Long-Run Perspective." Unpublished paper, Instituto Valenciano de Investigaciones Económicas (IVIE), Valencia.

Mas, Matilde, Francisco Pérez, and Ezequiel Uriel. 2002. *El stock de capital en España y su distribución territorial*. Bilbao: Fundación BBVA.

Notes

1. For a survey of the relevant literature, see de la Fuente Moreno (2006b).
2. Valencia (Va) and all the regions located to its left in figure 3 were Objective 1 regions in 1995—that is, their real income per capita was below 75 percent of the European Union average, and, as a result, they were entitled to special support from the European structural funds.
3. Being the seat of the national government and the headquarters of most large companies, Madrid has traditionally attracted large numbers of highly skilled people. Over the last 25 years, however, this factor has become increasingly less important as a result of decentralization and the creation of regional governments.
4. The (gross) university graduation rate was originally defined as the ratio between the total number of graduates in the universities of a region during a given academic year and the total population of the same region with the theoretical age of college graduation. I have corrected this variable so that it approximates the graduation rate by region of origin (rather than by location of the university).
5. We define the relative productivity of region i ($qrel_i$) as the difference between the region's log output per employed worker and the average value of the same variable in the sample. The contribution of human capital to relative productivity (cs_i) is obtained by multiplying the coefficient of this factor, β, by the relative level of schooling (measured in log differences with the geometric sample mean). After constructing these two variables for each region, we estimate a regression of the form $cs_i = a**qrel_i + e_i$, where e_i is a random disturbance. The coefficient obtained in this manner, $a \cong cs_i/qrel_i$, measures the fraction of the observed productivity differential that can be attributed to human capital in the sample as a whole.
6. See, for instance, Dabán and Lamo (1999); de la Fuente Moreno (2002); de la Fuente Moreno and Vives (1995); González-Páramo and Argimón (1997); and Mas and others (1995).

Family Migration: A Vehicle of Child Morbidity in the Informal Settlements of Nairobi City, Kenya?

ADAMA KONSEIGA

Sub-Saharan Africa has the lowest level of urbanization, but the fastest-growing urban population, in the world. Its urban population, which was 15 percent in 1950 and 32 percent in 1990, is projected to reach 54–60 percent by 2030 (United Nations 1998). While it is true that urban areas and cities offer the cost-reducing advantages of economies of agglomeration, scale, and proximity, as well as numerous economic and social externalities (such as skilled workers, cheap transport, and social and cultural amenities), the social costs of a progressive overloading of housing and social services, not to mention increased crime, pollution, and congestion, tend gradually to outweigh these historical urban advantages, especially in a context where urban growth is not accompanied by economic expansion. The unprecedented growth of urban areas in the context of declining economic performance (World Bank 2000), poor planning, and weak governance is creating a new face of poverty, whereby a significant proportion of the urban population lives below the poverty line in overcrowded slums and sprawling shantytowns in most African countries. An estimated 72 percent of all urban residents in Sub-Saharan Africa live in informal settlements, commonly known as slums (UN-Habitat 2003).

In Kenya, with an urban population of about 34 percent, an estimated 71 percent of all urban dwellers are living in informal settlements, which are characterized by extreme poverty, poor sanitation, inadequate social services, insecurity, social fragmentation, and poor livelihood opportunities. The situation is partly due to misguided urban planning policies and outmoded building codes that often make 80–90 percent of new urban housing illegal (United Nations 1991). Emerging evidence shows that the traditional advantage in health and social indicators that

Adama Konseiga is Affiliate at African Population & Health Research Center (APHRC) in Kenya, and Research Affiliate of GREDI (Research Group in Economics and International Development) in the Faculty of Administration at University of Sherbrooke in Canada.

Berlin Workshop Series 2009
© 2009 The International Bank for Reconstruction and Development/The World Bank

The author is grateful to Joost de Laat, who made these data available, and to the African Population and Health Research Center (APHRC) in Nairobi, for its support in understanding the complex setting of the Nairobi Urban and Health Demographic Surveillance System.

urban areas have enjoyed over rural areas has either drastically dwindled or even reversed in favor of rural areas (APHRC 2002; Brockerhoff and Brennan 1998; Dodoo, Sloan, and Zulu 2002; Mugisha and Zulu 2004). Between 1 million and 2 million migrants reside in cramped conditions in the slums of the capital city of Nairobi, which lack proper access to sanitation and affordable clean water. Children in such areas are exposed to enormous risks, health risks in particular. For example, a large demographic and health-focused survey conducted in various Nairobi slums in 2000 by the African Population and Health Research Center (APHRC) finds not only that morbidity risks for all major childhood illnesses (fever, cough, diarrhea) are higher for slum children than for children elsewhere in Kenya, but also that slum children have less access to health care, including immunization, and subsequently face higher mortality rates than even their rural counterparts.

One coping strategy for slum dwellers is to adopt split migration, whereby the wife and children are secured in the home village, while the head of household undertakes the income diversification and risk management[1] project that is migration to Nairobi. However, this strategy is often impaired by the important monitoring costs that the migrant incurs to ensure that the spouse fulfills the ex ante contract and does not divert the remittances into unproductive activities. The welfare implications of this information asymmetry are significant. Precious resources that could otherwise have been spent on, for example, health care or school fees, are spent on frequent, costly travel home. According to de Laat's estimations (de Laat 2005), the average migrant couple visits each other at least 12.6 times a year, with the husband making the majority (at least 9.5) of the trips. The combined travel cost of these visits is US$109, or 11.1 percent of his annual urban income. Some families for whom monitoring is simply too costly decide to move together to Nairobi, leaving children to be raised in precarious urban slum conditions, with obvious implications for their health and general well-being. For example, the major change in the living environment has been shown to have a more negative impact on the grade progression of children migrating from rural communities to large urban centers than on that of children moving from one rural community to another (Pribesh and Downey 1999).

It is against this backdrop that the current study seeks to understand the role of migration in the urbanization of poverty and poor health in the two slums (Korogocho and Viwandani) where the Nairobi Health and Demographic Surveillance System (NUHDSS) is ongoing. The paper focuses on under-five children living in Nairobi and compares them to under-five children living upcountry. The study examines the motivations behind the choice of joint migration as compared to split migration and the effect of joint migration on child morbidity, after controlling for incidental truncation and other socioeconomic factors. The study hypothesizes that children born to joint migrants and exposed to the slum environment are more likely to fall sick than children born to split migrants because of the poor socioeconomic conditions, poor environmental sanitation, and absence of alternative medical care in the slums. Slum settlements therefore expose children to high morbidity from preventable infectious diseases.

Conceptual Framework: Child Morbidity and Choice of Location

Health plays a dual role as input to the aggregate production function and as output, which places it at the heart of the modern concept of economic development. Health is central to well-being and essential for a satisfying and rewarding life. It is fundamental to the broader notion of expanded human capabilities, choice, and ability to participate. Health is a prerequisite for increases in productivity and a precondition for a successful education, especially for children.

Health is usually measured using infant mortality rates and life expectancy. Life expectancy can be very misleading because its increase may mask additional years of suffering and poor health (Todaro and Smith 2006). An alternative measure for the general well-being is the DALY: disability-adjusted life year. However, measures based on DALY have so far faced numerous data limitations. Child health remains one of the most popular development indicators because it does a relatively good job of measuring the quality of life in developing countries.

The world as a whole experienced dramatic improvements in health over the past half century, with under-five mortality in developing countries decreasing from 280 deaths per 1,000 live births in 1950 to 120 deaths per 1,000 live births by 2002 in low-income countries. However, developing countries face huge challenges compared to developed countries (seven deaths per 1,000 live births).[2] Each year, millions of lives could be saved simply by treating diarrhea: 2 billion of those who survive suffer malnutrition (lack of micronutrients) and infections. Every year, about 12 million children under 5 die in developing countries. Because most of these children die of causes that could be prevented for just a few cents per child, it has been rightly claimed that poverty is the underlying disease. In its 1993 report, the World Bank estimated that one-quarter of the global burden of disease was represented by diarrhea, childhood diseases including measles, respiratory infections, parasitic infections, and malaria (World Bank 1993). Similarly, the World Health Organization (WHO) has found that 5 conditions account for 70 percent of deaths among children under 5: acute respiratory infections, diarrhea, measles, malaria, and malnutrition.

Finally, average health levels can mask great inequality, especially among special populations and infants. Nairobi slum dwellers exhibit notably poor infant health outcomes (not less than 145 deaths per 1,000 live births, which is above the current world average). In order to achieve the Millennium Development Goals (MDGs), it is essential to assess the distribution of health, examine specific populations that are especially exposed to poverty, and shed light on the root causes of child mortality.

Urbanization of Poverty in Kenya

Urban population growth in Sub-Saharan Africa is driven principally by rural-urban migration of young adults seeking jobs and other livelihood opportunities in urban areas (Adepoju 1995; Anderson 2001). Given the increasingly poor living conditions and livelihood opportunities in most metropolitan centers in the region

(APHRC 2002; Brockerhoff and Brennan 1998; World Bank 2000), it appears paradoxical that many rural residents continue to flock to urban areas. Classical migration theories portray migrants as rational economic agents moving to areas that maximize their incomes and overall well-being (Harris and Todaro 1970). In this long-term endeavor, migrants account for their time horizon and probability of getting a job, which explains why younger and more educated individuals are more likely to migrate. In Nairobi, for instance, attempts to move squatter residents to better and more expensive housing have had limited success. Many prefer to live in the relatively cheap squatter settlements in order to accumulate savings for various investments in their home communities, while acquiring the city experience that prepares them for a more permanent formal urban job. This may explain the fact that the urban population growth rates have persisted at very high levels, despite the sustained economic downturn experienced over the past two to three decades. The short-run consequences are the growth of urban poverty and poor health performance, especially in the informal settlements.

Despite the fall in employment opportunities associated with the economic downturn in Kenya beginning in the 1980s, Nairobi's population continued to grow at about 5 percent a year between 1969 and 1999 (Agwanda and others 2004; Government of Kenya 2000). The city's population is composed largely of migrants; the proportion of city-born residents is no more than 20 percent up to age 35 and less than 10 percent after age 50. Half of the migrants came to Nairobi when they were between 17 and 23 years old (Agwanda and others 2004). In this context, income differentials between rural home and urban settlement and remittances cannot be the sole motivation for migration.

Relationships between Child Morbidity and Physical Environment

Parental migration is often found to be negatively correlated with child health in Africa, yet the causal mechanisms are poorly understood. This paper assumes that the health environment is an endogenous choice. Unlike previous studies, I assume that households first endogenously determine whether they will gain from participating in migration and, if they will, whether they will leave the children behind. The final choice is rationally made to ensure the optimal chances of survival for the child.

A basic specification of the resulting reduced-form child health output is based on Glewwe (1999). Child health depends on variable inputs such as health and nutritional inputs and some shifters (the environment and a child's health endowment).

$$H_i = f(HI_i; E_i, \varepsilon_i),$$ (1)

where H_i is the health of child i, HI_i is a vector of health inputs chosen by child 's household, E_i is a vector summarizing the environmental conditions surrounding child i, and ε_i is the child's genetic health endowment.

However, even though in optimizing child health the household head ultimately decides how to allocate health and nutritional inputs (prenatal care, breast milk, medicines, and medical care), it is clear that the environment is also his own endogenous choice to some extent. Survey data collected in two of Nairobi's informal settlement areas in 2004 indicate that, among married migrants,[1] 48 percent were split migrants and the remaining 52 percent were joint migrants.

At a first stage, the household is confronted with the decision about where they want their children to grow up with the optimal chances of survival. In particular, most households in the surveillance slums compare the health environment of the slum with that of the place of origin upcountry. The split-migration decision, which generally leaves the mother and children upcountry, increases the amount of time the mother works at the household's rural farm. Increased time of the mother at home has a direct positive impact on child health.

Given the national amenities and health facilities policy biased toward the formal sector, health-related reasons appear as the least important reason (0.36 percent) attracting rural residents into the slums. In comparison, health is a more important factor pushing slum residents to move back to the rural parts of Kenya (3.05 percent).[3] Even though the latter evidence encompasses older people and terminally ill people with HIV/AIDS, it clearly suggests that health outcomes are not generally neutral to choice of location. As pointed out in de Laat and Archambault (2007), large urban inequities exist in Nairobi, and among the urban poor, the advantages of urban social amenities and public services are questionable. Parents use perceptions of urban-rural differences in social amenities to carefully weigh concerns about child well-being when deciding whether to embark on family migration. This helps to explain why more than half of all children of married migrant men in the Nairobi slums are not living in Nairobi.

For slum residents ages 15 years and above by the end of 2004, NUHDSS data also show that family-related reasons (especially for females), better job prospects, and lower costs are the most important reasons why people across all ages move into the Demographic Surveillance System (DSA).[4] These responses are the ex ante perceptions of the migrants. However, for outmigration that occurs following the experience with living in a slum, figure 1 shows that family reasons are the most important reason among female out-migrants, while among males poor job prospects are the most important, together with poor amenities and social services (including health reasons). Among older individuals (60+), health-related reasons are among the most important factors that determine their migration out of the DSA.

---

[1] Heads of households born outside Nairobi and married formally or informally.

FIGURE 1. Reason for Outmigration in Kenya, by Gender

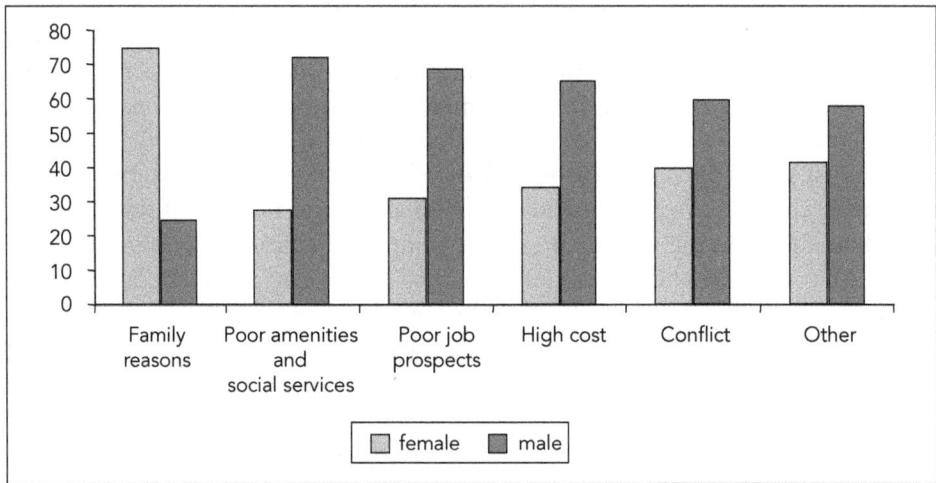

Source: 2004 NUHDSS data.

Additionally, de Laat and Archambault (2007) also find that security is Nairobi's main disadvantage, including the risk to children's health when living in the slums. Even though many of the people interviewed believe that the availability of health facilities is better in urban slums than in their rural homes, most perceive that the daily health risks to children living in the slums are much higher than in rural areas. Slums are characterized by polluted rivers and the lack of sewers, sanitation facilities, and garbage pick-up, thus exposing children to greater health risks.

Finally, migration out of rural areas and into the urban slums is a major environmental change for all members of migrant households, but especially for children (who suffer negative impacts on their grade progression as well as on their psychological and health development).

Data and Econometric Analysis

The following analysis is based on the 2004 Nairobi Informal Settlement Survey (2004 NIS), which collected data in two of Nairobi's slums, Korogocho and Viwandani (de Laat 2004). The survey was conducted between May 4, 2004, and June 27, 2004, on a subsample in these two communities where the NUHDSS operates.[5] Eligibility was defined as being "ever married" and between the ages of 24 and 56 years old. The primary objective of this research was to look at the health and education of children whose parents live in the Nairobi informal settlements (Korogocho and Viwandani).

The survey randomly selected 1,817 "eligible" heads of household; that is, heads of household who are divorced or separated (153 in total) or widowed (150); heads of household who are married and live with their spouse together in the Nairobi informal settlement (858 joint migrants in total); or heads of household who are married but live split from their spouse, who usually lives in the upcountry village (656 split migrants in total). There was no stratification by informal settlement area. A total of 37 household heads refused to participate in the NIS 2004, which represents only 2 percent of the initial sample. The most comprehensive survey questionnaire is that for the category of married household heads who live split from their spouse. The survey also contains relatively detailed information about family members who are not members of the household being interviewed. The following information is recorded in the database:

- All variables at the household level, including consumption

- All variables related to members of the household who are living in the Nairobi slums

- All variables related to the spouse(s) of the household head (called spousal household).

This paper focuses on the health of children whose parents are currently married. It is assumed that the groups of widowed, divorced, or separated households are independent from the study groups and can be left out. Two groups of households are then considered: household heads who live in the slums with their spouse(s) and children, and those who keep the whole family upcountry. Hereafter these groups are referred to respectively as joint migrants and split migrants (see table 1).

Comparing the two sources of information (the NUHDSS and the NIS), it appears that the major difference is that the split migrant's spouse and children are not observed in the risk set of the DSA. For this purpose, the survey included the additional module called spouses household roster. However, this has a strong methodological impact. Indeed, the current study disposes of a data set with 1,514 observations on the living arrangements of migrants (type of migration) in Viwandani and Korogocho. I have full data (no missing values) for all the covariates in the morbidity and migration type participation functions. I use the latter information to estimate a child morbidity function. This estimation needs to be corrected for selection into the DSA as a split or joint migrant. The problem can be summarized by considering data on the following:

- *"Split" subsample:* heads of households who are married but live split from their spouse, who usually lives in the upcountry village (656 in total)[6]

- *"Joint" subsample:* heads of households who are married and live with their spouse together in the Nairobi informal settlement (858 in total).

While the outcomes of the joint-migration children are observed, morbidity data on split-migration children are not observed in the same slum conditions and are obviously missing for the slum structural model. This entails a problem of incidental truncation that can be resolved using the Heckman model. The latter consists of using a sample (Joint+Split) to estimate the migration selection model and then uses a subsample (Joint) to estimate the child morbidity equation.

Methodological Approach

While some studies ask about the health and education of children, these studies often do not recognize that, while some people have their whole family in the urban slums, many others have children and spouses living upcountry. The objective of this section is to analyze the NIS data to understand why some parents have their children in the slums and others do not and what the effects are for the well-being of children. The findings may suggest relevant policies that may improve the lives of poor people living in cities, in line with the Millennium Development Goals.

Precisely the relationship between migration strategy and child health among slum residents is estimated. First, I describe the changes in child morbidity across

TABLE 1. Distribution of the Study Participants According to Migration Status and Age of the Slum Households

Indicator	Survey sample (household)		Household with children (estimation sample)		Child morbidity prevalence (household level)	
	Number	%	Number	%	Number	%
Total	1,514	100	951	100	951	100
Joint						
2004 NIS	858	57	557	59	241	43
Viwandani	470	31	294	31	117	40
Korogocho	82	5	49	5	20	41
Nyayo	306	20	214	23	104	49
Split						
2004 NIS	656	43	397	42	125	31
Viwandani	497	33	311	33	90	29
Korogocho	33	2	14	1	3	21
Nyayo	126	8	72	8	32	44
Age	945		62		945	
0 year	97	6	97	10	—	—
1 year	190	13	190	20	—	—
2 year	325	21	325	34	—	—
3 year	194	13	194	21	—	—
4 year	139	9	139	15	—	—

Source: 2004 NIS.

Note: Korogocho includes Nyayo in the definition of the NUHDSS. Nine households (three in Nyayo and six in Viwandani) have children both in the urban and rural places. This may be an interesting strategy where the head of a split household takes the older or most healthy children to Nairobi.

— Not available.

migration type. Second, I estimate an econometric model and investigate whether the impact of migration on child health is different across gender.

Slum dwellers are an important group to study because they are highly mobile (in- and outmigration rates describe a circular migration, in particular, between rural and urban places) and exhibit notably poor infant health outcomes (not less than 145 deaths per 1,000 live births, which is above the current world average).

Analytical Framework

This section provides a framework for thinking about the pathways by which choice of destination affects child health. The "new home economics" formalizes the process of time allocation within the household when labor has an opportunity cost (Sadoulet and de Janvry, 1995). Typically, labor can be used in production within the house, outside the house as a worker, or in leisure. While the narrow definition of leisure includes relaxation, pleasure, and sleep, it is broadly understood in the context of developing countries as home time. The latter is time not spent in directly productive labor market activities (family maintenance, family reproduction, socialization, and leisure). Therefore, utility is derived not directly from purchased goods, but from a vector of goods produced in the household with purchased goods and family time. Consumption decisions include a trade-off between the choice of time spent at home and the consumption of goods that would require more income and hence more work. The time allocated to family reproduction (pregnancy, childrearing, child health, and production) becomes increasingly costly, especially for the most educated households.

A demand for child well-being or children's health is derived from the application of Becker's theoretical framework. The household maximizes a utility function and chooses child health H, leisure L, and consumption of goods and services C.

The household problem can be specified as follows:

$$\underset{H,L,C}{Max}U = U\left(H, L, C; z_h, \mu\right), \tag{2}$$

where Z_h is a usual vector of household characteristics, including the education level of both the household head and his spouse and the household assets, and μ is the unobserved heterogeneity in preferences.

The household maximizes this utility function subject to two constraints: a health production function for child health status and a budget constraint.[7] Child health is generated by the following production function:

$$H_i = f\left(Y_i, z_i, z_h, z_c, \eta_i\right), \tag{3}$$

where Y_i is a vector of health inputs, which are nutrient intake, health care practices, time spent by parents taking care of children, and disease incidence, Z_i is a vector of child characteristics, which are body size, age, and gender, Z_h is a vector of community characteristics that may have a direct impact on child health, which are the accessibility and quality of health services and safe water, and η_i are unobservable individual health endowments such as the child's genetic inheritance.

In addition, the full income constraint includes the opportunity cost of leisure:

$$\pi^* = p_c C + wL + p_y Y + T, \tag{4}$$

where p_c, w, and p_y are the market prices of consumption goods, leisure, and health inputs, respectively, and π^* is the full household's income, including the value of the time endowment of the household and nonfarm income transfers.

Equation (1) above can then be derived as a reduced-form child health output.

Econometric Model

The importance of split migration has rarely been studied in the migration literature. Typically, split migrants are married heads of household who adopt a temporary move and live split from their spouse (who usually lives in the upcountry village with the children). This allows the family to protect the children's health from the poor environmental conditions of the destination. Among the study population, 62.8 percent have at least one child (951 households), and among them, 42 percent have left their children upcountry. The relevant sample for the current study is therefore composed of 557 joint households and 397 split households.

The distribution of the split-household sample suggests that 42 percent of the households who have children consider the migration project more beneficial if they leave their children upcountry, according to the theory. Analyzing the behavior of split-migration households from a population leads to an incidental truncation problem because these migrants are a restricted nonrandom part of an entire population. The households that supply migrants' labor may possess unobserved characteristics that are generally positively related to health and income, resulting in a sample-selection bias. With such a distortion, results from standard ordinary least squares (OLS) are simply biased. The regression model that includes the above selection issue is the migration model à la Nakosteen and Zimmer (1980). The simultaneous system writes the following:

Net benefit of moving:

$$V_i^* = \alpha' Z_i + \gamma' X_i + \varepsilon_i \qquad (1) \qquad (6)$$

Child morbidity outcomes of joint-migration households:

$$\log mo_{ji} = \beta_j' X_{ji} + \mu_{ji} \qquad (2) \qquad (7)$$

Child morbidity outcomes of split-migration households:

$$\log mo_{si} = \beta_s' X_{shi} + \mu_{si} \qquad (3) \qquad (8)$$

To estimate the simultaneous migration-type decision and child morbidity equations, it is assumed that v_i^* and $\log_{mo_i}$ have a bivariate normal distribution with correlation ρ. An analysis of morbidity in either subsample must account first for the structural differences of health and production markets in the related locations (slums and upcountry) and for the incidental truncation of the split migrant's (joint migrant's) morbidity on the sign of the net benefit. To face estimation problems of a model with sample selection, a Heckman two-step procedure is used to study joint migration. In this case, outputs are interpreted with split migrants as the reference category. The Heckman regression model adapted to the current situation, where the outcome variable is binary, can be written for the selected sample as in equations 6' and 7'-8'. For the selection model,

$$P_i^* = \alpha' Z_i + \gamma' X_i + \varepsilon_i \qquad (1)'(6')$$

where P^* is the probability of the variable indicator of the sign of the selection criteria that is the net benefit from joint migration. Z_i and X_i represent the independent variables of the selection equation identification and those of the morbidity equation, respectively.

For the morbidity model,

$$\log mo_i = \beta' X_i + \beta_\lambda \lambda_i + v_i \qquad (2\text{-}3)'(7'\text{-}8')$$

where the following relationship exists between the coefficient of the inverse Mills's ratio λ and the model statistics: $\beta_\lambda \ \rho\sigma_\mu$. The inverse Mills's ratio itself evaluates the ratio of the probability and cumulative density functions from the selection equation. Heckman (1979) argues that this function is a monotone decreasing function of the probability that an observation is selected into the analyzed sample.

The Heckman's two-step estimation procedure is applied to the select group of joint migrants, taking into account the fact that joint migrants and split migrants face distinct labor and production market structures, respectively, in their rural home and in the urban slums. The probit equation 6' is estimated to obtain estimates of α and γ and compute the inverse Mills's ratio. At a second step of the Heckman procedure, the inverse Mills's ratio is added to the child morbidity outcome equations 7'-8' to produce the consistent estimates of β and β_λ. However, the coefficients estimated in equation 6'—respectively, 7' and 8'—measure how the log-odds in favor of migrating (falling sick) change as the independent variables change by a unit. For the correct interpretation of these nonlinear outcomes, marginal effects should then be computed (Long and Freese 2001).

Model Variables and Estimation

The child health outcome depends on household characteristics, local community environment, and child endowment. This leads to the following principal variables:

- Household initial assets (toilet, water), parental education

- Health and education facilities in the community (social amenities, availability and accessibility of health services, parasites, contagious illnesses)

- Child's genetic endowment.

In this paper, child health status is quantified using self-reported morbidity data. Because of all the problems related to such data, it is important to explain in detail the outcome variable being used.

The Morbidity Variable and Reliability Issues

The dependent variable is an indicator of whether the household had a child who was sick in the month preceding the NIS 2004 survey or not. Table 1 shows that, while only 31 percent of split households had an under-5 child who was sick last month, about 43 percent of joint migrants had a child in the slums who suffered illness. Of all split households, I estimated that 61 percent have children under 5 years old who live upcountry (split-migration children). The proportion in the group of urban or joint households who have under-5 children is 64 percent. This may suggest that the two groups of the study population are comparable in terms of their fertility rates.

Although an important literature addresses migration and assimilation processes for understanding health differences, most suffer from a common limitation: they are based on data from the destination area (Landale and Oropesa 2001). Even though our data do not solve that problem, this rich survey has made an effort to overcome the limitation.

Typically, the main weakness of previous studies is that they are based on the same population at risk (located in the slums). These studies compare outcomes within a quite homogeneous group across generations of residence or according to duration of residence in the place of destination. Although such comparisons provide useful information (Zulu and others 2006), the evaluation of arguments stressing migration-related processes requires that migrants be compared with nonmigrants in the place of origin. This is the emphasis of the present study.

Comparing self-reported morbidity with indicators of morbidity from physicians' evaluations, Ferraro and Farmer (1999) find that self-reported morbidity is equal or superior to physician-evaluated morbidity in a prognostic sense. When data from respondents and physicians do not agree, the presumption is that respondents are underreporting or overreporting medical conditions. However, the study suggests that biopsy or autopsy may be the gold standard. The study suggests that self-reported data should not axiomatically be characterized as inferior solely because they come from respondents. The accuracy of survey data remains an empirical question. Most of the time responses from survey participants are likely to be biased by the assumptions that the respondents apply to the problem. The type of information collected and the context of the questioning are also important when attempting to understand discrepancies between self-reported data and other sources of information. For instance, questions regarding sexually transmitted diseases probably contain more bias than questions regarding conditions such as heart attacks or child health.

The data collected on self-reported morbidity outcomes, especially for children staying upcountry, may have some measurement errors. This may not be a major problem, as morbidity is the primary dependent variable of interest. Indeed, measurement error in an explanatory variable traditionally has been considered a much more important problem than measurement error in the response variable (Wooldridge 2002). Self-reporting may be a mismeasurement of actual child health, but all economic decisions (for instance, the decision to return upcountry or to regroup the family in one place) by the household head are conditioned by his perceptions of child well-being upcountry relative to child well-being in the slums. When estimating a linear equation with measurement error in the dependent variable under OLS conditions, what is important is how the error is related to other factors (Wooldridge 2002). It is possible to ignore the fact that the dependent variable is an imperfect measure and obtain consistent estimators of the regression parameters if the measurement error is statistically independent of each explanatory variable. In this context, the measurement error may only affect the intercept if the former does not have zero mean. However, it is possible to assume that the measurement error is not independent of migration status. Even in the scenario where the split head of household may underreport sickness of his children upcountry due to lack of contact (at least 11 percent of the urban annual income is spent on frequent travel upcountry, not including phone communications), the error term is negatively correlated with migration status. The correction for the downward bias in the split-migration parameter involves instrumental variables estimation, which is done in the Heckman procedure used below.

In this study, attempts to control for measurement bias do not show any significant evidence of information bias on reporting sickness upcountry versus urban location. The respondent bias is captured as an indicator of a household head who did not know about the sickness status of his children living upcountry (missing, refuse to answer, or don't know as response) but did know the morbidity status of household members in the slums.

Finally, it is important to compare the current findings with data collected using more reliable measurements of child health, such as using anthropometry or biomarkers to measure nutritional status of children and mothers, or using WHO and other quality of life measurements for child and adult health focused on disability, mental health, and so forth.

Table 2 shows the total morbidity rate in the two slums of Nairobi at the individual level—that is, 23.2 percent for the whole population. However, child morbidity reached 39 percent in 2004. There appears to be no significant difference by gender of the study population as regards under-five morbidity. However, under-five children in the slums tend to be sicker than their rural counterparts, especially girls (7 percentage points difference).

The covariates used in the Heckman model to identify the selection equation and explain morbidity outcomes in the slums are summarized in table A.1 and include the following:

- *Selection variable:* migration status (joint versus split migration)

TABLE 2. Gender and Morbidity Profile in the Slums and Upcountry (Individual Level) of Kenya

Population	Total		Male		Women	
	Number	%	Number	%	Number	%
Urban population						
Total	5,733	100	3,165	55	2,568	45
Sick	1,331	23	737	13	594	10
Upcountry population						
Total	2,773	100	1,144	41	1,629	59
Sick	511	19	214	8	297	11
Under-five urban population						
Total	865	100	420	49	445	51
Sick	337	39	164	19	173	20
Under-five upcountry population						
Total	531	100	293	55	238	45
Sick	146	27	75	14	71	13

Source: 2004 NIS.

- *Control variables:* age of the children, average educational attainment of the household, literacy of the household head in the urban settlement, religion, gender of the household head, orphan status, ethnicity, total size of the household, caregiver, social network in the place of origin, wealth index, production factors (land and labor), and location of the household head.

Empirical Results

This section implements the econometric analysis and interprets the reduced form of the selection of migration type and the morbidity outcome model. The latter evaluates the impact of the covariates corrected for selection bias.

Table 3 indicates that the bivariate effect of choosing the joint-migration strategy is significantly high. The risk of having a child fall sick is 39.2 percent higher in the slums than in the rural place of origin.

A more elaborate estimation that controls for selection bias and other covariates follows in table 4. The results in regression 1 in table 4 show that the child morbidity of joint-migration households in the slums of Nairobi is a positive function of the level of schooling of the household but a negative function of the education level of the head of household as compared to the reference group of split migrants. This suggests two findings. First, the average level of education of the urban household plays against the health of children. This is explained by the fact that educated adults tend to leave children with caregivers while at work. In the poor sanitation conditions of the slums, the younger children suffer the most (negative impact of age of under-five children). In particular, educated spouses spend more time in the urban labor market and therefore spend less time in reproduction activities (less time spent breastfeeding, for example).

TABLE 3. Morbidity of Slum Children in Joint-Split Households

Explanatory variables	Sick last month
Married under joint migration	0.331***
	(3.90)
Constant	−0.482***
	(−7.35)
Observations	945
Log likelihood	−623.2

Source: Author's calculations.

Note: z statistics in parentheses.

*** Significant at 1 percent.

Additionally, the presence of an educated head (joint migration) is very important for the health of children. Children born to educated household heads who stay far from the family may be sicker. In the case of a missing or imperfect labor market, the household must rely on family labor, and thus sending a household member (the head in this case) may stop the household from moving toward local high-return activities (farm and health production). The adverse effect of lost labor may be higher when migrants tend to be younger and better educated than the average rural laborer.

Similarly, the regression shows that children without a father who are raised in the slums suffer more diseases than others.

Children born to a Protestant family appear to be less sick than children from the other religious groups. This suggests that the Protestant social network and level of cooperation work better in the conditions of city life. Being from a Luhya family exposes children to higher health risks than being from other ethnic groups such as Kikuyu.

The likelihood that the household will migrate jointly (regression 2 in table 4) is significantly dependent on median size of social network, the wealth index, and the availability of agricultural factors. Compared to households who know 1 to 10 people in their community of origin, households who know between 11 and 30 people are more likely to choose split migration. The social network literature argues that knowing more people enables the migrant to leave for the city. In the 2004 NIS survey, it is found that monitoring costs in terms of controlling the work effort and investment behavior of the spouse are very high (at least 11 percent of urban annual income is spent on frequent travels upcountry). The most frequent and costly monitoring mechanism is frequent travel upcountry, and the split migrant can substitute this by delegating some monitoring activities to his relatives who are left behind. One explanation of the advantaged health status of the upcountry resident also emphasizes the role of culture in fostering family cohesion and providing social support. Because close friends and family members often encourage health-promoting behavior, especially by being an important source of information through their childcare experiences, social support may play an important role in the positive health practices and outcomes of those staying upcountry as compared with slum migrants.

TABLE 4. Morbidity of Slum Children in Joint-Split Households

Covariate	Sick last month (1)	Joint migrant (2)
Average years of schooling of the household	0.0519**	
	(2.14)	
Average age of children under 5	−0.0640	
	(−1.34)	
Religion = Protestant	−0.122	
	(−1.09)	
Urban head is literate = Yes	−0.781*	
	(−1.75)	
Has lost father in the last 10 years	0.264**	
	(2.19)	
Female household head	0.465**	
	(2.35)	
Ethnicity = Luhya	0.328**	
	(2.11)	
Slum = Nyayo	0.172	
	(1.45)	
Social network from origin community = 0		0.0396
		(0.30)
Social network from origin community = 11–30		−0.343***
		(−3.21)
Social network from origin community = 31–50		0.00173
		(0.011)
Social network from origin community = 50+		−0.0132
		(−0.082)
Members in spousal + urban household		−0.201***
		(−8.62)
Own land or houses in Nairobi		0.0481**
		(−2.30)
Available agricultural production factors		0.00811**
		(2.18)
	0.108	1.299***
	(0.20)	(9.72)
	946	946
	−955.9	

Source: Author's calculations.
Note: z statistics are in parentheses.
*** Significant at 1 percent.
** Significant at 5 percent.
* Significant at 10 percent.

Finally, households that are better endowed with production factors (land and labor) or richer (own houses in Nairobi) can afford to undertake split migration, leaving the family members to work on the agricultural farm, while being able to face important monitoring costs.

Conclusion

To provide better education and health services to everyone as required by the Millennium Development Goals, it is important to understand why some parents allow their children to live in the slums and others do not, and what the effects are, for the children.

This study examines the joint migration of the whole family to the slums of Nairobi and estimates the effect of such a strategy on child morbidity. On the one hand, the likelihood of the household migrating jointly is significantly higher for households with poor social networks in their community of origin, which makes it impossible for the household head to face the high monitoring (especially travel) costs related to split migration. Households that are better endowed with production factors (land and labor) or richer (own houses in Nairobi) can afford to undertake split migration.

The findings indicate that the bivariate effect of choosing the joint-migration strategy is significantly high. The risk of falling sick for a child is 39.2 percent higher in the slums than in the rural place of origin. Moreover, the morbidity of joint-migration households in the slums of Nairobi negatively depends on the education level of the head of household as compared to the reference group of split migrants. This suggests that the presence of an educated household head is very important for the health of children. Children born to an educated household head who stays far from the family may be sicker. In the case of a missing or an imperfect labor market, the household must rely on family labor, and thus sending a household member (the head in this case) may prevent the household from moving toward local high-return activities (farm and health production). The adverse effect of lost labor may be higher when migrants tend to be younger and better educated than the average rural laborer.

Finally, the research indicates that, in the poor sanitation conditions of the slums, the younger children suffer the most, especially when adults (especially the mother) allocate time away from home to the urban labor market. Similarly, children who have lost their father but are raised in the conditions of the slums suffer more diseases than others.

The study suggests several ways to ensure better health of slum children by promoting the split-migration strategy or compensating the welfare of children living in the slums. A constructive urban policy is necessary to realize the potential of cities to foster successful development, while at the same time giving more balanced treatment to development in rural areas to avoid urban bias. These findings can be validated using the rich longitudinal data collected by the NUHDSS, which, unlike the cross-sectional NIS survey, may enable researchers to study the time dimension and vulnerability by monitoring changes in health status of the urban poor.

References

Adepoju, Aderanti. 1995. "Emigration Dynamics in Sub-Saharan Africa." *International Migration; Special Issue: Emigration Dynamics in Developing Countries* 33 (3-4): 315–90.

Agwanda, Alfred O., Philippe Bocquier, Anne Khasakhala, and Samuel O. Owuor. 2004. "The Effect of Economic Crisis on Youth Precariousness in Nairobi: An Analysis of Itinerary to Adulthood of Three Generations of Men and Women." DIAL Working Paper DT/2004/4, Développement Institutions e Analyses de Long Terme, Paris. http://www.dial.prd.fr/dial–publications/PDF/Doc–travail/2003-09.pdf.

Anderson, J. A. 2001. "Mobile Workers, Urban Employment, and 'Rural' Identities: Rural-Urban Networks of Buhera Migrants, Zimbabwe." In *Mobile Africa: Changing Patterns of Movement in Africa and Beyond,* ed. M. Dedruijn, R. Van Dijk and Dick Foeken. Lieden, the Netherlands: Brill.

APHRC (African Population and Health Research Center). 2002. *Population and Health Dynamics in Nairobi Informal Settlements.* Nairobi: APHRC.

Bassolé, Léandre. 2007. "Child Malnutrition in Senegal: Does Access to Public Infrastructure Really Matter? A Quantile Regression Analysis." Working Paper, CERDI-CNRS, Université d'Auvergne.

Sadoulet, Elisabeth, and Alain de Janvry. 1995. *Quantitative Development Policy Analysis.* Baltimore: The Johns Hopkins University Press.

Brockerhoff, Martin, and Ellen Brennan. 1998. "The Poverty of Cities in Developing Countries." *Population and Development Review* 24 (1): 75–114.

de Laat, Joost. 2004. "2004 Nairobi Informal Settlement Survey." Brown University, Providence, RI; APHRC, Nairobi.

———. 2005. "Moral Hazard and Costly Monitoring: The Case of Split Migrants in Kenya." Job Market Paper, Brown University, Providence, RI.

de Laat, Joost, and Caroline Archambault. 2007. *Child Well-Being, Social Amenities, and Imperfect Information: Shedding Light on Family Migration to Urban Slums.* New York: Population Association of America.

Dodoo, F. N ii-Amoo, Melissa Sloan, and Eliya M. Zulu. 2002. "Space, Context, and Hardship: Socializing Children into Sexual Activity in Kenyan Slums." In *Fertility and Reproductive Health in Sub-Saharan Africa: A Collection of Microdemographic Studies,* ed. Samuel Agyei-Mensah and John B. Casterline, 147–60. Westport, CT: Greenwood Press.

Ferraro, Kenneth F., and Melissa M. Farmer. 1999. "Utility of Health Data from Social Surveys: Is There a Gold Standard for Measuring Morbidity?" *American Sociological Review* 64 (2): 303–15.

Glewwe, Paul. 1999. "Why Does Mother's Schooling Raise Child Health in Developing Countries? Evidence from Morocco." *Journal of Human Resources* 34 (1): 124–59.

Harris, John R., and Michael P. Todaro. 1970. "Migration, Unemployment, and Development: A Two Sector Analysis." *American Economic Review* 60 (1): 126–42.

Heckman, James J. 1979. "Sample Selection Bias as a Specification Error." *Econometrica* 47 (1): 153–61.

Kenya, Government of. 2000. *Second Report on Poverty in Kenya.* Vol. I: *Incidence and Depth of Poverty.* Nairobi: Central Bureau of Statistics, Ministry of Planning and National Development. http://www4.worldbank.org/afr/poverty/pdf/docnav/02880.pdf.

Landale, Nancy S., and R. S. Oropesa. 2001. "Migration, Social Support, and Perinatal Health: An Origin-Destination Analysis of Puerto Rican Women." *Journal of Health and Social Behavior* 42 (2): 166–83.

Long, Scott J., and Jeremy Freese. 2001. *Regression Models for Categorical Dependent Variable Using Stata.* College Station, TX: Stata Press.

Mugisha, Frederick, and Eliya M. Zulu. 2004. "The Influence of Alcohol, Drugs, and Substance Abuse on Sexual Relationships and Perception of Risk to HIV Infection among Adolescents in the Informal Settlements of Nairobi." *Journal of Youth Studies* 7 (3): 279–93.

Nakosteen, Robert A., and Michael A. Zimmer. 1980. "Migration and Income: The Question of Self-Selection." *Southern Economic Journal* 46 (3): 840–51.

Pribesh, Shana, and Douglas B. Downey. 1999. "Why Are Residential and School Moves Associated with Poor School Performance?" *Demography* 36 (4): 521–34.

Stark, Oded. 2003. "Tales of Migration without Wage Differentials: Individual, Family, and Community Contexts." ZEF Discussion Paper on Development Policy 73, Center for Development Research. http://www.zef.de/publications.htm.

Todaro, Michael P., and Stephen C. Smith. 2006. *Economic Development,* 9th ed. Boston: Pearson Addison Wesley.

United Nations. 1991. *World Urbanization Prospects*, New York: United Nations, Department of Economic and Social Affairs, Population Division.

United Nations. 1998. *World Urbanization Prospects: The 1996 Revision.* New York: United Nations, Department of Economic and Social Affairs, Population Division.

UN-Habitat (United Nations Human Settlement Programme). 2003. *Slums of the World: The Face of Urban Poverty in the New Millennium?* Nairobi: Global Urban Observatory.

Wooldridge, Jeffrey M. 2002. *Econometric Analysis of Cross Section and Panel Data.* Cambridge, MA: MIT Press.

World Bank. 1993. World Development Report: Investing in Health. Oxford: Oxford University Press.

World Bank. 2000. *World Development Report 1999/2000: Entering the 21st Century.* New York: Oxford University Press.

Zulu, Eliya M., Adama Konseiga, Eugene Darteh, and Blessing Mberu. 2006. "Migration and the Urbanization of Poverty in Sub-Saharan Africa: The Case of Nairobi City, Kenya." Population Association of America, Los Angeles.

Notes

1. For further details, see Stark (2003).
2. Nairobi slum dwellers exhibit notably poor infant health outcomes (not less than 145 deaths per 1,000 live births, which is above the current world average).
3. Figures are estimated from a livelihood survey conducted in May 2003 in Korogocho and Viwandani.
4. The reasons for in-migration into the DSA were recoded into five categories: family-related reasons, which include marriage, moving with the family, and moving to live near relatives; better amenities and social services, which include housing- and health-related attributes; better job prospects; lower cost; and other reasons.
5. APHRC is conducting an extensive Health and Demographic Surveillance System, which served as sampling frame for the NIS survey. The data collection procedures include visits to all 23,000 households in the DSA every four months to update information on all vital events (births, deaths, movements, vaccinations, and pregnancies). Movements include change of residence and migrations.
6. In fact, this group is reduced to 652 cases of split migrants who have information on their spouse upcountry.
7. See also Bassolé (2007).

Appendix. Descriptive Statistics

TABLE A.1. Descriptive Statistics, by Migration Status

Variable and migration status	Number	% missing	Mean	Standard deviation
Average years of schooling of the household				
Split	403	0	9.26	2.43
Joint	543	0.91	7.67	2.56
Average age of children under 5				
Split	397	1.49	2.26	1.19
Joint	548	0	2.09	1.16
Income activity last month = Yes				
Split	403	0	0.98	0.14
Joint	548	0	0.98	0.13
Religion = Catholic				
Split	403	0	0.36	0.48
Joint	548	0	0.3	0.46
Religion = Protestant				
Split	403	0	0.54	0.5
Joint	548	0	0.49	0.5
Religion = Other Christian				
Split	403	0	0.04	0.2
Joint	548	0	0.09	0.29
Religion = Muslim				
Split	403	0	0.02	0.13
Joint	548	0	0.05	0.21
Religion = No religion				
Split	403	0	0.03	0.16
Joint	548	0	0.05	0.21
Literate = Yes				
Split	403	0	0.98	0.15
Joint	548	0	0.98	0.13
Has lost father in the last 10 years				
Split	403	0	0.17	0.37
Joint	548	0	0.3	0.46
Female household head				
Split	403	0	0.01	0.12
Joint	548	0	0.09	0.28
Ethnicity = Luhya				
Split	403	0	0.07	0.26
Joint	548	0	0.15	0.36
Social network from origin community = 0				
Split	403	0	0.11	0.32
Joint	548	0	0.14	0.35

Variable and migration status	Number	% missing	Mean	Standard deviation
Social network from origin community = 1–10				
Split	403	0	0.42	0.49
Joint	548	0	0.48	0.5
Social network from origin community = 11–30				
Split	403	0	0.3	0.46
Joint	548	0	0.2	0.4
Social network from origin community = 31–50				
Split	403	0	0.07	0.26
Joint	548	0	0.08	0.27
Social network from origin community = 50+				
Split	403	0	0.08	0.28
Joint	548	0	0.08	0.27
Members in spousal + urban household				
Split	403	0	5.7	1.98
Joint	548	0	4.61	1.69
Own land or houses in Nairobi				
Split	403	0	1.83	13.34
Joint	548	0	1.04	9.7
Available agricultural production factor				
Split	403	0	8.94	66.52
Joint	548	0	6.74	65.97
Slum = Nyayo				
Split	403	0	0.18	0.39
Joint	548	0	0.39	0.49

Source: Author's calculations.

TABLE A.2. Morbidity of Slum Children in Joint-Split Households

Variable	Sick last month (1)	Joint migrant (2)
Average years of schooling of the household	0.0396*	
	(1.65)	
Average age of children under 5	–0.0670	
	(–1.41)	
Income activity last month = Yes	–0.480	
	(–1.12)	
Religion = Catholic	0.175	
	(1.39)	
Religion = Other Christian	0.0930	
	(0.47)	
Religion = Muslim	–0.153	
	(–0.54)	
Religion = No religion	0.0218	
	(0.079)	
Head is literate = Yes	–0.743*	
	(–1.68)	
Has lost father in the last 10 years	0.286**	
	(2.37)	
Female household head	0.528***	
	(2.66)	
Ethnicity = Luhya	0.343**	
	(2.20)	
Social network from origin community = 0		0.0415
		(0.31)
Social network from origin community = 11–30		–0.344***
		(–3.23)
Social network from origin community = 31–50		0.000640
		(0.0040)
Social network from origin community = 50+		–0.0121
		(–0.075)
Members in spousal + urban household		–0.201***
		(–8.61)
Own land or houses in Nairobi		–0.0479**
		(–2.29)
Available agricultural production factor		0.00808**
		(2.16)
	0.562	1.299***
	(0.84)	(9.72)
	946	946
	–956.0	

Source: Author's calculations.
Note: z statistics are in parentheses.
*** Significant at 1 percent.
** Significant at 5 percent.
* Significant at 10 percent.

Remittances and Their Impact on the Macroeconomic Situation of and Financial Sector Development in the Kyrgyz Republic

ROMAN MOGILEVSKY AND AZIZ ATAMANOV

This report has been prepared within the framework of the Asian Development Bank (ADB) study on remittances and poverty in Central Asia and South Caucasus. It complements a parallel study on remittances and poverty in the Kyrgyz Republic.

The study aims to analyze the impact of remittances on the macroeconomic situation in the Kyrgyz Republic and on development of the country's financial sector. The paper has six sections and two appendixes. The first section addresses definitions, measurement techniques, amounts, and structure of remittances in the Kyrgyz Republic. The second assesses the relationship between remittances and recent macroeconomic variables. The third provides information on individual and household characteristics of the senders and recipients of remittances, pattern of remittance sending, and use of remittances at the micro level. The fourth discusses remittance channels used in the country and competition in the remittance marketplace. The fifth reviews the Kyrgyz financial sector and opportunities for its development related to remittance inflow. A final section summarizes the paper's contents and formulates recommendations for economic policy regarding remittances and related issues. Appendix A provides background information on migration in the Kyrgyz Republic. Appendix B contains tables and graphs, which provide additional details on remittances and remitters in the country.

Remittance Flows in the Kyrgyz Republic

Massive cross-border monetary flows involving individuals have characterized the Kyrgyz Republic since independence. This is due to several factors:

Roman Mogilevsky is Executive Director of the Center for Social and Economic Research (CASE) in Kyrgyzstan.

Berlin Workshop Series 2009

- *Large permanent migration.* After the breakup of the former Soviet Union (FSU), many ethnic minority groups in their respective republics started moving to the republics of the FSU or to other countries where they comprise a majority of the population (see appendix A). In the Kyrgyz Republic, many Russians, Germans, and other minority groups moved to the Russian Federation, Germany, and other countries, while a smaller but significant number of ethnic Kyrgyz people returned to the Kyrgyz Republic. This permanent migration required the cross-border movement of property and increased the frequency of intrafamily monetary transfers, as many families were separated by the new borders.

- *Widespread shuttle trade.* During the period of independence, shuttle trade largely replaced official trade implemented by legal entities concerning imports and, later, exports of goods.[1] Shuttle trade required traders to bring with them large amounts of money (either in cash or via the financial system) from the Kyrgyz Republic to other countries and back.

- *Liberal regime of foreign currency circulation in the Kyrgyz Republic.* Since the early years of independence, the Kyrgyz Republic has had a liberal currency regime. As early as 1993, the national currency was introduced; thereafter, there were practically no restrictions on the exchange of national to foreign currency and vice versa—either for individuals or for other legal entities (corporations and financial institutions). This allowed migrants and shuttle traders to have the foreign and national currencies necessary for their operations.

Only in 2002–03 did professional and political discussions focus on remittances in the Kyrgyz Republic. This happened for two key reasons. First, migration of Kyrgyz workers to Russia and Kazakhstan increased swiftly due to robust economic growth and fast-growing demand for labor in these oil-rich countries coupled with a large wage differential between these countries and the Kyrgyz Republic. Second, measures to achieve macroeconomic stabilization and strengthen the financial sector that were implemented after the 1998–99 financial crisis created a better environment in the early 2000s for the expansion of financial services. As a result, the Kyrgyz Republic experienced an increase in the activity of monetary transfer operations (MTOs) and a surge in money transfers via this channel. This made a considerable part of long-existing flows (shuttle traders' operations) visible for everybody. Both trends developed further from 2004 to 2007. Currently, labor migration and remittances have become a big issue in the Kyrgyz Republic because they have significantly affected the domestic labor market, private consumption, imports, government budget, family relations, and many other components of the socioeconomic situation in the country.

Another important process that has been developing during the same period is the maturing of some segments of the informal economy, especially garment production and exports, and the conversion of the Kyrgyz Republic into a regional center of reexporting activity. Many thousands of people are employed in the Kyrgyz garment and trade industries. The open market, *Dordoi*, which is near Bishkek, has become the largest distribution center serving the whole of Central Asia and many parts of the Siberia and Ural regions of Russia. Commodities imported from the People's Republic of China, Turkey, and the United Arab Emirates as well as those produced in the Kyrgyz Republic (mainly garments) are sold in the open market to traders or individuals from the Kyrgyz Republic and other Central Asian republics who, in turn, reexport them to other countries. Another large market in Kara-Suu in the southern part of the Kyrgyz Republic serves a similar role for the densely populated region of Fergana Valley. These activities involve massive cross-border financial transactions implemented by individuals and may expand because of the significant growth of consumption throughout Central Asia and the Asian part of Russia.

Previous Studies of Remittances in the Country

Two known papers are devoted to the issue of remittances in the Kyrgyz Republic and their impact on the economy. The first was prepared by the Economic Policy Institute (2005) and the second by Japarov and Ten (2006). Additionally, a publication by Mansoor and Quillin (2006) from the World Bank covers the issue of remittances in Central and Eastern Europe and the FSU including the Kyrgyz Republic.

To assess the role of remittances in the Kyrgyz economy and to evaluate their magnitude, in 2005 the Economic Policy Institute conducted a survey of 1,177 respondents comprising labor migrants or their family members. The sample does not pretend to be representative of the country. According to the survey results, two-thirds (67 percent) of respondents go to Russia and 19 percent go to Kazakhstan. Remittances come mainly in cash (61 percent), and only 34 percent of the respondents send money through the banking system. Half of remittances reportedly are spent on daily needs, 10 percent are directed to investments, and the remainder are spent on items such as health care, education, and durable goods. The average size of remittances is an estimated US$1,419 per migrant per year.

This paper uses two approaches to estimate the total value of remittances. The first approach uses official numbers about money transfers from the National Bank of the Kyrgyz Republic (NBKR). As official numbers only reflect money transferred through the financial system, they are too low and should be increased 66 percent to account for money entering through informal channels.[2] Using this approach, the total volume of inbound remittances in 2003 was estimated at US$207 million (the official number from NBKR was US$70.3 million). The second uses the number of labor migrants and the average size of remittances. As there are no official data on the number of labor migrants, data from various sources are used, and several assumptions are made. In particular, information about 350,000 labor migrants in Russia and Kazakhstan is taken from the International Organization for Migration (IOM). In addition, it is assumed that 50,000 labor migrants are working in other countries. Using these numbers, the volume of remittances in 2003 was estimated at US$520 million. This number forms 27 percent of gross domestic product (GDP) and 158 percent of the budget expenditure in 2003. Remittances clearly play a crucial role in the socioeconomic development of the Kyrgyz Republic, accelerating economic growth by increasing consumption and decreasing poverty. The accuracy of these estimates depends on the accuracy of the underlying data on remittances sent via formal channels, assumptions on the number of labor migrants, and representativity of the survey sample. As the Economic Policy Institute (2005) notes, none of these estimates is guaranteed, and all should be viewed as indicative only.

Japarov and Ten (2006) estimate the size of remittances in 2005 using an approach similar to that of the Institute for Economic Policy. The only difference is that they assume that 44 percent of the money transferred entered through the banking system. They estimate remittance inflow to the Kyrgyz Republic in 2005 as between US$520 million and US$750 million. To verify this range, the authors compare data from the National Statistical Committee (NSC) on the population's monetary income with data on the turnover of retail trade and paid services. Excessive consumer expenditures over monetary income appear to be close to the estimated remittances.

Mansoor and Quillin (2006) focus on trends in international migration and remittances in Eastern Europe and the FSU countries. It analyzes the situation in the Kyrgyz Republic based on official statistics, household budget surveys, and a survey of returned migrants. It finds that Kyrgyz citizens favored Russia and Kazakhstan as migration destinations. In 2002 more than 75 percent of remittances went to rural areas. An analysis of data from household budget surveys conducted in six European and Central Asian countries shows that richer households receive more remittances than poor households. For instance, only 0.8 percent of households received remittances in the poorest quintile of the Kyrgyz Republic, compared with 7.0 percent in the richest quintile. In addition, among all countries under consideration, only in the Kyrgyz Republic is the ratio of remittances to consumption higher for richer households than for poorer ones. Aggregate information from the six countries also shows that a larger part of remittances is used for food and clothing, but a significant share (more than 10 percent) is used for savings and education. The majority of migrants prefer to spend shorter times abroad and then to return home. During their stay in Russia, many migrants from the Kyrgyz Republic and Tajikistan work in low-skill sectors.

Measuring Remittances in the Kyrgyz Republic

This section considers the financial flows that are associated with remittances in the Kyrgyz context.

According to the fifth edition of the *Balance of Payments Manual* of the International Monetary Fund (1993), remittances consist of three components:

- *Employee compensation*, which comprises wages, salaries, and other benefits earned by individuals for work performed for and paid by residents of economies other than those in which the employee is a resident.

- *Worker remittances*, which cover current transfers by migrants, defined as persons who come to an economy and stay there or expect to stay there for a year or more.

- *Migrant transfers*, which consist of the flow of goods and financial exchanges that arise from the migration of individuals from one economy to another.

NBKR, which is responsible for compiling the balance of payments of the country, has limited information on these monetary flows. Therefore, the remittance-related methodology of NBKR is based on sensitive assumptions.[3]

NBKR has the following information on cross-border monetary flows involving participants in the Kyrgyz Republic:

- Data on repatriated wages and salaries of foreign employees who are not residents of the Kyrgyz Republic and are working on large joint ventures in the Kyrgyz Republic such as Kumtor Operating Company, the country's largest gold-mine enterprise

- Data on international monetary transfers to and from the Kyrgyz Republic done by individuals through banking accounts including card accounts, money transfer systems (for example, Western Union and the like), as well as the postal system

- Data on the number of permanent migrants to and from the Kyrgyz Republic and the estimated average value of the property that they bring with them to the country of destination.

In the majority of cases, apart from data on repatriated wages or salaries of foreign employees working in the Kyrgyz Republic, NBKR has no information on the migrant or worker status of people sending money to or from the Kyrgyz Republic or on the economic nature of such transactions (for example, intrafamily transfer, payment for goods and services, and person-to-person loan disbursements). Therefore, NBKR uses the following rules:

- Repatriated wages and salaries of foreign employees working in the Kyrgyz Republic are considered outgoing compensation of employees.

- All incoming and outgoing monetary transfers to and from the Kyrgyz Republic sent by individuals via MTOs and the postal system are considered worker remittances.

- All incoming and outgoing monetary transfers to and from the Kyrgyz Republic sent by individuals via banking accounts with amounts below or equal to US$3,000 are considered worker remittances, while transfers that are US$3,000 and above are considered business transactions and are not counted as remittances.

- Migrant transfers are estimated as a product of the number of immigrants and emigrants and the average value of each migrant's property.

According to this approach, there is no incoming compensation of employees on the Kyrgyz balance sheet. In addition, NBKR has no information about and does not attempt to account for international informal cash transfers done by individuals (cash brought by migrants or their agents to and from the Kyrgyz Republic).

As a result of the incomplete information on the amount and economic nature of transborder financial flows as well as the need to employ assumptions, this methodology suffers from some important shortcomings:

- *Lack of accounting for informal transfers.* These transfers may compose a significant share of total remittance inflow and outflow.

- *Risk of misinterpreting the economic nature of financial transfers.* For example, all transfers via MTOs, which are a major part of all financial flows currently identified as remittances in the Kyrgyz Republic, and the postal system are considered worker remittances. However, other options are equally possible: (a) repatriation of money earned as employee compensation in Russia or in other countries by Kyrgyz citizens who stay there for less than a year, (b) repatriation of money earned in Russia or in other countries by Kyrgyz citizens who stay there for a year or more (worker remittances there would not be an interpretation error in this case only), (c) compensation of the costs of goods brought by Kyrgyz shuttle traders to other countries (goods exported at free-on-board prices), (d) compensation for transportation and other costs associated with bringing goods from the Kyrgyz Republic to other countries, (e) export credit resources sent by a trader in another country to a Kyrgyz counterpart (a credit operation that is to be included in the financial account of the balance of payments), and (f) international intra-family transfers (other transfers in the balance-of-payments classification). Obviously, other options are also possible.

- *Risk of misidentifying worker remittances and business transactions.* Similarly, the threshold of US$3,000, which is used to separate worker remittances from business transactions, runs the risk of misidentifying transfers via banking accounts.

Thus of the three components of remittance inflows, only two—worker remittances and migrant transfers—are estimated by NBKR. Only one—worker remittances—is relevant to labor migration and is capable of influencing the Kyrgyz economy and its financial sector.[4] The estimated amount of worker remittances, however, most probably represents a mixture of components with different economic meanings.

Remittance Dynamics

Remittances[5] grew very quickly in 2002 to 2006 (see figure 1; quarterly data on remittances and their components are provided in table B.1). The average annual growth rate of remittance inflow (credit) for these five years is 125 percent (that is, on average, remittances more than doubled every year). The growth rate was somewhat reduced in 2005 to 2006, but, for these years, it was still 50 percent and more per year. This dynamic has been driven mainly by the inflow of worker remittances, which, on average, tripled yearly. Inflows of migrant transfers, in contrast, were almost constant over this period, at less than US$10 million per year.

FIGURE 1. Dynamics of Remittance Inflow into the Kyrgyz Republic, 2000–06

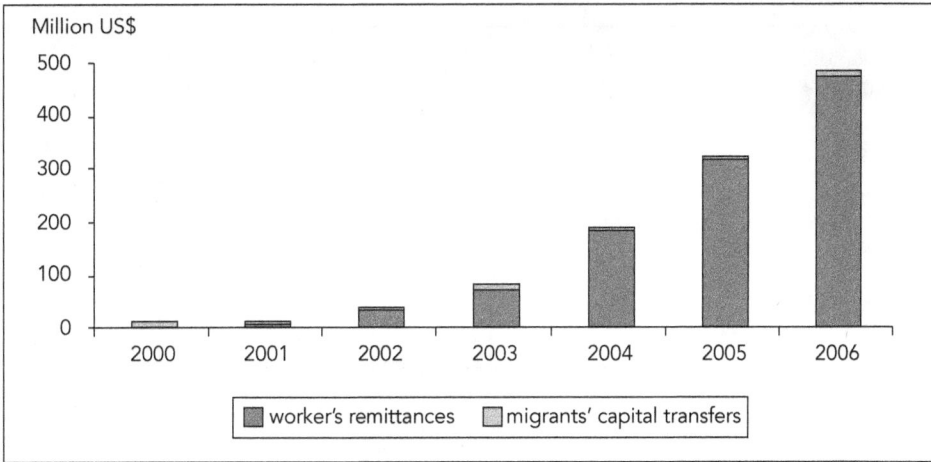

Source: NBKR and authors' estimates (for 2006).

There was also a growing outflow of remittances in these years (debit in table B.1). The average annual growth rate of total remittance outflow in 2002 to 2006 was 22 percent. This outflow was driven by worker remittances, which increased from zero in 2001 to more than US$40 million in 2006. This growth may reflect an increase in the activity of Chinese traders as well as Tajik and Uzbek hired workers in the Kyrgyz Republic and the expansion of international intra-family (and possibly business) transfers involving Kyrgyz citizens. Another growing item of remittance outflow was migrant transfers. This reflects an increase in permanent emigration from the Kyrgyz Republic and in the estimated value of emigrants' properties. However, inflow of remittances has been growing much faster than outflow, so net total remittances are growing quickly as well.

As noted, these data do not account for informal money transfers of migrants. Some indirect information on these informal transfers may be derived from the analysis of the balance-of-payments item on "net errors and omissions." This item, in essence, is a balance of all informal foreign currency transactions in the Kyrgyz economy. These informal transactions include imports and exports implemented by shuttle traders (only a small part of these trade flows are covered by official statistics); smuggling of some commodities such as gasoline from Kazakhstan and Uzbekistan, where prices for these commodities were and still are subsidized; other receipts from illegal activities; and, among others, informal transfers of Kyrgyz workers abroad. As shown on figure 2, until 2003 net errors and omissions fluctuated—sometimes with large amplitude—around zero. This means that different components of informal foreign currency flows were basically balanced. However, since 2003, this item has increased significantly, indicating a growing inflow of foreign currency to the Kyrgyz Republic. Of course, it is not known which components of informal flows have contributed to this growth, but it is possible to presume that some part of this growth is related to informal transfers.

FIGURE 2. Net Errors and Omissions in the Balance of Payments of the Kyrgyz Republic, 1997–2006

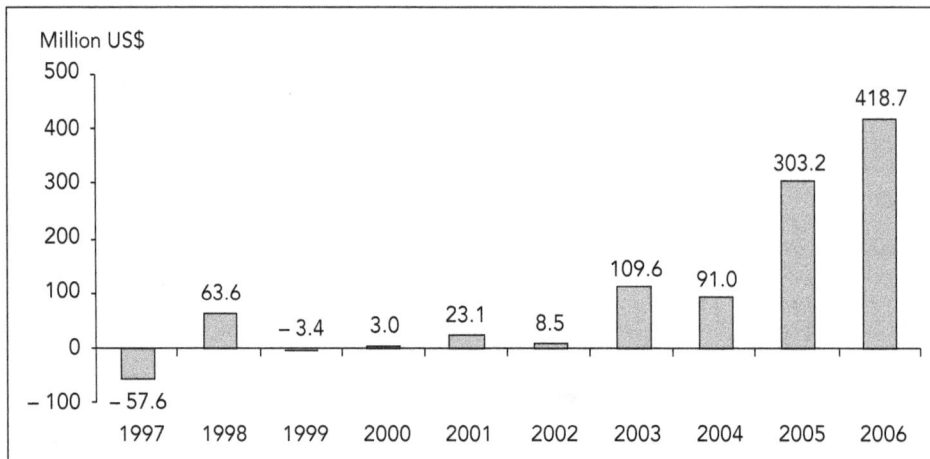

Source: NBKR.
Note: The 2006 data are preliminary.

Figure 3 compares the quarterly dynamics of worker remittances (transfers through formal channels) and net errors and omissions (a possible proxy for informal transfers) in 2003 to 2006. Both variables have similar upward trends (dash lines in figure 3) and a similar seasonal pattern of change (see figure 4). These similarities,[6] especially the similarity in seasonality, may indicate that these two flows originate from the same source. This does not mean, however, that all errors and omissions can be attributed to worker remittances. On the contrary, remittances of formal workers are a mixture of components, including remittances, as are net errors and omissions.

FIGURE 3. Dynamics of Net Errors and Omissions versus Worker Remittances, 2003–06

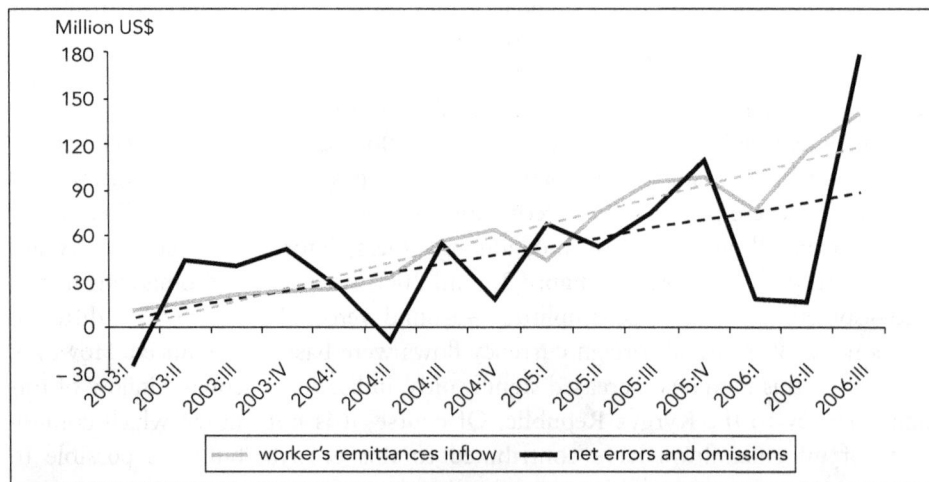

Source: NBKR.

FIGURE 4. Seasonality of Remittances and Net Errors and Omissions, 2002–05

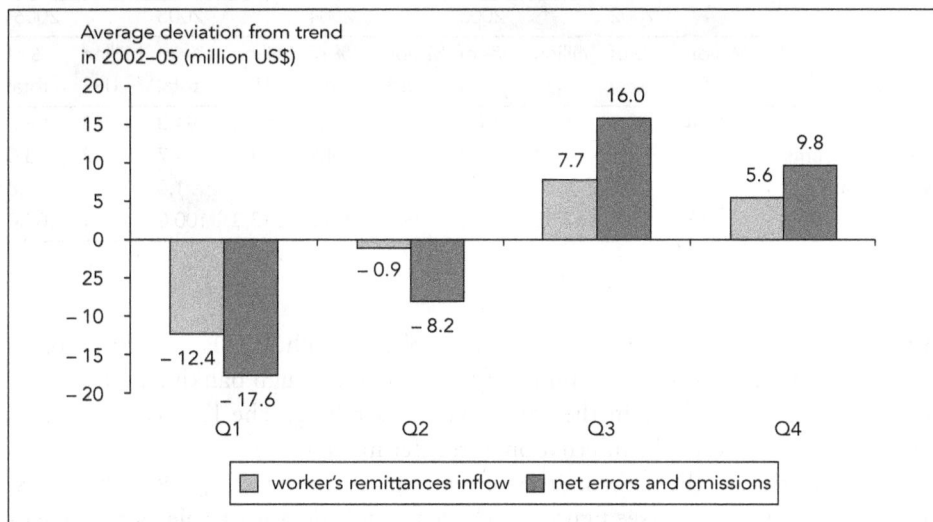

Source: NBKR and authors' calculations.

The distinct seasonality of both formal and informal transfers—their relative increase in the third and fourth quarters and decrease during the first quarter of every year—may be linked to the pattern of cross-border movement of Kyrgyz workers and shuttle traders who are not residents of their country of migration. During winter, they usually stay home and do not earn any income, which is the source of remittances, nor do they have a need to send home remittances. Such need typically appears closer to the end of their stay abroad, which is the second part of the year.

Composition of Remittance Inflows

Disaggregated data on international monetary transfers, available at NBKR, allow analyzing the geography of transfers and their composition in terms of transaction value. NBKR collects information from commercial banks. This is the main source of information on the country's balance of payments regarding transfers from individuals. The database contains the following information: country from which the money is sent, money transfer channel, date of transfer, and amount transferred in U.S. dollars. There are some other fields in the database (such as commercial bank mediating the transaction), but these pieces of information are not available for research purposes according to the regulations on banking secrecy. NBKR started to compile the database in 1999, and data for 1999 (seven months) up to 2006 are used for the analysis here.

As mentioned, there are three formal channels for sending remittances: MTOs, banking accounts, and transfers via Kyrgyz Post (the postal service). The relative role of these channels in the total inflow of worker remittances is shown in table 1.

TABLE 1. Inflow of Worker Remittances, by Sending Channel, 2002–06

Channel	2002 Million US$	% of total	2003 Million US$	% of total	2004 Million US$	% of total	2005 Million US$	% of total	2006[a] Million US$	% of total
MTOs	24.4	80.5	62.8	89.3	167.0	93.3	295.4	94.3	455.3	96.2
Banking accounts	2.2	7.1	4.4	6.2	8.7	4.8	14.7	4.7	14.2	3.0
Kyrgyz Post	3.8	12.4	3.2	4.5	3.4	1.9	3.2	1.0	3.6	0.8
Total	30.3	100.0	70.3	100.0	179.1	100.0	313.3	100.0	473.1	100.0

Source: NBKR.
[a] Preliminary data.

Almost all remittances enter the Kyrgyz Republic through MTOs, and their role is growing with time. Absolute amounts of money sent through banking accounts are increasing, but their share in the total amount is falling. The Kyrgyz Post serves only a small segment of the international transfer market.

Two countries are the main sources of remittances for the Kyrgyz Republic: Russia and the United States (see figure 5). The Russian Federation's role as a source of remittances, which started in 2002, is growing steadily. In 2005 transfers from Russia accounted for 86 percent of the total amount of remittances sent, while those from the United States accounted for 11 percent. The role of other countries is much less important. The third and fourth important sources of remittances, Kazakhstan and the United Kingdom, together account for less than 3 percent of the total number of transactions and less than 1 percent of the total amount of remittances. The unexpectedly low share of Kazakhstan, which is considered the second largest labor market for Kyrgyz migrants, may be due to two factors: (a) migrants' preference for using informal channels to send money to and from the relatively geographically close country and (b) the unfriendly legal environment in Kazakhstan for nonresident use of the services of financial institutions.

To understand trends in remittances, it is worth looking at the distribution of transactions by country, channel, and size (see figure B.1, panels A through D). The pattern of transfers from Russia via MTOs has been changing since 2002 (see figure B.1, panel A). There were few large transactions before 2002, but from 2002 to 2004, the value and number of transactions grew two to three times (and more) each year, accompanied by a reduction in the median size of transfer. Starting in 2005, the trend changed again. The median size of transfer grew along with the number of transactions. Such dynamics could reflect changes in the composition and income of senders. Mass labor migration started in 2002. Since then, among all senders, labor migrants started to dominate, sending relatively small amounts of money. This led to a decline in the median size of transaction. However, with the passage of time, people adapted to the situation in the receiving country, and their incomes as well as monetary transfers grew in size. Migrants also mastered some cost-reducing techniques such as consolidation of remittances,[7] leading to an increase in the median size of transfers. Other factors affecting both the number and the size of transactions could be the growing confidence in the reliability of

FIGURE 5. Worker Remittance Inflows from Main Countries of Origin, 2000–06

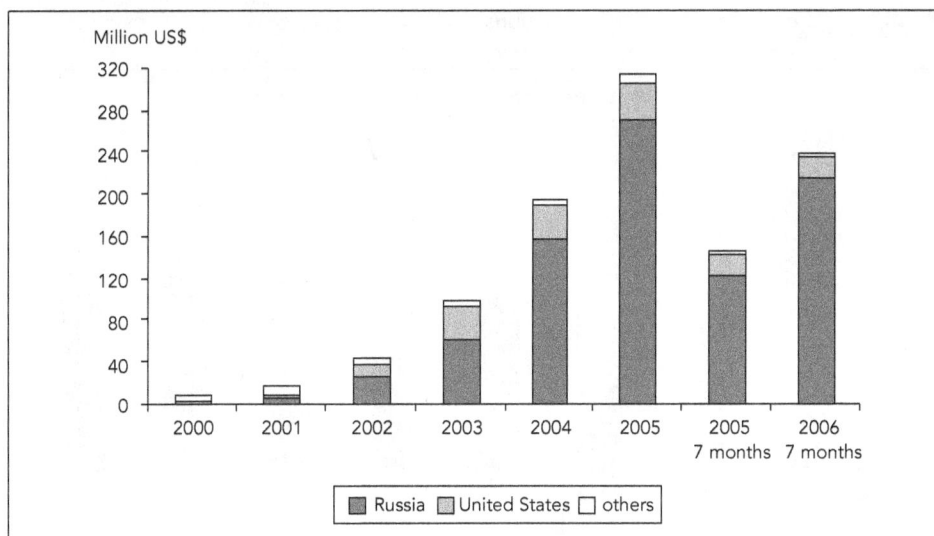

Source: NBKR.

transactions mediated by financial institutions and the expansion in the number and location of retail outlets serving MTO clients in the Kyrgyz Republic.

The pattern of transfers via MTOs from the United States also changed somewhat (figure B.1, panel B). Similar to Russia, a growing number of smaller transactions from 2002 to 2004 replaced the smaller number of larger transactions from 1999 to 2001. However, in 2005, the number of transactions fell almost sixfold, with a drastic increase in the median (11 times more!) and mean size of transfer. Reasons for such a sharp change are unclear.

The existence of a threshold of US$3,000 for transfers via banking accounts to be considered as remittances explains why there is no trend in the size of transactions (figure B.1, panels C and D). Larger transactions are censored from the database. However, mean and median sizes of transfers via banking accounts from the United States are considerably larger than those from Russia.

The large difference between mean and median size of transactions made via MTOs (see figure B.1, panels A and B) suggests the presence of very large single transactions, which account for a large portion of the total amount of remittances. The distribution of transfers via MTOs by transaction value is shown in figure 6, panels A and B. These figures show that large (US$10,000–US$50,000) and very large (more than US$50,000) transactions make up a relatively small (while growing with time) share in the total number of transactions, but a very large and growing share in the total amount of transactions. In 2005 large transactions accounted for 22 percent, and very large transactions accounted for 72 percent of the total amount of remittances sent via MTOs, leaving just 6 percent for smaller transactions. On the contrary, very small (less than US$100) and small (US$100.01–$500) transactions constituted 30–50 percent of the total number of transactions in 2001

FIGURE 6. Worker Remittance Inflows from Main Countries of Origin, 2000–06

A. Share in the total number of transactions

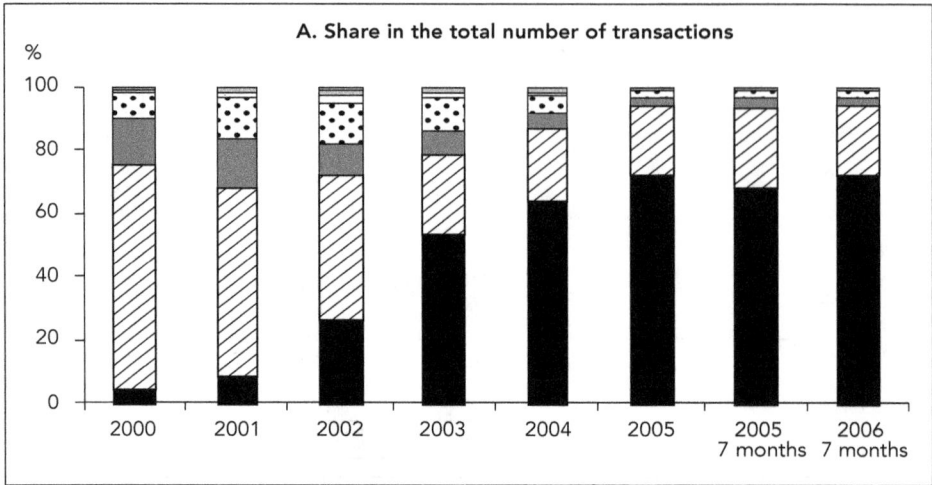

Source: NBKR.

B. Share in the total value of remittances

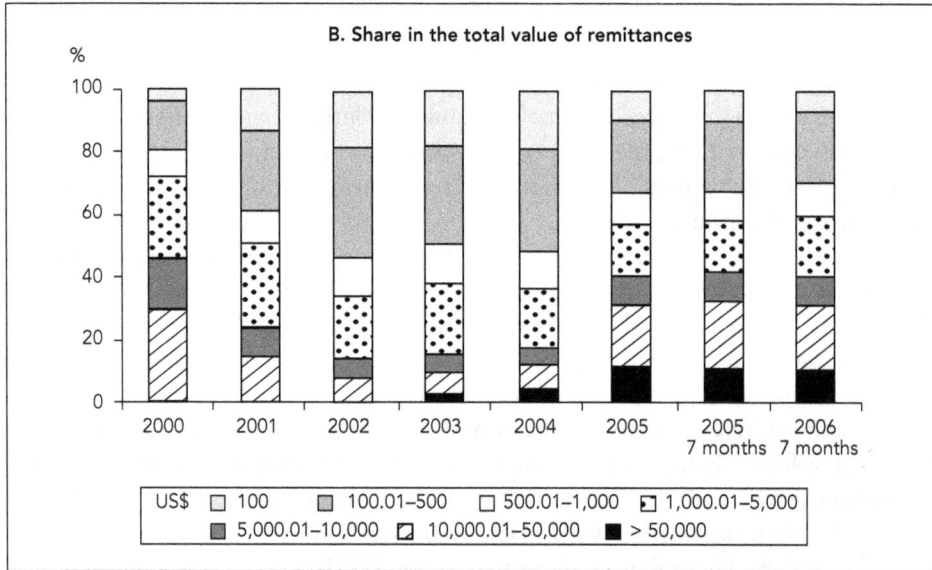

Source: NBKR.

to 2006 (with a maximum of 51 percent in 2004), while their share in the total value of remittances was small and falling, from 1.6 percent in 2001 to 0.3 percent in 2005 to 2006. Thus small and medium (US$500–US$10,000) transactions dominate the total number of transactions, but large and very large transactions prevail in the total value of remittances.

In 2005, 3,002 transactions were in the range of US$10,000–US$50,000, and 1,549 transactions were above US$50,000. The maximum transaction registered was US$779,000. In the first seven months of 2006, the maximum single transaction was US$2,101,122, and five transactions exceeded US$1 million! Moreover, the number of large transactions, their share in the total value of remittances, and the maximum value of transactions increased with time. So the growth in remittances in 2002 to 2006 should be attributed to the growth in large and very large transactions. This trend coincided with the revival of the Kyrgyz financial market.

This prevalence of large transactions raises a question about their economic interpretation and their relationship to labor migration. Taking into account the typical income of Kyrgyz-hired workers in Russia, which ranges from several hundred to a few thousand U.S. dollars per month for highly skilled workers, and the fact that they could save only a portion of it, their savings could only be a source of very large transactions if the remittances of a group of hired workers were consolidated. Although such consolidation does take place, the amounts consolidated could hardly exceed US$50,000. Therefore, the massive migration of Kyrgyz citizens to Russia and Kazakhstan and their eventual employment in construction, municipal services, and other relatively low-paying jobs do not seem to be a major source of remittance growth. Therefore, the increase in remittances is not necessarily associated with growth in the number of labor migrants.

A much more realistic explanation for large transactions and the growth in their number and amount is that these transfers represent revenues from and loans for the trade operations of Kyrgyz wholesale shuttle and retail traders in the markets of Russian cities. If this is the case, the larger part of what is called "worker remittances" is a mixture of revenues from exports of goods and services, trade credits, as well as mixed income of Kyrgyz retail traders operating in Russia.[8] The growth in remittances then should be attributed to a shift in the pattern of revenue repatriation—from informal to formal (mainly MTO) channels—and to expansion of the Kyrgyz shuttle trade.

Macroeconomic Effect of Remittances

In recent years, remittances have been growing so quickly that they have become the second largest source of foreign currency for the country after exports of goods (see table 2). In 2002 to 2005, the inflow of remittances grew much faster than the exports of goods and services, foreign direct investment, and official development assistance—all positive items on the balance sheet of the Kyrgyz Republic. In the first three quarters of 2006, the only source of foreign exchange with a growth rate higher than remittances was the export of tourism services. However, this item is much smaller than remittances. The share of remittances in GDP at market exchange rates is also growing, from 12.7 percent in 2005 to an estimated 16.8 percent of GDP in 2006.

TABLE 2. Worker Remittances as a Percent of Other Important Sources of Foreign Exchange, 2000–06

Source	2000	2001	2002	2003	2004	2005	2006
Exports of goods	0.3	0.4	6.1	11.9	24.4	45.6	58.3
Exports of services	2.1	2.4	21.4	44.4	85.4	122.6	126.3
Exports of tourism services	8.5	7.8	85.2	146.9	236.9	429.0	283.3
Gross foreign direct investment	1.5	2.1	26.3	47.8	102.0	148.9	141.0
Official development assistance and other government receipts in foreign currency	0.7	1.2	8.6	27.1	69.0	152.1	515.3
Worker remittances as % of GDP[a]	0.1	0.1	1.9	3.7	8.1	12.7	16.8

Source: NBKR, NSC, and World Bank.
[a] At market exchange rate.

In the small open economy of the Kyrgyz Republic, such significant inflows of money could affect virtually all economic variables. There are several potential mechanisms through which remittances influence other macroeconomic variables. Households receiving remittances could increase their consumption; therefore, remittances could have a positive effect on private consumption. Moreover, the share of imported consumer goods in total consumption is high,[9] so part of the remittances could be spent on imported consumer goods. Arguably, one would not expect remittances to have a considerable impact on investments in fixed capital. On the one hand, the inflow of remittances in many households is positively associated with savings, so growth in remittances could cause growth in domestic savings. This does not mean, however, that increased savings result in the growth of investments. Many households prefer to save by acquiring real estate, which is confirmed by the rise in the price of apartments and houses in Bishkek and Osh during the last several years. Obviously, this type of saving behavior does not contribute much to investments and GDP growth.[10] So remittances can be expected to have a positive impact on GDP overall, but it will be smaller than the impact on private consumption. Increased domestic production of consumer goods and services induced by remittances could cause some growth in employment. However, this growth may not be registered because a large part of consumer goods and services is produced in the informal economy.

Imports are a key source of government revenues in the Kyrgyz Republic. The state's custom committee collects value-added tax, excises, and custom duties on imports that, altogether, exceed 50 percent of the total tax collections. Therefore, an increase in imports—an expected outcome of the inflow of remittances—should result in the growth of government revenues.

On the one hand, remittances, which strengthen the current account, could also encourage appreciation of the exchange rate. On the other hand, they may fuel inflation if NBKR tries to sterilize the inflow of foreign currency by purchasing currency on the open market, accumulating net international reserves that, until very recently, were at a rather low level if measured in months of imports; this causes an increase in money supply in the economy.

Obviously, many other factors influence the country's economic development. Therefore, it is necessary to test the hypotheses presented here by looking at actual trends of the variables under consideration. In the period under consideration, almost all variables experienced upward trends; so, of course, all these variables were strongly correlated with remittances. However, these correlations could be spurious, as many other growth-inducing forces and exogenous shocks were present in the Kyrgyz economy apart from remittances. All these variables also have very large and similar seasonality, which increases the probability of spurious correlation. Therefore, the correlation of growth rates of seasonally adjusted variables seems to be a more reliable (but still imperfect) indicator of the existence of a causal relationship between remittances and other variables. The shortness of available time series (three to five years only) precludes the use of more sophisticated methods of time-series analysis such as co-integration.

With regard to the relationship of remittances to personal consumption and GDP, figure 7 shows that the share of remittances in GDP and personal consumption was growing steadily in 2001 to 2005 (preliminary data for 2006 show continuation of this trend). In relation to share of GDP, this is a result of the rapid growth of remittances, while the average annual GDP growth rate for 2001 to 2006 was just 3.6 percent. This relatively low and unstable growth rate is explained partially by problems in the Kumtor gold mine, which is a major contributor to Kyrgyz GDP. In 2002 and 2005, Kumtor had technological accidents that significantly decreased its production. NSC also publishes data on GDP without Kumtor; according to NSC data, the average annual growth rate of GDP without Kumtor in 2001 to 2006 was 4.5 percent. This number is not very high when compared with the growth rates of other Commonwealth of Independent States (CIS) countries,

FIGURE 7. Worker Remittances as a Percent of GDP and Private Consumption, 2001–05

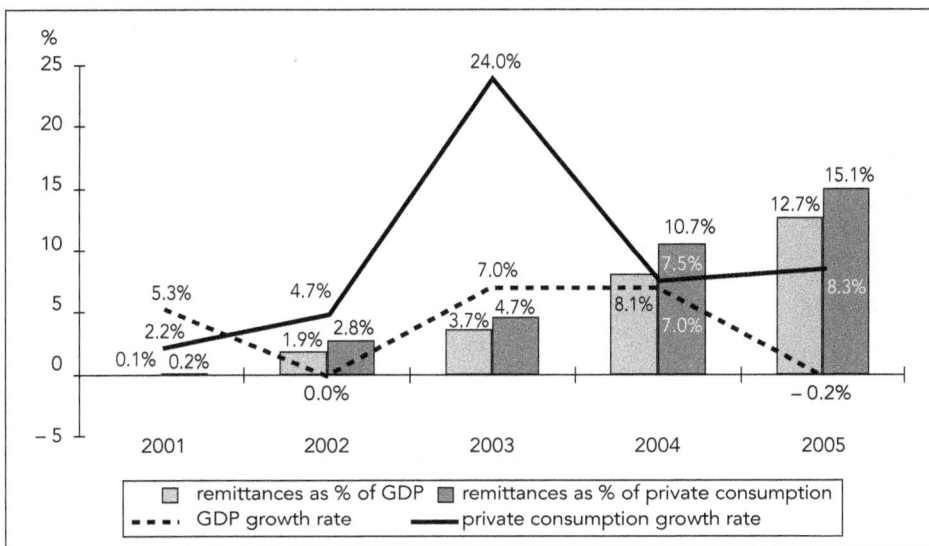

Source: NBKR and NSC.

which are closer to 10 percent a year. So far, the fast growth of worker remittances has not been associated with comparable GDP growth. However, analysis of a cross-correlation of remittances and GDP real growth rates in the quarterly series from 2002 to 2006 indicates a statistically significant (at 5 percent), yet not very strong,[11] positive correlation between the growth of remittances and the growth of GDP five quarters later (figure B.2, panel A). Therefore, it seems that data provide some evidence of a marginally significant positive impact of remittances on GDP growth.

Growth of private consumption in 2001 to 2006 was much larger than growth of GDP. The average annual growth rate for this period was 11.2 percent. Wide fluctuations in the growth of private consumption (from 2.2 percent in 2001 to 24.0 percent in 2003 and to 22.1 percent in 2006) somewhat erode the correlation between private consumption and remittances. Still, a cross-correlogram shows a 5 percent statistically significant positive correlation between remittances and private consumption four and five quarters later (figure B.2, panel B).[12] Thus private consumption seems to be influenced by remittances, while, of course, remittances have not become a major driving force for consumption (for example, performance of the agriculture sector has a stronger and more immediate effect on this variable).

The relationship between remittances and imports is much stronger (see figure 8). Both variables have similar upward time trends. Yet the absolute growth of imports is always considerably larger than the absolute growth of remittances. This suggests that there should be other sources of financing of imports (such as exports of goods and services, foreign credit to the private sector) apart from remittances.[13] A cross-correlogram indicates a statistically significant positive correlation between remittances and imports with a five-quarter lag (figure B.2, panel C).

FIGURE 8. Remittances, Imports, and Government Revenues, 2001–06 (US$ in millions)

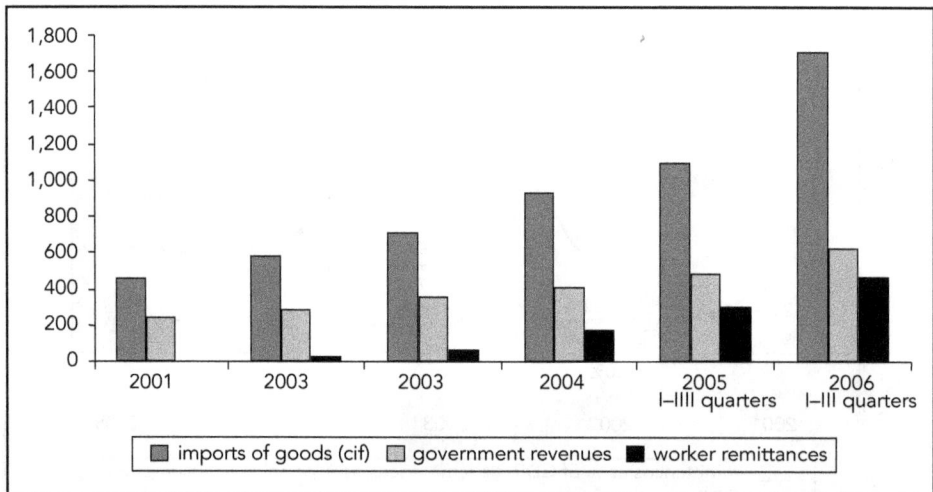

Source: NBKR and NSC.
Note: U.S. dollar values of government revenues have been estimated at current exchange rate for each quarter. CIF = cost, insurance, freight.

The relationship between imports and government revenues is also weaker than expected, while there is a statistically significant immediate positive correlation between these variables (figures 8 and B.2, panel D). According to expectations, there appears to be a statistically significant positive correlation with a five-quarter lag between remittances and government revenues (figure B.2, panel E).

As figure B.3 indicates, investments in fixed capital declined in 2001–03 and started to grow again only in 2004. This investment growth in the last two to three years was closely associated with a big inflow of foreign direct investment in 2002–06. Gross foreign direct investment (in U.S. dollars) was almost four times larger in 2006 than in 2001. Given the very small degree of conversion of remittances into deposits, the small role of banking credit in financing capital investments, and the weak propensity of recipients to invest their remittances in business, there is virtually no evidence that remittances have an impact on investments in the Kyrgyz Republic.

The impact of remittances on employment is difficult to measure because of the existence of a very large informal labor market, which includes mainly agriculture, trade, construction, and other market services as well as some manufacturing industries (for example, garment and food production). The formal market covers non-market services (education, health, government, as well as social and municipal services) and industries represented by large enterprises (for example, mining, power generation, railroad, and communications). Figure 9, panel A, shows a permanent downward trend in employment in the formal labor market. Obviously, remittances do not have a positive impact on this component of employment. Neither do they have a negative impact on formal employment; this decline in formal sector employment started well before the increase in remittances and labor migration. The reduction in formal employment is linked to imperfections in the coun-

FIGURE 9. Formal and Informal Employment in the Kyrgyz Republic, by Sector, 2001–05

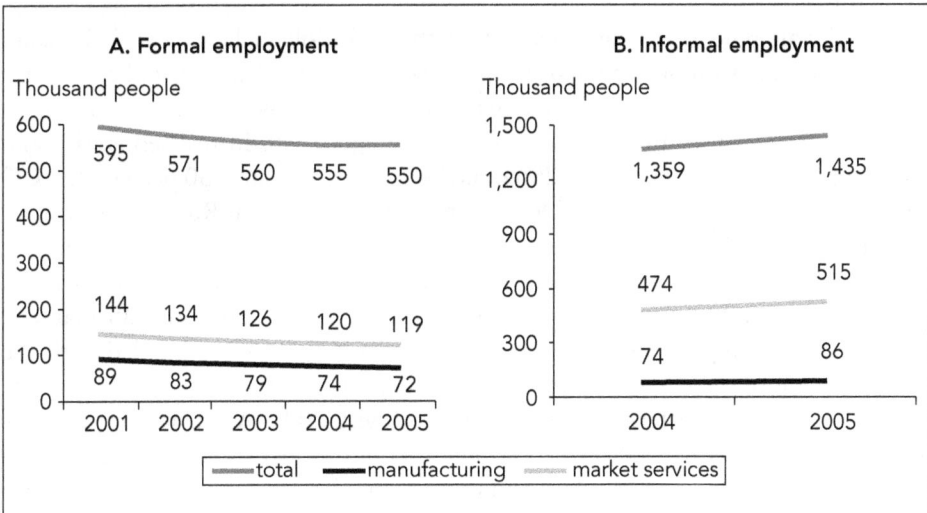

Source: NSC.

try's business climate and a heavy tax burden—notably the payroll tax—on formal enterprises. Recently, NSC published data from a household survey on informal employment in 2004–05 (figure 9, panel B). These data conform to the expectations that remittances have a positive influence on employment in market services and sectors producing consumer goods.

Inflow of remittances, together with tourism export revenues and some other balance-of-payments items, leads to an increase in the supply of foreign exchange in the domestic currency market.[14] NBKR is a major buyer of foreign currency. In 2001–06, the net cumulative purchase of NBKR on the interbank currency market was US$375 million; of that amount, US$186 million was for 2006 only. This allowed NBKR to increase its net foreign reserves from som 2.6 billion (US$55 million) in 2001 to som 24.7 billion (US$647 million) in 2006. This policy resulted in a larger money supply. Monetary aggregate M2x grew from som 8.2 billion (US$172 million) at the end of 2001 to som 32.3 billion (US$847 million) at the end of 2006. Remarkably, until 2007 this rapid growth in the supply of money (31.5 percent a year on average) did not cause serious inflation. The average annual inflation rate (based on the consumer price index) in 2002 to 2006 was just 4.0 percent. This is a good result, accounting for numerous unfavorable external shocks (such as an increase in the price of oil and gas). Obviously, the surge in money supply has been absorbed by the growing demand for money. Monetization of the economy increased from 11.1 percent of GDP in 2001 to 28.5 percent of GDP in 2006, the result of a deeper financial market, a reduction of in-kind settlements between economic agents, and, probably, some substitution of foreign currency by soms in domestic economic transactions and savings of the population. However, the inflation situation changed dramatically in 2007; in the first 10 months of 2007 the consumer price index grew 20.1 percent, which is more than its cumulative growth in four previous years. While this inflation hike was triggered by external price shocks, the inflationary pressure of the quickly growing money supply also had a role.

The global trend of the depreciation of the U.S. dollar also affected the som, which appreciated strongly (by more than 20 percent) versus the U.S. dollar in nominal terms in 2001 to 2006. This nominal appreciation, however, does not mean an overall appreciation of the Kyrgyz currency (see figure 10). In real terms, the som appreciated 17 percent for non-CIS countries, but depreciated 30 percent for CIS countries—mainly vis-à-vis the ruble—due to higher inflation in Russia and stronger nominal appreciation of the ruble versus the U.S. dollar. Therefore, exchange rate developments increased the competitiveness of imports from non-CIS countries in the domestic market and the competitiveness of Kyrgyz exports in CIS markets. Stronger price competitiveness of Kyrgyz goods in CIS markets, coupled with the robust growth of these economies, led Kyrgyz exports to these countries to increase 2.2 times in U.S. dollar terms in 2006 compared with 2001. As mentioned, imports also strongly increased in 2001–06, but only part of this increase could be related to real exchange rate developments, as imports from CIS countries grew even faster than imports from non-CIS countries, despite unfavorable real exchange rates.

In summary, the inflow of worker remittances to the Kyrgyz economy (a) has a positive impact on GDP and personal consumption; (b) contributes to the growth of imports and, indirectly, of government revenues; (c) is associated with some growth of employment in the informal economy; (d) does not produce any measurable effect on investments; and (e) has no negative consequences for inflation and the real exchange rate.

Pattern of Remittances at the Micro Level

To understand the factors driving remittance flows, it is necessary to examine the individuals and households that send and receive these money transfers. In the context of this study, key issues for consideration are the composition of senders and recipients, their preferences regarding transmission channels for remittances, the impact of remittances on their savings as well as business activities, and the attitude of recipients toward services currently offered to them by the Kyrgyz financial sector.

Analysis in this section is based on data from two surveys conducted in the framework of the ADB project. The first is a representative household survey covering 3,997 households in all parts of the Kyrgyz Republic which provides information on household characteristics, welfare, migration, and remittances. Methodological details of this survey are provided in the Asian Development Bank report on remittances and poverty in the Kyrgyz Republic (ADB 2008).

Another source of data is a remittance recipient survey (RRS), which was conducted in October 2006 in Bishkek and Osh at the premises of different branches of four banks: Amanbank, Bank Kyrgyzstan, Ecobank, and Settlement and Saving Company. Three hundred and six randomly selected recipients of remittances were interviewed. Table B.2 provides a composition of the sample. This survey is not representative of the country's population because the sampling method led to a disproportionately high share of urban residents in the sample. Despite that, this survey provides useful information on the composition and behavior of senders and recipients of remittances. The survey included questions on the social and demographic profile of recipients and senders, details of money transfers, savings, business activities, and experience with the financial sector. Some questions were asked in both surveys, and an analysis of similarities of and discrepancies in the data collected by the two surveys is provided in this section to shed additional light on the pattern of remittances at the household level.

Profiles of Remittance Senders and Recipients

Household survey data provide information on the characteristics of Kyrgyz migrants (table B.3). An absolute majority of migrants come from rural areas, but urban areas other than Bishkek provide the largest share of migrants in the total population. Bishkek provides the smallest share of migrants. This is understandable because the capital city has the best employment situation, while other urban areas have the worst. By educational status, an absolute majority of migrants (77 percent) have completed secondary education, 16.5 percent have completed education higher than secondary (secondary special, higher, and postgraduate levels), and 6.4 percent have completed education below secondary. The share of migrants with higher education is significantly larger in Bishkek (41.8 percent); about five of six migrants (82.5 percent) go to Russia, 12 percent go to Kazakhstan, and only 5.5 percent go to other countries. However, a higher share of Bishkek migrants go to Kazakhstan and other countries—16.5 and 16.6 percent, respectively. The majority of migrants stay abroad for a short period. The median stay is 1.2 years (two years for Bishkek). By occupational status, the majority (71.6 percent) are employed in the private sector; 19.5 percent are self-employed, which is a relatively high share, 5.8 percent are employed in the public sector, 1.4 percent are students, and 1.7 percent have other types of occupation. Again, migrants from Bishkek demonstrate a somewhat different picture. Fewer are employed in the private sector (51.9 percent), considerably more are employed in the public sector (12.7 percent), and 25.3 percent are self-employed. Two main sectors of employment of Kyrgyz migrants are construction (45 percent) and trade (30.4 percent). Migrants from Bishkek work in more diverse sectors, with much fewer working in the construction industry. It is clearly necessary to distinguish between migrants originating from Bishkek and those originating from other areas.

FIGURE 10. Exchange Rate Dynamics in 2000–06

REAL effective exchange rate = 100 for 2000

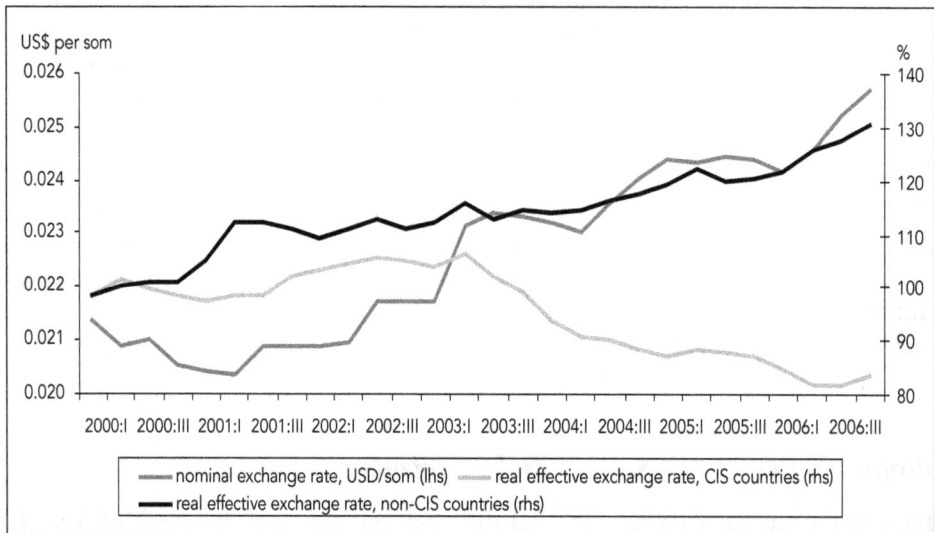

Source: NBKR.

FIGURE 11. Characteristics of Migrants Sending Remittances

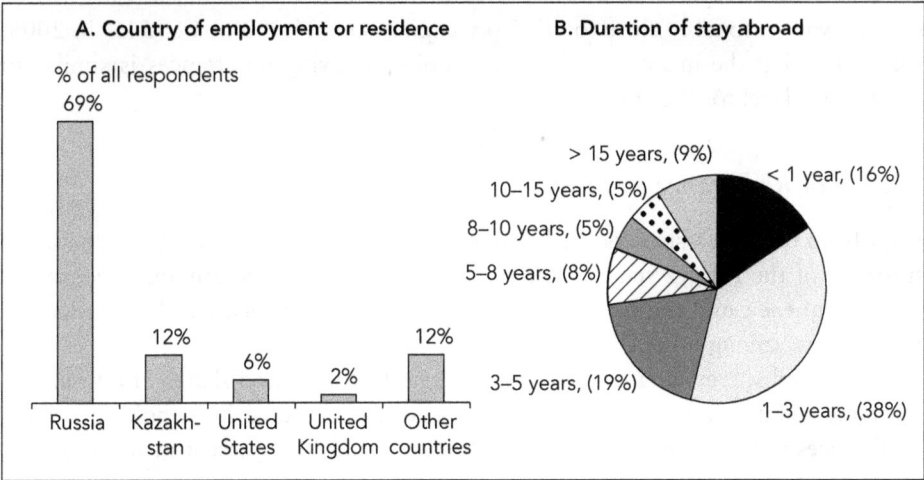

Source: RRS data.

The survey of recipients receiving remittances provides a similar picture with regard to migration geography (see figure 11, panel A). Russia (with a big lead) and Kazakhstan are again the two main destinations of migrants; the United States and the United Kingdom are the most frequent destinations outside the CIS. The lower share of Kyrgyz migrants in Russia, compared with the household survey, is due to the large share of Bishkek residents in this survey; Bishkek migrants go less frequently to Russia and more frequently to other countries (table B.3).

RRS data on duration of stay abroad are also generally consistent with the results of the household survey for Bishkek (figure 11, panel B). They show that more than one-third (38 percent) of the migrants work outside the Kyrgyz Republic for one to three years. The share of migrants who stay abroad for three to five years (19 percent) and of newcomers who stay abroad less than one year (16 percent) is also significant; 27 percent of all migrants stay abroad for more than five years. In 14 percent of cases, people continue to remit money after staying 10 and more years abroad. This is evidence of stable family relations in many Kyrgyz households.

TABLE 3. Respondents' Household Annual Income per Capita, by Location
thousand soms

Location	Mean	Median
Bishkek	40.4	28.0
Osh	22.5	13.0
All samples	31.3	18.0

Source: RRS data.

Data on income of respondents correspond to the well-known fact that incomes are higher in Bishkek than in Osh (see table 3). Median per capita income for the sample was reasonably close to GDP per capita (som 21,900 or US$545) in 2006, suggesting that the income level of households receiving remittances is similar to the average level for the country.

Pattern of Remittance Transfer

Data from these two surveys shed light on the preferences pertaining to remittance transfers of the Kyrgyz senders and receivers. These relate to amount, geography, form, frequency, and channel of remittances, preferred currency, and consolidation of transfers, among others.

Household survey data on remittance amounts, forms, and shares of households receiving remittances are provided in table 4. The share of households receiving remittances is 16 percent in the Kyrgyz Republic and 11.2 percent in Bishkek. The total amount of remittances is estimated at US$256.4 million (9 percent GDP). This amount differs considerably from official estimates and from numbers circulating in the Kyrgyz media. Remittances are composed of cash and goods: 95 percent of remittances are in cash and 5 percent are in the form of goods. In Bishkek, the share of in-kind remittances approaches 10 percent. The average amount of remittances per receiving household for the country is US$1,380 a year, varying from US$1,283in rural areas to US$1,865 in Bishkek.

RRS gives quite similar estimates for average amounts per household. In this survey, respondents (mostly Bishkek residents) reported median remittances of US$1,800. This is very close to the estimate for Bishkek provided in table 4. According to the RRS data, 95 percent of respondents get their money in cash. This

TABLE 4. Amount of Remittances Received by Households, by Location

Indicator	Kyrgyz Republic	Bishkek	Other urban areas	Rural areas
Households receiving remittances (%)	16.0	11.2	18.1	16.8
Total amount of remittances (million US$)	256.4	47.8	52.7	156.0
Share of cash remittances in total amount of remittances (%)	95.0	90.3	94.8	96.5
Average amount of remittances a year				
Cash remittances per household (US$)	1,334	1,691	1,373	1,255
In-kind remittances per household (US$)	387	733	354	298
Total remittances per household (any form)	1,380	1,865	1,385	1,283
Share of remittances in total income of receiving households (%)	50.0	41.6	51.5	51.2

Source: Household survey data.

coincides exactly with the value for the country and is higher than, but still close to, the value for Bishkek from the household survey.

According to household survey data, more than 80 percent of all remittances come from Russia (see figure 12), slightly less than 10 percent come from Kazakhstan, and another 10 percent come from other countries. Regarding Russia, these data are consistent with the NBKR data on geography of transfers (figure 5). However, one can see a difference between these two sources of information regarding Kazakhstan and the United States. Kazakhstan is the second largest source of remittances in the household survey, but not an important source of remittances in the NBKR database. The situation of remittances from the United States is, in some sense, the reverse. The United States is the second largest source of remittances in the NBKR data, but a very small source in the household survey. In the RRS, 7 percent of the respondents reported having relatives in the United States and receiving remittances from them. These are mainly people living in Bishkek, who have more education and income than the average. Obviously, this group is small in absolute numbers, although they may receive a significant portion of total remittances entering the country. Therefore, recipients of remittances from the United States apparently have not been sufficiently covered by the household survey.

The household survey data provide the geographic distribution of recipients of remittances within the country (see figure 13). Almost three-quarters of all cash remittances go to the southern part of the country—Osh City, Osh oblast, and Jalalabat as well as Batken oblasts. Batken oblast, which is one of the poorest regions of the country, receives a disproportionately high share of remittances compared to its population. Labor migration and remittances are especially important for this oblast. Bishkek's share of remittances is roughly equal to its share of the country's population. More economically developed Chui and Issykkul oblasts receive a small fraction of remittances.

Information on the frequency and amount of remittance transfers in the household survey allows us to estimate the distribution of transfers by transaction value (see figure 14). According to these data, more than half of all transfers are in the range of US$100–US$500, with a median value close to US$300. Large transfers (more than US$5,000) constitute just 0.3 percent of the total number of transactions. These results differ significantly from those shown on figure 6, panel A,[15] indicating that households reported much smaller amounts of remittances than shown in the NBKR data (even controlling for the possible consolidation of remittances sent). This confirms the idea that a large part of the money entering the country via large transactions (through MTOs) is not from worker remittances but from trade- and other business-related monetary flows.

Apart from the amount of remittances, another relevant issue is the selection of remittance channels by migrants and their households. It is possible to distinguish formal channels of money transfer (for example, MTOs, banking accounts, and the postal service) and informal channels (migrant and individual intermediaries). The household survey provides information on the current practices of migrants (see table 5). The majority of migrants (78.5 percent) use a bank account or an MTO to

TABLE 5. Channels for Cash Remittances

Channel	% of households receiving remittances using this channel[a]	Average amount of remittance (US$ per receiving household)	Channel as % of total amount of cash remittances
Bank or MTO	78.5	1,330	78.2
Postal service	1.3	320	0.3
Carried by household migrant	25.6	898	17.2
Carried by friend or relative	6.9	646	3.3
Carried by other individuals	1.3	987	1.0

Source: Household survey data.
[a] More than one answer was possible.

transmit money—that is, a formal channel—and most remittances (78.2 percent) enter the country through this channel. Another formal channel—the postal service—has a negligible role. The second important channel of transmission is hand carrying the money by the migrants themselves; 25.6 percent of all receiving households hand carry money, and 17.2 percent of all cash remittances enter in this way. Many migrants commute, so they travel home often and have a chance to bring money with them. The role of intermediaries appears to be relatively low—just 8.2 percent of all households use this channel—and individual intermediaries bring in only 4.3 percent of the total amount of cash remittances. The amounts sent through formal channels (apart from the postal service, which limits the amount transmitted) are larger than the amounts entering through informal channels.

Among MTOs, the best known and popular are Western Union, Anelik, and UNIstream (see table 6). People interviewed by the RRS are aware of, more or less,

FIGURE 12. Remittances, by Country of Origin

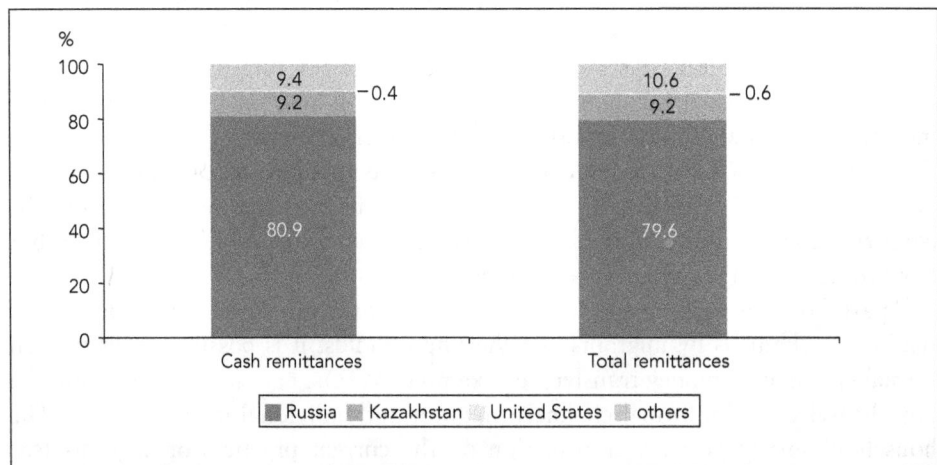

Source: Household survey data.

TABLE 6. Use of Money Transfer Systems of All Respondents (by percentage)

System	Aware of the system	Ever used	Used last time	Used most often
RRS (% of all respondents)				
Western Union	69	44	21	22
MIGOM	26	16	11	11
Money Gram	16	3	1	1
Contact	17	8	4	5
Leader	7	1	0	1
Anelik	50	33	20	17
Xpress Money	5	1	0	1
UNIStream	51	39	29	30
Travelex	11	3	1	1
Zolotaya Korona	6	1	1	1
Bystraya Pochta	14	5	4	3
Kyrgyz Transfer	4	0	0	0
Allure	5	1	0	0
Interexpress	2	1	1	1
Argymak	2	0	0	0
Country Express	1	0	0	0
Eco-perevod	19	7	3	3
Blizko	1	0	0	0
Household survey (% of all households receiving remittances)				
Western Union	72	51	38	38
Anelik	38	21	12	13
Bystraya Pochta	3	0	0	0
MoneyGram	13	3	2	2
UNIStream	23	11	5	5
Contact	14	5	3	3
Interexpress	8	0	0	0
MIGOM	11	4	2	2

Source: Data from the household survey and RRS.

and have used MIGOM, Contact, Eco-perevod, MoneyGram, and Bystraya Pochta. These data are broadly consistent with the data of NBKR, although in the latter, Contact is much more important and MIGOM as well as Eco-perevod are much less important. This discrepancy may be due to the selection of respondents at the premises of only a few banks (more than half of the respondents were contacted at the Ecobank premises in Bishkek and Osh). Similar questions were asked in the household survey, while fewer MTOs were listed directly in the questionnaire. The results appear to be reasonably consistent with those of the RRS (table 6). Answering questions about the advantages of MTOs, people stressed that money transfers are quick, secure, and convenient and that money collection procedures are simple.

FIGURE 13. Cash Remittances, by Oblast

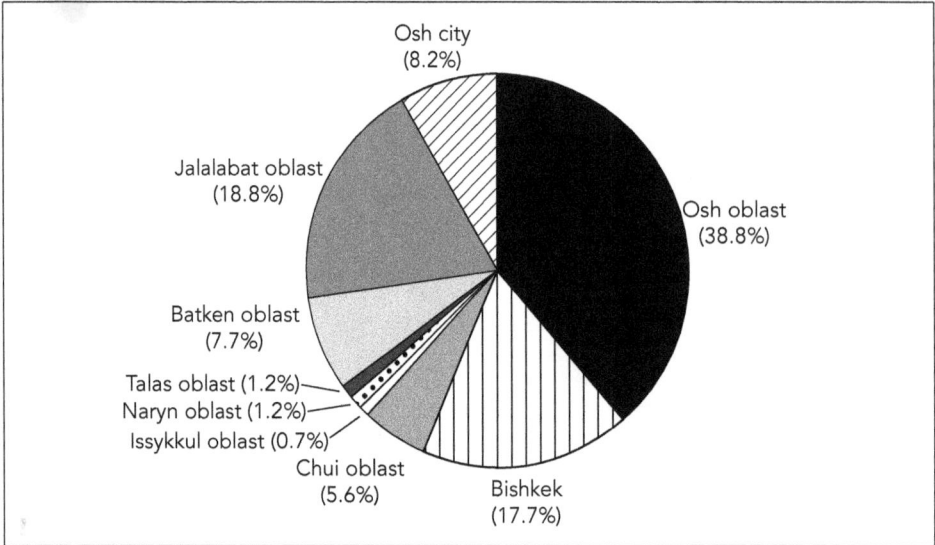

Source: Household survey data.

FIGURE 14. Distribution of Cash Remittance Transfers, by Transaction Value and percent of Total Number of Transactions

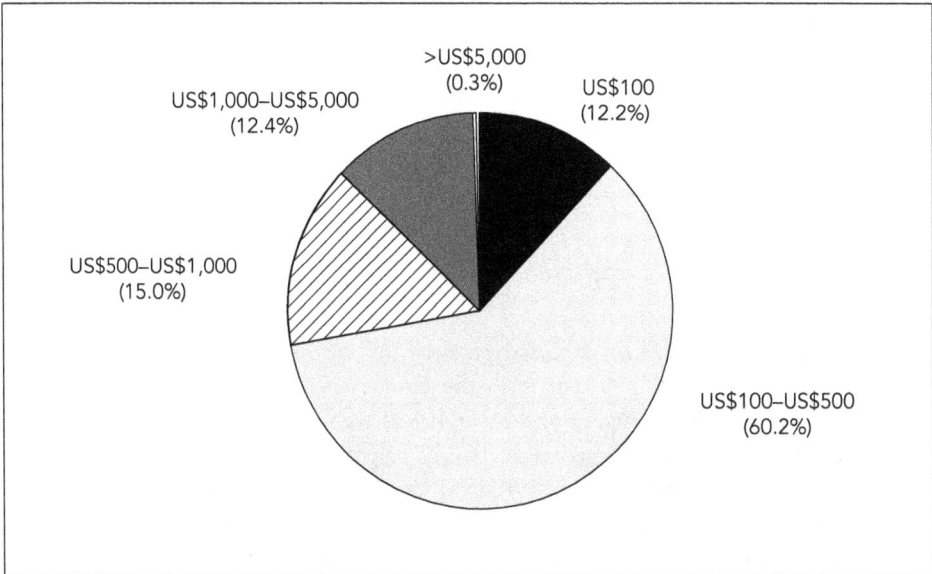

Source: Household survey data.

TABLE 7. Use of Informal Money Transfer Channels (% of all respondents)

Informal channel	Aware of the channel	Ever used	Used last time	Used most often
Conductor	25	4	1	1
Private person	34	11	7	4
Bus driver	19	6	3	2
Truck driver	5	1	1	1
Tourist agency	4	1	0	0
Stewardess	3	1	0	0

Source: RRS data.

Respondents in the household survey also consider informal channels to be secure and reliable (especially when a migrant carries money home), cheap, and readily available, but slow, which is the main disadvantage in the eyes of remitters.

In the RRS, by the very design of the survey, all respondents use formal channels. Still, they were asked about their attitude toward informal ones. Relatively few people reported using or even being aware of informal channels of money transfers (see table 7): 96 percent of respondents said that they prefer formal ways of sending money, and only 4 percent prefer informal channels. The dominant reasons for preferring formal channels are their quickness, security, and convenience of use. The most popular informal way of sending money is through private persons (relatives or friends).

In the RRS, in a majority of households (83 percent), the sender decides on the type of money transfer system to be used, and in the remaining 17 percent of households, the recipient determines the system to be used. The senders notify 96 percent of the recipients about the money transfer, and only 3 percent receive this information from an MTO. In the household survey, the responses were similar. Senders select the MTO to be used in 95 percent of cases, and only in 5 percent are decisions made by or with the participation of the recipient. In 99.7 percent of households in the household survey, the sender notifies the recipient of the transfer.

According to the RRS data, 73 percent of respondents receive information about the transfer within one day, 25 percent in two to three days, and 3 percent in a week. Moreover, 12 percent of the respondents pay a commission to the money transfer company when receiving money; 88 percent pay nothing. For those paying a commission, the charge varies from 0.1 to 10 percent of the transaction amount, with a median of 1.5 percent. Only 36 percent of respondents can get money immediately after receiving notification of a money transfer, and 64 percent wait for their money. Waiting time varies from a few minutes to three days, and the median reported time is one hour. In the household survey, respondents (mostly rural people) reported that more time is needed to collect money, with a median of four hours, which is still reasonably quick.

Both surveys provide similar data on the currency of transfers (see figure 15). Three-quarters of all recipients obtain their money in U.S. dollars. In some cases, people receive soms (much more often in the household survey) and rubles (in the

RRS). Considerably more people prefer receiving money in the national currency. This may indicate that remittances are mainly used for consumption, which is usually done in the national currency; rather than for saving, which is often done in U.S. dollars or the appreciating Russian ruble.

In contrast to the previous indicators, information on the frequency of sending remittances differs significantly between the two surveys (see figure 16). Respondents in the household survey reported much lower frequencies of sending money. More than 70 percent said that they receive money transfers one to three times a year. In the RRS, only 25 percent of respondents receive transfers one to three times a year. Just 6 percent of households receiving remittances get transfers more than 10 times a year; in the RRS, this share is as high as 37 percent. One possible explanation for this discrepancy could be a difference between rural residents (prevailing in the household survey) and urban residents (prevailing in the RRS). Rural dwellers have less access to key remittance channels than urban dwellers, which suggests that their frequency of transfers is lower too.

Data for length of receiving remittances by households from the two surveys are not fully comparable because of differences in the formulation of questions. However, comparison is still possible (see figure 17), and it shows that respondents in the RRS (predominantly urban residents) receive remittances for a longer period than respondents in the household survey (predominantly rural residents), in which more than half (58 percent) reportedly receive remittances for less than a year. If one takes into account the fact that migration decisions and remittances associated with them depend on the available information and that urban people have much more access to information than rural people, these results seem reasonable. In both surveys, the share of households receiving remittances for more than five years is about or below 10 percent.

Household survey data show considerable correlation between migrants' length of stay abroad and the length of period they send remittances. The correlation coefficient is 0.56 for migrants who are members of receiving households and 0.48 for migrants who are not members of receiving households. This indicates that family ties between migrants and their relatives in the Kyrgyz Republic are rather strong and are uninterrupted for a period of time.

Finally, in the RRS, 73 percent of all respondents collect the money sent to them, 14 percent collect money sent to other people (for example, urban people collect money for their rural relatives), and 13 percent participate in bulk remittance transactions (that is, they own only part of the money received). The share of bulk remittances is considerable. Pooling remittances may be related to the remitters' desire to minimize both the costs (such as reducing the costs of traveling to MTO outlets, which may be relatively far from the migrants' workplace, or realizing economies of scale by using regressive transfer fee schemes offered by some MTOs and banks) and the risks associated with the remittance-sending procedure.

Remittances and Business Activities of Recipient Households

Inflow of remittances significantly increases the amount of disposable income of receiving households that can be used not only for consumption but also for savings and investments in business activities. The surveys under consideration provide some information on savings and own businesses of households.

More than half of all households receiving remittances reported the availability of some savings (59.9 percent in the household survey and 68 percent in the RRS). In the household survey, only 37.3 percent of households that do not receive remittances have savings, and the majority of households receiving remittances save money in the form of cash in domestic (54.3 percent of all households in this category) or foreign (22.1 percent) currency. The third popular form of saving is the purchase of consumer goods for future consumption (16.9 percent). Only 6.3 percent of households receiving remittances invest their money in businesses. Fewer people than expected, just 3.5 percent, reported investing in real estate, and only 1 percent of respondents save money in the form of bank deposits. Among households without remittances, 94 percent of those that save do so in cash (soms). The preference for domestic currency as an instrument for savings is a new phenomenon. Previously, people generally saved in U.S. dollars. This behavioral change may be related to low inflation in the 2000s and a strong and steady nominal appreciation of the som against the U.S. dollar.

Whether a household receives a remittance or not, 73 percent of all respondents mainly use cash savings in emergencies; 20 percent use cash for special events, 15 percent use cash for the purchase of consumer goods, and 9 percent use cash for educational purposes. In emergencies, when their savings are insufficient, respondents in both surveys reportedly resort to the financial support of relatives and friends living in the Kyrgyz Republic or in other countries. Meanwhile, the proportions relying on relatives at home or abroad are somewhat different. In the household survey, 81 percent of respondents receiving remittances rely on relatives and friends living in the Kyrgyz Republic, and 60 percent resort to the assistance of relatives or friends living abroad (more than one answer on this question was possible). In the RRS, 47 percent of all respondents said that they request assistance from family members living in other countries (only one answer was possible here), and 40 percent ask for help from family members living in the Kyrgyz Republic. In households without remittances, 92 percent rely on their relatives and friends in the Kyrgyz Republic, and 17 percent resort to a community member or neighbor. People do not rely on the support of or borrow from official organizations, including banks. In the RRS, only 3 percent of respondents consider going to a bank for a loan in an emergency. This reliance on relatives abroad indicates that recipients of remittances see migration as a way to diversify household risk. For example, a bad harvest or natural disaster would affect households with migrants less than households without migrants; all members and relatives would be adversely affected in equal portion.

Of all households (both receiving and not receiving remittances), 12 percent reported having a business or entrepreneurial activity owned or carried out by

FIGURE 15. Currency of Money Transfers

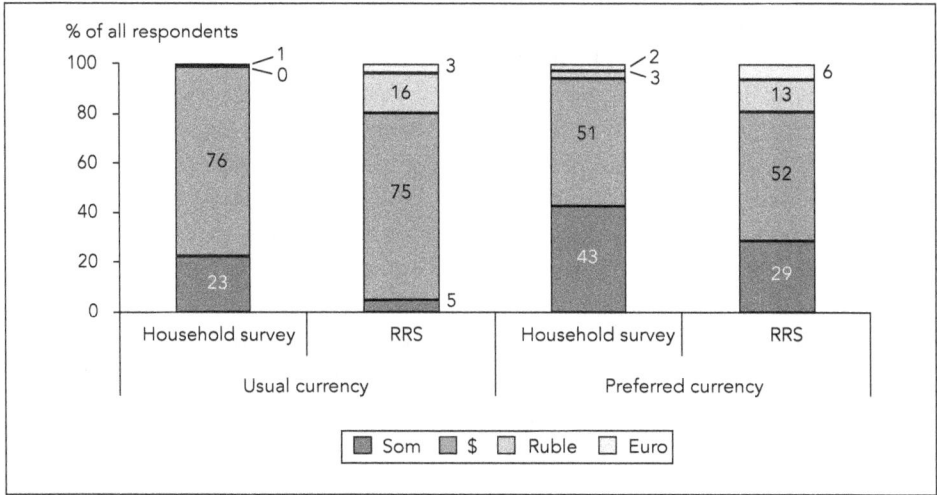

Source: Data from household survey and RRS.

household members. Only 18 percent of these businesses have hired labor (22 percent in the case of households receiving remittances), and in all other cases people are self-employed. The median number of hired workers is two, and the median time of business operations is 29 months. Households running their own business make some investments in them, and the median reported amount of investments for both households receiving and not receiving remittances is som 20,000 (close to US$500). Thus receiving remittances does not affect the households' propensity to have a business or their method of operating it.

FIGURE 16. Number of Money Transfers per Year Received by the Respondents

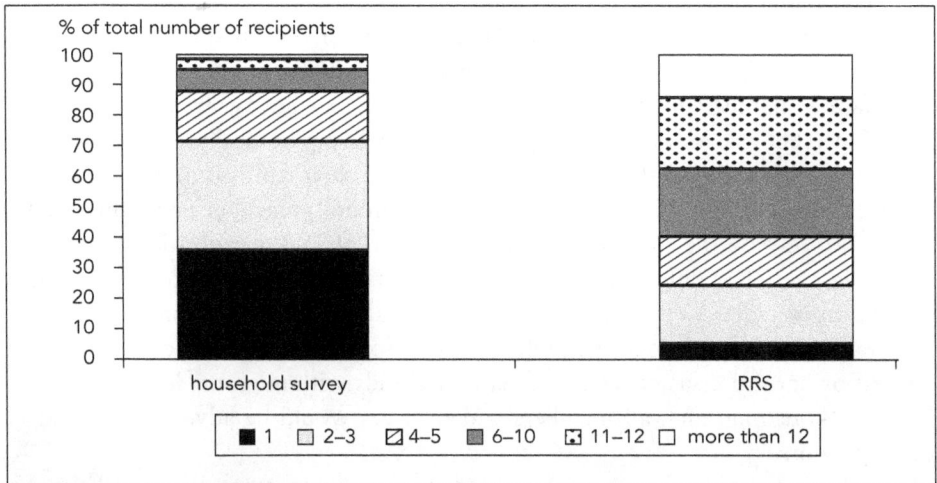

Source: Data from household survey and RRS.

Remittance Recipients and the Financial Sector

Financial activities of households considered in this section include borrowing, lending, and cashless settlement. Both surveys provide information on these issues.

According to the household survey, households receiving remittances and those not receiving them are similar in their use of and attitude toward financial services (see table 8). Less than 13 percent of households borrow money from any source, 1.7 percent lend money, and less than 1 percent have a bank account or any type of banking card; 14.5 percent of households give money away, and 26.9 percent contribute to community or religious organizations.

Among those who borrow money, 55 percent borrow from their relatives and friends, 22 percent borrow from microfinance organizations and credit unions, and 17 percent borrow from banks. The relative popularity of nonbank financial institutions (NBFIs) as suppliers of credit may be related to their proximity (compared with banks) to rural respondents, who predominated in the survey. The amount of debt outstanding is not large; the median is som 10,000 (approximately US$260). People borrow to pay for business investments (22 percent), consumption of goods (17 percent), health (9 percent), education (6 percent), and rituals (10 percent).

Key reasons for not having a bank account are lack of money to keep or maintain an account (72.4 percent of households do not have an account) and "no need of a bank account" (44.8 percent). Low trust in the banking system is a much less frequent answer (18 percent). Respondents do not consider technical issues such as "no bank near my house" (12.2 percent) and "complicated procedure for opening a bank account" (8 percent) as main impediments to having a bank account. Regarding geographic proximity of banking infrastructure to the respondents, the median distance to a bank is 5 kilometers, and the median time to get to a bank branch is 25 minutes.

Regression analysis of factors influencing the probability of a household having a bank account indicates that this probability is higher for households with higher income (without remittances), with higher education of household head, living in

FIGURE 17. Number of Years Respondents Have Received Remittances

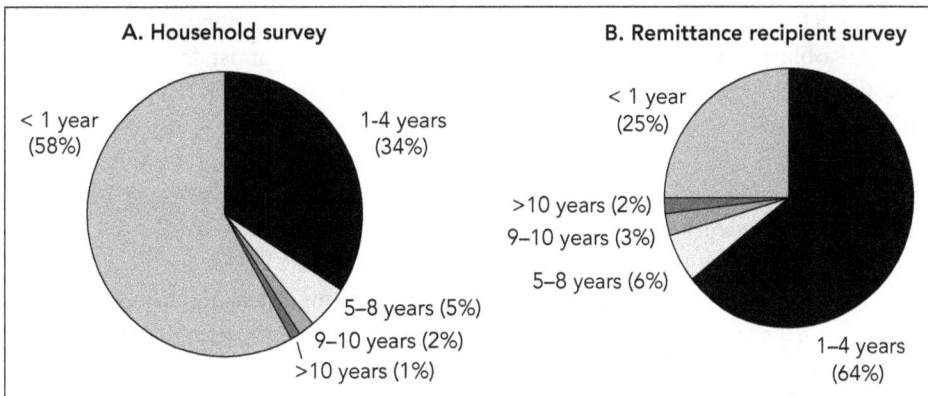

Source: Data from household survey and RRS.

an urban area, and with savings (see table B.4). The amount of remittances received, involvement in entrepreneurial activity, and gender of the household head do not appear to be significant determinants of access to bank services. These results are consistent with other data showing that (a) urban people with higher income and educational status constitute a narrow group of banking system clients and that (b) receiving remittances does not produce a measurable increase in the probability of a household having closer contact with the banking sector.

The RRS survey provides somewhat different results regarding access to financial services. Among these predominantly urban respondents, 23 percent have bank accounts, 8 percent have a credit or a debit card, and 6 percent use automated teller machines (ATMs)—that is, 10 to 20 times more than in the household survey. Among respondents with a bank account, 55 percent have one with Ecobank, 13 percent with Kyrgyz Bank, and 10 percent with Settlement and Saving Company;[16] fewer people reported accounts in seven other banks. Of those receiving remittances through a bank, 85 percent take the whole amount in cash, while 15 percent take part of the money in cash and leave the rest in their bank account.

The most popular reason for not having a bank account are "I do not need a bank account" (48 percent of those answering this question) and "I do not have enough money to keep or maintain a bank account" (38 percent); 6 percent do not trust banks. Compared with answers received in the household survey, lack of money is the second, not the most, important reason; respondents in the RRS apparently have more income than respondents in the other survey.

People did not express much enthusiasm when answering the question on potential incentives and banking services to make them keep part of their remittances in a bank; 68 percent did not respond at all. Among those who responded to this question, the most popular answers were to "provide higher interest rates on deposits" and "help open a bank account." Obviously, the majority of the respondents do not understand the purpose of banks or how to use them. In large part, this is a consequence of lack of previous banking experience, which points to the need to educate people on the use of financial services and the potential advantages of different financial products. This is an area where the government, financial institutions, and international organizations may undertake joint efforts.

In the RRS, 39 percent of respondents reported the availability of some kind of financial obligations. Of those with such obligations, the most frequent types of obligations are related to business (17 percent), consumer credit (15 percent), and support of family members living separately from the household (13 percent). Of these obligations, 47 percent are with family members, 27 percent are with a bank, and 13 percent are with a private lender. These obligations typically are associated with running a business and paying for education.

In summary, the population, especially those individuals from rural areas and the poor, has limited access to financial services. On the one hand, the Kyrgyz population has a generally low level of income and welfare: people simply do not have enough money to save or enough assets to serve as collateral for borrowing. On the other hand, financial services suffer from various perceptual problems. Both financial institutions and their potential clients consider using financial services as a luxury accessible only to people with higher income and educational status or to people with lower-than-usual risk and an aversion to transparency. This view has its roots in the turbulent history of the Kyrgyz economy and its financial sector in the 1990s up to the early 2000s. Because of such attitudes, the number of clients of banks and other institutions is small. Banks do not enjoy economies of scale and must keep their prices prohibitively high for the majority of the population. This, in turn, constrains access of the population to financial services. However, conditions in the financial sector and living standards of the population are gradually improving. It is time for financial institutions to invest in confidence building and in educating people on the use of financial services. The government and international development organizations should support such efforts.

Issues and Patterns of Remittance Transfer Businesses

Inbound and outbound money transfers in the Kyrgyz Republic are regulated by laws governing transactions with foreign currency, banks and banking activities, and licensing. Several regulations issued by NBKR are related to money transfer operations. No specific legislation on international money transfers currently exists.

The regulatory and legal framework establishes that only commercial banks and exchange offices with a special license issued by the NBKR have a right to undertake professional transactions in a foreign currency with individuals. Legally, no regulation restricts organizations from providing money transfer services. According to NBKR specialists, a license to provide money transfer services is being developed. A new license will include requirements regarding organizational form, liquidity, and type of operators eligible to provide international money transfer services. Before introducing this license requirement, NBKR feels that it is necessary to

TABLE 8. Involvement of Households in Financial Activities (% of all households)

Activity	All households	Households receiving remittances	Households not receiving remittances
Borrow from any source	12.6	11.5	12.8
Lend money	1.7	2.5	1.5
Give money	14.5	19.3	13.6
Donate money to community or religious organizations	26.9	29.6	26.3
Have bank account	0.7	1.3	0.6
Have credit card	0.4	0.8	0.4
Have debit card	0.2	0.4	0.1
Use ATM	0.2	0.6	0.1

Source: Household survey data.

assess the possible impact of the legislation on the market, but it does not have enough resources and capacity to do that.

The foreign exchange regime in the Kyrgyz Republic is very liberal. There are no restrictions on transactions and savings in foreign currency for either residents or nonresidents. International travelers (both leaving and entering the country) may hold unrestricted amounts of foreign currency in cash, subject only to a customs declaration.

There are no legal restrictions on the size of outbound transfers. The size of inbound remittances is regulated by legislation in the country of origin[17] or by internal rules of MTOs. For example, Kyrgyz Post limits the size of a single transfer within the Kyrgyz Republic to a maximum of som 10,000 (US$250 in 2006). Restrictions on cross-border postal and telegraphic transfers depend on bilateral agreements between countries and are revised periodically.

In 2006 a new law preventing money laundering and financing of terrorism was enacted. According to this law, a banking transaction should be checked, and information about it should be transferred to the Financial Intelligence Unit under the Ministry of Finance if the transaction amount is equal to or above som 1 million or its equivalent in foreign currency (slightly more than US$26,000 in mid-2007). The following transactions are subject to mandatory control when they exceed this threshold: all internal and external operations of depository institutions, foreign exchange operations, real estate deals where the threshold is som 4.5 million or US$118,000, remittances, all suspicious deals and transactions, and so forth. At the time of writing, little is known about the practical implementation of this very recent law.

The Kyrgyz Republic is a member of the Eurasian Economic Community along with Belarus, Kazakhstan, Russia, Tajikistan, and Uzbekistan. The aim of this international organization is to elaborate unified foreign economic policies, tariffs, prices, and other operational components of the common market. Members of the community inform each other about local laws regulating cross-border money transfers.

The monitoring body for international money transfers is the Department of Balance of Payment at NBKR. Each month, all commercial banks and the Kyrgyz Post report their inbound and outbound money transfers. The information is expressed in U.S. dollars (the currency of the balance sheet compiled by NBKR) irrespective of the currency of transaction.

Money Transfer Operators in the Kyrgyz Republic

While there are no legal restrictions, in practice, only commercial banks handle money transfers. The only nonbanking institution operating in this market is the state enterprise, Kyrgyz Post. According to NBKR specialists, commercial banks dominate the provision of international money transfer services because only they have adequate liquidity and resources to work with asymmetrical flows of money transfers, as inbound remittance flows are much larger than outbound ones.

As noted, remittances enter the Kyrgyz Republic mainly through money transfer companies. These companies operate via their agents, Kyrgyz commercial banks. The banks offer two channels for remittances: banking accounts (including credit card transactions) and MTOs. Practically all active banks operating in the Kyrgyz Republic (19 of 21) are involved in the business of money transfers.

Sixteen MTOs are present in the Kyrgyz Republic, including two major global organizations (Western Union and MoneyGram). Practically all MTOs are operating in the CIS: Allure (formerly STB Express), Anelik, Blizko, Bystraya Pochta (Fast Post), Contact, Country Express, Faster, InterExpress, Leader (formerly VIP Money Transfer/VMT), MIGOM, Travelex Money Transfer, UNIStream, Xpress Money, and Zolotaya Korona (Golden Crown). In addition, there are three domestic money transfer systems: Argymak, Eco-perevod, and Kyrgyz Transfer. Usually, MTOs partner with several banks in the country[18] and vice versa; banks serve more than one MTO simultaneously.[19] Technologically, Kyrgyz commercial banks usually use payment platforms of partner MTOs for transacting, sharing information, and monitoring. Systems are well tested, which allows reliable performance and does not raise any concerns on the Kyrgyz bankers' side.

The network of outlets opened by commercial banks to serve international money transfers is geographically dense throughout the country. These outlets are located inside all bank branches, but most are located outside them. Numerous MTO outlets are located in the two largest cities, Bishkek and Osh, in practically all smaller towns, and in many large and even medium-size villages. For example, according to the data of MTO Web sites, UNIStream has outlets in 57 towns and villages of the Kyrgyz Republic, Contact is present in 55 settlements, Anelik is present in 63 locations, and Western Union has 140 outlets in Bishkek only. The MTO network is well represented in the areas experiencing massive labor emigration, which are in the south of the country.

An important and attractive feature of transfers through MTOs is that it is not necessary to disclose any information about the sender and recipient of the transfer (apart from personal identification) or about the economic nature of the transaction. The absence of transfer taxation also seems a crucial factor in the popularity of this remittance channel.

All commercial banks provide international money transfer services via banking accounts. However, this option is much less popular than the use of money transfer systems that do not require opening a bank account (table 1). Urban people with relatively high levels of education and income are the principal users of transfers through bank accounts. There could be several reasons for the relatively low popularity of bank accounts as a money transfer tool:

• It is not always legally possible for a Kyrgyz migrant to open an account in the country of destination. This problem is especially typical in Kazakhstan.

• There are much fewer bank branches than MTO outlets in the country. Banks are located mainly in cities (Bishkek has 48) and towns.

- Opening a bank account is costly and burdensome (at least for less educated people). Many perceive these costs as being high and do not understand the benefits of using a bank account for purposes such as deposits, loans, and credit cards.[20]

- Some types of transfer operations have relatively high transaction costs.

- According to bank representatives, the introduction of anti–money laundering legislation has caused many clients to leave commercial banks. According to this legislation, banks must report to the authorities all very large transactions, which compose the bulk of remittances entering the country. This deters many clients from using bank accounts as a transmission channel.

- Finally and closely related to that, Kyrgyz shuttle traders are competitive in large part due to informality and the associated reduction in tax payments (substituted by much smaller payments to officials in customs or the open market). From this point of view, using MTO services—implying a quick contact with the banking system—is more attractive than opening a bank account.

In recent years, NBKR with the support of donors—mainly the World Bank—has paid a lot of attention to modernizing the country's payment system. One activity directly related to international money transfers has been the creation of an interbank collective point for SWIFT (Society for Worldwide Interbank Financial Telecommunications) at NBKR in 2002. This substantially increased the number of banks connected to SWIFT—currently, there are 20—and reduced the costs of its use. To establish a unified national interbank cashless settlements system and to introduce the national banking card, commercial banks, with the participation of NBKR, established Elcard, an interbank processing center. This center started operating in December 2006. Currently, 13 banks are members of the system, and six accept payments with this card.

Bank cards, which are one of the most convenient methods of transferring money internationally via the banking system, are not popular in the Kyrgyz Republic. Use of bank cards implies high fixed and variable costs for customers. The two domestic card systems are not integrated with international ones. The ATM and postal terminal network is being developed, and at this point having or maintaining a bank card is a luxury affordable by only a few people. By the end of 2006, there were only 19 ATMs, 324 postal terminals, and 13 imprinters for international cards in the country. Only 11,800 cards of VISA and MasterCard have been issued by Kyrgyz banks. In 2006 cardholders made 242,000 transactions with their international cards. In more than 90 percent of cases, these transactions were cash withdrawals from ATMs; settlements with cards in nonfinancial enterprises are still infrequent.

The situation with bank cards illustrates the slow introduction of new financial services and technologies in the country. In interviews bankers said that they are interested in introducing new technological solutions like mobile banking,[21] but they need technical assistance in designing new financial products affordable for potential clients. The key problem, which so far has prevented banks from introducing many advanced technologies, is the high fixed costs of equipment, software, and system design, which cannot be covered by charging high user fees because the demand for this kind of service is very elastic.

Although mobile telephony initially faced a similar problem in the country, timely investments accompanied by an aggressive advertising campaign made this sector one of the most profitable and fastest growing in the Kyrgyz Republic. Currently, five mobile phone operators working in three standards provide services that are accessible in all populated areas of the country. The number of mobile telephony subscribers is almost doubling each year, according to the consulting agency, Expert. This number exceeded 900,000 people at the end 2006 and approached 1.3 million, or 25 percent of the country's total population, in April 2007. According to the same source, in Bishkek—the national capital—mobile telephony coverage exceeded 80 percent at the end of 2006. Therefore, the penetration of mobile telephony is already deep enough to make the introduction of mobile banking a practical undertaking.

The Kyrgyz Post, which provides the third remittance channel, is a state-owned enterprise with the widest network of offices in the country. It delivers money (postal money orders, pensions, and government allowances) to doorsteps. Similarly, its partners—other countries' postal services—have very good coverage in the destination countries of Kyrgyz migrants. This network could give Kyrgyz Post an important comparative advantage in the remittance market, but it has not taken advantage of it. The postal service has a marginal and diminishing share of inbound transfers (table 1). The postal service's remittance transmission services are the most expensive in the market. This state-owned enterprise does not have enough incentives or capacity to expand its role in the money transfer business. The Kyrgyz government is discussing a plan to establish a postal bank based on the postal service network.[22] Perhaps this would provide an opportunity to revive this remittance channel.

One more channel for transferring money internationally is the so-called informal transfers, which include bringing in cash to the country by migrants or their agents (typically relatives or friends). Recently, this was the most popular way of sending money back to the Kyrgyz Republic. In early 2005 an estimated two-thirds of all transferred amounts entered the country through this channel; of these, around 30 percent were made through agents or intermediaries (Economic Policy Institute 2005). However, during the last two years, the situation has changed dramatically. Interviews with migrants, diaspora representatives, and bankers as well as data from the household survey and the RRS indicate that the majority of migrants have switched to using formal channels (mainly MTOs). The reduction in the role of informal intermediaries is especially striking. According to survey data, less than 5 percent of all remittances enter through informal intermediaries, and less than 10 percent of recipients frequently use their services. MTOs' affordable costs, reliability, and wide network of outlets have eliminated the main advantages of informal transfers. People still bring considerable assets with them when returning to the Kyrgyz Republic, but these are frequently in the form of commodities to be sold in the domestic market, transforming remittances into imported goods.

Competition in the Remittance Market

The growing demand for international money transfer services has attracted many suppliers of these services to the market. The availability of numerous MTOs and consumers—combined with the existence of a competitive and reasonably regulated banking sector, very liberal regulatory regime for international money transfers, and low barriers to entry (such as affordability of the costs of equipment and expertise needed for commercial banks to start operations)—has made this market truly competitive in the Kyrgyz Republic. Competition has at least three facets: (a) between MTOs, (b) between banks, and (c) between transfer-sending channels.

Table 9 provides a list of the most popular MTOs. There is no obvious leading organization in the market. In different periods and by different indicators, Anelik, Contact, UNIStream, and Western Union have been in the lead position. In the early development of the international money transfer business (2000–03), Western Union was the undisputed leader in the market. It had the largest market share both in the number of transactions and in the amount of money transferred. This is natural, as Western Union is a relatively old MTO that developed its business in other regions of the world and was prepared to step into the Kyrgyz market quickly. MoneyGram, another global provider of these services, has been less successful in this market and plays only a secondary role. With the passage of time, however, CIS-based MTOs have taken over the leading positions. First Anelik and then Con-

TABLE 9. Share in Total Number and Amount of Incoming Transfers in the Kyrgyz Republic, by MTO, 2000–06 (by percentage)

Indicator	2000	2001	2002	2003	2004	2005	2005 7 months	2006 7 months
Share in total number of transactions conducted through MTOs								
Anelik	0	5	29	27	14	21	19	15
Contact	0	5	8	23	41	42	41	44
Leader	0	0	0	0	4	2	2	6
MIGOM	0	0	0	3	4	3	3	4
MoneyGram	0	9	5	3	1	1	1	0
UNIStream	0	0	0	0	4	7	7	9
Western Union	100	81	58	44	29	20	22	18
Other MTOs	0	0	0	0	2	4	5	3
Share in total amount of money transfers sent through MTOs								
Anelik	0	1	8	34	34	25	27	16
Contact	0	1	5	15	17	9	10	10
Leader	0	0	0	0	1	1	1	3
MIGOM	0	0	0	1	3	4	4	3
MoneyGram	0	3	7	4	2	1	1	1
UNIStream	0	0	0	0	13	30	25	40
Western Union	100	95	81	45	28	24	26	19
Other MTOs	0	0	0	0	1	6	5	7

Source: NBKR.

FIGURE 18. Mean and Median Amount of Transaction for Leading Money Transfer Operators, 2005

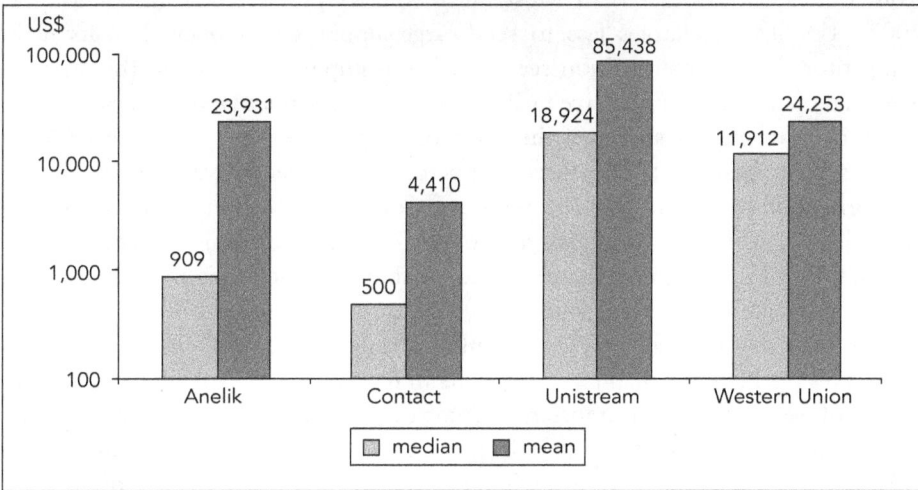

Source: NBKR.

tact as well as UNIStream have gained the largest shares of the market. Currently, leadership in the market is split between these systems. In the number of transactions, Contact has the largest share, approaching 50 percent of the total number of incoming transfer operations. Western Union and Anelik are also popular. From the point of view of the share of money remitted, the situation is different. UNIStream is now the largest channel for transfers; its market share was one-fourth of all money in 2005 and 40 percent in seven months of 2006. Shares of Anelik and Western Union have been gradually declining, but they still hold the second and third places.

The fact that Contact, which handles the largest number of transactions, is only fourth in share of total amount of money transferred means that it remits smaller amounts per transaction than other MTOs. As figure 18 shows, the mean and median amounts of transactions for Contact are much smaller than for other major MTOs. UNIStream is another extreme case. It handles much fewer transactions, but these transactions are large or very large (the mean transfer in 2005 exceeded US$85,000).

Analysis of transfers via MTOs by country provides further insight into market structure. The situation with transfers from Russia (figure B.4, panels A and B) is similar to the aggregate picture: Contact handles a large number of relatively small transactions, while UNIStream handles a small number of very large transactions; Anelik is number two; and Western Union is number three for either indicator. However, the picture of transfers from the United States is somewhat different (figure B.4, panels C and D). Western Union is an absolute leader here, in both the number and the amount of transactions. MoneyGram is the only competitor, with a considerable share of the total amount of transfers. In 2005 to 2006 Anelik completely lost its market share in the United States, which was large in 2002 to 2004.

Another factor that could affect the MTOs' ability to compete is the cost of transactions. Table 10 shows the costs of sending some typical transfer amounts from Russia (cities other than Moscow) to the Kyrgyz Republic (as of May 1, 2007). UNIStream charges less to send large amounts of money than its main competitors.[23] Price competition seems to be an important factor in this market. Many companies offer regressive tariffs in an effort to attract larger transactions. A comparison of market shares of the five most popular systems in Russia with the systems' transaction costs (measured as a percentage of median transfer) shows that the correlation coefficient between market shares and transaction costs is –0.56 and is significantly different from zero at the 5 percent significance level. The negative correlation may be a consequence of the flexibility of the remitters, who tend to switch to the cheapest system available.

It follows that different MTOs prevail in specific segments of the market. Contact serves mainly individual labor migrants in Russia, which explains the predominance of relatively small transfers. UNIStream is oriented more toward bulk remittances and merchant transfers from Russia. Western Union is a leader in the U.S. market. However, the situation is very dynamic, and market shares of different companies rise and fall quickly. Many factors affect market share: (a) proximity of retail outlets to the migrants, which is a function of the number and geographic coverage of their networks and the extent to which these networks match the location of the majority of Kyrgyz migrants in Russia, the United States, and other countries; (b) size of transaction costs; (c) density of MTO outlets in the Kyrgyz Republic and their proximity to the recipients of remittances; and (d) convenience and quality of services provided to clients. Acute competition has meant that all leading MTOs have well-developed networks. However, this is more a result of the work of Kyrgyz banks than of MTOs themselves. Quality of services is also similar for all existing MTOs. Therefore, the first two factors—density of networks outside the Kyrgyz Republic and transaction costs—seem to explain the current position of MTOs in the market. Moreover, these are exactly the factors primarily affecting senders, usually the party deciding which remittance channel to use.

TABLE 10. Transaction Costs for Transferring Money from Russia to the Kyrgyz Republic, by MTO Transfer Amount

MTO	US$500	US$3,000	US$5,000	US$10,000
Allure	2.0	2.0	1.6	1.0
Anelik	3.0	0.9	0.8	0.7
Contact	3.0	3.0	3.0	3.0
Leader	1.5	1.5	1.5	1.5
MIGOM	2.4	2.0	2.0	2.0
MoneyGram	4.6	3.2	2.1	1.8
Travelex	3.6	2.9	1.9	—
UNIStream	1.5	1.5	1.5	1.5
Western Union	4.8	3.3	3.6	3.8

Source: Web sites of MTOs.
— Not available.

Commercial banks form another group of competitors in the Kyrgyz remittance market. By estimates, Ecobank is an absolute leader in the market,[24] followed by Kyrgyzstan Bank, Amanbank, and Settlements and Savings Company. These banks are the most active market participants from the point of view of number of partner MTOs, number and geographic diversity of retail outlets, as well as advertisement efforts (for example, television, magazines, newspapers, booklets, and newsstands), both within the Kyrgyz Republic and among migrants in the countries of their destination, mainly Russia. Representatives of banks visit the workplaces and residences of migrants in Russia, board trains frequented by migrants (the practice of Ecobank) to distribute booklets and leaflets promoting their services, and collaborate with diasporas and embassies of the Kyrgyz Republic in Russia and other countries (the approach of Amanbank). Ecobank also has agreements with Russian banks, and police stations to distribute their information through these channels. All banks extend their networks of retail outlets and tailor the working hours (including weekends) of their branches and outlets in the Kyrgyz Republic to be more accessible and convenient for clients. In selecting their partner banks and MTOs in Russia, Kyrgyz banks try to collaborate with those that are well represented in areas where Kyrgyz migrants are located (Moscow, Siberia, St. Petersburg, and Urals) and have the most client-friendly atmosphere. Anelik, with its long experience of working with Armenian labor migrants, is such a partner. The banks make much less effort to serve Kyrgyz migrants in Kazakhstan or China. Banks do not attempt to develop approaches specific to different types of migrants (for example, shuttle traders versus construction workers). No bank has made a serious effort to strengthen its position in the market by introducing new technological solutions or providing complementary financial services on conditions that are sufficiently attractive for their clients. Bankers seem to believe that their own financial services are not affordable for the majority of senders and recipients of remittances.

Money remitters may choose not only between MTOs and commercial banks, but also between sending channels. As noted, sending transfers via MTOs without opening a bank account is the most common channel. Apart from structural problems, which could explain the underuse of bank accounts and marginalization of postal and telegraphic transfers, there is the issue of transaction costs. Postal services are the most expensive because their transfer fee can be as high as 10 percent of the transferred amount. This, of course, excludes the postal service from any serious participation in the market. The costs of transferring money through a bank account are much lower. A typical transaction may cost 0.2–0.5 percent (but not less than US$20–US$25) on the sender's side plus 1.04 percent (1 percent fee plus 0.04 percent retail sales tax) for cashing the transferred amount in the bank on the recipient's side. This makes transaction costs for banking accounts higher than those for some MTOs, even for large transfers. For small amounts, below US$500, using a bank account makes no economic sense because the transaction costs would exceed 5 percent.

Thus the money transfer market has experienced a dynamic period of development in the last four to five years and has become a healthy, competitive segment of business activity of the Kyrgyz financial sector. Commercial banks have established themselves as a reliable remittance channel. Many market participants seem to have matured and have entered the next stage of development: that is, offering money transfer services with other financial sector products.

Remittances and Financial Intermediation

The financial sector of the Kyrgyz Republic consists of a two-tier banking system and NBFIs.[25] The regulatory body for the Kyrgyz financial sector is NBKR, whose status, tasks, functions, organization, and principles are legally set by the constitution of the Kyrgyz Republic and the Law on the NBKR of July 29, 1997. The main goal of NBKR is to achieve and support price stability by means of relevant monetary policy. The main objective is to support the purchasing power of the national currency and to ensure the security and reliability of the banking and payment system (Article 3). To carry out its tasks, NBKR organizes and carries out its activity independent of the state authorities. NBKR has the following functions:

- Developing and conducting monetary policy in the Kyrgyz Republic

- Regulating and supervising activities of banks and other financial as well as credit institutions licensed by NBKR

- Working out and implementing a unified exchange rate policy

- Possessing an exclusive right to issue bank notes

- Promoting effective functioning of the payment system

- Establishing rules of banking transactions, accounting, and reporting for the banking system.

In the 1990s the Kyrgyz financial sector experienced several severe crises, which substantially reduced its role in the economy and undermined the trust of economic agents in banking and nonbanking institutions. These crises were the result of macroeconomic instability and inappropriate financial regulation. In the early 2000s the government and NBKR undertook significant corrective measures, reducing the government's budget deficit, curbing inflation, and putting in place a much more rigorous regulatory system for financial institutions. Therefore, beginning in 2001 and starting from a very low base, the Kyrgyz financial sector began to develop into a considerably different and healthier sector than before.

In terms of banking regulation and supervision, the main laws regulating these issues in the Kyrgyz Republic are the Law on the National Bank and the Law on Banks and Banking. According to these laws, NBKR is solely responsible for banking supervision and has the right to issue regulations and instructions to oversee bank activities. The government cannot interfere with its activities. NBKR has the exclusive right to license banks. Should a bank fail to comply with its requirements,

NBKR has the right to impose penalties and corrective measures. In extreme cases, it may suspend or revoke a license. NBKR conducts regular extensive off- and on-site inspections, and these include regular stress testing of banks. Significant efforts were made to introduce International Accounting Standards, and since 2003, commercial banks have been publishing financial statements according to these standards. By assessment of the International Monetary Fund and the European Bank for Reconstruction and Development, compliance with the Basel Core Principles for Effective Banking Supervision Assessment is generally "medium" in the Kyrgyz Republic. The main deficiencies are in the transfer of ownership and major acquisitions, supervision of overseas operations of domestic banks and local operations of foreign banks, risk management, and governance and auditing. NBKR is continuing its efforts in the regulatory area. Minimum capital requirements for banks were increased to som 60 million in early 2006; a further increase to som 100 million (around US$2.6 million) is scheduled for 2008. NBKR has developed a supervisory framework for market, country, and transfer risk and has instructed banks to maintain adequate capital to cover these risks effective January 2007. NBKR has also introduced regulations for consolidated supervision to monitor risks faced by financial institutions in line with the recommendations of the Basel Core Principles. A bill before Parliament seeks to amend the central bank charter to enhance its autonomy and ensure legal protection of its employees in performing official duties. Apart from commercial banks, NBKR supervises nonbanking credit institutions. All other financial institutions are supervised by the State Agency on Financial Surveillance and Reporting.

As of end 2006, the Kyrgyz Republic had 21 active commercial banks with 171 branches or 3.3 branches per 100,000 people (3.6 branches per 100,000 people in Bishkek). The branch density has not changed much since 2000, when it was 3.2. This indicator is low by international standards, well below the average of 4.9 for low- and middle-income countries (according to World Development Indicators data for 2004). Apart from the active banks, 11 commercial banks are in the process of external administration, conservation, or liquidation.

Table 11 provides key cumulative indicators of the Kyrgyz banking system. The period from 2001 to 2006 brought the rapid expansion of total assets, liabilities, and own capital of commercial banks. In 2006 alone the capital of the banks increased 48 percent, assets increased 29 percent, and liabilities increased 26 percent. Still, GDP shares of these indicators are lower than in the majority of CIS countries.

An analysis of the structure of banking assets in 2005 to 2006 shows that, as expected, the largest bank asset consists of net credits to nonfinancial corporations and individuals (see figure 19). However, a large part of assets consists of highly liquid assets, which yield little or no income, money on "nostro" accounts in foreign banks, excessive reserves on correspondent accounts in NBKR,[26] and cash. This means that the asset allocation of banks is generally very conservative. At the end of 2006, the liquidity ratio for the banking system was 77.9 percent, that is, it was much higher than NBKR's normative of 30 percent. Similarly, the capital ade-

TABLE 11. Assets and Liabilities of Active Commercial Banks, 2001–06

Indicator	2001	2002	2003	2004	2005	2006
Total assets of active commercial banks						
Million soms	4,958	7,836	11,274	17,471	21,709	28,057
% of GDP	6.7	10.4	13.4	18.5	21.5	24.8
Total liabilities of active commercial banks						
Million soms	3,427	6,191	9,377	15,107	18,528	23,353
% of GDP	4.6	8.2	11.2	16.0	18.4	20.6
Total capital of active commercial banks						
Million soms	1,530	1,645	1,897	2,364	3,182	4,704
% of GDP	2.1	2.2	2.3	2.5	3.2	4.2

Source: NBKR.

quacy ratio (capital-to-risk-weighted assets) was 28.3 percent compared with a normative of 12 percent. This excessive liquidity reflects a response to the maturity mismatch of banking loans and deposits. As of the end of 2006, the average duration of loans was 20.1 months, while the average duration of deposits was just 2.6 months. The short duration of deposits is a result of the prevalence of call deposits; the share of time deposits in the total amount of deposits (stability ratio) is as low as 22.4 percent. Still, liquidity reserves of the banking system are very large and sufficient to cover any disintermediation risk.[27] Under the country's conservative credit policy, banks have significant liquidity reserves. Some recently received a significant inflow of capital from their domestic and foreign owners. This weakens the

FIGURE 19. Banking System Assets, 2005–06

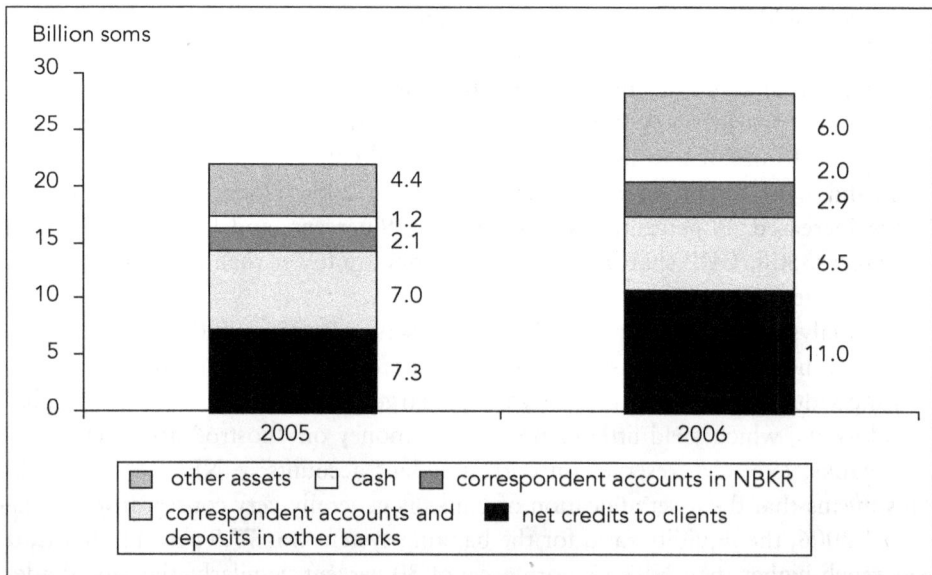

Source: NBKR.

interest of banks in remittances as a source of capital. So far, their main incentive to work with remittances has been to earn income from money transfer services.

In 2006 the share of credit in total assets grew significantly, reflecting the rapid expansion of banking credit to the economy (see also table B.5), which could be seen as a positive sign of increasing intermediation of the financial system. Another positive sign is some improvement in the quality of the credit portfolio; the share of classified credits declined from 10.7 percent in 2000 and 8.2 percent in 2005 to 6.1 percent in 2006. Further good news on the lending activity of Kyrgyz banks is related to the increase in the share of longer-term loans (with maturity of more than one year), from 30.4 percent in mid-2005 to 36.4 percent in mid-2006; 2006 also marked an end to the long trend of increasing dollarization of deposits and credits. In 2006 the share of domestic-currency deposits in total deposits increased for the first time since 2001, from 27 percent in 2005 to 34 percent in 2006; the share of domestic-currency credits in total credits also increased, from 29 percent in 2005 to 31 percent in 2006.

The economic sector receiving the largest share of all credit is trade. For the last three years, the share of trade was in the range of 43–47 percent of total credits. The second large sector is industry; its share, however, fell from 21.7 percent at the end of 2003 to 12.7 percent in mid-2006. Consumer credit to households is the third largest segment of the credit market, with 7–9 percent of all credits. Mortgage credit is the fastest-growing sector; its share increased from 3.1 percent at the end of 2003 to 8.6 percent in mid-2006. Thus consumer and mortgage credit to households have become an increasingly important part of financial services. This provides an opportunity to bring the recipients of remittances into closer contact with the financial sector.

Disinflation, growing supply of credit, and improved efficiency in the banking sector have led to a considerable reduction in the interest rates on credit, which declined from 54.8 and 32.3 percent a year on credit in domestic and foreign currency, respectively, in 1999 to more realistic (but still high) values of 24.6 and 18.9 percent, respectively, in 2004 (table B.5). In 2005 to 2006 interest rates rose slightly, reflecting growing demand for credit and, perhaps, a perception of higher risk of political instability.

Deposits of legal persons or entities and individuals are the main components of commercial bank liabilities (see figure 20). The share of deposits of individuals increased from 14.5 percent in 2005 to 17.8 percent in 2006. The share of call deposits in total deposits of legal persons or entities is very high and growing, increasing from 83 percent in 2005 to 90 percent in 2006 (table B.5). Call deposits of legal persons are the largest component (more than 40 percent) of Kyrgyz banks' liabilities and explains a large part of the high liquidity of the banking system.

FIGURE 20. Banking System Liabilities, 2005–06

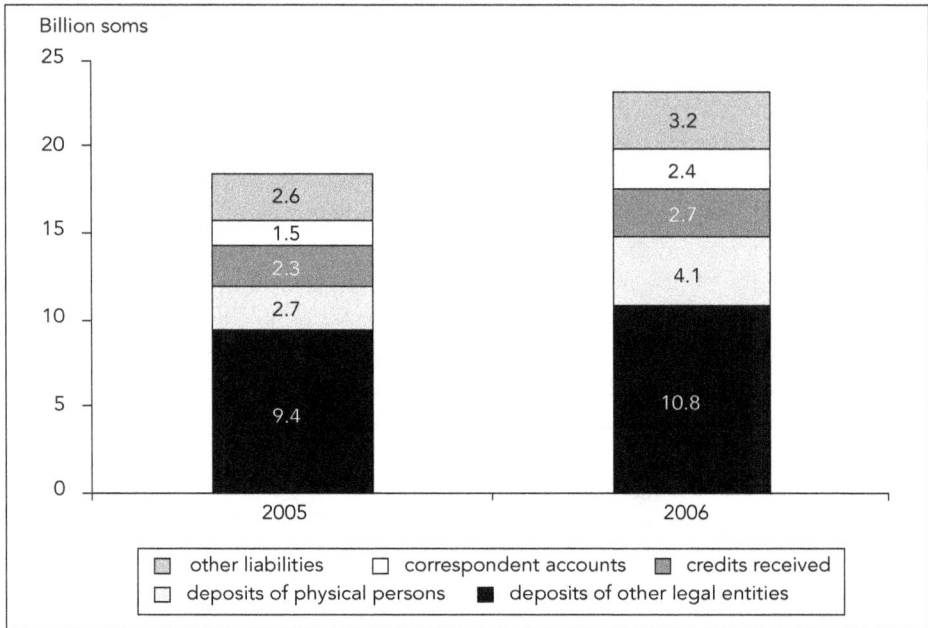

Source: NBKR.

Interest rates on time deposits are low compared with the rates on credit (table B.5) and are declining. In 2006 the real weighted interest rate on deposits in domestic currency was slightly higher than zero. Nominal rates are somewhat higher (around 10 percent a year in domestic currency) for deposits with maturity longer than 12 months, but the share of such deposits in total deposits is relatively small.

Thus the Kyrgyz financial sector has substantially expanded its intermediation in recent years. The share of total deposits in GDP increased from 3.5 percent in 2001 to 14.9 percent in 2006. Aggregate credit of banking and NBFIs to nonfinancial corporations and individuals grew from 3.4 percent of GDP in 2001 to 14.6 percent in 2006 (table B.5). Yet financial intermediation is small in the Kyrgyz Republic compared with other countries. For example, according to the World Development Indicators, in 2005, domestic credit provided by the banking sector (not including NBFIs) was 20.7 percent of GDP in Russia, 21.7 percent in Georgia, 24.7 percent in Kazakhstan, 32.3 percent in Moldova, 35.5 percent in the region of Europe and Central Asia, and 48.3 percent in low-income countries. In number of deposits per 1,000 people (table B.5), the Kyrgyz Republic is far behind countries such as Armenia (111.4 in 2004) or Central and Eastern European countries (in the range of 1,000–2,000).[28]

To boost confidence in the banking system and foster financial deepening, NBKR plans to introduce a deposit insurance scheme for small depositors by late 2008.[29] Enabling legislation on deposit insurance has already been submitted to Parliament, and NBKR has drawn up the modalities for commercial bank participation. It has estimated the level of protection, total cost, and cost sharing between banks and the government. To help lenders to gather information on debtors, NBKR created the Credit Information Bureau in 2000, which became an independent credit bureau in 2003. To establish effective contract enforcement mechanisms, the government and NBKR plan to amend the civil, housing, and land codes as well as the laws governing collateral to harmonize provisions on collateralized lending by financial institutions and facilitate collateral seizure in cases of default.

Expansion of all activities of the Kyrgyz banking sector has led to some improvement of its financial results (see figure 21). In 2006 all relevant indicators such as gross and net interest income, noninterest income, net operating income, net profits, return on assets (ROA), and return on equity (ROE) improved compared with 2005. Net profits increased from som 430 million (US$10.5 million) in 2005 to som 791 million (US$19.7 million) in 2006, growing 84 percent. This improvement in profitability is partially a result of a reduction in the tax rate on profits from 20 to 10 percent, which became effective in 2006. ROA and ROE increased from 2.3 and 17.6 percent, respectively, in 2005 to 3.3 and 22.4 percent in 2006. Noninterest income of commercial banks approached their gross interest income and exceeded net interest income, indicating that other financial services, including MTOs, are as important for banks as intermediation activities (deposits and credits).

The banking sector of the Kyrgyz Republic is relatively small. There is no obvious leader in the market. During 2002 to 2006, in different years, nine banks ranked as the top three banks by at least one of four indicators: statutory capital, assets, deposits, and credits. AsiaUniversalBank has always been the largest bank in terms of deposits and assets and one of the leaders in terms of statutory capital. In term of credit, the leading position belongs to Ineximbank, which was also in the top three on all other indicators in 2004 to 2006. In 2002 to 2006 the share of the largest bank in any of these four indicators was in the range of 13–29 percent, and the share of the three largest banks was in the range of 37–54 percent. As shown on table 12, concentration in the banking sector, which showed no clear trend in 2002 to 2005, declined significantly in 2006.

TABLE 12. Herfindahl Index, 2002–06

Indicator	2002	2003	2004	2005	2006
Statutory capital	0.0854	0.0848	0.0823	0.0869	0.0768
Assets	0.0916	0.0901	0.1215	0.1147	0.0909
Deposits	0.1349	0.0913	0.1249	0.1348	0.1089
Credits	0.1202	0.1012	0.1034	0.0986	0.0895

Source: www.bankir.kg and authors' calculations.

Among active commercial banks, two—Aiyl Bank and SSC—are owned by the state, and there are plans to privatize them. The government is a minority shareholder of KICB. All remaining banks are private. Fifteen banks have foreign shareholders, and in 10 banks foreign participation exceeds 50 percent. Large banks from Kazakhstan play a leading role in or have full control over five banks in the Kyrgyz Republic. Ownership structure somewhat influences bank strategies in the Kyrgyz market, and there are three classes of ownership: (a) predominantly domestic ownership, (b) full or partial ownership by Kazakh banks, and (c) full or partial foreign ownership.

The foreign-ownership group concentrates on transactions with the owners' country of origin or joint ventures with the participation of companies from these countries. With few exceptions, these banks are less active in other segments of the Kyrgyz financial market. Banks affiliated with Kazakh ones are well capitalized and aggressive in the Kyrgyz domestic market, including its money transfer segment.[30] Of course, they also serve transactions with Kazakhstan and Kazakh companies operating in the Kyrgyz Republic. Domestically owned banks are more active in the regions of the Kyrgyz Republic and in the retail segment of the market. This category of bank is much less capitalized (only two are in the top 10). This may be one reason why this group of banks is the most active in the market for international money transfers and why this group is interested in offering advanced services to the senders and recipients of remittances and in retaining their resources in banking accounts. They are explicitly interested in collaborating with ADB on these issues. Two other groups demonstrated much less interest in this business. Domestically owned banks make some efforts to transform recipients of remittances into bank customers. They open branches near typical workplaces of their customers (in open markets), develop new deposit schemes for the recipients of remittances (with no requirement for the minimum sum of deposit), and so forth. In spite of these efforts, they have made little progress, and most recipients of remittances use money for consumption only and do not use other banking services. No bank monitors the extent of financial intermediation to recipients of remittances. In addition, even the banks that are most interested and active in the remittance market make no effort to hire special staff to transform recipients of remittances into full-scale customers. The banks very often do not know what kind of products could or should be developed, how to sell these products to remittance clients, and how to use remittances for leveraging and capitalizing on incoming flows.

As of the end of 2006, NBFIs included the Kyrgyz Agricultural Financial Corporation (KAFC),[31] the Financial Company for Support and Development of Credit Unions, which provides credits to credit unions, 12 insurance companies, 164 microfinance organizations, 308 credit unions, 145 pawnshops, 269 exchange offices, five investment funds, three stock exchanges, one private pension fund, and 79 other financial institutions (for example, financial brokers, investment consultants).

NBFIs are an important source of credit for the economy. In 2006 NBFIs provided credit to the nonfinancial sector in the amount of som 4.81 billion or US$120 million (table B.5), 22.8 percent more than in 2005; this is more than 40 percent of banking credit to the economy. Of this amount, KAFC provided som 2.07 trillion (US$51.5 million), more than any commercial bank. Other lending NBFIs are microfinance organizations (som 2.05 billion or US$51.2 million of credits in 2006), credit unions (som 674 million or US$16.8 million), and pawnshops (som 20 million or US$0.5 million). In 2006, 54.2 percent of all NBFI credits went to agriculture and 31.5 percent went to trade; the share of mortgage loans was 3.2 percent. KAFC was created and is capitalized by concessional loans of international financial institutions to supply relatively cheap credit to farmers and rural entrepreneurs. As a result, KAFC interest rates on credit are the lowest in the country (table B.5), and KAFC credit has longer maturity, usually from two to five years.

The securities market in the Kyrgyz Republic is rather weak. The most significant segment of this market is trade with Treasury bills. In 2006 the volume of outstanding T-bills was som 1.26 billion (US$31.4 million or 1.1 percent GDP). T-bills gradually have become longer-term financial instruments, and short-term (three- and six-month) bills have been almost completely replaced by 12-, 18-, and 24-month bills. This has led to a change in the previous trend of weighted yield on T-bills. In 2000 to 2005, the yield fell from 14.2 to 7.1 percent a year (reflecting little interest on the part of government to borrow in the domestic market). However, in 2006 the yield rose to 9.5 percent, with an increase in the share of T-bills with 18- and 24-month maturity in the total amount of outstanding bills. The market for corporate shares and bonds is small. In 2006 there were only 2,200 transactions (roughly nine transactions a day) on the Kyrgyz Stock Exchange. The total volume of trade was som 3.9 billion (US$97 million or 3.5 percent GDP), of which only som 840 million (US$21 million) were transactions with securities listed on this exchange. Yet this market was much more active in 2006 than in previous years.

In sum, the Kyrgyz financial market is growing quickly from a very low base. Largely, this growth is a consequence of macroeconomic stabilization, considerably stronger regulation, inflow of foreign direct investment, and competition. Still, the country's financial market is shallow, and financial intermediation is insufficient to meet the country's needs. Banks consider remittances to be a source of noninterest income and make little effort to provide intermediary services to the senders or recipients of remittances. However, with some revival of consumer finance, growing competition in the banking sector, and adaptation of households receiving remittances to contacts with the banking sector, chances for more successful financial intermediation are improving.

Issues and Recommendations

In the last four to five years, remittance flows have had a significant impact on the economic and financial development of the Kyrgyz Republic. Remittances contributed to the growth of household consumption and extended contacts of the population with the financial sector as never before. This had numerous spillover effects on different segments of the national economy.

The inflow of remittances also raised several issues that need to be addressed by the authorities and the business community of the Kyrgyz Republic:

- Clarifying the notion of remittances in the Kyrgyz context and refining the methodology of their measurement and tracking

- Creating an enabling environment for converting remittances into investments in the Kyrgyz economy

- Increasing and broadening the scope of financial services offered to and used by senders and recipients of remittances.

Official data on worker remittances also include revenues from exports of goods and other types of economic flows. For this reason, actual remittances related to Kyrgyz migrants' labor abroad are somewhat smaller, but still significant, for the country. A new remittance-measuring methodology needs to be introduced, which would allow excluding irrelevant flows and accounting for remittances entering through informal channels.

The impressive growth of the remittance transfer industry and the voluntary switching of remitters from informal to formal remittance-sending channels, which took place in just a few years, may be attributed to liberal rules governing foreign currency, competitive environment, and improved general regulation in the banking sector. The service providers, because of acute competition in the market, have lowered their initially high transaction costs for transmitting remittances. It is remarkable that stakeholders (recipients of remittances, bankers, regulators) generally are satisfied with the quality of transfer services, which means that the market perfectly regulates itself. From this point of view, the plans to introduce new remittance-related legislation as well as the application of existing anti–money laundering legislation, which seem to be impeding the development of normal banking practices, may require reconsideration to avoid unnecessary distortions in the market.

Macroeconomic and microeconomic consequences of the inflow of remittances appear to be generally positive. Apart from an increase in household consumption, it has caused the development of a services sector, increased imports and government budget revenues, and expanded domestic employment opportunities (mostly in the informal economy). The remittances so far have exerted little influence on investments because of the poverty of the majority of households receiving remittances and the lack of experience of the majority of the population with financial services. However, frequent and trouble-free contacts with the banking system create a basis for building the population's confidence in the banking system, which is a key prerequisite for an increase in financial intermediation.

Commercial banks have developed a dense network of MTO outlets. This has contributed to the expansion of this money transfer channel and to the growth in banks' noninterest income. However, they have been less successful in providing the senders and recipients of remittances with other financial services. Now is the moment for banks to begin an aggressive campaign to involve the senders and recipients of remittances in the financial sector in ways other than money transfer services. To do this, banks will have to adopt a strategic, flexible approach and be prepared to educate their current and potential clients.

The rest of this section offers recommendations to the Kyrgyz authorities, donors, and the banking community. The following recommendations are geared specifically to the government and the national bank:

- Introduce a new remittance-measuring methodology and coordinate it with other remittance-receiving countries of the region

- Establish a system of regular periodic collection, analysis, and reporting of data on remittance as well as migration flows in the country

- Negotiate with Russia, Kazakhstan, and other remittance-sending countries measures to improve migrants' status and facilitate remittance flows using bilateral and multilateral frameworks (for example, that of the Central Asian Regional Economic Cooperation Programme)

- Provide financial literacy training to remitters and their families and introduce such training into the school curriculum

- Review comprehensive financial legislation to amend and enhance the introduction of modern remittance technologies such as mobile banking

FIGURE 21. Income and Expenditures of Commercial Banks, 2005–06

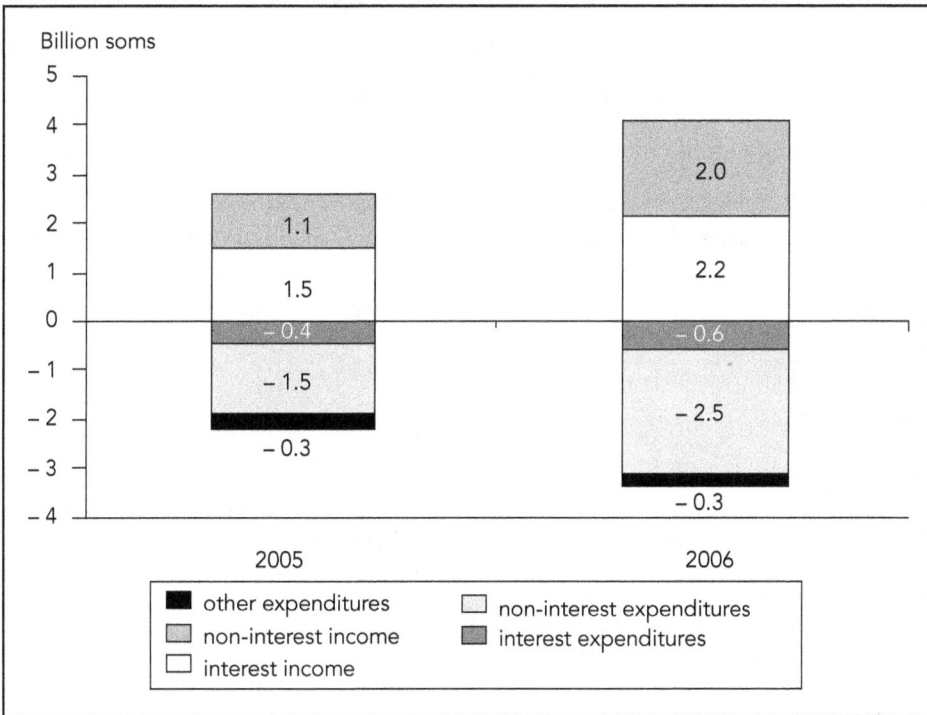

Source: NBKR.

- Revise anti–money laundering legislation and its application to avoid discouraging clients from using the banking sector

- Refrain from introducing specific remittance regulations and instead strengthen general banking regulation

- Avoid introducing any form of remittance taxation.

The following recommendations are geared to donor organizations:

- Support the adoption of legislation in sending countries (such as Kazakhstan), which would enable or ease the access of Kyrgyz migrants to banking services

- Provide technical assistance and, possibly, financial resources to Kyrgyz banks for developing financial products (for example, mobile banking) that are attractive and affordable for senders and recipients of remittances

- Provide training programs in financial education for senders and recipients of remittances.

The following recommendations are geared to Kyrgyz commercial banks:

- Develop a long-term strategy to develop banking for recipients of remittances by investing in infrastructure and new technological solutions (for example, mobile banking), possibly forming consortia for these purposes

- Lower the fees for clients and make services more convenient for recipients of remittances on the condition that they use complementary banking services (for example, waive cashing fees if the client puts the remittance on time deposit or takes a loan from the bank)

- Conduct more aggressive and more targeted advertising campaigns explaining the long-term benefits of the extensive use of financial services, especially for investments, bulky expenditures (ritual expenses or education), and retirement.

References

ADB (Asian Development Bank). 2006. *Central Asia: Increasing Gains from Trade through Regional Cooperation in Trade Policy, Transport, and Customs Transit*. Manila: ADB.

———. 2008. "A Study on International Migrants' Remittances in Central Asia and South Caucasus." Country Report on Remittances of International Migrants and Poverty in the Kyrgyz Republic. Manila: ADB.

Economic Policy Institute. 2005. *Estimation of the Remittances from Labor Migrants*. Bishkek: Аки Press.

IMF (International Monetary Fund). 1993. *Balance of Payments Manual*. Washington, DC: IMF.

Japarov, Akylbek. and L. Ten. 2006. *Estimation of the Remittances from Labor Migrants*. Bishkek: Аки Press.

Mansoor, Ali, and Bryce Quillin. 2006. *Migration and Remittances: Eastern Europe and the Former Soviet Union.* Europe and Central Asia Region. Washington, DC: World Bank.

NBKR (National Bank of the Kyrgyz Republic). 2006. *2006 Balance of Payments.* Bishkek: NBKR.

Notes

1. See, for example, ADB (2006).
2. Calculated as 100 percent less 34 percent coming via formal channels.
3. In June 2007 the National Bank of the Kyrgyz Republic introduced important modifications of its methodology of estimating remittance flows. NBKR (2006) contains revised (upward) estimates of remittance flows for 2002–06. It states that the amount sent via official channels is adjusted for informal cash transfers by multiplying on an unspecified coefficient, which is greater than 1. This information is insufficient for this paper's analytical purposes; therefore, this paper is based on the NBKR's initial data and methodology.
4. Estimated migrant transfers have no link to labor migration or to any phenomena associated with it.
5. The quantitative estimates of remittances are published by NBKR in the *Balance of Payments*.
6. The fast growth of formal transfers compared with net errors and omissions conforms to the assumption that formal transfers will gradually replace informal ones as the Kyrgyz financial system becomes stronger.
7. In the survey of recipients of remittances conducted in Bishkek and Osh in October 2006, 13 percent of respondents indicated that they received bulk remittances.
8. Interviews with representatives of some Kyrgyz diaspora organizations in Russia show that these organizations try to consolidate transfers of their fellow citizens (mainly traders) into large and very large bulk transactions.
9. According to NBKR data, imports of consumer goods in 2006 amounted to US$497.5 million or som 20 billion (at current exchange rate), which is 18 percent of total private consumption.
10. Of course, the rising price of apartments creates more incentives for residential construction. Despite signs of increased construction activities in Bishkek, so far this economic sector is not a major contributor to the country's GDP.
11. Correlation coefficient of 0.51.
12. There is also a marginally significant immediate (with zero lag) negative correlation between these two variables. The correlation coefficient sign is counterintuitive and may be a purely statistical phenomenon.
13. This is especially relevant for 2006. According to preliminary data, the absolute growth of imports was US$617 million, while the absolute growth of net worker remittances was only US$150 million. In other words, more than three-quarters of the absolute increase in imports were covered by sources other than remittances.
14. Of course, not all of these currencies enter the currency market because a large part of domestic turnover and a major part of savings are in U.S. dollars or other foreign currencies.

15. While these figures are not fully comparable, more than three-quarters of cash remittances in the household survey come via MTOs or the banking system, so the distribution of remittances via this channel is similar to the distribution of all cash transfers.

16. These results may also be a consequence of the method undertaken in selecting the respondents in the survey.

17. There is a restriction on money transfers through MTOs for residents of Russia. A single transaction through an authorized bank during a working day cannot exceed US$5,000. There is no limitation on the amount of money transfers for nonresidents. A federal unitary enterprise, Russian Post/Pochta Rossii, provides electronic money transfer services to Kazakhstan and Belarus, while only postal transfers are available for other CIS countries. Starting in 2005, the maximum amount of a postal money transfer for an individual is Rub 100,000 (close to US$4,000). The number of transfers is unlimited.

18. For example, in 2006, UNIStream had 11 bank partners, Western Union had 9, Anelik had 8, and Contact had 7.

19. Ineximbank has 10 MTO partners, Ecobank has 9, and Kyrgyzstan has 8.

20. For example, account opening fee (up to US$25), notarial attestation of signatures, and other documents for entrepreneurs (up to US$10).

21. Some Kyrgyz banks had planned to introduce mobile banking, but recent political instability and associated change in ownership of the largest mobile operator—which was expected to be a partner in this business—did not allow these plans to become a reality.

22. Some of the post offices in this network already provide banking services, as Kyrgyz Post rented them to commercial banks.

23. Anelik's rates, shown in the table, were introduced recently. In 2005 to 2006, Anelik had a flat rate of 3 percent, which was much higher than UNIStream. The "Super-Anelik" tariff with rates below 1 percent, which was introduced at the end of 2006, could be seen as an attempt to cut prices.

24. Despite Ecobank's share in this market (about 40 percent), this bank has no instrument with which to exercise market power. Therefore, its big market share does not limit competition in the market.

25. This paragraph is based on information on the NBKR Web site.

26. In 2002 to 2006, excessive reserves of commercial banks in NBKR were always in the range of 50–60 percent of mandatory reserves.

27. Such as a massive premature withdrawal of deposits from banks.

28. The source of data is the World Development Indicators for 2006.

29. This paragraph is based on the IMF (1993).

30. In recent years, they received substantial capital injections from their mother banks, and all five are in the top 10 Kyrgyz banks in terms of statutory capital.

31. In December 2006 KAFC received its banking license and has been converted into Aiyl (Rural) Bank. This paper covers activities of the organization only in the capacity of an NBFI.

Appendix A. Migration Patterns

The tremendous social and economic change related to the breakup of the former Soviet Union strongly affected the demographic situation in the Kyrgyz Republic. Fertility and birth rates dropped, and the death rate declined following the transition to independence and a market economy, accompanied by sharp political and economic shocks as well as a period of continuous instability, a sudden shift to a new environment with significantly greater risks and uncertainties, an end to massive subsidies from the central Soviet budget, and the resulting decline in the quantity and quality of social services. The natural population growth rate fell from 24.1 percent in 1987 (the last "quiet" year of the Soviet period) to 15.9 percent in 2006. Still, the population is growing relatively quickly. In 2007, it reached 5.2 million people or 0.7 million more than in 1991, when the country gained independence.

The population is predominantly rural (65 percent) and young (children and adolescents compose 34 percent of the population, while 57 percent are of working age). The issue of employment, especially rural employment, is therefore acute. While official unemployment figures are rather low—registered unemployment is just 3 percent, and estimated unemployment according to the International Labour Organisation's (ILO) definition is 9 percent—these figures presume that all peasants with a piece of land are employed. Because land and agrarian reform in the 1990s gave land to virtually every peasant, there is no rural unemployment according to official records. In reality, however, since the collapse of the previous mode of agricultural production based on the extensive use of resources and permanent inflow of subsidies to large agricultural enterprises, agricultural activities have not been able to feed the growing rural population. A natural response to this situation is the migration of young people from rural to urban areas and, increasingly, abroad in search of employment opportunities. Labor migration has become a major social and economic phenomenon in the Kyrgyz Republic.

Migration both from and to the Kyrgyz Republic has been traditionally large since the end of the nineteenth century. However, in the pre-Soviet and especially in the Soviet period, migration was mainly immigration from Russia and Ukraine and was forced or organized (Cossack settlers in pre-Soviet times, evacuees during World War II, specialists and skilled workers participating in postwar industrialization, and students); voluntary migration was marginal. The situation changed dramatically after independence. There was a large outflow of people in the early 1990s (see figure A.1). All these people emigrated voluntarily for ethnic identity and economic reasons. All these migrations—apart from those of students—were associated with a permanent change of residence.

FIGURE A.1. Emigration from and Immigration to the Kyrgyz Republic, 1991–2004

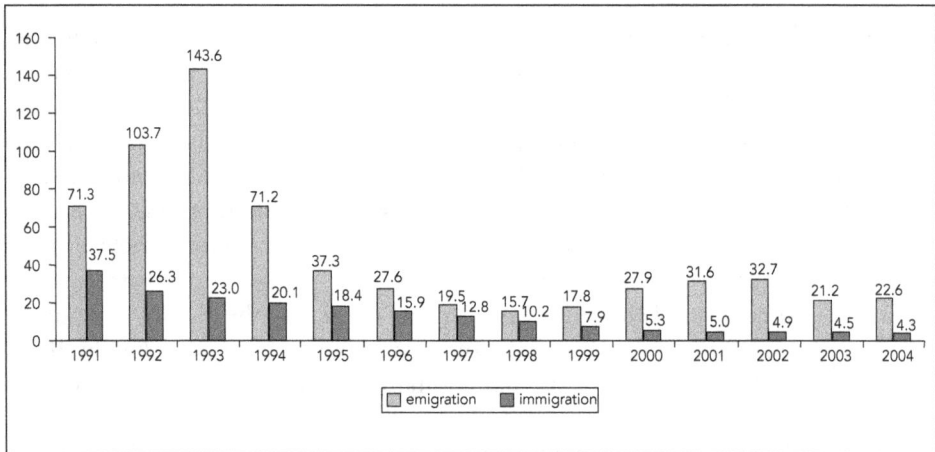

Source: NSC.

Recently, however, there has been a new trend: temporary migration driven by exclusively economic reasons. The temporary migrants are mainly ethnic Kyrgyz, but ethnic minorities are also well represented. This makes the phenomenon different from the permanent migrations, where the migrants were mostly minorities (mainly Russians, Ukrainians, and Germans). The main destinations of the temporary migrants are Kazakhstan and the Russian Federation, but Kyrgyz migrants can be found in many other countries as well. Currently, there are no reliable estimates of the number of international labor migrants in the Kyrgyz Republic. In 2003 the National Statistical Committee of the Kyrgyz Republic (NSC) conducted a one-time survey of labor migration, but did not disseminate the survey results. According to the International Organization for Migration, the majority of labor migrants work in Russia (300,000) and in Kazakhstan (50,000). Journalists even say that the total numbers are closer to 500,000–700,000, but these figures seem too subjective and unfounded.

The reasons for migration are mostly economic. Living standards, wages, employment, and market opportunities are significantly higher in oil-rich Kazakhstan and the Russian Federation than in the Kyrgyz Republic, Tajikistan, or Uzbekistan. The migrants fill niches in the labor markets of Kazakhstan and Russia that citizens do not find as attractive as other employment options. Apart from economic reasons, the migrants choose to go to Kazakhstan and Russia because they speak Russian—universally spoken by people in their 30s and 40s in the Kyrgyz Republic, but less common among younger people—or the Kazakh language, which is similar to the Kyrgyz language, and they feel a cultural kinship with the other former Soviet republics.

Internal migration is also large. According to NSC estimates, the total number of internal migrants in 1999 to 2005 exceeded 350,000. Most internal migrants (72.8 percent) come from densely populated rural areas to Bishkek and Chui Valley.

Similar to international labor migration, internal migrants are mainly young people.

The Kyrgyz Republic not only supplies labor migrants to other countries but also receives them from other countries, mainly from Tajikistan and Uzbekistan. These immigrants work in agriculture and construction and successfully compete in the domestic labor market of the Kyrgyz Republic with their attractive combination of skill, readiness to work for modest pay (even by standards of the Kyrgyz Republic), and good work ethic. Again, there are no reliable statistics on these immigrants, as they work largely on an informal basis, but there are thousands of immigrant workers during the agricultural season in the Kyrgyz Republic. Chinese traders also are a visible component of foreign labor in the country.

Appendix B. Complementary Tables and Graphs

TABLE B.1. Balance-of-Payments Data on Remittance Flows, by Quarter, 2000–06 (million US$)

Indicator	2000				2001		
	I	II	III	IV	I	II	III
Net compensation of employees	(2.5)	(2.8)	(2.6)	(2.5)	(2.3)	(2.4)	(2.9)
Credit	0.0	0.0	0.0	0.0	0.0	0.0	0.0
Debit	2.5	2.8	2.6	2.5	2.3	2.4	2.9
Net worker remittances[a]	0.3	0.3	0.3	0.4	0.4	0.4	0.6
Credit	0.3	0.3	0.3	0.4	0.4	0.4	0.6
Debit	0.0	0.0	0.0	0.0	0.0	0.0	0.0
Net migrants' capital transfers	(4.6)	(7.6)	(8.4)	(6.9)	(4.7)	(8.8)	(13.1)
Credit	1.1	1.8	2.0	1.6	0.9	1.7	2.5
Debit	5.7	9.4	10.4	8.5	5.6	10.5	15.6
Net total remittances[b]	(6.8)	(10.1)	(10.7)	(9.0)	(6.6)	(10.8)	(15.4)
Credit (gross inflow)	0.3	0.3	0.3	0.4	0.4	0.4	0.6
Debit	7.1	10.4	11.0	9.4	7.0	11.2	16.0

Indicator	2004				2005		
	I	II	III	IV	I	II	III
Net compensation of employees	(2.9)	(2.8)	(3.1)	(4.9)	(4.1)	(4.0)	(4.8)
Credit	0.0	0.0	0.0	0.0	0.0	0.0	0.0
Debit	2.9	2.8	3.1	4.9	4.1	4.0	4.8
Net worker's remittances[a]	22.8	30.2	51.6	59.1	38.9	64.7	87.0
Credit	25.0	32.7	57.0	64.4	44.3	74.5	95.3
Debit	2.2	2.5	5.4	5.3	5.4	9.8	8.3
Net migrants' capital transfers	(7.3)	(10.8)	(12.6)	(13.1)	(8.7)	(16.7)	(20.4)
Credit	1.8	3.6	2.1	2.0	2.0	1.9	2.2
Debit	9.1	14.4	14.7	15.1	10.7	18.6	22.6
Net total remittances[b]	12.6	16.6	35.9	41.1	26.1	44.0	61.8
Credit (gross inflow)	26.8	36.3	59.1	66.4	46.3	76.4	97.5
Debit	14.2	19.7	23.2	25.3	20.2	32.4	35.7

Source: NBKR and authors' estimates.
[a] Data on 2000–01 are estimates, as only net values of worker remittances have been published.
[b] No data on worker remittances, the main component of total remittances, were published before 2000.

IV	2002				2003			
	I	II	III	IV	I	II	III	IV
(2.7)	(3.0)	(2.7)	(2.9)	(3.7)	(3.1)	(3.2)	(3.0)	(3.3)
0.0	0.0	0.0	0.0	0.0	0.0	0.0	0.0	0.0
2.7	3.0	2.7	2.9	3.7	3.1	3.2	3.0	3.3
0.5	4.4	6.4	8.4	9.1	9.0	13.3	20.4	22.3
0.5	4.7	7.2	8.9	9.6	9.8	15.5	21.5	23.4
0.0	0.3	0.8	0.5	0.5	0.8	2.2	1.1	1.1
(8.0)	(5.5)	(10.0)	(12.6)	(8.5)	(4.6)	(7.3)	(9.3)	(7.8)
1.5	1.3	1.4	1.9	1.8	1.6	1.7	2.1	2.4
9.5	6.8	11.4	14.5	10.3	6.2	9.0	11.4	10.2
(10.2)	(4.1)	(6.3)	(7.1)	(3.1)	1.3	2.8	8.1	11.2
0.5	6.0	8.6	10.8	11.4	11.4	17.2	23.6	25.8
10.7	10.1	14.9	17.9	14.5	10.1	14.4	15.5	14.6

IV	2006		
	I	II	III
(4.5)	(5.1)	(4.7)	(4.7)
0.0	0.0	0.0	0.0
4.5	5.1	4.7	4.7
89.7	68.5	103.8	128.3
99.1	75.6	115.0	140.6
9.4	7.1	11.2	12.3
(17.8)	(11.1)	(16.2)	(21.7)
2.6	1.9	2.2	2.1
20.4	13.0	18.4	23.8
67.4	52.3	82.9	101.9
101.7	77.5	117.2	142.7
34.3	25.2	34.3	40.8

TABLE B.2. Sample Composition in the Remittance Recipient Survey

Composition	Bishkek		Osh		All samples	
	Number	%	Number	%	Number	%
Number of respondents	153	100	150	100	303	100
Urban residents	135	88	108	72	243	80
Rural residents	18	12	42	28	60	20
Women	90	59	84	56	174	57
Age < 21	13	8	3	2	16	5
Age 21–59	70	46	76	51	146	48
Age 60+	7	5	5	3	12	4
Men	63	41	65	44	128	43
Age < 21	4	3	4	3	8	3
Age 21–59	57	37	57	38	114	38
Age 60+	2	1	4	3	6	2

Source: RRS data.

TABLE B.3. Profile of Migrants (% of all migrants, unless otherwise noted)

Characteristic	Kyrgyz Republic	Bishkek	Other urban areas	Rural areas
Migrants				
Number (thousands)	251.5	26.2	52.4	173.0
% of total population	5.0	3.6	6.2	4.9
% of working-age population	8.1	5.4	10.0	8.3
Female migrants as a % of all migrants	27.5	40.5	26.8	25.7
Age of migrants (years)				
Minimum	15	18	15	15
Median	28	32	31	27.5
Maximum	67	63	66	67
Education of migrants				
Less than completed secondary education	6.4	2.5	10.0	6.0
Completed secondary education	77.1	55.7	72.6	82.0
Above secondary education	16.5	41.8	17.4	11.9
Destination country				
Russian Federation	82.5	67.1	81.1	85.2
Kazakhstan	12.0	16.5	10.0	11.9
Other countries	5.5	16.6	8.9	2.9
Duration of stay abroad (years)				
Minimum	0.1	0.1	0.1	0.1
Median	1.2	2.0	1.5	1.0
Maximum	24.0	24.0	10.4	11.0
Occupation abroad				
Self-employed	19.5	25.3	18.4	19.0
Entrepreneurial activity (with hired employees)	0.0	0.0	0.0	0.0
Employed in the public sector	5.8	12.7	7.9	4.2
Employed in the private sector	71.6	51.9	70.0	75.0
Unpaid family work (help on the farm, housework)	0.7	0.0	1.1	0.7
Unemployed and looking for work	0.4	3.8	0.0	0.0
Unemployed and not looking for work	0.0	0.0	0.0	0.0
Student	1.4	2.5	2.1	1.0
Retiree with pension	0.2	1.3	0.0	0.2
Others	0.4	2.5	0.5	0.0

Characteristic	Kyrgyz Republic	Bishkek	Other urban areas	Rural areas
Sector of employment or entrepreneurial activity abroad				
Agriculture (including hunting, forestry, and fishing)	1.4	2.5	3.2	0.7
Mining and quarrying industry	0.0	0.0	0.0	0.0
Processing industry	6.6	10.1	8.4	5.5
Power, gas, and water supply	0.7	3.8	0.0	0.5
Construction	45.0	17.7	44.2	49.3
Wholesale and retail trade	30.4	27.9	26.8	31.9
Transport and communications	3.8	8.9	4.7	2.7
Financial sector	0.6	2.5	0.5	0.3
Public administration and defense	0.4	2.5	0.5	0.0
Education, health care, and social protection	0.6	3.8	0.5	0.2
Other	7.8	12.7	7.9	7.0
Seasonal workers	44.1	26.6	43.7	46.8

Source: Household survey data.

TABLE B.4. Logit Model Describing Probability for Household to Have a Banking Account

Variable	Coefficient	Standard error	z statistic	p value
Urban	0.826	0.444	1.859	0.063
TOT–MON–REM	$2.69 \cdot 10^{(6)}$	$2.01 \cdot 10^{(6)}$	1.336	0.182
Gender	(0.360)	0.479	(0.752)	0.452
Education	1.005	0.461	2.179	0.029
Business	0.672	0.438	1.535	0.125
Income–WR	$1.36 \cdot 10^{(5)}$	$3.73 \cdot 10^{(6)}$	3.655	0.000
Savings	0.719	0.403	1.783	0.075
Constant	(6.796)	0.512	(13.272)	0.000
LR statistic (7 df)	43.32			
Probability (LR statistic)	$2.89 \cdot 10^{(7)}$			
McFadden R^2	0.12612			

Source: Household survey data and authors' estimates.

Note: The dependent variable is Y. The method is ML–binary logit. Included observations are 3,997. Convergence was achieved after 12 iterations, and the covariance matrix was computed using second derivatives. Variables are defined as follows. Y is a binary variable equal to 1 for households with at least one member having a banking account and 0 otherwise. Urban is a binary variable equal to 1 for households living in an urban area and 0 for rural households. TOT–MON–REM is total cash remittances received by household (soms). Gender is a binary variable equal to 1 for households in which the household head has higher education and 0 otherwise. Business is a binary variable equal to 1 for households that are involved in entrepreneurial activity and 0 otherwise. Income–WR is income without remittances (soms). Savings is a binary variable equal to 1 for households that reported availability of savings and 0 otherwise.

TABLE B.5. Deposits and Credits, 1996–2006

Indicator	1996	1997	1998	1999	2000	2001	2002	2003	2004	2005	2006
Deposits of individual(s) and other legal entities in national currency (end of period)											
Million soms	483.9	894.5	947.9	1,212.8	1,175.6	1,068.5	1,385.9	1,823.5	2,460.9	3,539.7	5,771.2
% of GDP	2.1	2.9	2.8	2.5	1.8	1.4	1.8	2.2	2.6	3.5	5.1
Deposits of individual(s) and other legal entities in foreign currency (end of period)											
Million soms	390.7	643.3	1,173.8	1,418.1	1,617.6	1,526.9	2,256.4	3,195.2	5,745.0	9,512.4	11,035.7
% of GDP	1.7	2.1	3.4	2.9	2.5	2.1	3.0	3.8	6.1	9.5	9.8
Total deposits											
Million soms	874.7	1,537.8	2,121.7	2,630.8	2,793.22	595.351	3,642.3	5,018.7	8,206.0	13,052.1	16,806.9
% of GDP	3.7	5.0	6.2	5.4	4.3	3.5	4.8	6.0	8.7	13.0	14.9
Banking credit to nonfinancial corporations and individuals in national currency (end of period)											
Million soms	250.1	453.0	479.5	439.0	457.2	654.2	847.3	1,127.4	1,723.9	2,207.1	3,469.0
% of GDP	1.1	1.5	1.4	0.9	0.7	0.9	1.1	1.3	1.8	2.2	3.1
Banking credit to nonfinancial corporations and individuals in foreign currency (end of period)											
Million soms	157.1	470.1	1,235.9	982.7	998.3	863.3	1,164.1	1,767.1	4,081.5	5,505.0	7,881.3
% of GDP	0.7	1.5	3.6	2.0	1.5	1.2	1.5	2.1	4.3	5.5	7.0
Total banking credit to nonfinancial corporations and individuals (end of period)											
Million soms	407.2	923.1	1,715.3	1,421.7	1,455.6	1,517.4	2,011.4	2,894.6	5,805.3	7,712.2	11,350.3
% of GDP	1.7	3.0	5.0	2.9	2.2	2.1	2.7	3.5	6.2	7.7	10.0
NBFI credits to nonfinancial corporations and individuals (end of period)											
Million soms	—	—	—	—	—	874.0	1,256.8	2,010.1	2,772.0	3,922.2	4,817.7
% of GDP	—	—	—	—	—	1.3	1.8	2.6	3.2	4.2	4.6
Weighted average interest rate on new time deposits (percent)											
National currency	35.0	36.9	37.8	38.4	26.6	16.6	11.5	8.7	8.3	9.4	6.6
Foreign currency	—	—	—	—	7.5	5.8	5.5	3.6	4.3	3.1	5.3
Weighted average interest rate on new banking credits (percent)											
National currency	58.3	49.9	42.5	54.8	50.1	36.4	30.2	25.1	24.6	25.4	25.6
Foreign currency	31.2	34.7	26.5	32.3	31.4	25.0	22.6	19.2	18.9	16.8	17.3
Kyrgyz Agricultural Financial Corporation weighted average interest rate in national currency (%)	—	—	—	—	—	27.4	21.3	17.3	17.0	15.8	14.2
Bank deposits per 1,000 people	—	—	—	—	21.5	19.1	24.6	31.3	34.6	44.8	—

Sources: NBKR and NSC.
— Not available.

FIGURE B.1. Mean and Median Size of Transfer, by Country and Mode of Transfer, 2000–06

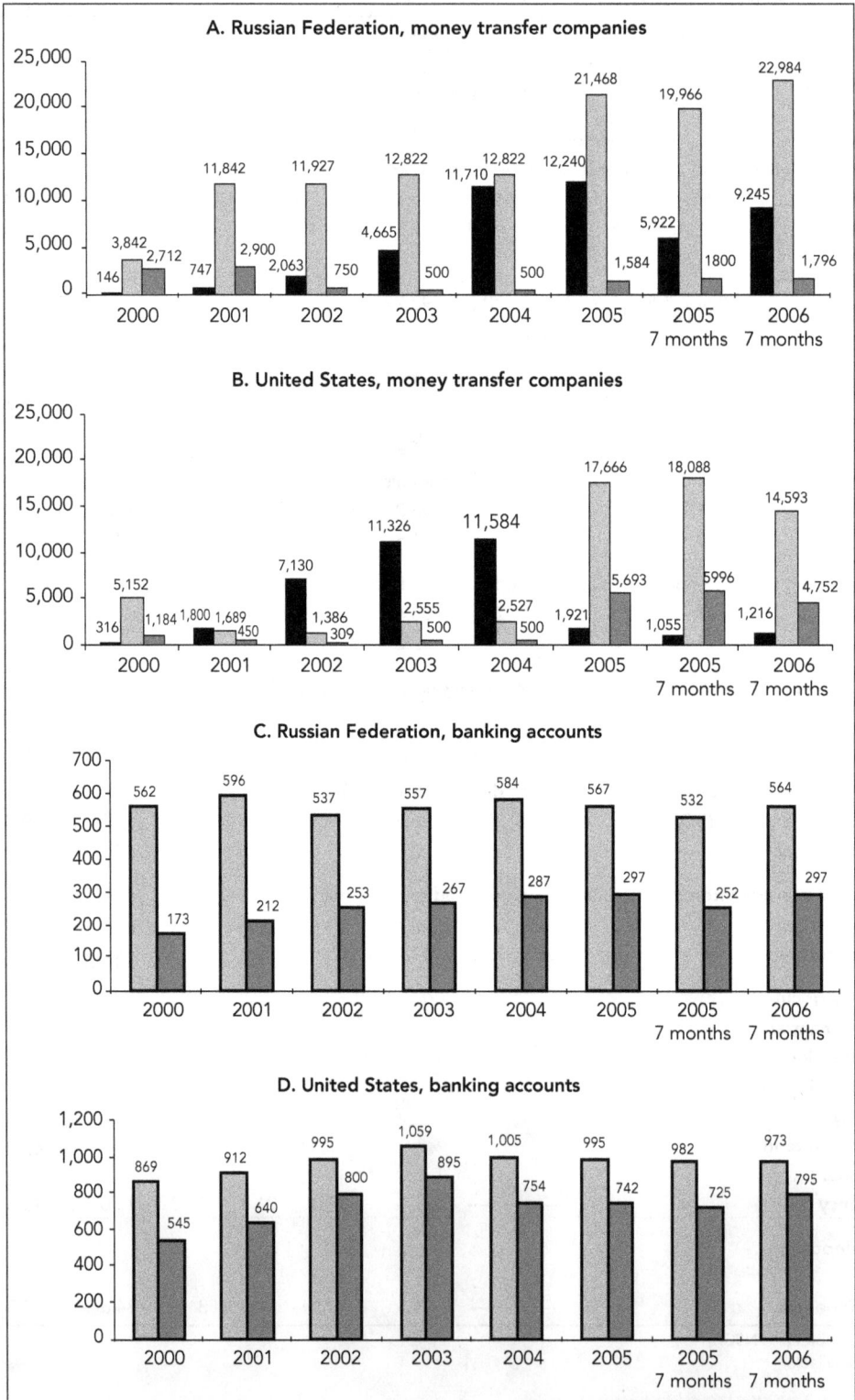

A. Russian Federation, money transfer companies

B. United States, money transfer companies

C. Russian Federation, banking accounts

D. United States, banking accounts

Sources: NBKR and authors' calculations.

FIGURE B.2. Cross-Correlograms of Remittances and Key Macroeconomic Variables

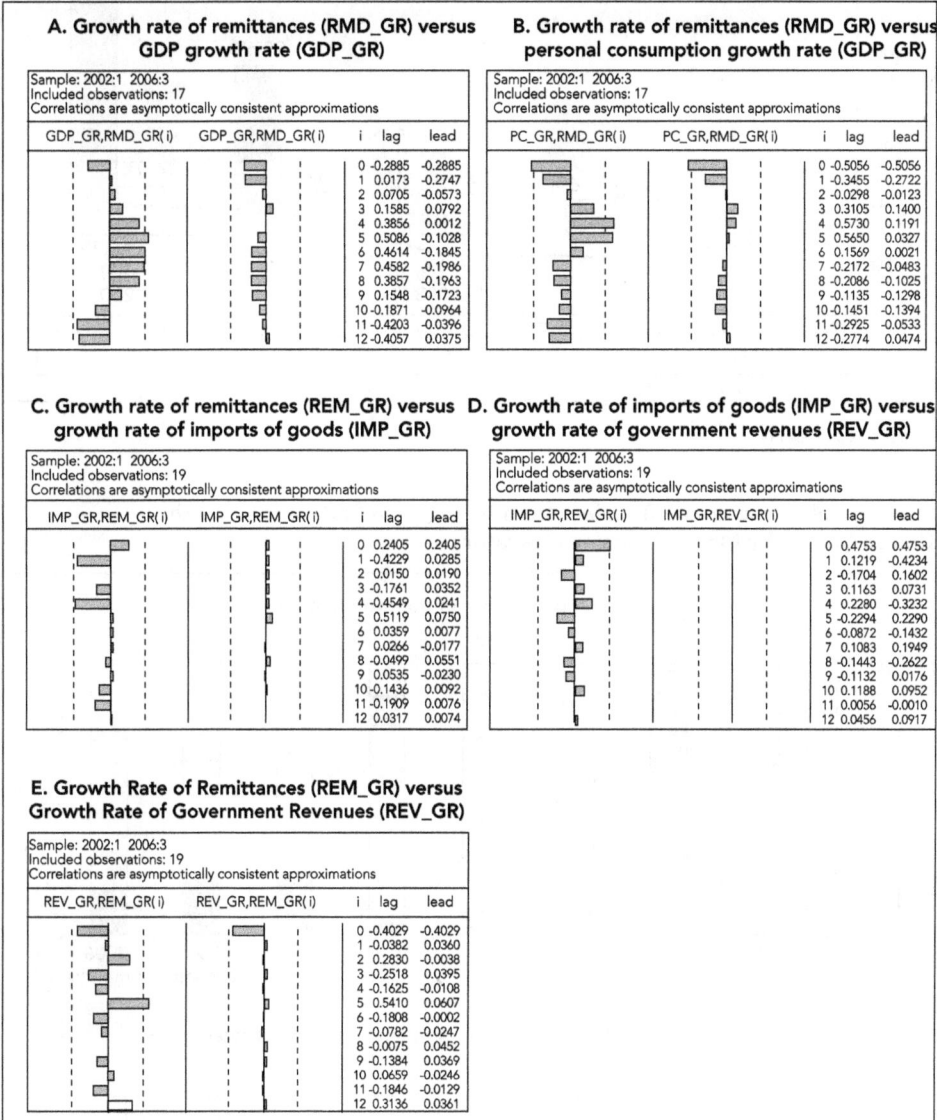

A. Growth rate of remittances (RMD_GR) versus GDP growth rate (GDP_GR)

Sample: 2002:1 2006:3
Included observations: 17
Correlations are asymptotically consistent approximations

GDP_GR,RMD_GR(i)	GDP_GR,RMD_GR(i)	i	lag	lead
		0	-0.2885	-0.2885
		1	0.0173	-0.2747
		2	0.0705	-0.0573
		3	0.1585	0.0792
		4	0.3856	0.0012
		5	0.5086	-0.1028
		6	0.4614	-0.1845
		7	0.4582	-0.1986
		8	0.3857	-0.1963
		9	0.1548	-0.1723
		10	-0.1871	-0.0964
		11	-0.4203	-0.0396
		12	-0.4057	0.0375

B. Growth rate of remittances (RMD_GR) versus personal consumption growth rate (GDP_GR)

Sample: 2002:1 2006:3
Included observations: 17
Correlations are asymptotically consistent approximations

PC_GR,RMD_GR(i)	PC_GR,RMD_GR(i)	i	lag	lead
		0	-0.5056	-0.5056
		1	-0.3455	-0.2722
		2	-0.0298	-0.0123
		3	0.3105	0.1400
		4	0.5730	0.1191
		5	0.5650	0.0327
		6	0.1569	0.0021
		7	-0.2172	-0.0483
		8	-0.2086	-0.1025
		9	-0.1135	-0.1298
		10	-0.1451	-0.1394
		11	-0.2925	-0.0533
		12	-0.2774	0.0474

C. Growth rate of remittances (REM_GR) versus growth rate of imports of goods (IMP_GR)

Sample: 2002:1 2006:3
Included observations: 19
Correlations are asymptotically consistent approximations

IMP_GR,REM_GR(i)	IMP_GR,REM_GR(i)	i	lag	lead
		0	0.2405	0.2405
		1	-0.4229	0.0285
		2	0.0150	0.0190
		3	-0.1761	0.0352
		4	-0.4549	0.0241
		5	0.5119	0.0750
		6	0.0359	0.0077
		7	0.0266	-0.0177
		8	-0.0499	0.0551
		9	0.0535	-0.0230
		10	-0.1436	0.0092
		11	-0.1909	0.0076
		12	0.0317	0.0074

D. Growth rate of imports of goods (IMP_GR) versus growth rate of government revenues (REV_GR)

Sample: 2002:1 2006:3
Included observations: 19
Correlations are asymptotically consistent approximations

IMP_GR,REV_GR(i)	IMP_GR,REV_GR(i)	i	lag	lead
		0	0.4753	0.4753
		1	0.1219	-0.4234
		2	-0.1704	0.1602
		3	0.1163	0.0731
		4	0.2280	-0.3232
		5	-0.2294	0.2290
		6	-0.0872	-0.1432
		7	0.1083	0.1949
		8	-0.1443	-0.2622
		9	-0.1132	0.0176
		10	0.1188	0.0952
		11	0.0056	-0.0010
		12	0.0456	0.0917

E. Growth Rate of Remittances (REM_GR) versus Growth Rate of Government Revenues (REV_GR)

Sample: 2002:1 2006:3
Included observations: 19
Correlations are asymptotically consistent approximations

REV_GR,REM_GR(i)	REV_GR,REM_GR(i)	i	lag	lead
		0	-0.4029	-0.4029
		1	-0.0382	0.0360
		2	0.2830	-0.0038
		3	-0.2518	0.0395
		4	-0.1625	-0.0108
		5	0.5410	0.0607
		6	-0.1808	-0.0002
		7	-0.0782	-0.0247
		8	-0.0075	0.0452
		9	-0.1384	0.0369
		10	0.0659	-0.0246
		11	-0.1846	-0.0129
		12	0.3136	0.0361

Sources: NBKR, NSC, and authors' calculations.

FIGURE B.3. Remittances and Investments in Fixed Capital, 2001–05

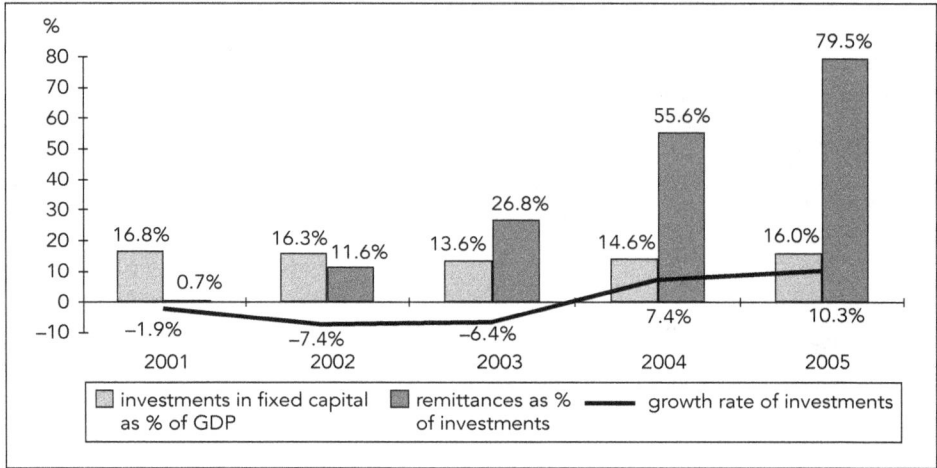

Sources: NBKR and NSC.

FIGURE B.4. Structure of Transfers from the Russian Federation and the United States, by Money Transfer Operator

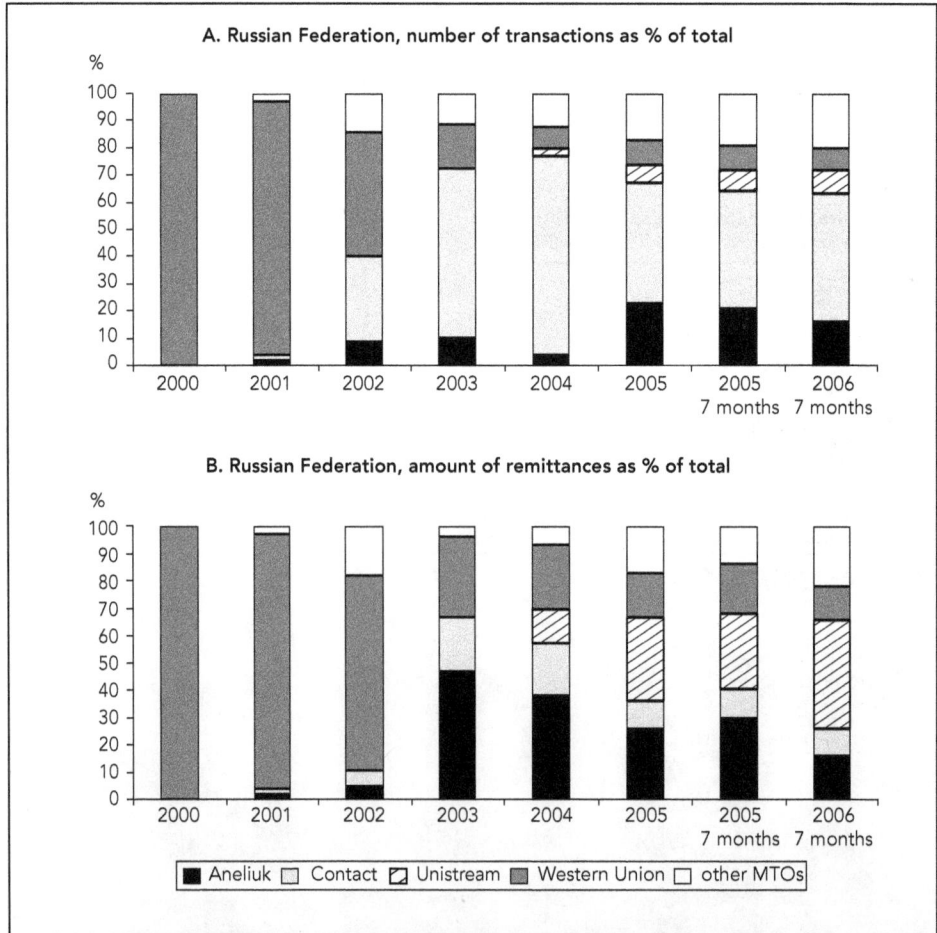

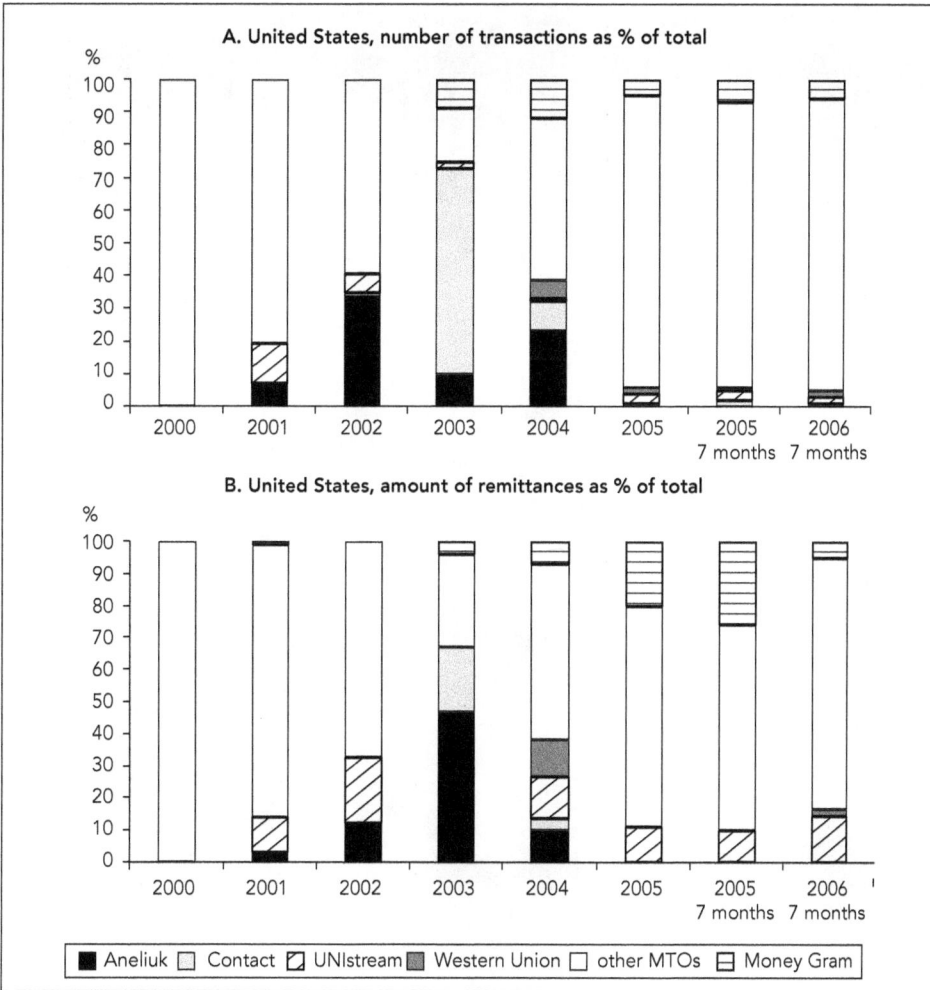

A. United States, number of transactions as % of total

B. United States, amount of remittances as % of total

Aneliuk ☐ Contact ▨ UNIstream ▦ Western Union ☐ other MTOs ⊟ Money Gram

Source: NBKR.

Part V:
Africa—Rethinking Growth and Regional Integration

Spatial Development Patterns and Policy Responses: A South African Case Study

HASSEN MOHAMED

Regional disparities are characteristic of all economies. South Africa is no exception. Like all countries, the subnational regional patterns of development have evolved historically and culturally over a long period of time. Two main processes have shaped South Africa's space economy.

At one level the space economy is a product of historical patterns of growth and preexisting geographic differences such as natural, locational, and community endowments. However, and significantly, South Africa's spatial configuration is also the product of apartheid spatial planning, which appropriated land, wealth, and opportunities for the benefit of a minority. Black people were turned into "unfree" cheap labor on white-owned farms, a trend that continued until and beyond the discovery of diamonds and gold in 1867 and 1886, respectively, in the former Transvaal—the hinterland—which became the launching pad for South Africa's industrialization. The apartheid policy consolidated the dispossession and subjugation of black people, Balkanizing the country into ethnically based homelands where black people were forced to live away from economic activity of any significance. The economically important and dynamic parts were designated as white South Africa. Black people were only useful in white South Africa as cheap labor, in particular in the gold and diamond mines. At a micro level apartheid spatial policy was reinforced particularly in the planning of human settlements, where black townships were located farthest from areas of economic activity, and significant investment was directed only to areas where white people lived. South Africa's uneven spatial development must be understood as the result of a brutal and oppressive system of land dispossession of black people by white settlers spurred on by a deliberate policy of apartheid and historical dynamics and patterns of growth. The confluence of these processes left the post-apartheid democratic state with a terrible legacy of huge spatial disparities in income and welfare.

Hassen Mohamed is Chief Director of the Planning, Policy Coordination and Advisory Unit for The Presidency in South Africa.

Berlin Workshop Series 2009

South Africa's Space Economy

On a macro scale the polarized nature of the South African space economy finds expression in two clearly distinguishable sets of spatial arrangements and patterns of economic activity: concentrated areas of high economic activity, with high population densities and high levels of poverty, and areas where economic activities are at a low ebb, also with high population densities and high levels of poverty.

The core of South Africa's space economy is made up of 26 areas.[1] These, together with their immediate hinterlands (within a 60-kilometer-proximity radius), make up 31 percent of the land surface, but account for 84 percent of the population, 77 percent of the poor,[2] and almost 96 percent of national income (see table 1). Hence the policy objectives of promoting sustainable economic growth and attacking poverty operate largely in the same space.

TABLE 1. Economic Indicators in South Africa, by Economic Area

Area	National population	People under minimum living level	National gross value added (rand)	Land surface (hectares)
26 economic core areas				
Number	29.3 million	12.5 million	940 billion	12.7 million
Percent	62.62	53.21	77.04	27.15
Areas of economic significance extended into an accessibility radius of 60 kilometers[a]				
Number	39.6 million	18.2 million	1.167 billion	38 million
Percent	84.46	77.31	95.59	31.24

Source: Presidency, Republic of South Africa (2006).
[a] In which R1 billion of gross value added is generated annually.

One of the abiding legacies of the apartheid system of separate homelands (the despised Bantustan system) is the high concentration of people living in extreme poverty in barren backwaters. Some 1.9 million people (or 4 percent of the national population) and about 1.5 million (or 6.5 percent of the total number living below the minimum living level) are concentrated in dense settlements in areas with an extremely frail and underdeveloped economic base.[3] Average per capita annual income is at about R2,374 (US$330) or approximately 9 percent of the national average. There is 1 employed person for every 10 people on average. Economic activity is largely survivalist, and state transfers and grants are the main source of income. Outmigration toward towns and cities particularly of the young and economically active exacerbate their vulnerability and marginality. Of the 47 district municipalities, 34 (or 72 percent) mainly rural districts experienced net outmigration to the major metropolitan centers and secondary towns and cities (Presidency, Republic of South Africa 2006). Quite clearly these areas have substantial thresholds to overcome and, as a result, continue to lag behind the established core economic regions.

Research into the spatial structure of economic growth in South Africa reveals that existing patterns of growth reflect a structure that has been in existence since the early twentieth century (McCarthy 2000), and convergence is not much in evidence. This seems to support the argument that convergence between developed and undeveloped regions takes a long time, and regions and countries with unequal spatial economies, such as South Africa, converge at a very slow pace (if at all).

Policy Response: The National Spatial Development Perspective

The stark social and economic dualism and unevenness of the national space economy prompted the South African government to confront a fundamental question: what kind of spatial arrangements will enable the country to bring about democratic nation building, address poverty and inequality, and promote sustainable growth?

Given the uneven pattern of social and economic development, how should policy interventions impinge on spatial disparities? Specifically, the following questions arise:

- Are infrastructure investments in areas with low economic potential effective in reducing poverty?

- What types of investments are effective in areas with poor natural resources and economic potential?

- What kinds of areas afford the poor greater protection against the deleterious effects of economic shocks and ability to diversify income sources?

- Is the aggregate impact on poverty reduction greater by focusing on areas with high poverty rates or high poverty densities?

- Is it possible in all circumstances to locate jobs where people reside, or does it make more sense to link people to areas with job opportunities?

How these questions are answered may lead to different policy responses and approaches. Some (in the name of so-called balanced development) misguidedly call for the redirection of public investment from the economically dominant regions to the lagging regions. South Africa, however, has taken a distinctive approach to dealing with the massive spatial disparities based on its unique history and context.

Given South Africa's uneven pattern of spatial development, in 2003 the government adopted the National Spatial Development Perspective (NSDP) as a principle-based overarching framework to contribute to government's broader growth and development objectives.[4] The NSDP arose as an initiative to improve the coordination of government infrastructure spending and ensure that the investments in infrastructure and development programs achieve better spatial outcomes. Given the objectives to stimulate the economy, create jobs, address poverty, and promote social cohesion, the NSDP enables government to confront three fundamental planning questions:

- Where should government direct its investment and development initiatives to ensure sustainable, maximum social and economic impact?

- What kinds of spatial forms and arrangements are conducive to achieving the objectives of democratic nation building and social and economic inclusion?

- What is the best way to capitalize on complementarities and facilitate consistent decision making within government and achieve coordinated and integrated action?

In order to respond to these questions, contribute to the broader growth and development policy objectives of the South African government, and respond to the disparate spatial contexts, the NSDP puts forward a set of five normative principles to guide government infrastructure investment and social spending (Presidency, Republic of South Africa 2006):

- *Principle 1.* Rapid economic growth that is sustained and inclusive is a prerequisite for the achievement of other policy objectives, among which poverty alleviation is key.

- *Principle 2.* Government has a constitutional obligation to provide basic services to all citizens (water, sanitation, energy, health, and educational facilities) wherever they reside.

- *Principle 3.* Beyond the constitutional obligation identified in principle 2, government spending on fixed investment should be focused on localities of economic growth and economic potential in order to gear up private sector investment, stimulate sustainable economic activities, and create long-term employment opportunities.

- *Principle 4.* Efforts to address past and current social inequalities should focus on people, not places. In localities where there are both high levels of poverty and demonstrated economic potential, this could include fixed capital investment beyond basic services to exploit the potential of those localities. In localities with low demonstrated economic potential, government should, beyond the provision of basic services, concentrate primarily on developing human capital by providing social transfers such as grants, education and training, and poverty relief programs and on reducing migration costs by providing labor market intelligence so as to give people better information, opportunities, and capabilities to enable them to gravitate, if they choose, to localities that are more likely to provide sustainable employment and economic opportunities. Moreover, sound rural development planning, aggressive land and agrarian reform, and expansion of agricultural extension services should serve as the bedrock of sustainable rural development.

- *Principle 5.* In order to overcome the spatial distortions of apartheid, future opportunities for settlement and economic development should be channeled into activity corridors and nodes that are adjacent to or link the main growth centers. Infrastructure investment should primarily support localities that will become major growth nodes in South Africa and the South African Development Community (SADC) region to create regional gateways to the global economy.

From the preceding discussion on South Africa's spatial economy, it is strikingly evident that the focus on people and on localities with demonstrated economic potential is far from narrow. Unlike in many other developing countries, in South Africa the analysis reveals that economic potential and large concentrations of poverty often coincide. Thus the policy objectives of promoting broad-based economic growth and addressing poverty operate largely in the same geographic spaces.

This is not to ignore the existence of spatial poverty traps in parts of the country where households are marginalized from economic activities (circled areas in figure 2). In areas where economic development is at a very low ebb and prospects for sustaining livelihoods well into the future appear slim, the NSDP advocates improvements in the "aspatial aspects" (particularly human capital) and a focus on redistributive intervention mechanisms to increase productivity of households' own income (see principle 4).

In generating the principles, the NSDP has been informed by international theory and domestic and international case studies showing the following:

- Unfocused infrastructure spending does not necessarily result in improved gross domestic product (GDP) growth.

- Unfocused human resources development does not improve GDP growth.

- Regions that already have some economic success are more likely to grow than other regions because successful regions have individuals, firms, and industries with the wherewithal to learn from concrete experience.

- Successful learning occurs when institutions and incentives work and institutions are locally specific.

- Success is often achieved through focused, polarized investment.

- Redirecting public investment from economically dominant regions to lagging regions has not automatically spurred economic activity in lagging regions.

In terms of poverty eradication, the NSDP advocates the view that poverty is not necessarily best addressed where it manifests itself. Ellis and Harris (2004) argue, "The poor benefit when they have more options to which to turn, and more options are created in the vortex of dynamic growth processes, not in the declining sectors that are left behind." From a spatial point of view, local as well as international studies (Kanbur and Venables 2003) have shown that the impact on poverty depends crucially on the proximity of poor households to centers of economic activity and the extent to which these households are connected to such economic activities.

The NSDP argues that the following conditions are critical in order to turn the tide against poverty (Presidency, Republic of South Africa 2006):

- Location is critical for the poor to exploit growth opportunities.

- The poor who are concentrated around economic centers have greater opportunity to gain from economic growth.

- Areas with demonstrated economic potential provide greater livelihood and income protection because of a greater diversity of income sources.

- Areas with demonstrated economic potential are most favorable for overcoming poverty.

- The poor make rational choices about relocating to areas with greater economic opportunities.

- Government has to ensure that policies and programs are in place to ensure that the poor are able to benefit fully from growth and development opportunities in such areas, including easing the transaction costs of migration for poor families.

The NSDP and Regional Development

In line with current thinking about regions as the critical foundations of development processes, the NSDP argues that, while macroeconomic considerations are important, development ultimately is strongly shaped by processes on the ground in the specific 26 core economic regions.

Successful regions are the building blocks of economic development and innovation, and the health of the national economy depends on the growth potential of these regions and their ability to compete nationally and internationally.

Regions are not uniformly good at everything and have unique trajectories, strengths, and weaknesses. The logic underpinning the NSDP principles for regional development can be summarized as follows:

- Dynamic qualities of areas are developed historically and culturally over a long period of time.

- Subnational regions are not uniformly good at everything, and it is not possible for social and economic development and potential to be distributed evenly across geographic space.

- Different regions have different economic potential, and the spatial variations in the incidence of poverty are vastly different.

- The policy response itself should be differentiated and should correspond to the specificity of the different subnational contexts.

Conclusions

In the South African context, a national spatial perspective is invoked as the crucial instrument to support the development of regions through the coordination of policies and programs according to set principles and guidelines.

To give effect to the principles of the NSDP, government has adopted a subnational approach (a decentralized regional development approach) to tackling poverty and promoting growth. Recognizing the importance of regions in economic development and the insufficiency of national efforts alone, government has designated district and metropolitan municipalities together with provincial governments as the pivotal sites for facilitating coordinated planning and action drawing together state and other actors in a process of joint decision making and collaborative action.

References

Ellis, Frank, and Nigel Harris. 2004. "New Thinking about Urban and Rural Development." Keynote paper delivered at the Department for International Development Sustainable Development Retreat, University of Surrey, July.

Kanbur, Ravi, and Anthony J. Venables, eds. 2003. *Spatial Inequality and Development.* Oxford: Oxford University Press.

McCarthy, Jeff. 2000. "The Changing Spatial Structure of Economic Growth in South Africa Over 50 Years." A research paper prepared for The Presidency, South Africa, January. http://www.idp.org.za/NSDP/documents/mccarthy%20final.pdf.

Presidency, Republic of South Africa. 2006. *National Spatial Development Perspective.* Pretoria: Presidency of the Republic of South Africa.

Notes

1. A map of South Africa's space economy is available at the following link: http://www.thepresidency.gov.za/main.asp?include=docs/pcsa/planning/nsdp/main.html.
2. As measured by the minimum living level measure, which is defined as the minimum monthly income needed to sustain a household and varies according to household size. The larger the household, the larger the income required to keep its members out of poverty. Minimum living level includes food, clothing, payments to municipalities in respect of rent, utilities, washing and cleaning, education, transport, contribution to medical and dental expenses, replacement of household equipment, and support of relatives.
3. A poverty map of South Africa is available at the following link: http://www.thepresidency. gov.za/main.asp?include=docs/pcsa/planning/nsdp/main.html.
4. The full version of the NSDP is available on www.thepresidency.gov.za/publications.

Geography and Regional Cooperation in Africa

WIM NAUDÉ

Africa's relatively poor economic performance remains a cause for concern. In a comprehensive recent review of this performance, Ndulu and others (2007a) describe four "policy syndromes" as central to Africa's problems: state controls, adverse redistribution, intertemporally unsustainable spending, and state breakdown.

This paper departs from this view by positing that, in addition to these policy syndromes, "geographic syndromes" are also central to Africa's poor economic performance. Two elements of this are a "proximity gap" (the cumulative result of long distances to markets, being landlocked, and suboptimal patterns of agglomeration) and a "health gap" (the result of tropical diseases and adverse climatic and soil conditions). This paper focuses on Africa's "proximity gap," conveying the message that much can be done to reduce it, particularly through regional cooperation.

Proximity and African Development

Productivity in Africa is low because of insufficient proximity between economic agents. This has two dimensions: a lack of proximity (a) between African countries and international markets and (b) between economic agents within Africa due to insufficient agglomeration (Naudé and Krugell 2006; Venables 2006). Low productivity limits industrialization and urbanization.

Africa's lack of proximity is due to adverse geography (Naudé 2004). First-nature geography limits development through geographic isolation, a disease bur-

Wim Naudé is a Senior Research Fellow at UNUWIDER in Finland.

Berlin Workshop Series 2009

© 2009 The International Bank for Reconstruction and Development/The World Bank

An earlier version of this paper was presented at the International Policy Workshop on Spatial Disparities and Development Policy in Preparation of the World Development Report 2009, Berlin, Germany, October 2, 2007. The author is grateful to the participants for their constructive comments. An extended version of this paper is available as a World Institute for Development Economics Research of the United Nations University discussion paper at http://www.wider.unu.edu/publications/working-papers/discussion-papers/2007/en–GB/dp2007-03/.

den due to its largely tropical location, scarcity of large, navigable rivers, lack of alluvial plains, high rates of evaporation, a "curse" of abundant natural mineral resources (Sachs and Warner 2001; Sachs and others 2004), and the North-South orientation of the continent, which has made technological transfers, especially in agriculture, difficult (Diamond 1997).

Second-nature geography, reflected in the large number of landlocked countries in Africa, increases proximity in three ways. First, the distance to international markets is great and entails the need to cross a large number of borders (Ndulu and others 2007b). Second, small internal markets cannot easily gain from specialization. Third, landlocked countries often have neighboring countries that are economically poorly performing, in conflict, or both (Collier 2006a). This creates a proximity gap by reducing interactions among economic agents across countries. Consequently, the positive spatial spillover effects of growth are low in Africa (Collier and O'Connell 2007).

This geography makes investment more expensive in Africa than elsewhere (Ndulu and others 2007b). It increases transport costs through distance (Martínez-Zarzoso, García-Menéndez, and Suárez-Burguet 2003), being landlocked (Hausmann 2001), and the inability to reap economies of scale (Naudé and Matthee 2007).

Regional Cooperation and the Proximity Gap

Overcoming the proximity gap may require a "big push" in infrastructure (United Nations Millennium Project 2005). Due to the cross-border nature of such infrastructure, regional cooperation is important. Reducing the proximity gap requires at least four longer-term issues to be prioritized in regional cooperation: transport infrastructure, trade facilitation, decentralization or local economic development, and migration.

Transport Infrastructure

Transport infrastructure is subject to network effects, threshold effects, and compatibility requirements that necessitate regional coordination. Despite these, cooperation might not be simple because the incentives to cooperate are asymmetrical. This is because, first, for transport infrastructure connecting the interior with the coast, the benefits are often smaller for the coastal country than for the landlocked country. Two, customs officials may have a negative attitude toward transit trade because it does not imply revenue (Zanamwe 2005). Three, transit trade creates risks for transit countries because transit goods may be diverted into them. Guarantees required for such trade are thus high and often cannot be met due to the poor development of banking and insurance (Zanamwe 2005).

Given that the incentives for coordination are not symmetrical, there is the danger that commitments in regional trade agreements will not be credible—that is, they will be exacerbated by a lack of third-party enforcement. Thus a call may be made for transport infrastructure to be included in World Trade Organization (WTO) binding rules on trade facilitation.

Additional measures to improve the incentives for cooperation could include the design of transport corridors to maximize the mutual advantages of countries—for instance, by fast-tracking transit trade—and for landlocked countries to apply peer pressure collectively on their neighbors (Collier 2006b).

Trade Facilitation

In trade facilitation, African countries should have three explicit aims: to ensure (a) appropriate physical infrastructure and facilities for the movement of goods, (b) the harmonization and effectiveness of customs procedures, and (c) the upgrading of information and communication technology (Zanamwe 2005).

Countries should also use the opportunities afforded within the WTO negotiations concerning global rules on trade facilitation. The current negotiations are limited to issues of transparency and the administration of trade regulations. African priorities thus may not be reflected in these negotiations (Zanamwe 2005). However, African countries should commit to broad and binding rules on trade facilitation and link these to foreign aid (in technical assistance, capacity building, and infrastructure investment).

Decentralization and Local Economic Development

It is not only international transport infrastructure and costs that matter, but also domestic infrastructure and costs (Elbadawi, Mengistae, and Zeufack 2006). The development of these will benefit from fiscal decentralization and an emphasis on local economic development, which should include the promotion of investment and the marketing of localities. When local politicians are required to improve the attractiveness of their localities to investors, they become aware of shortcomings in transport and related infrastructure.

A precondition for the role of local authorities in local economic development is to deepen local democracy and strengthen local government capacity (Jansen van Rensburg and Naudé 2007). Decentralization and local economic development should be on the regional cooperation agenda: local communities can better use benefits of cross-country infrastructure if they are involved in the planning and implementation thereof.

Migration

Because Africa's population is concentrated in landlocked countries (40 percent) and these face geographic constraints, migration will continue. Without migration, the costs of adverse geography are borne disproportionately by labor (Venables 2006). Migration is not exclusive to Africa: on a global scale, populations are moving from poor inland regions toward the coast (Venables 2006). Climate change and growing productivity in African urban areas may further encourage this migration (Stern 2006).

Facilitating migration and explicitly recognizing the greater overall efficiency of the resulting distribution of the African labor force should be high on the regional agenda.

The Role of the International Community

Regional cooperation could be supported by the international community in at least four ways. The first is by according higher levels of foreign aid, including nonfinancial aid such as technical assistance, and by linking aid with commitments to binding rules on trade facilitation. Nonfinancial aid and security guarantees will be more credible if transport infrastructure is improved (Collier 2006a). Funding for infrastructure should also be accompanied by measures to reduce the potential for corruption in infrastructure construction (Collier 2006a).

The second is by ensuring adherence to international laws on the rights of landlocked countries to have access to the sea (Zanamwe 2005). The third is by extending trade preferences to African countries. According to Collier and Venables (2007), African countries need to overcome a threshold effect if they are to become a location for international production. An additional case made here is that the investments required in transport infrastructure in Africa need to be supported by higher volumes of trade, which trade preferences can help to establish. Trade preferences may even be in the interest of developed countries, which are likely to be involved in the financing of bulk infrastructure. However, care must be taken to design these preferences so as not to undermine the ability of African countries to diversify their exports (Gamberoni 2007).

The fourth is by ensuring consistency of the currently negotiated Economic Partnership Agreements and regional integration efforts (such as the South African Development Community Free Trade Area, which commenced in 2008). By the time of writing, accusations were leveled that Economic Partnership Agreements were undermining regional integration in Africa.

The question of Africa's relationship with Asia, and in particular China, is crucial for its development. Too often the position is that the European Union (EU) is Africa's main market and that Africa merely competes against Asia there. Asia should not be considered a mere competitor with Africa. It is an important market in itself for African goods (Zafar 2007).

Concluding Remarks

Greater spatial inequalities may result as Africa achieves economies of scale and specialization in manufacturing and reaps the benefits of growing cities. Similar processes are playing out in China. As long as these spatial inequalities are accompanied by the migration of the population to denser, richer areas, they could be seen as an important route for closing the global spatial disparities between Africa and the rest of the world.

References

Collier, Paul. 2006a. "African Growth: Why a 'Big Push'?" *Journal of African Economies* (AERC supplement 2): 188–211.

———. 2006b. "Assisting Africa to Achieve Decisive Change." Centre for the Study of African Economies, Oxford University, Oxford.

Collier, Paul, and Stephen O'Connell. 2007. "African Economic Growth: Opportunities and Choices." In *The Political Economy of African Economic Growth 1960–2000*, ed. Benno Ndulu, Robert Bates, Paul Collier, and Stephen O'Connell. Cambridge, U.K.: Cambridge University Press.

Collier, Paul, and Anthony J. Venables. 2007. "Rethinking Trade Preferences: How Africa Can Diversify Its Exports." *World Economy* 30 (8): 1326–45.

Diamond, Jared. 1997. *Guns, Germs, and Steel: The Fates of Human Societies*. New York: W.W. Norton.

Elbadawi, Ibrahim, Taye Mengistae, and Albert Zeufack. 2006. "Market Access, Supplier Access, and Africa's Manufactured Exports: A Firm-Level Analysis." *Journal of International Trade and Economic Development* 15 (4): 493–523.

Gamberoni, Elisa. 2007. "Do Unilateral Trade Preferences Help Export Diversification?" HEI Working Paper 17/2007, Graduate Institute of International Studies, Geneva.

Hausmann, Ricardo. 2001. "Prisoners of Geography." *Foreign Policy* 122 (January): 44–53.

Jansen van Rensburg, Linda, and Wim A. Naudé. 2007. "Human Rights and Development: The Case of Local Government Transformation in South Africa." *Public Administration and Development* 27 (5): 393–412.

Martínez-Zarzoso, Inmaculada, Leandro García-Menéndez, and Celestino Suárez-Burguet. 2003. "Impact of Transport Costs on International Trade: The Case of Spanish Ceramic Exports." *Maritime Economics and Logistics* 5 (2): 179–98.

Naudé, Wim A. 2004. "The Effects of Policy, Institutions, and Geography on Economic Growth in Africa: An Econometric Study Based on Cross-Section and Panel Data." *Journal of International Development* 16 (6): 821–49.

Naudé, Wim A., and Willem F. Krugell. 2006. "Economic Geography and Growth in Africa: The Case of Sub-National Convergence and Divergence in South-Africa." *Papers in Regional Science* 85 (3, August): 443–57.

Naudé, Wim A., and Marianne Matthee. 2007. "The Significance of Transport Costs in Africa." UNU Policy Brief 6/2007, United Nations University, Tokyo.

Ndulu, Benno, Robert Bates, Paul Collier, and Stephen O'Connell. 2007a. *The Political Economy of African Economic Growth 1960–2000*. Cambridge, U.K.: Cambridge University Press.

Ndulu, Benno J., Lopamudra Chakraborti, Lebohang Lijane, Vijaya Ramachandran, and Jerome Wolgin. 2007b. *Challenges of African Growth: Opportunities, Constraints, and Strategic Directions*. Washington, DC: World Bank.

Sachs, Jeffrey D., John M. McArthur, Guido Schmidt-Traub, Margaret Kruk, Chandrika Bahadur, Michael Faye, and Gordon McCord. 2004. "Ending Africa's Poverty Trap." *Brookings Papers on Economic Activity* 1: 117–216.

Sachs, Jeffrey D., and Andrew M. Warner. 2001. "The Curse of Natural Resources." *European Economic Review* 45 (4-6): 827–38.

Stern, Nicholas. 2006. *The Economics of Climate Change [The Stern Report]*. Cambridge, U.K.: Cambridge University Press.

United Nations Millennium Project. 2005. *Investing in Development: A Practical Plan to Achieve the Millennium Development Goals; Overview*. London: Earthscan Publications. http://www.unmillenniumproject.org/reports/index–overview.htm.

Venables, Anthony J. 2006. "Shifts in Economic Geography and Their Causes." Paper presented at the Federal Reserve Bank of Kansas City's Symposium on the New Economic Geography, Jackson Hole, WY, August 24.

Zafar, Ali. 2007. "The Growing Relationship between China and Sub-Saharan Africa: Macroeconomic, Trade, Investment, and Aid Links." *World Bank Research Observer* 22 (1): 103–30.

Zanamwe, Gainmore. 2005. "Trade Facilitation and the WTO: A Critical Analysis of Proposals on Trade Facilitation and Their Implications for African Countries." TRALAC Working Paper 5/2005, Trade Law Center for South Africa, Stellenbosch.

Part VI: Learning from Europe's Efforts at Integration and Convergence

The Role and Objectives of European Cohesion Policy

NICOLA DE MICHELIS

When looking at the rationale of a policy, it is crucial to start from the basics. In the case of European cohesion policy, these are defined in the treaty establishing the European Community. In Article 158, the treaty says that the European Community should aim to reduce disparities between the levels of development of the various regions and the backwardness of the least favored regions. In Article 159, the treaty says that, for European cohesion policy to function, other policies need to move in the same direction, notably, national policies and other European Community policies. This dimension is often forgotten in the debate on objectives, operation, and effectiveness.

These two articles summarize the main features of European cohesion policy and its rationale. First, the policy contributes to the integration of the European Union (EU). At the moment of the launch of the single-market project, it was recognized that opening capital, financial, and labor markets would have asymmetric impacts on different parts of the EU and that there would be winners and losers. Rather than counting on labor mobility as the only adjustment mechanism, it was decided to set up an accompanying investment-based instrument—that is, cohesion policy—to promote the full use of the capacity of regions to contribute to and benefit from creation of the single market.

From this stems the structural role of European cohesion policy. Contrary to widespread belief, European cohesion policy is not about compensating disadvantage, and it is not about revenue and income support; rather it is about ensuring that regions are able to unlock their underused potential. In this sense, the policy fulfills a very important allocative function by conditioning its support on targeting the financial resources made available on investments that support key growth-enhancing areas, administrative and institutional modernization, and networking and exchange of experience between local and regional actors. The policy pursues

Nicola de Michelis is Head of Unit, Development of Cohesion Policy for the European Commission in Brussels.

Berlin Workshop Series 2009
© 2009 The International Bank for Reconstruction and Development/The World Bank

this objective throughout the European Union, by modulating its financial support on the basis of the "ability to pay" of the actors concerned.

The second objective of European cohesion policy is to promote solidarity between the citizens of the EU and between the regions; resources are redistributed according to the relative wealth of the recipient member states and regions.

Finally, the policy promotes EU legitimacy by strengthening the support of European citizens for the EU by addressing their expectations of a rightful citizenship independent of where they live. Successive surveys have shown that European cohesion policy emerges as one of the only policies that are perceived locally as a guarantee that the EU will not favor one place over another and that it will operate as a balancing institution to reduce tensions between countries and regions.

The Organisation for Economic Co-operation and Development (OECD) has been arguing over the past few years that a new paradigm is emerging whereby public policies are shifting increasingly from sectoral to multisectoral, multidisciplinary approaches; from direct subsidies to the provision of public goods; and from central governance of those policies to multilevel governance systems.

European cohesion policy, in many respects, reflects most of this paradigm shift. It operates on the basis of place-based economic development strategies promoting integration of different sectors (such as infrastructure, services to enterprises, research and development, innovation, education, and skills upgrading) and areas (for example, between rural and urban areas). It has, over time, shifted its focus toward the environment in which firms and economic agents operate and away from direct aid to those agents, trying to reduce the perverse dependence on public aid that certain regions may have had in the past. And it is operated through a system of multilevel governance based on a "contract" between the European Community, the national, and the regional levels.

This latter dimension is particularly important and deserves a few additional words. It is important because European cohesion policy allows addressing effectively issues of information incompleteness and heterogeneity of preferences, which are typical of any public intervention. Member states or nations in general have the resources, but they often lack the knowledge of local and regional assets and therefore lack the capacity to target investment. Regions do have that knowledge but often lack the strategic vision. And both regional and national governments lack the knowledge of the private sector in deciding where to locate investment.

The question is not whether multilevel governance is important, but how it needs to be implemented.

Some aspects of the policy obviously need and can be improved to avoid, for example, having resources be captured by local interests and diverted toward objectives other than those pursued by the policy. Another difficult problem that the policy faces and for which it is often criticized is related to the difficulty of properly assessing its impact. Investment supported by European cohesion policy is influenced by many other variables, such as the overall macroeconomic framework, the functioning of financial and labor markets, the quality of the public administration, and the operation of the other national and regional investment policies that sometimes operate in a different direction from European cohesion policy. While these are problems that most public policies face, it is clear that more needs to be done, whether by clarifying the objectives of the policy, by developing new, more solid statistics and indicators, or by improving the contracting arrangements between the different levels of government involved.

Nonetheless, European cohesion policy remains the only continent-wide experiment of a place-based public investment policy, with strong conditionality, to which 27 countries have agreed to participate.

European cohesion policy in this respect provides a very interesting case study for other countries outside the EU to study how these contractual mechanisms between different levels of government could be put in place.

Its implementation is governed by a series of key principles that have changed and modernized the functioning of public decision making and policy design. It is based on the principle of partnership, whereby all the actors—vertically and horizontally—need to discuss and agree ex ante what sort of strategies and investments need to be pursued. It has improved the evaluation of public policies in all member states of the EU. While evaluation can and should be improved in all member states, evaluation has become part and parcel of public policy design through ex ante evaluations during the programming period, with feedback mechanisms that allow governments to adapt the policy and reorient its direction, and ex post evaluations. It is based on multiannual programming, moving away from a project-based approach to a system whereby resources are made available for a seven-year period on the condition that an overall development strategy is agreed by the EU, national, and subnational levels. It is not a blank check. Countries are obliged to cofinance investment so as to ensure accountability and ownership. The principle of additionality is respected. This principle states that the money coming from the European budget does not replace public resources, but is additional to them.

These are some of the reasons why many countries outside the EU are looking with increasing interest to this policy. The European Commission has signed memoranda of understanding with Brazil, China, and the Russian Federation, and contacts are in place with the Republic of Korea, many countries in South and Central America, and Africa.

Learning from Europe's Efforts at Integration and Convergence: Lessons for Developing Countries' Integration Policies

ROLF J. LANGHAMMER

The theoretical underpinnings of convergence funds are rooted in the new theories of economic geography and the endogenous growth models. They explain persistent spatial disparities between core and peripheral regions in the process of economic growth as being the result of the attractiveness of core regions for mobile resources that are absorbed by economic activities with increasing returns to scale. Core regions can thus collect the gains of geographic specialization from agglomeration effects as long as these effects are not jeopardized by congestion effects. Given technical indivisibilities of lump-sum infrastructure investment with long gestation periods, imperfect foresight of private capital markets in financing such investment, and their character as collective goods (nonrivalry, nonexcludability), convergence funds are financed from public funds, in particular by taxing activities and factors of production in core regions. To be effective in terms of not substituting for own funds in the recipient countries that could be used otherwise (fungibility problem), recipients must be fungibility constrained—that is, external savings should add to but not replace local savings. Analogies to development aid inflows come to mind. Development aid can prevent fungibility problems from becoming serious if the recipients are poor and if the projects to be financed are characterized by lumpiness. Regions benefiting from convergence funds are the more fungibility constrained, the more such funds finance infrastructure with a high minimum amount of capital binding and the more they change supply conditions and thus raise income and domestic savings. In order to give full justice to convergence funds, opportunity costs for those financing the funds must be taken into consideration as much as the beneficial effects of some degree of regional disparities.

This calls for distinguishing the effects of convergence funds seen from a single recipient's view and those seen from the net view of recipients and donors. While the recipient's assessment can easily be positive if domestic infrastructure could

Rolf J. Langhammer is Professor and Vice-President of Kiel Institute of World Economics in Germany.

Berlin Workshop Series 2009

have been financed from nonlocal sources only, donors may forgo growth if financing infrastructure in donor regions would have been more productive.

Have European Union Convergence Funds Lived Up to Expectations?

Unlike so-called shallow integration schemes focusing on internal free trade only (like the North American Free Trade Agreement [NAFTA]), the European Union (EU) stands alone as a model of deep integration with common policies and supranational institutions. Consequently, the EU is the only regional integration scheme whose long-standing history with convergence policies using structural funds can be assessed.

In a meta analysis, Dall'erba and de Groot (2006) first take stock of the econometric literature on the funds' impact on economic growth and then use formal meta regression analysis techniques to explain why outcomes from the first step show such divergence in results. In fact, the variance in results is striking. Studies find that structural funds have a range of effects on economic growth, from statistically positive effects, which nonetheless have certain side conditions, to statistically insignificant or even negative effects. Side conditions comprise a number of "good policy conditions" such as low unemployment, high research and development, or no impact of corruption on the allocation of funds. Side conditions affecting structural funds in a negative way are expenditures for the Common Agricultural Policy (CAP) and a high degree of centralization in national tax collection.[1] There is strong similarity to arguments in the debate regarding the effectiveness of development aid, which stresses the indispensable nature of a "good policy" environment and struggles with the diminishing returns issue, the endogeneity problem, and the reverse causality issue between growth and structural funds or aid, respectively, Likewise, as in the recent aid literature, affiliation of authors to countries or institutions benefiting from the allocation of funds is found relevant in the Dall'erba and de Groot analysis. As a result, the authors suggest meta analysis techniques in which the variable to be explained is the size of effect. The size of effect is derived from comparing the outcomes of several individual studies on the effect of a 1 percent increase in the amount of structural funds received on the growth rate under different definitions of funds' resources and growth.

Insights and Limits to Findings from Research on EU Structural Funds

What the studies cited above have in common is the importance of the institutional environment in which EU structural funds are embedded, mobilized, allocated, and disbursed. Such environment comprises general indicators such as the Sachs-Warner index of institutional quality but also digs deeply into EU specifics when it comes to the CAP or the degree of fiscal decentralization, which differs by member states.

While the common result is helpful for focusing on the degree of institutional quality in regional integration schemes among developing or least developed countries, it is also disenchanting, as it impedes the transferability of EU experiences to other integration schemes that fail to operate common policies or to host common institutions.

Pure developing-country South-South integration schemes that exist without membership of industrial economies (South-North integration) can be categorized into two groups: an Asian and a Latin American–African type. The Asian type is informal, minimizes contractual commitments, stresses "open regionalism," pools national sovereignties but does substitute them for communitywide sovereignty, and thus survives with a minimum level of "bindingness." Extreme heterogeneity in historical roots, economic structures, and size has made this nonbinding type of integration the only credible option.

The other type has been very much influenced by the EU experience and for many years has sought to establish formal commitments, milestones, targets, contracts, and stepwise integration processes. The list of failures including disintegration steps, dissolution, stagnation, and decay is almost as long as the list of new endeavors, especially since the early 1990s, when a second wave of integration (after the first one in the 1960s) inspired many countries to follow the European single market program. Therefore, it does not come as a surprise that the largest similarity between EU policies and the past experiences in South-South integration schemes has its roots in the second type of integration in Africa.

In the francophone West African Economic and Monetary Union, for instance, a so-called community solidarity tax exists that compensates net importers (basically the landlocked Sahel countries) for tariff revenue lost due to the removal of internal tariffs. Part of the proceeds from this tax may be used to finance the cost of eliminating regional disparities (Doe 2006). In the companion scheme of Central Africa, a similar tax existed in the early days of Central African integration. Finally, the South African Customs Union (SACU) provides for a common external tariff and a common excise tariff for this common customs area. All customs and excise taxes collected in the common customs area are paid into South Africa's national revenue fund. The revenue is shared among members according to a revenue-sharing formula as described in the agreement. South Africa is the custodian of this pool. Only the member states' shares of Botswana, Lesotho, Namibia, and Swaziland are calculated, with South Africa receiving the residual. SACU revenues constitute a substantial share of the state revenue of these four countries.[2]

Neither in Latin American nor in Asian integration schemes were intraregional tax sharing or allocation of public funds negotiated with the goal of removing regional disparities. Yet it is evident that, due to weak institutional foundations of regional integration in Africa (including lack of enforcement capacities), the modest schemes like the solidarity tax were unable to reduce regional disparities.

This is not to say that the issue of regional disparities has not been tackled in Latin America and Asia. Yet, because of the national rather than supranational approach to integration to which Latin American member states and those of the

Association of South East Asian Nations (ASEAN) adhere, regional disparities were tackled mainly through a special regional focus of infrastructure projects financed by the two regional development banks: the Inter-American Development Bank (IDB) and the Asian Development Bank (ADB). The latter, for instance, was the driving force behind the Greater Mekong Subregion Project, which promoted transport capacities in the backward area linking the Indochinese states and the Yunnan Province of China to the more advanced ASEAN economies (Cuyvers 2002). Salazar and Das (2007) argue that, except for Brunei, Singapore, and to lesser extent Malaysia, the other founding member states of ASEAN have limited capacity to provide financial support and to transfer resources to the poorer Indochinese states of Cambodia, the Lao People's Democratic Republic, Myanmar, and Vietnam. As a result, fiscal redistribution between richer and poorer member states mostly did not occur.

A Viable Option

Standard Heckscher-Ohlin-Samuelson trade theory suggests that the poorer the median member state in South-South integration is, the more such integration is income diverging (Venables 2003). The reason is that freeing internal trade leads the costs of trade diversion to fall on the poorest state. This is the country that has the most abundant unskilled labor and thus, prior to integration, tended to import relatively capital-intensive goods from the cheapest source. After integration, the more industrialized member state benefits from trade that gets diverted from outside to inside the integration scheme. This suggests that regional disparities in South-South integration will not be eroded but, at least in the short run, will be cemented or even extended. The postwar experience of South-South integration provides ample evidence for many distributional conflicts after divergence has occurred, irrespective of whether or not such disparities would have shown up without integration anyway. Thus there is demand for policies to reduce regional imbalances. Yet, with weak regional institutions, weak tax bases, and low initial economic interdependence, neither the domestic private sector nor the domestic public sector is likely to support and operate an EU type of structural fund. Nor will a horizontal fiscal redistribution scheme be established. Time preference rates in these regions are notoriously high, so the future benefits of redressing regional disparities are given low priority in domestic policies. If international development policies have lower time preference rates (which is likely), they could become financiers and managers, provided that they can withstand the pressure of local pressure groups to distort the regional allocation of infrastructure funds toward projects of national importance only. The historical experience of the Southern African Development Cooperation Conference (until 1993), which became eligible for external funding of infrastructure projects of regional importance, points to the risk of mislabeling infrastructure projects with a national scope as "regional" projects.

Nevertheless, the EU in particular should feel responsible for keeping regional imbalances in Sub-Saharan African integration schemes at bay. In the context of European Partnership Agreements, the EU will conclude four bilateral free trade arrangements comprising all Sub-Saharan African states. After long transition periods, the agreements will ultimately end with free trade conditions inside the four groups and with the EU. As argued, trade theory signals welfare-impeding trade diversion effects to the detriment of the poorest member states, unless they are offset by the positive effects of opening EU markets fully to African products. European Partnership Agreements seem well designed to host structural funds financed by the EU in favor of peripheral African states, which are threatened by marginalization should the EU enforce South-South integration. Rather than just spending project funds in a focused spatial way, the EU could also think of preferred budget financing in favor of backward states by simultaneously hardening the budget constraints for the more advanced countries in order to maintain a budget cap for the African integration scheme in total.

Success, however, seems conditioned on taking the lessons of EU structural funds seriously. Often structural funds are threatened by redundancy: that is, by "doing what comes naturally" or by doing it in an unconditional way. There are too many critical views on the ineffectiveness of EU structural funds that one could easily ignore if the transferability of the concept to poor developing countries is on the agenda.

References

Bähr, Cornelius, Ulrike Stierle von Schütz, and Matthias Wrede. 2007. "Dezentralisierung in den EU-Staaten und räumliche Verteilung wirtschaftlicher Aktivitäten." *Perspektiven der Wirtschaftspolitik* 8 (2): 110–29.

Beugelsdijk, Maaike, and Sylvester Eijffinger. 2005. "The Effectiveness of Structural Policy in the European Union: An Empirical Analysis for the EU-15 in 1995–2001." *Journal of Common Market Studies* 43 (1): 37–51.

Cappelen, A., F. Castellaci, J. Fagerberg, and B. Verspagen. 2003. "The Impact of EU Regional Support on Growth and Convergence in the European Union." *Journal of Common Market Studies* 41 (4): 621–44.

Cuyvers, Ludo. 2002. "Contrasting the European Union and ASEAN Integration and Solidarity." Fourth EU-ASEAN Think Tank Dialogue, European Parliament, Brussels.

Dall'erba, Sandy, and Henri L. F. de Groot. 2006. "A Meta-Analysis of EU Regional Policy Evaluation." Unpublished paper, Vrije Universitet, Amsterdam. http://www.ecomod.org/files/papers/1277.pdf.

Doe, Lubin. 2006. "Reforming External Tariffs in Central and Western African Countries." IMF Working Paper 06/12, International Monetary Fund, Washington, DC.

Ederveen, Sjef, Henri L. F. de Groot, and Richard Nahuis. 2006. "Fertile Soil for Structural Funds? A Panel Data Analysis of the Conditional Effectiveness of European Cohesion Policy." *Kyklos* 59 (1): 17–42.

Esposti, Roberto, and Stefania Bussoletti. 2004. "Regional Convergence, Structural Funds, and the Role of Agriculture in the EU: A Panel-Data Approach." Quaderno di ricerca, Università Politecnica delle Marche, Dipartimento di Economia.

Rodriguez-Pose, Andrés, and Ugo Fratesi. 2004. "Between Development and Social Policies: The Impact of European Structural Funds in Objective 1 Regions." *Regional Studies* 38 (1): 97–113.

Salazar, Lorraine C., and Sanchita B. Das. 2007. "Bridging the ASEAN Developmental Divide Challenges and Prospects." *ASEAN Economic Bulletin* 24 (1): 1–14.

Venables, Anthony J. 2003. "Winners and Losers from Regional Integration Agreements." *Economic Journal* 113 (490): 747–61.

Notes

1. For a positive yet conditioned assessment, see Beugelsdijk and Eijffinger (2005); Cappelen and others (2003). Insignificant results are noted by Rodriguez-Pose and Fratesi (2004), while others stress the importance of binding factors like institutional quality (Ederveen, de Groot, and Nahuis 2006) and fiscal decentralization (Bähr, Stierle von Schütz, and Wrede 2007). The negative impact of the CAP is underlined by Esposti and Bussoletti (2004).

2. http://www.dfa.gov.za/foreign/Multilateral/africa/sacu.htm.

The Geography of Inequalities in Europe

PHILIPPE MARTIN

The concern for cohesion is an important feature of the process of European integration. While the single market offered the promise of increased output and efficiency for the European Union (EU) as a whole, it is often argued that the viability of the project, in social and political terms, requires that the gains be distributed fairly across countries and regions. This has led to a large increase in funds for regional policies and an explicit mention of the objective of reducing regional disparities in the Single European Act (Article 1). The EU has been devoting an increasing share of its budget to regional policies. The structural funds and the cohesion fund represent more than one-third of the 2004 European Community budget.

At the European level, the goal of the cohesion policy is not defined precisely: it can be interpreted broadly as being to reduce the welfare differences among European regions. Article 158 of the amended Treaty of Amsterdam (European Union 1997) establishing the European Community reads, "The Community shall aim at reducing disparities between the levels of development of the various regions and the backwardness of the least favored regions or islands, including rural areas." This is broad because it could be interpreted as reducing inequalities between countries or between regions inside countries. Moreover, regional policies are often presented by policy makers as part of a broader objective to reduce inequalities between the poor and the rich. Regional cohesion is seen as a prerequisite for social cohesion, and this is the main reason that regional inequalities should be reduced. There is an implicit assumption here: the spatial dimension of inequalities is an important determinant of inequalities between individuals at the national level. This assumption is important because it implies that social transfers that are not spatially defined (such as unemployment benefits, national income taxes, and social security transfers) are not enough to ensure social cohesion at the national level.

Philippe Martin is in the Paris School of Economics at Université Paris 1, Panthéon Sorbonne in France.

Berlin Workshop Series 2009
© 2009 The International Bank for Reconstruction and Development/The World Bank

The author would like to thank two referees as well as Karolina Ekholm for helpful suggestions.

In this paper, I argue that regional policies, as they exist today in Europe, are based on shaky grounds both from an empirical and a theoretical point of view. It starts by reviewing the existing evidence that European integration has led to a process of convergence between countries, but not between regions inside countries, and suggests some mechanisms through which trade integration in Europe can lead to a process of convergence between countries, but not between regions inside countries. This will be so in particular if, due to European structural and institutional features, poor regions cannot exploit their comparative advantage relative to rich regions as well as if poor countries cannot exploit their comparative advantage relative to rich countries. As evident in the example of France, in the past 20 years regional divergence in production has indeed occurred. However, the geography of incomes has, during the same period, become more equal, producing a "scissors effect" between the geographies of production and income. This suggests that transfers, which have nothing to do with regional policies, have, at least in France, more than compensated the increase in production inequality. Hence, "regional convergence" is not a synonym of "regional cohesion," at least at the national level.

I then review evidence on a possible trade-off between growth and regional inequalities to suggest that efficiency motives cannot easily be used to defend regional policies. Both evidence and theory suggest that regional concentration leads to efficiency gains so that regional policies that attempt to reduce such spatial concentration cannot be based on strong efficiency grounds. This also implies that the EU is faced with a choice it has tried to avoid until now. Either it puts its effort into slowing or even reversing the process of spatial economic concentration at the national level or it concentrates on policies to speed up the convergence between poor and rich countries. Finally, I analyze the relation between spatial and social inequalities and report empirical evidence that suggests a strong empirical relation between the two in the EU.

Regional Convergence and Divergence in Europe

Spatial inequalities have developed among the European countries and among the countries' own internal regions in different ways. Table 1 illustrates the development of those disparities measured by the standard per capita gross domestic product (GDP) deviation for the NUTS2 (Nomenclature of Territorial Units for Statistics, level 2) regions for the year 1990 and the period 1995–2000. In eight countries internal regional disparities increased after 1995. The two last lines of the table also show that, while inequalities among countries diminished, those among the countries' own internal regions on average increased a little. The data also suggest that disparities increased especially in countries with initially low disparities and decreased in countries with initially high disparities.

Detailed studies have shown that up to the mid-1980s GDP per capita inequalities among member states represented half of the inequalities among the European

TABLE 1. Regional Disparities in per Capita GDP within the Member States, NUTS2, 1990 and 1995–2000

STANDARD deviation of index EU15 = 100

Member state	1990	1995	1996	1997	1998	1999	2000
Belgium	25.1	40.8	41.6	41.6	41.6	40.2	39.4
Germany[a]	21.8	20.1	20.5	20.9	21.0	21.5	22.1
Greece	6.3	10.4	10.3	9.5	9.5	9.5	9.6
Spain	14.9	16.8	17.1	17.4	17.4	18.1	18.1
France	28.9	28.2	27.9	27.3	26.6	27.5	28.3
Italy	24.8	28.5	28.9	27.7	28.1	27.8	27.2
Netherlands	10.6	13.5	14.6	15.3	15.7	15.8	15.5
Austria	27.5	25.4	24.8	23.6	22.7	22.5	23.9
Portugal	13.5	15.2	15.4	17.3	17.9	17.6	16.6
Finland	17.9	19.5	21.2	20.8	23.9	24.2	25.0
Sweden	10.9	12.0	13.0	15.2	16.3	20.1	20.9
United Kingdom	20.2	31.5	32.0	34.0	35.6	34.2	34.2
EU15 (by member state)	12.5	12.5	11.8	11.6	11.7	11.0	11.4
EU15 (within member states)	26.5	28.3	28.1	28.2	28.5	28.2	28.5

Source: European Commission 2002.
[a] Excludes New Länder.

regions and that inequalities among regions within each state represented the other half (Duro 2001). Since then, inequalities among states have diminished 25 percent, but regional inequalities within the states have increased 10 percent. As a result, regional inequalities in Europe are explained mainly by inequalities within countries. Thus Europe is experiencing a process of convergence among countries at the same time as it is experiencing a process of nonconvergence or divergence among the countries' own regions: all of the convergence among the regions in Europe at the European level is thus explained by the convergence among countries.

Further evidence on the subject is given by Midelfart-Knarvik and Overman (2002). Figure 1 shows the coefficient of variation (the standard deviation divided by the mean) for the distribution of manufacturing activity across states and regions in the EU. At the national level this index of geographic concentration has remained roughly constant over time. At the regional level, however, geographic concentration is more pronounced and has been increasing over time.

At the EU level, a similar development in spatial polarization may be described for unemployment. Overman and Puga (2002) show that, since the mid-1980s, regions starting with a low or high unemployment rate have not experienced much change in their relative situation. Regions with intermediate unemployment rates have developed toward extremes. Overman and Puga interpret this result as an effect of the spatial polarization of economic activities due to economic integration. They show that the fate of the regions in terms of unemployment is linked much more closely to the results of the neighboring regions (whether or not they belong to the same country) than to the results of the respective country itself.

FIGURE 1. Geographic Concentration of Economic Activity

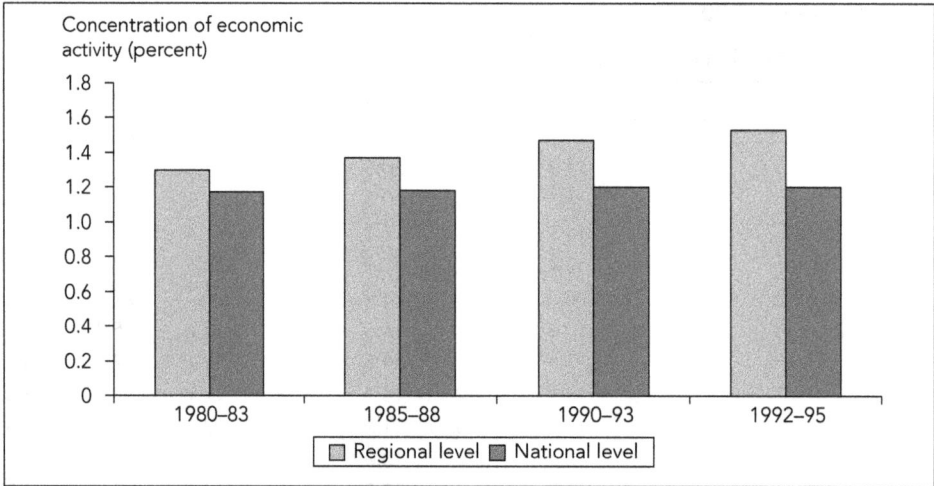

Note: Coefficient of variation for four-year averages of shares in total EU manufacturing.
Source: Midelfart-Knarvik and Overman 2002.

To sum up, trade integration in Europe has fostered convergence between countries. It has not fostered convergence between regions inside countries. In some cases, regional disparities have increased. The spatial polarization has occurred in terms of both income and unemployment.

Divergent Geographies of Production and Income: The French Case

This picture is misleading if it suggests that social inequalities have increased between regions inside Europe. A contradictory image may emerge if one looks at regional inequalities of disposable income—that is, income net of transfers. Here we only look at the French example. For French regions the difference is quite

FIGURE 2. Coefficient of Variation: GDP per Capita, French NUTS2 Regions, 1981-2004

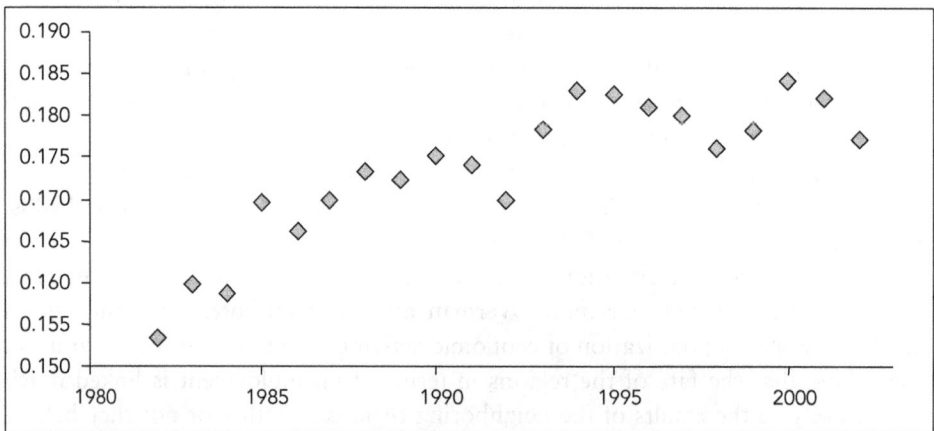

Source: Insee.

FIGURE 3. Coefficient of Variation: Unemployment Rate, French NUTS2 Regions, 1981-2004

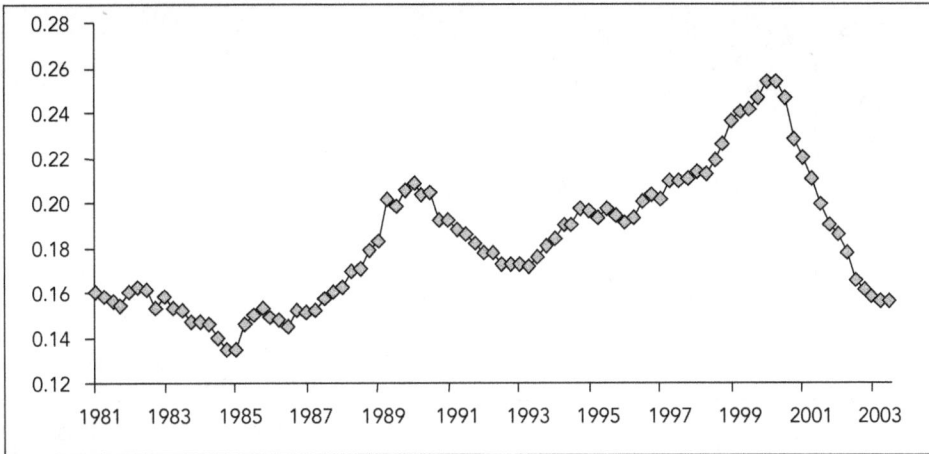

Source: Insee.

striking. Figure 2 shows the coefficient of variation across French NUTS2 regions from 1982 to 2002. There is a clear upward trend of regional inequalities in production during the period.

Figure 3 gives the same measure of regional inequalities for the unemployment rate from 1981 to 2004. In the 1980s up to the 1990s, regional inequalities also increased. However, and quite surprising, the recent years show a dramatic decrease in this measure of inequality. It is known that regional inequalities in unemployment are countercyclical (high-unemployment regions have more stable unemployment rates than low-unemployment regions), so the latest drop is partly cyclical and reflects the recent increase in unemployment in France.

Figure 4 gives a very different picture. It shows the coefficient of variation of disposable income for NUTS regions from 1982 to 1999 (more recent data are not available). First, and not surprising, the inequality is less for disposable income per capita than for GDP per capita. On average the regional inequality in GDP per capita is more than double the inequality in disposable income. More surprising, even though the first measure increased by more than 2 percentage points, the second measure decreased by 2 percentage points. As Davezies (2001) stresses, there is a growing disconnect between the geography of production (becoming more unequal) and the geography of incomes (becoming more equal), so that "regional convergence" is not a synonym of "regional cohesion." The reason for this is that interregional income transfers are important even though nothing much is known about them. In particular, it is difficult to quantify the impact of public versus private transfers in the difference between GDP and income at the regional level.

This French disconnect between the geography of production and the geography of income is not a general phenomenon. Unfortunately, we do not have data for other countries from which to draw general conclusions. There is, however, evidence that in the United Kingdom both types of regional inequalities (in terms of

FIGURE 4. Coefficient of Variation: Disposable Income per Capita, French NUTS2 Regions,1982-99

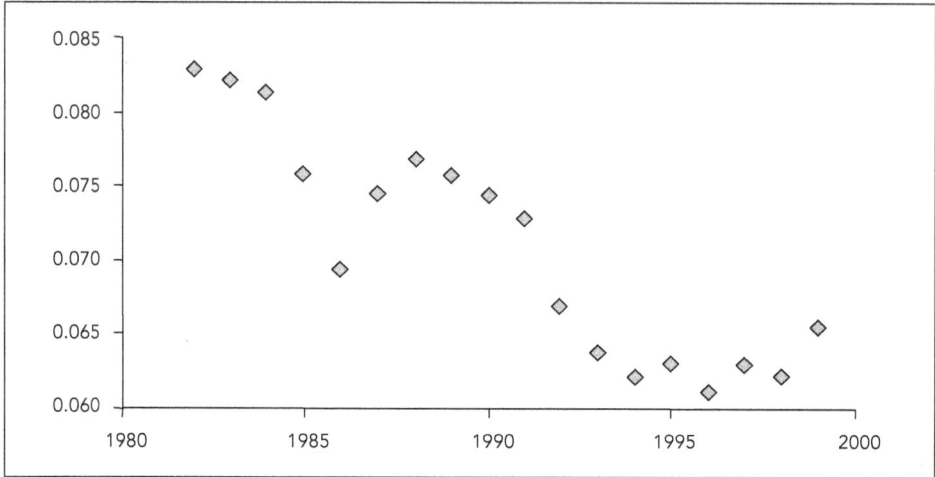

Source: Insee.

GDP per capita and disposable income) have increased in the past 20 years (see Monastiriotis 2003). This suggests that the evolution of the welfare state is key. Whereas in France, during the past 20 years, transfers (due to the progressivity of the income tax, social security, and unemployment benefits) have increased, this has not occurred in the United Kingdom. The important point is that regional policies certainly do not explain much of the difference between the United Kingdom and France. In France national regional policies that attempt to give incentives (essentially through tax cuts) for firms to locate in the poorest regions (the *politique d'aménagement du territoire*) are very active, although it is difficult to evaluate their real impact, in part because the government does not provide much data. In the United Kingdom these policies are much less important. This suggests that interregional transfers are very large and growing in France. It also suggests that they are mostly due to progressive income taxes and the welfare state, not to spatially defined policies such as regional policies.

A Tentative Explanation for Global Convergence and Local Divergence

The presence of economies of scale and trade costs may explain why regions with no obvious comparative advantage in certain activities can become centers of production of those activities. A model of the underlying mechanisms was introduced by Krugman (1991), who was at the origin of the so-called new economic geography. The central finding of this literature is that the reduction of trade costs may engender a concentration of economic activities in certain regions that have better access to the large markets even if they do not have the lowest production costs. This spatial concentration is advantageous because of the existence of economies of scale conducive to limiting production locations, and it is made possible by trade integration, which, while reducing transaction costs, does not oblige enterprises to be located close to all their consumers.

Here we analyze very briefly some of the necessary conditions for a process of "local divergence" with "global convergence" to follow trade integration. The interaction of economies of scale, comparative advantage, and trade costs is essential. The purpose of the small "model" provided here is simply to illustrate a mechanism that may be more general. Suppose there are three regions. The first one, which for illustrative purposes is called the Ruhr, is a rich, central region with high wages and high labor costs. The second region, Catalonia, is a middle-income region close to the large European markets. A third region, Andalusia, is a peripheral region with low wages and low labor costs. Economies of scale play a major role in the sense that average production costs increase with the number of locations due to fixed costs. Let us assume that the firm can produce in the three regions or in only one.[1] The choice of location is simply a minimization of the sum of production and trade costs.

If the firm decides to produce in the three regions, its total cost is as follows:

$$TC(R + C + A) = 3F + c_R S_R + c_C S_C + c_A S_A, \tag{1}$$

where F is the fixed cost associated with each plant, $c_R, c_C,$ and c_A are the marginal costs of production (which can be interpreted as the wage costs), respectively, in the Ruhr, Catalonia, and Andalusia. We assume that $c_R > c_C > c_A$. $S_R, S_C,$ and S_A are the market sizes, respectively, in the Ruhr, Catalonia, and Andalusia. We assume that $S_R > S_C > S_A$. In this situation, the firm pays no trade or transport costs, as it produces in all three locations.

If the firm produces in the Ruhr only, its total cost is as follows:

$$TC(R) = F + c_R(S_R + S_C + S_A) + t_I(S_C + S_A) + t_D S_A, \tag{2}$$

where t_I is the international trade cost that the firm located in Germany has to pay to sell in Catalonia and Andalusia. To sell in Andalusia, the firm also has to pay the domestic Spanish trade cost (which can be interpreted as a transport cost), as this region is in the periphery.

If the firm produces in Catalonia only, its total cost is as follows:

$$TC(C) = F + c_c(S_R + S_C + S_A) + t_I S_R + t_D S_A, \tag{3}$$

so it pays the international trade cost to sell in Germany and the domestic Spanish cost to sell in Andalusia.

Finally, if the firm decides to produce in Andalusia, its total cost is as follows:

$$TC(A) = F + c_A(S_R + S_C + S_A) + (t_I + t_D)S_R + t_D S_C, \tag{4}$$

Suppose we start from a situation where international trade costs t_I are very high. In this situation, which we interpret as the pattern before the European integration process, the firm will want to locate some activity in the three locations. It is easy to check, and it is intuitive indeed that if t_I is high enough (and domestic transport costs are not too low either), then or any other location equilibrium. This just says that if trade costs are high, firms will want to be close to all their consumers.

Suppose now that Spain and Germany lower their trade costs t_I. In a highly stylized way, we interpret the scenario of "global convergence with local divergence" as a case when the firm chooses to locate in Catalonia only. In this case, Spain as a whole gains some economic activity, but Andalusia loses it.

This will be the case under the following conditions:

- Condition 1. $TC (R + C + A) > TC$,

- Condition 2. $TC (R) > TC (C)$,

- Condition 3. $TC (A) > TC (C)$.

Condition 1 is fulfilled when fixed costs are sufficiently high, international and domestic trade costs are sufficiently low, the international cost advantage of Spain over Germany is sufficiently high, but the cost disadvantage of Catalonia is relatively small compared to Andalusia. Condition 2 applies for some of the same characteristics as for condition 1, but it also requires that the overall Spanish market is not too small compared to the German market. Finally, condition 3 requires on top of some these three characteristics that the domestic cost in Spain is not too low.

Figure 5 shows an example of some possible outcomes of locations depending on combinations of international trade costs t_I and national cost differences between the two Spanish regions, $c_C - c_A$. It illustrates that the scenario of global convergence and local divergence (going from location pattern $R + C + A$ to the location

FIGURE 5. The Possibility of Global Convergence and Local Divergence following European Trade Integration

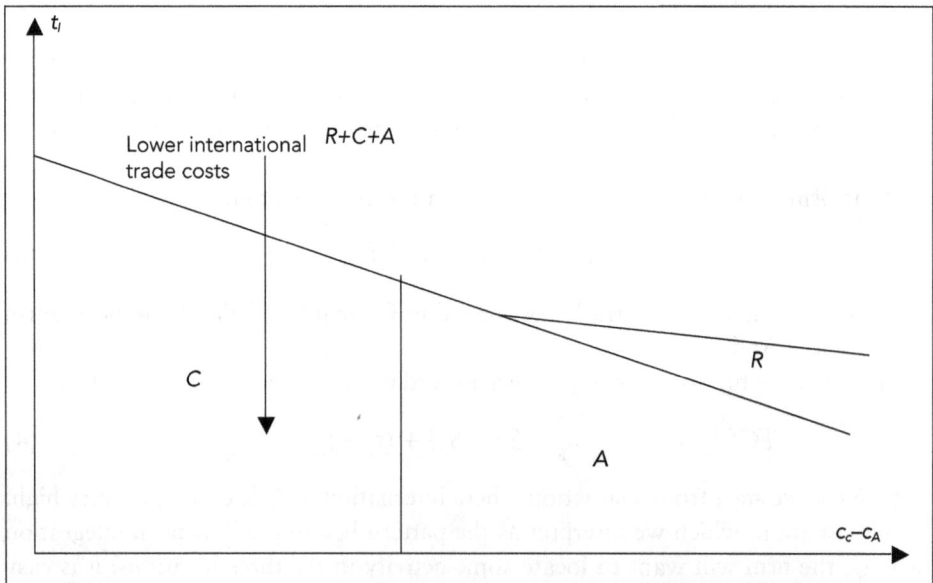

in C only) is possible when international trade costs are lowered, but the difference in production costs between C and A is low enough.

Overall, this example suggests that international integration (lower t_I) can lead to global convergence and local divergence, if the international cost advantage of the poorer country is larger than the national cost advantage of the poorer region. One can think that the European practice of nationally uniform minimum wages (and more generally of labor institutions) coupled with different labor costs between countries can produce exactly such a situation. The example also suggests that such a scenario will occur in countries for which the richest region has both a large domestic market and good market access to other rich regions. In this case, market access is the main driving force of location between regions inside countries, and differences in the costs of production are the main driving force of location between countries.

Lower domestic transport costs in Spain, due, for example, to infrastructure projects financed by structural funds, may not produce local convergence. This has been shown, for example, in Martin and Rogers (1995). In this example, when domestic trade costs are high, the firm prefers to locate production in both Spanish regions, in order to serve the market of the poor region. At intermediate levels, the firm prefers to concentrate its production in the richest of the two and save on transport costs. At low levels of transport costs, the difference in production costs becomes the most important factor determining the firm's choice of location, which presumably favors the poorest region. However if, again for institutional reasons, differences in production costs between regions inside countries are constrained to be small, then regional policies that build transport infrastructure between rich and poor regions will only emphasize the differences in market size between those regions.

Overall, this analytical framework suggests quite intuitively that the interaction of economies of scale and trade costs may produce a scenario of global convergence with local divergence following trade integration if poor countries—but not, or to a lesser extent, poor regions—can take advantage of their "natural" comparative advantage. This same mechanism that leads to the phenomenon of global convergence and local divergence can also explain why regional policies emphasizing transport infrastructure may not be successful in decreasing inequalities between poor and rich regions (see Martin 2003 for a review of the evidence on the effects of regional policies in Europe).

Regional Policies and the Possibility of a Trade-Off between Equity and Efficiency

A motivation for public intervention at the regional level, put forward by the commission, is that of efficiency. It sees in geographic disequilibria "an under-utilization of economic and social potentials and an inability to take advantage of opportunities that could be beneficial to the Union as a whole."

This motivation is much less clear than the equity-based motivation. If the phenomenon of spatial concentration is explained by the existence of economies of scale, this means that spatial agglomeration is at the origin of economic gains. This will be the case if firms can benefit from the proximity of other enterprises in the same sector to diminish their costs (transport costs or fixed costs). This will also be the case if such concentration makes it possible to increase the firms' productivity through localized spillover effects—that is, if the firms can receive transfers of knowledge from other neighboring businesses. These localized spillovers have been documented in numerous studies (see, for example, Jaffe, Trajtenberg, and Henderson 1993), and the existence of agglomeration gains has been discussed extensively by economists since Marshall described them in 1890. The example of Silicon Valley shows the advantage a country can obtain from a very heavy spatial concentration of activities with positive technological externalities. The stronger spatial concentration of innovation-based activities in relation to production activities thus has an economic rationale, and the benefits of this spatial concentration go beyond private gains. Another gain from agglomeration, both for workers and for firms, is labor pooling: firms benefit from a large spatial concentration of specialized workers in an area because they can easily hire from this large pool.

The objective of policies promoting a greater dispersal of economic activities is based on the assumption that the economic geography produced by market forces alone is too concentrated. However, the efficiency argument may demand more or less spatial concentration: on the one hand, the economic gains of spatial agglomeration and, on the other, the effects of congestion (as, for example, reflected in pollution or the high price of fixed factors such as land). The fact that in Europe the convergence of countries is accompanied by national divergence makes one think that the former type of argument—efficiency gains with spatial concentration—has pride of place. In this case, a trade-off between equity and spatial efficiency appears (see Baldwin and others 2003; Martin 1998, 1999). It is difficult to assess this trade-off quantitatively. Figure 6 shows the relation between the levels of regional disparities and

FIGURE 6. GDP per Capita and Regional Disparities, 2000

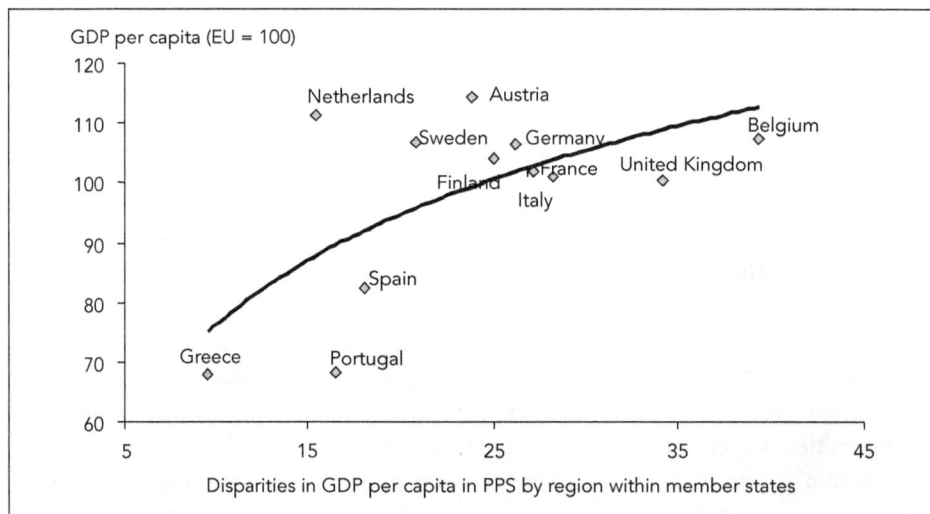

Source: Eurostat.

FIGURE 7. Growth and Regional Disparities, 1995-2000

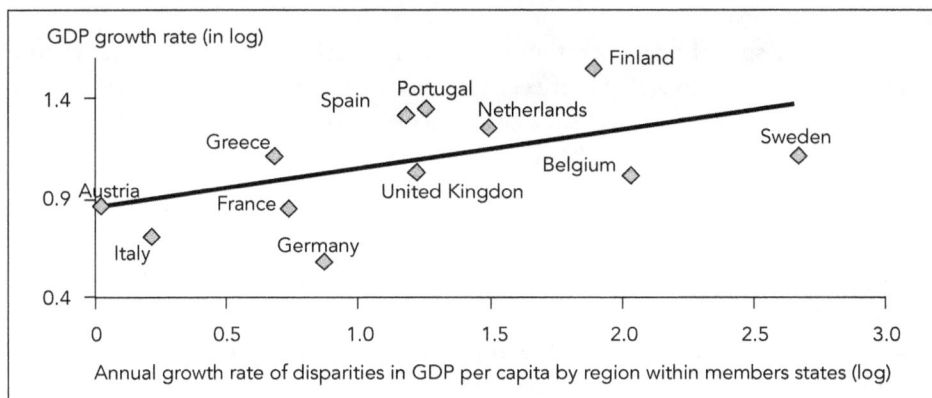

Source: Eurostat.

GDP per capita in the larger EU15 countries. Denmark, Ireland, and Luxembourg are excluded because regional data are lacking for those small countries. Two groups appear clearly. The three poorest countries (Greece, Portugal, and Spain) have the lowest level of regional disparities. The second group of countries (the relatively rich) have an average level of regional disparities that is clearly above the first group. However, inside this group no obvious relation appears. The positive relation between a country's growth of GDP overall and the growth of regional disparities during the period 1994–2000 appears more clearly in figure 7.[2] Of course, this positive correlation should be taken with much caution. It suggests the possible existence of a trade-off between spatial equity and growth, but such correlation may not be causal.

Other evidence is provided by Ciccone and Hall (1996) for the United States and Ciccone (2002) for Europe. Both find that employment density has a positive effect on productivity levels. Recent econometric work by Crozet and Koenig (2005) gives a more precise picture of this trade-off in Europe. They find a positive relation between the growth of GDP per capita of a region and the change in the level of inequalities inside the region. The effect is economically significant: a 10 percent increase in the standard deviation index of GDP per capita within a NUTS1 region leads to a 1.6 percent increase in regional GDP per capita.

The existence of such a trade-off has consequences for the definition and quantification of the objectives of regional policies, in particular for the case of new entrants. It implies that a strategic choice has to be made between the objective of lowering or stabilizing the absolute differences in GDP per capita between regions inside countries and the objective of achieving rapid convergence toward the rest of the EU. The decisions of which infrastructure projects to finance and where to locate them are obviously dependent on this strategic choice between external and internal convergence. In this matter, Ireland made an interesting choice, deciding to be defined as a single NUTS2 region rather than as several small regions, which gave rise to a high degree of spatial inequalities. As Davezies (1999) emphasizes, Ireland took the risk of being excluded more rapidly from the benefit of the structural funds, but it could choose to develop projects in those regions that provided the highest national return.

To sum up, spatial agglomeration of economic activities may (at least up to a certain point where congestion effects may become too large) have positive efficiency effects and may be a welcome consequence of trade integration. This implies a trade-off for regional policies between efficiency and equity.

Inequalities between Regions and Inequalities between Individuals

Equity is, after efficiency, the other traditional motivation of regional policies. Certain economic agents—be they workers or consumers—are not mobile and are therefore condemned to live in poor or declining regions from which the mobile factors (capital and highly skilled workers) have departed. Because of the lower labor demand in such regions, real wages will adjust downward or, if real wages do not adjust because of labor market rigidities, unemployment will increase. In both cases, the welfare of the inhabitants will deteriorate. As consumers, those agents will also see their welfare deteriorate because certain goods and services will no longer be produced locally (the businesses will have left for more wealthy regions). In certain cases, in particular for certain services, the transaction costs will become so high that they can no longer be consumed by those agents. Thus the diversity of consumable goods and services in the poor region will decline. Moreover, the most mobile agents are in general those with the highest level of human capital (education, experience). Such agents, thanks to the possession of "positive externalities" in the form of localized social interactions, have a positive impact on productivity and thus on the real wages of other workers. By leaving a region in decline, the most productive workers also have a negative impact on the productivity of the remaining workers, that is, those who are the most disadvantaged. There is an absence of market coordination, given that, when certain agents decide on their location, they do not take into account the effect of their choice on the other agents. From that standpoint, the possibility of a market failure, with the consequent increase in inequalities that is specific to the spatial dimension of the economy, exists and may thus serve as motivation for public intervention.

There are several ways to analyze the impact of the agglomeration phenomenon on the least mobile agents. The first is to refuse to see it as a problem of equity and to interpret it as coming from a specific market failure. In Europe, except in the United Kingdom, promoting the spatial mobility of workers is not considered a solution to the problems of regional inequality. This is legitimate, but only partially, because cultural and social obstacles mean that there will always be a substantial fringe of workers who will be harmed by geographic inequalities. The vision of regions empty of both inhabitants and economic activities (such as the Dakotas in the United States) is unacceptable in Europe.

Are Spatial Inequalities in Production Correlated with Social Inequalities?

Policy makers often argue that a strong rational for decreasing regional inequalities is that part of the wider objective is to decrease inequalities between individuals. Spatial cohesion is part of an overall objective of social cohesion. This is based on the belief that there is a strong relation between spatial inequalities and individual inequalities so that regional policies that decrease spatial inequalities can also decrease individual inequalities.

From a theoretical point of view, it is not obvious that countries that are more unequal spatially are those that have more unequal income distribution. The problem comes from aggregation, which is well known to those who have studied the dynamics of inequalities at the international level.

Take a simple example of two countries, A and B, each of them comprising two regions, 1 and 2, each with the same population of 50 individuals. Both countries have the same average GDP and GDP per capita. Country A has no spatial inequality; its two regions have the same income per capita. However, in both regions the distribution of income is highly unequal. Say, 10 percent of individuals each earns 10 and 90 percent of the population earns 1. So the overall inequality, as measured by the percentage of total income that goes to the richest 10 percent, is 100 / 190 = 53 percent. This is a very unequal society, even though there is no spatial inequality. The other country has a different distribution of total income. In region 1, 20 percent of the population earns 5.5, and 80 percent earns 1.5, so average income per capita in the region is 2.3. In the other region, all earn 1.5. Hence spatial inequality is quite large in this case, as income per capita in the rich region is more than 50 percent more than in the poor region. However, the distribution of income at the country level is much less unequal than for country A: the percentage of total income that goes to the richest 10 percent of the population (all in the richest region) is 55 / 190 = 29 percent.

This example shows that higher spatial inequality measured by differences in income per capita across regions does not automatically generate a more unequal distribution of income. Moreover, in this example, a spatially based redistributive policy would seem unfair to the "poor" of the rich region. An income transfer from region 1 to region 2, even if financed by the rich of the richest region, would artificially create an inequality between the "poor" of the rich region and the poor of the poor region. Such a transfer from the rich to the poor region would increase certain measures of income inequality.

An obvious question is whether there is a relation between spatial and social inequalities. One way to check whether such a relation exists is to regress a measure of interpersonal inequality (namely, the log of the ratio of the mean net income of the top decile to the bottom decile) on likely determinants of interpersonal inequality as well as a measure of spatial inequality. Table 2 shows the results of such regressions for pooled data of 12 countries (Austria, Belgium, Finland, France, Germany, Greece, Italy, the Netherlands, Portugal, Spain, Sweden, and the United Kingdom) and the seven years available (1995 to 2001). Again, the three countries (Ireland, Luxembourg, and Denmark) with no NUTS2 regional data are excluded.

The measure of spatial income inequality (SPATIAL) is the log of the coefficient of variation of income per capita at the NUTS2 level.

TABLE 2. Income Inequality and Spatial Inequality

DEPENDENT variable: log of the ratio of the mean net income of the top decile to the bottom decile at country level

Variable	(1)	(2)	(3)	(4)	(5)
SPATIAL	0.772**	0.805**			0.972***
	(0.238)	(0.234)			(0.205)
COHESION			0.107	0.093	−0.039
			(0.110)	(0.139)	(0.094)
INCPERCAP	0.096	−0.020	0.134	0.190	0.036
	(0.170)	(0.176)	(0.076)	(0.163)	(0.203)
SOCIAL		0.143		−0.087	−0.076
		(0.176)		(0.299)	(0.251)
Year fixed effects	Yes	Yes	Yes	Yes	Yes
Country fixed effects	Yes	Yes	Yes	Yes	Yes
Number of observations	81	71	81	71	71
R^2 (within)	0.96	0.96	0.96	0.96	0.97

Source: Eurostat/Region.

Note: Standard errors are in parentheses. The constant and dummy coefficients are not reported. All variables are in log.

*** Significant at 1 percent.

** Significant at 5 percent.

* Significant at 10 percent.

The first column shows the regression of inequality on the coefficient of variation (SPATIAL) and the log of income per capita (INCPERCAP), as it can be argued that richer countries are less unequal than poorer ones. Year dummies are added to control for purely cyclical effects and country dummies for any omitted variables that are country specific. Spatial inequality is indeed positively correlated with individual inequality. Income per capita has a negative impact on interpersonal income per capita only in (unreported) regressions when country dummies are not included. An important question is whether, once national transfers are taken into account, spatial inequality still affects individual income inequality. If, when such transfers are controlled for, spatial inequalities no longer affect individual inequalities, it can then be argued that national redistribution tools are sufficient for cohesion. To test this, the log of per capita expenditure on social transfers (SOCIAL) is added, which is interpreted as measuring the preference of the country for redistribution. These are measures of national redistribution and not of regional policies. The interesting result is that introducing this crude measure of the national redistributive policy does not reduce the coefficient on spatial income inequality (SPATIAL). If anything, it increases the correlation between social and spatial inequalities.

In columns 3 and 4, we redo the exercise using a different measure of spatial inequality. Spatial inequality is now in terms of unemployment using the European Commission measure "Cohesion," which measures regional dispersion of unemployment rates for each country. In this case, this measure of spatial inequality is not significantly correlated with income inequality. When both measures of spatial inequality are included in the regression (column 5), only the spatial inequality in incomes is significantly correlated with individual inequalities. The correlation is also quantitatively quite large. Given that the variables are in logs, the estimated coefficients can be interpreted as elasticities. Hence, a 10 percent increase in spatial inequalities of income is correlated with a 9.7 percent increase in individual incomes, even after controlling for regional inequalities in unemployment, income per capita, social transfers, year, and country fixed effects.

This exercise should be interpreted with caution, as many other determinants can affect individual income inequalities. The sense of causality is not obvious. Clearly, spatial inequalities could affect individual inequalities, but individual inequalities could also lead to spatial inequalities if agents (rich and poor) agglomerate in different regions. The link between regional and social inequalities seems strong even when controlling for year and country-specific effects, and national redistribution policies seem unable to eliminate the full impact of regional income inequalities on social inequalities.

Is There a Spatial Component to Wage Inequalities?

An alternative way to analyze the relation between spatial and social inequalities is to look at the determinants of wage inequalities. If a large part of wage inequalities between individuals is explained by geographic factors, then regional policies that induce the relocation of industries toward poor regions may help to decrease individual inequalities, even though they may not be the most efficient way to do this. Work by Duranton and Monastiriotis (2002) and Gobillon (2002) suggests that this is only partially the case. The first paper uses data on average regional earnings in the United Kingdom during the 1982–97 period. It shows a worsening of U.K. regional inequalities and a rise in the north-south gap. However, differences in education account for most of the aggregate divergence. London gained because its workforce became relatively more educated over the period. Second, returns to education increased nationwide, which favored the most educated regions (that is, London). Third, returns to education were initially lower in London, but they (partially) caught up with the rest of the country. Had returns to education and their distribution across U.K. regions remained stable over the period, the U.K. north-south divide would have decreased.

Gobillon (2002) uses individual French data on wages to quantify the determinants of local disparities in wages during the 1978–90 period. He finds that two-thirds of regional inequalities in wages are explained by the individual characteristics of the workers; in particular, his or her level of education. Of course, this leaves one-third unexplained, but this is the maximum that geographic factors could account for.

These two studies suggest that a major reason for the increase in regional inequalities inside European countries may have little to do with the geography of production per se. If returns to education have increased since the 1980s, which most labor economists believe, then the increase in regional inequality is at least partially a consequence of the increase in individual inequalities itself caused by the increase in the return to education. A plausible story is that initially rich regions were well endowed with workers with high levels of education so that the increase in regional disparities in GDP per capita reflected the association of a general increase in the return to education and the initial geographic disparity in education levels. Furthermore, it is well known that better educated workers are more mobile, so they may have concentrated in the richer regions too.

Can Regional Policies Increase Social Inequalities?

The type of instrument used by regional policies also has important implications for the link between individual and regional inequalities. Most countries subsidize investment rather than employment at the regional level, and this translates into subsidies to capital rather than labor (see Fuest and Huber 2000; Yuill, Bachtler, and Wishlade 1997). An important example is the subsidy program provided to eastern Germany. According to Fuest and Huber (2000), 90 percent of the subsidies to firms locating in eastern Germany take the form of investment subsidies. At the European level, more than 400 types of subsidies exist that can help firms in poor regions. They take so many forms that it seems quite safe to characterize them as a complicated mix of subsidies to capital and labor.

Regional policies consisting of subsidizing industries so as to give them an incentive to relocate in disadvantaged regions may have perverse effects on individual inequalities. If capital is mobile, subsidizing the return on that capital in one region amounts to increasing its return in all regions. The reason is that, if the return to capital is higher in one region than in another, in the long term, delocation will take place until the returns are equalized (see Dupont and Martin 2003). Regional policies that subsidize capital in poor regions may imply transfers from the poor to the rich region, as the increase in the return to capital will benefit the region with the highest share of capital ownership. Hence, even if they succeed in reducing regional inequalities, such subsidies to capital can end up increasing inequalities between individuals. This may be an extreme scenario, but it serves as a reminder that the choice of instruments used by regional subsidies is extremely important.

To sum up, a large share of regional inequalities comes from individual inequalities themselves produced by individual characteristics—in particular, differences in the education level. This implies that regional policies that offer subsidies to firms that locate in poor regions or that finance infrastructure projects in those regions may have only limited effects on regional inequalities and that policies concentrating on education may be more efficient.

Conclusions

Public economic intervention must be based on considerations of either efficiency or equity. This paper has argued that the legitimacy of regional policies in Europe is not strong on either ground. A major rethinking is required, based on simple principles in economics. On the efficiency motive, we have argued that increasing returns, which explain spatial economic concentration, also point to the efficiency gains of this process. Recent econometric evidence shows, in the European context, that these gains should be taken into account when defining regional policies. In the light of the recent enlargement, this is a crucial trade-off. On the equity motive, the evidence suggests that national redistribution schemes (income taxes, social transfers) that are not spatially defined do reduce spatial inequalities (at least in the French example), but they may not be sufficient instruments to reduce social inequalities.

Regional policies in Europe do not take into account the fact that richer countries can redistribute from rich to poor regions through national redistribution more easily than poor countries. Corsica, even if it has the same GDP per capita as some regions in poorer countries, benefits heavily from transfers from Ile de France, but this is not taken into account when designing European regional policies. Given the existence of these transfers at the national level, it is not obvious why European regional policies should focus on regional inequalities within nations. From this point of view, the recommendation of the Sapir report to renationalize regional policies to focus the impact of structural funds on inequalities between countries makes sense (Sapir, Aghion, and Bertola 2004). The priority, especially after the enlargement, should be to speed up convergence between countries in Europe. It might be argued that this is at odds with the finding that European integration has fostered convergence between countries, but not between regions inside countries, so that regional policies are not necessary for global convergence, but they are necessary for local convergence. However, inequalities between countries remain much larger, in level, than inequalities between regions inside countries, and national redistribution policies are powerful instruments to reduce the latter.

References

Baldwin, Richard, Rikard Forslid, Philippe Martin, Gianmarco Ottaviano, and Frederic Robert-Nicoud. 2003. *Public Policies and Economic Geography.* Princeton, NJ: Princeton University Press.

Ciccone, Antonio. 2002. "Agglomeration Effects in Europe." *European Economic Review* 46 (2): 213–27.

Ciccone, Antonio, and Robert Hall. 1996. "Productivity and the Density of Economic Activity." *American Economic Review* 86 (1, March): 54–70.

Crozet, Matthieu, and Pamina Koenig. 2005. "The Cohesion vs. Growth Trade-off: Evidence from EU Regions (1980–2000)." Unpublished paper. http://team.univ-paris1.fr/teamperso/crozet/trade-off–July2005.pdf.

Davezies, Laurent. 1999. "Un essai de mesure de la contribution des budgets des pays membres à la cohésion européenne." *Economie et Prévision* 138-139 (April-September): 163–96.

———. 2001. "Revenu et territoires." In *Aménagement du territoire.* Conseil d'Analyse Economique. http://www.cae.gouv.fr/.

Dupont, Vincent, and Philippe Martin. 2003. "Regional Policies and Inequalities: Are Subsidies Good for You?" Unpublished paper, CERAS-ENPC, Paris.

Duranton, Gilles, and Vassilis Monastiriotis. 2002. "Mind the Gaps: The Evolution of Regional Inequalities in the U.K. 1982–1997." *Journal of Regional Science* 42 (2): 219–56.

Duro, Juan Antonio. 2001. "Regional Income Inequalities in Europe: An Updated Measurement and Some Decomposition Results." Instituto de Análisis Económico, Consejo Superior de Investigaciones Científicas.

European Union. 1997. *Treaty of Amsterdam.* Luxembourg: Office for Official Publications of the European Communities.

Fuest, Clemens, and Bernd Huber. 2000. "Why Do Governments Subsidise Investment and Not Employment?" *Journal of Public Economics* 78 (1-2): 171–92.

Gobillon, Laurent. 2002. *Mobilité résidentielle et marché locaux de l'emploi.* Ph.D. dissertation, Ecole des Hautes Etudes en Sciences Sociales.

Jaffe, Adam, Manuel Trajtenberg, and Rebecca Henderson. 1993. "Geographic Localization of Knowledge Spillovers as Evidenced by Patent Citations." *Quarterly Journal of Economics* 108 (3): 577–98.

Krugman, Paul. 1991. *Geography and Trade.* Cambridge, MA: MIT Press.

Martin, Philippe. 1998. "Can Regional Policies Affect Growth and Geography in Europe?" *World Economy* 21 (6): 757–74.

———. 1999. "Public Policies, Regional Inequalities, and Growth." *Journal of Public Economics* 73 (1): 85–105.

———. 2003. "Public Policies and Economic Geography." In *European Integration, Regional Policy, and Growth,* ed. Bernard Funk and Lodovico Pizzati. Washington, DC: World Bank.

Martin, Philippe, and Carol Ann Rogers. 1995. "Industrial Location and Public Infrastructure." *Journal of International Economics* 39 (3): 335–51.

Midelfart-Knarvik, Karen Helene, and Henry G. Overman. 2002. "Delocation and European Integration: Is Structural Spending Justified?" *Economic Policy* 17 (35): 321–59.

Monastiriotis, Vassilis. 2003. "Union Retreat and Regional Economic Performance: The U.K. in the 1990s." LSE Working Paper, London School of Economics, London.

Overman, Henry, and Diego Puga. 2002. "Unemployment Clusters across European Countries and Regions." *Economic Policy* 17 (34): 117–47.

Sapir, André, Philippe Aghion, and Giuseppe Bertola. 2004. *An Agenda for a Growing Europe: The Sapir Report.* Oxford : Oxford University Press.

Yuill, Douglas, John Bachtler, and Fiona Wishlade. 1997. *European Regional Incentives 1997–98,* 17th ed. London: Bowker-Saur.

Notes

1. Of course, the firm could produce in two regions, a possibility that would complicate the presentation without adding much.
2. The relation is given in log because it does not appear to be linear.

Part VII: Spatial Policy for Growth and Equity

Cohesion and Convergence: Synonyms or Two Different Notions?

GRZEGORZ GORZELAK

"Cohesion" has become one of the most important phrases in current policies conducted within the European Union (EU) member states and the European Union as such. It is a relatively new term: it was first brought into the *acquis communautaire* of the European Communities in the Single European Act of 1986, which emphasized the need to enhance the social and economic cohesion of the European Community with a view to leveling regional disparities and their potential growth, an anticipated result of the introduction of the single market. The notion of cohesion did indeed take root in the Maastricht Treaty establishing the European Union. Since then, especially after the cohesion fund was brought into being, cohesion became one of the leading directives of the EU policies.

Cohesion as a policy directive has three dimensions: economic, social, and territorial. The last has been formally approved only recently, in the Treaty of Lisbon, which states, "It [the Union] shall promote economic, social, and territorial cohesion and solidarity among Member States."

Since the very beginning, cohesion has been understood simply as convergence. These two terms have been used as synonyms, although cohesion is clearly viewed in terms of its equalizing function. To reach a state of cohesion means to eliminate territorial disparities in the level of economic development (economic cohesion) and in the access to labor and income (social cohesion). Such an approach to cohesion coincides with the regional policy of the European Union (formerly the European Community), which allocates about 60 percent of its funding to support regions with a low level of development—less than 75 percent of the EU average gross domestic product (GDP) per capita, using purchasing power parity.

The member states, especially those that benefit the most from structural funds and cohesion funds, follow the commission's principles in their own cohesion

Grzegorz Gorzelak is Professor of Economics and Director of the Centre for European Regional and Local Studies at Warsaw University in Poland.

Berlin Workshop Series 2009
© 2009 The International Bank for Reconstruction and Development/The World Bank

policies. In most, if not in all, of them we also find the synonymy between cohesion and convergence.

Yet the goal of territorial convergence is hardly, if at all, achievable. This conviction has emerged even within the Directorate-General for Regional Policies (at that time DG 16), which wrote in the third report on regional policy that reaching a state of cohesion within the community was a task the fulfillment of which was rather distant in time (CEC 1987). With the passage of time, however, these reservations were been reduced, and a general belief that achieving cohesion by implementing convergence can constitute the basis for the regional policy of the EU has spread widely among the commission, the governments, regions, and localities within the European Union.

The empirical evidence demonstrates a strong persistence of historical regional patterns, even if these patterns were to be changed by massive external assistance rendered to the less well-off regions. Central Appalachia is still the internal periphery of the United States in spite of the fact that it has enjoyed the greatest share of the Appalachian Program. Mezzogiorno has not entered the path of fast growth and has not demonstrated the abilities of the Third Italy that emerged without any help from the Italian government and the EU. The most recent example of the former German Democratic Republic dramatically shows that a massive inflow of financial and technical help from the outside leads nowhere and may be counterproductive by killing individual motivation and attitudes of self-reliance and self-responsibility.

There are several positive cases of sudden advancement of some backward countries and regions. Ireland is the one most often quoted. But it is often forgotten that the external assistance for the EU did not bring any reward until 1994, and then the aid was coupled with massive inflow of foreign (U.S.) investment in computer and pharmaceutical industries. Moreover, Ireland achieved national success at the expense of growing internal regional differentiation, since most of the growth was concentrated in the south, leaving the north behind.

Ireland is a clear example of a process of polarization that is a product of the slow growth of lagging regions and the rapid advancement of metropolitan cores. "Metropolises govern the world," as Castells says. This is because they became the nodes of the "economy of flows," to use another term publicized by Castells (see Castells 1997).

This process is clearly pronounced in the countries that are undergoing accelerated transformation: the Central and Eastern European (CEE) new member states. There is a positive relationship between the initial level of development and its dynamics (see figure 1).

Similar regional patterns can be found in CEE countries. Capital city regions "escape" the rest of the country, and the regions that contain big cities follow them. The border regions—both located at the external borders of the EU as well as those located along the internal border—do display slow growth; at the same time, these usually are the less developed regions in all CEE countries. Thus divergence is a matter of fact, which may be attributed to relatively fast growth that is concentrated mostly in capital and big city regions.

FIGURE 1. GDP per Inhabitant, 1995, and GDP Growth, 1995–2004

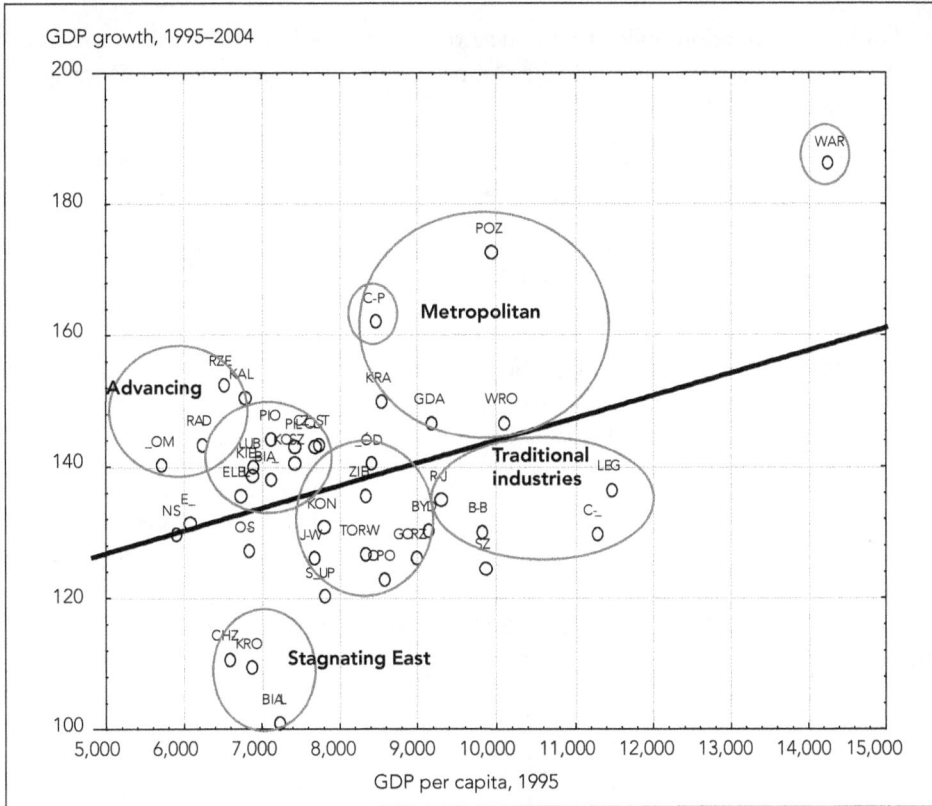

Source: Bank of Regional Data, Central Statistical Office, Warsaw. See also Bachtler and Gorzelak 2007.

The picture for the regions of the EU is more complicated. As indicated in the fourth cohesion report (CEC 2007), there is a negative relationship between the level of GDP per inhabitant and its dynamics. However, the national and regional processes are not separated, and the overall pattern is a cross-product of these two dimensions (see figure 2).

We therefore observe convergence on the national level and divergence on the regional level. It is doubtful whether these two levels may parallel each other. It may even be that regional divergence is a condition of national convergence, since it does not seem that we can overcome the "equity-efficiency" dilemma, fundamental for regional policy.

So, what is wrong with a cohesion policy that aims to achieve convergence? Several answers have been given to this question, and the most important ones are found in classical papers by Boldrin and Canova (2001), Sapir and others (2003), Rodriguez-Pose and Fratesi (2004), and the less known, but more critical of cohesion policy, work by Ederveen, de Groot, and Nahuis (2006). Their arguments may be summarized as follows (compare Bachtler and Gorzelak 2007):

- Cohesion policy is mostly social in meaning and does not contribute to growth (Boldrin and Canova 2001).

- Traditional cohesion policy that concentrates on "hard" infrastructure and assistance to firms does not increase the competitiveness of lagging regions (Rodriguez-Pose and Fratesi 2004).

- This policy may even depress growth in countries with poor institutions, high corruption, and lack of openness (Ederveen, de Groot, and Nahuis 2006).

- Only assistance to education (Rodriguez-Pose and Fratesi 2004) and institution building (Ederveen, de Groot and Nahuis 2006) may create grounds for long-lasting development of such regions.

- To achieve these goals, the EU policies have to be remodeled, to increase outlays for competitiveness and innovativeness, at the expense of the Common Agricultural Policy and traditional regional policy (Sapir and others 2003).

For much of the past 20 years, the use of cohesion policy resources has been governed by the assumptions of "traditional" regional policies of the postwar period originating in Keynesian doctrine and state interventionism in a resource-based

FIGURE 2. Growth of GDP per Capita, 2000–04, GDP per Capita, 2004, and Hypothetical Regional Patterns of New and Old Member States

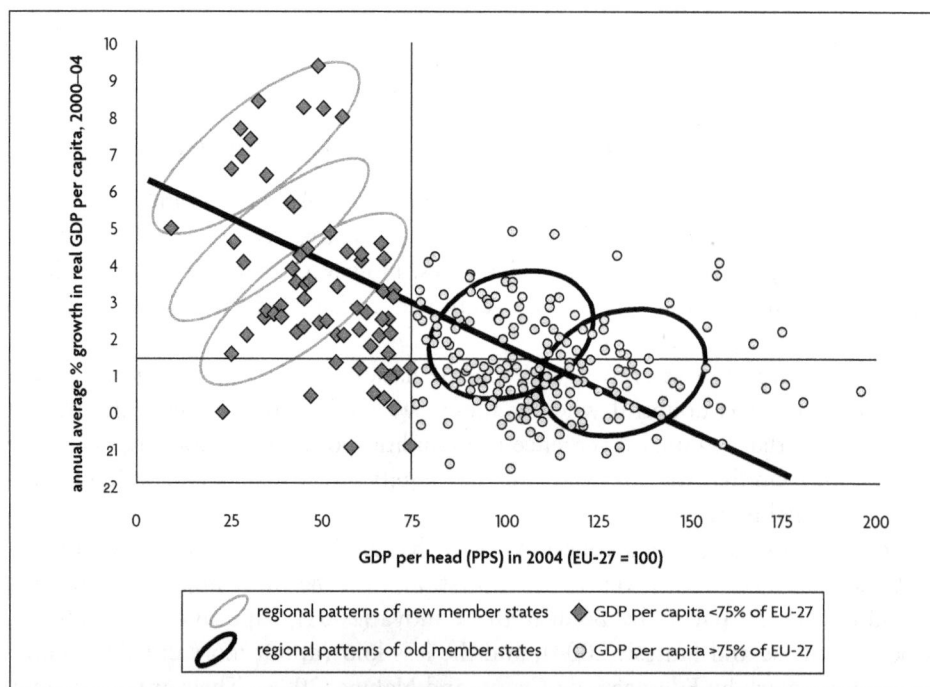

Source: Based on figure 1.6 in fourth cohesion report (CEC 2007: 10).
Note: Three regions are beyond the scale of this chart: Brussels with an index of 248 and growth of 0.93 percent; Luxembourg with an index of 251 and 1.9 percent; and Inner London with an index of 303 and growth of 1.7 percent. EU-27 average growth is 1.4 percent.

economy. Traditional regional policy was both formulated and pursued in what Castells (1997) dubs the "economy of places," an economic reality where specialized economic and urban systems functioned much more in isolation from one another than is now the case. As a result of the shift to an open, knowledge-based economy and from quantitative to qualitative development factors, traditional approaches have become much less effective. Castells calls the current model the "economy of flows"—that is, a mutually interdependent system—with a dominant role for the flows of goods, people, capital, and, especially, information. In the current era, countries and regions will only gain lasting competitive advantage if they can produce innovation on a steady basis. Exerting an influence on this new economic model must take different forms than was the case under the previous paradigm.

The paradigm shift has been partly recognized by the European Commission in its development of new assumptions for cohesion policy for 2007–13, drawing on the Lisbon strategy (CEC 2006): "These strategic guidelines should give priority to … investment in innovation, the knowledge economy, the new information and communication technologies, employment, human capital, entrepreneurship, support for SMEs [small and medium enterprises], or access to risk capital financing." It is instructive to note that the commission's original version of the guidelines (CEC 2005) was considerably more definitive in the need for a shift in policy focus but was "diluted" at the insistence of the member states.

Maintaining such a direction in reforming cohesion policy also calls for reconsidering the concept of cohesion. Arguably, *cohesion* should be understood in functional terms and not as an effort to reach *convergence*. Convergence is an approximation of static states, whereas cohesion is dynamic by nature, being the opposite of entropy. Moreover, convergence is difficult to achieve, certainly with the limited resources available at the EU level. Cohesion should be liberated from its "equalization" underpinnings and should be understood rather as harmony and collaboration (economy of flows), lack of destructive pressures and irresolvable conflicts, and the possibility for coexistence and cooperation between individual components. Following this line of argument, an alternative understanding of the individual aspects of cohesion would involve a policy focus on three elements: *economic cohesion,* denoting the possibility for achieving effective cooperation between economic agents, lowering transaction costs, and harmonizing relationships between businesses and their institutional environment; *social cohesion,* eliminating barriers to horizontal and vertical mobility by helping to overcome differences in levels of education, career advancement, and material status; and *territorial cohesion,* removing constraints on spatial development that restrict the achievement of social and economic cohesion, such as eliminating barriers to transport, connecting the major nodes of European and national space, and developing research and business networks.

References

Bachtler, John, and Grzegorz Gorzelak. 2007. "Reforming EU Cohesion Policy: A Reappraisal of the Performance of the Structural Funds." *Policy Studies* 28 (4): 309–26.

Boldrin, Michelle, and Fabio Canova. 2001. "Inequality and Convergence in Europe's Regions: Reconsidering European Regional Policies." *Economic Policy* 16 (32): 205–53.

Castells, Manuel. 1997. *The Information Age: Economy, Society, and Culture: The Rise of Network Society*, vol. 2. Oxford: Blackwell.

CEC (Commission of the European Communities). 1987. *The Regions of the Enlarged Community: Third Periodic Report on the Social and Economic Situation of the Regions of the Community.* Brussels: CEC.

———. 2005. *Communication from the Commission Cohesion Policy in Support of Growth and Jobs: Community Strategic Guidelines, 2007–2013.* COM(2005) 0299. Brussels: CEC.

———. 2006. "Council Decision of 6 October 2006 on Community Strategic Guidelines on Cohesion." In *Official Journal of the European Communities.* L291/11, 21 (October). Brussels: CEC.

———. 2007. *Growing Regions, Growing Europe: Fourth Report on Economic and Social Cohesion.* Brussels: CEC, Directorate-General for Regional Policies.

Ederveen, Sjef, Henri de Groot, and Richard Nahuis. 2006. "Fertile Soil for Structural Funds? A Panel Data Analysis of the Conditional Effectiveness of European Cohesion Policy." *Kyklos* 59 (1): 17–42.

Rodriguez-Pose, Andrés, and Ugo Fratesi. 2004. "Between Development and Social Policies: The Impact of European Structural Funds in Objective 1 Regions." *Regional Studies* 38 (1): 97–113.

Sapir, André, with Philippe Aghion, Giusepe Bertola, Martin Hellwig, Jean Pisani-Ferry, Dariusz Rosati, José Viñals, and Helen Wallace. 2003. *An Agenda for a Growing Europe: Making the EU Economic System Deliver.* Report of an Independent High-Level Study Group established on the initiative of the president of the European Commission. Brussels: European Commission. http://www.euractiv.com/ndbtext/innovation/sapirreport.pdf.

Regional Development as Self-Organized Converging Growth

PETER NIJKAMP

Regional development is not only an efficiency issue in economic policy; it is also an equity issue due to the fact that economic development normally exhibits a significant degree of spatial variability. Over the past decades this empirical fact has prompted various strands of research literature, in particular, on the measurement of interregional disparity, the causal explanation for the emergence or persistence of spatial variability in economic development, and the impact assessment of policy measures aimed at coping with undesirable spatial inequity conditions. The study of socioeconomic processes and inequalities at meso and regional levels positions regions at the core of policy actions and hence warrants intensive conceptual and applied research efforts.

For decades, the unequal distribution of welfare among regions and cities has been a source of concern for both policy makers and researchers. Regional development is about the geography of welfare and its evolution. It has played a central role in disciplines such as economic geography, regional economics, regional science, and economic growth theory. The concept is not static in nature; instead, it refers to complex space-time dynamics of regions (or an interdependent set of regions). Changing regional welfare positions are often hard to measure, and in practice we often use gross domestic product (GDP) per capita (or growth of GDP per capita) as a statistical approximation (see, for example, Stimson, Stough, and Roberts 2006). Sometimes alternative or complementary measures are also used, such as per capita consumption, poverty rates, unemployment rates, labor force participation rates, or access to public services. These indicators are more social in nature and are often used in United Nations welfare comparisons. An example of a rather popular index in this framework is the Human Development Index, which represents the welfare position of regions or nations on a 0–1 scale using quantifiable standardized social data (such as employment, life expectancy, or adult liter-

Peter Nijkamp is Professor in the Department of Spatial Economies at Free University of Amsterdam in The Netherlands.

Berlin Workshop Series 2009
© 2009 The International Bank for Reconstruction and Development/The World Bank

acy; see, for example, Cameron 2005). In all cases, however, spatial disparity indicators show much variability.

Clearly, the concept of a region is problematic in empirical research, as the spatial scale of regions may exhibit much variation, ranging, for example, from the larger U.S. states to relatively small regions in Europe, even sometimes down to the municipal level. A key feature of any region—in contrast to a nation—is its relative openness (see, for example, Blanchard 1991). From a statistical viewpoint, regions are often administrative spatial units with a certain competence for socioeconomic policy and planning. The relatively small scale of a region leads normally to a high degree of heterogeneity and interaction with each other, as a result of locational features such as local production factors, institutions, transport infrastructures, and local market size (see also Armstrong and Taylor 2000).

Regional disparities may have significant negative socioeconomic costs, for instance, because of social welfare transfers, inefficient production systems (for example, due to an inefficient allocation of resources), and undesirable social conditions (see Gilles 1998). Given a neoclassical framework of analysis, these disparities (in terms of per capita income) are assumed to vanish in the long run, because of the spatial mobility of production factors, which eventually causes an equalization of factor productivity in all regions. Clearly, long-range factors such as education, research and development (R&D), and technology play a critical structural role in this context. In the short run, however, regional disparities may show rather persistent trends (see also Patuelli 2007).

Disparities can be measured in various relevant categories, such as (un)employment, income, investment, and growth. Clearly, such indicators are not entirely independent, as is, for instance, illustrated in Okun's law, which assumes a relationship between economic output and unemployment (see Okun 1970; Paldam 1987). Convergence of regional disparities is clearly a complex phenomenon, which refers to the mechanisms through which differences in welfare between regions may vanish (Armstrong 1995). In the convergence debate, we observe increasingly more attention being paid to the openness of spatial systems, reflected inter alia in trade, labor mobility, and commuting (see, for example, Magrini 2004). In a comparative static sense, convergence may have varying meanings in a discussion of a possible reduction in spatial disparities among regions, in particular (see also Barro and Sala-i-Martin 1992; Baumol 1986; Bernard and Durlauf 1996; Boldrin and Canova 2001):

- β-convergence: a negative relationship between per capita income growth and the level of per capita income in the initial period (for example, poor regions grow faster than initially rich regions)

- σ-convergence: a decline in the dispersion of per capita income between regions over time.

The convergence hypothesis in neoclassical economics has been widely accepted in the literature, but it is critically dependent on two hypotheses (Cheshire and Carbonaro 1995; Dewhurst and Mutis-Gaitan 1995):

- Diminishing returns to scale in capital, which means that output growth will be less than proportional with respect to capital

- Technological progress, which will generate benefits that also decrease with its accumulation (that is, diminishing returns).

Many studies have been carried out to estimate the degree of β-convergence and σ-convergence (see, for example, Barro and Sala-i-Martin 1991, 1992). The general findings are that the rate of β-convergence is on an order of magnitude of 2 percent annually, while the degree of σ-convergence tends to decline over time, for both U.S. states and European regions. Clearly, there is an ongoing debate worldwide on the type of convergence, its speed, its multidimensional conceptualization, and its causal significance in the context of regional policy measures (see, for example, Fagerberg and Verspagen 1996; Fingleton 1999; Galor 1996). Important research topics in the current literature appear to be the role of knowledge and entrepreneurship, spatial heterogeneity in locational or sociocultural conditions, and institutional and physical barriers. An important new topic in the field has become group convergence (or club convergence; see, for example, Baumont, Ertur, and LeGallo 2003; Chatterji 1992; Chatterji and Dewhurst 1996; Fischer and Stirböck 2006; Islam 2003; López-Bazo and others 1999; Quah 1996; Rey and Montouri 1999; Sala-i-Martin 1996). Thus the research field of spatial disparities is still developing, giving rise to fascinating policy issues. The rest of this paper addresses prominent policy questions as they have emerged over the years.

Spatial Disparities: Productivity Is the Key

Spatial disparities may manifest themselves at different geographic levels, ranging from nations to urban districts. The lower the geographic scale, the larger the geographic variation in the welfare variable(s) considered. This scale dependence of spatial disparities calls for great caution in comparing the performance of nations or regions. But in most cases, differences in spatial performance (for example, income per capita or employment growth) are directly or indirectly related to differences in productivity among regions. Clearly, such differences may be ascribed to physical geography, to inefficient use of human resources, to inadequate availability of physical or human capital, and to lack of resources, among others, but overall deficiencies on the supply side of production factors—whatever the cause of these deficiencies may be—lead to lower performance of the region concerned. And, therefore, the measurement and evaluation of total factor productivity are of great importance for understanding spatial welfare disparities.

The motives for measuring regional development are manifold. But a prominent argument over the years is that welfare positions of regions or nations may exhibit great disparities that are often persistent in nature (see Fingleton 2003). These translate into large disparities in living standards. For example, in 1960, the world's richest country had a per capita income that was 39 times greater than that of the world's poorest country (after correcting for purchasing power), while by 2000 this gap had increased to 91 (Abreu 2005). Not only do regions in our world have significant differences in welfare positions, but it sometimes takes decades or more to eliminate them. As an illustration, take Tanzania (the world's poorest country in 2000), which experienced on average a modest growth rate of 0.6 percent a year over the period 1960–2000. In order to reach the world's average per capita income of US$8,820 per year at its current rate of growth, Tanzania would need another 485 years. Even if the annual growth rate were to increase to 1.8 percent (the world's current average), Tanzania would need 161 years to close the gap. And if it were to grow at the rate of the Republic of Korea (the fastest grower over the period concerned), it could close the gap in just 49 years. Persistent regional welfare disparities are a source of frustration for both economists and policy makers (Lucas 1988).

Regional development is clearly a multidimensional concept with a great variety that is determined by a multiplicity of factors such as natural resource endowments, quality and quantity of labor, capital availability and access, productive and overhead investments, entrepreneurial culture and attitude, physical infrastructure, sectoral structure, technological infrastructure and progress, public support systems, and so forth (see Blakely 1994). By focusing the attention on regional differences in welfare, we touch on a centerpiece of the evolution of growth in and between regions.

In the past half a century, we have witnessed an avalanche of studies in regional differences in welfare. The literature on regional development has usually centered around two dominant issues: how is regional welfare created, and how can we cope with undesirable interregional welfare discrepancies? The first question, normally referred to as "allocative efficiency," addresses the optimal use of scarce resources (that is, inputs such as capital, labor, physical resources, and knowledge) to generate a maximum value of output. The second question is sociopolitical equity in nature and addresses the mechanisms and conditions (economic, policy interventions) that may help to alleviate undesirable development disparities in the space economy. Normally, regions that operate efficiently tend to grow faster than regions that have less favorable development conditions, so that there is a built-in tension between efficiency and equity within a system of regions, at least in the short run. The efficiency-equity dilemma is without doubt one of the most intriguing issues in regional development policy (Baldwin and others 2003; Brakman, Garretsen, and van Marrewijk 2001; Fujita and Thisse 2003; Puga 1999). But have we gained sufficient new insight in order to assist regional development policy?

The policy response to undesirable discrepancies in international welfare has usually been to start a subsidy program, in the form of either infrastructure provision (and other regional development factors) or social welfare transfers. In many cases, the size of these transfers exceeds by far regional development expenditures, but these transfers are only of a consumptive nature (for example, short-term income subsidies) and do not have a productive meaning; their long-range impact on the reinforcement of regional economic structures is almost negligible.

There is another striking fact. The great many studies on the effect of regional policy measures on regional welfare are often not leading to conclusive findings that would warrant an intensification of regional development policy. Of course, there may be many reasons for this disappointing observation, such as the long-term nature of regional development efforts in which a time span of one generation is not unusual, the lack of distinction between static allocation effects and long-range dynamic generative effects, the insufficient attention given to the difference between internal and external border areas, and the methodological flaws inherent in tracing the effects of individual projects or programs on a total regional economy. In addition, the focal point of regional policy is not always clear, as it might differ according to spatial unit, sector, or socioeconomic target group.

Regional development policy clearly is fraught with many uncertainties. This paper aims to shed light on the complexity of regional development. It starts from the heart of regional economics—location and allocation theory—and includes an exposition on neoclassical factor endowment and infrastructure theory. Next, a more contemporaneous contribution is offered on the modern drivers of regional development—knowledge and entrepreneurship—while also paying attention to recent advances in endogenous growth and the new economic geography. It then pays attention to an important and often less tangible issue—the effect of social capital—and addresses more explicitly the so-called convergence debate and the role of governments in regional development policy. It concludes with some retrospective and prospective remarks on the future of regional development policy and research.

Spatial Accessibility: A Prominent Competitive Factor

In the history of economic development, we have observed that spatial accessibility offers many opportunities for economic progress. Riverbanks and coastal areas were often forerunners in acquiring welfare gains. Indeed, the history of mankind has exhibited a dynamic geographic pattern, where accessibility through proper infrastructure and favorable physical-geographical conditions (climate) were decisive factors for the settlement of people and firms. These areas created the foundations for large agglomerations (such as Cape Town, London, New York, Tokyo, or Venice). Regional development appeared to find favorable breeding places in accessibility and large economic attraction poles. It is evident that differences in geographic accessibility ultimately caused spatial disparities. Even nowadays, persistent discrepancies in regional welfare have historical roots in the locational conditions of such high-potential areas. The present figures of our world are striking: approximately 1 billion people live on less than a dollar a day, while more than 2 billion people have no access to adequate sanitation. And the gap between poor and rich is formidable and even increasing. For example, the top 20 percent of the world's population consumes about 85 percent of the world's income, while the bottom 20 percent lives on approximately 1.5 percent of the world's income. And things get worse: a generation ago, people in the top 20 percent were 30 times richer than those in the bottom 20 percent; nowadays, they are more than 70 times richer (see Serageldin 2006). In general, the more prosperous places are those with a high degree of accessibility.

The dispersion of economic activity in our world shows a great variation. And hence, location theory has played a central role in explaining not only the spatial distribution of economic activity, but also the dispersion of welfare among regions or cities. Consequently, regional development theory is deeply rooted in location theory (Martin and Ottaviano 2001). Location theory has a long history in regional economics and economic geography. Starting off from path-breaking ideas set forth by Von Thünen, Christaller, Lösch, Isard, Hoover, and many others, modern location theory has moved into a strong analytical framework for regional economics and economic geography. Cost minimization and profit maximization principles are integrated in a solid economic setting, in which both partial and general spatial equilibrium studies on the space economy highlight the geographic patterns of industrial and residential behavior. Furthermore, the theory encapsulates the impact of public actors, for instance, through the provision of space-opening or accessibility-enhancing infrastructure (as can be observed in regional development policy). Thus the fundamentals of classical location theory are made up of a blend of physical geography (determining the accessibility of a location and the availability of resources) and smart economic behavior (through a clever combination of production factors and market potentials in space; for a review, see Capello 2006; Davis and Weinstein 1999; Fujita and Thisse 2002). Location and accessibility are essentially two sides of the same coin.

However, location patterns are never static; instead, they have an endogenous impact on newcomers (residents and firms) in addition to various spatial externalities. Thus incumbent firms may attract others through scale, localization, and urbanization advantages (for example, in the form of spatial-economic externalities in a Marshallian district; see Asheim 1996). Consequently, agglomerations tend to become self-reinforcing spatial magnets affecting the entire space economy. Such concentrations of economic activity create welfare spin-offs for a broader regional system and thus determine the geographic patterns of welfare and regional development. Seen from this perspective, a blend between location theory and urban economics (or urban geography) is plausible (see also the so-called new economic geography; Fujita, Krugman, and Venables 1999; Hanson 1996).

In the past decades, we have witnessed the emergence of the digital economy through which actors can be networked worldwide. As a consequence, the interaction between industrial networks and location as well as the access to networks have gained much interest (see Nijkamp 2003 for a review). Locations that offer the best available network services are the proper candidates for many firms in the information and communication technology (ICT), high-tech, and high-services sectors and are able to generate a high value added for regional development. Despite many statements on the "death of distance," physical distance still matters. ICT may enhance spatial productivity of actors by expanding their action radius, but evident substitution mechanisms have so far not been found (with a few exceptions on a local scale).

The availability of and access to infrastructure are critical factors for successful regional development (Davis and Weinstein 1999). In addition to the impact of labor as capital on traditional factor inputs, interest is growing in measuring the impact of infrastructure on regional development. Especially in a world with shrinking distance, space-time accessibility of regions becomes a critical determinant of relative regional-economic positions. Transport economics and transport geography have offered an abundance of theoretical and empirical evidence on the importance of physical infrastructure for regional growth. An extensive review can be found in Nijkamp (2003). The uneven provision of infrastructure has also been identified as a key determinant of regional income disparities in less developed countries (World Bank 2006: 168–74). However, it is not the pure supply of infrastructure, but rather its effective use that determines its productivity-enhancing potential.

Entrepreneurship, Innovation, and the Knowledge Economy

Spatial dynamics (including the emergence of spatial disparities) is the result of changing patterns in the activity of people and firms, including geographic mobility. Since the good old days of Marshall, Schumpeter, and Kirzner, we know that innovation and entrepreneurship are the driving factors behind economic growth. There is an avalanche of literature on the importance of entrepreneurship for enhancing the innovative capacity and growth potential of regions (see, for example, Acs, Carlsson, and Karlsson 1999; Audretsch and others 2002). Entrepreneurs are change agents with a high potential for innovation.

In recent years, we have witnessed increasing interest in entrepreneurship. Entrepreneurship is a complex, multifaceted phenomenon that finds its roots in risk-taking behavior of profit-seeking individuals in a competitive economy. But its determinants also have clear correlations with gender, age, education, financial support systems, administrative regulations, risk tolerance, and market structures (Kirchhoff 1994; Storey 1994). Entrepreneurship lies at the heart of innovation as the art of doing creative things for the sake of achieving a competitive advantage in an open economy. The debate on entrepreneurship and innovation has, from a geographic perspective, prompted the emergence of new concepts such as innovative regions, innovative milieus, learning regions, or knowledge-based regions (see, for example, De Groot, Nijkamp, and Stough 2004; Florida 1995; Malecki 2000; Simmie 1997). Innovation is the factor critical to survival in a competitive space economy and determines the direction and pace of regional development. A key aspect of innovation in a modern space economy is the use of and access to the ICT sector. Consequently, ICT infrastructure is increasingly seen as a necessary resource for regional development with a high degree of productivity-enhancing power.

The emergence of ICT has prompted speculative ideas on e-economics, e-societies, e-governments, or e-firms. Indeed, it goes almost without saying that ICT is a necessary ingredient of a modern knowledge-based economy. And that also holds for regions and cities. Clearly, knowledge is a composite good with many facets, but from an economic perspective knowledge serves to enhance productivity and induce innovations. There is indeed an ongoing debate on the unidirectional or circular relationship between knowledge and development, and this forms one of the central issues in endogenous growth theory (see also Krugman 1991; Markusen 1985). Endogenous growth theory seeks to offer a microeconomic foundation for economic dynamics where traditional fixed factors are seen as a result of intrinsic economic forces.

Endogenous growth theory has played a central role in the growth debate since the 1990s. The main idea of these new contributions is that technological progress is not exogenously given, but rather an endogenous response of economic actors in a competitive business environment. Consequently, in contrast to earlier macroeconomic explanatory frameworks, the emphasis is much more on the economic behavior of individual firms (see, for example, Aghion and Howitt 1998; Barro and Sala-i-Martin 1997). In this way, it can be demonstrated that regional growth is not the result of exogenous productivity-enhancing factors but is the result of deliberate choices of individual actors (firms and policy makers). This implies that governments are not agents "above the actors," but rather agents "among the actors" in a dynamic economy.

Furthermore, the importance of knowledge for innovation and entrepreneurship is increasingly recognized. The spatial distribution of knowledge and its spillovers are considered as an important factor for successful regional development in an open, competitive economic system. Thus the geographic patterns of knowledge diffusion as well as the barriers to access to knowledge are decisive for regional development in a modern, global, and open space economy. Consequently, knowledge policy—often instigated by ICT advances—is a critical factor for the creation of regional welfare (see, for example, Acs, de Groot, and Nijkamp 2002; Döring and Schnellenback 2006; Keeble and Wilkinson 1999). With more economies depending on knowledge-intensive products, the importance of a dedicated knowledge policy is increasingly recognized.

Regional development policy appears to move increasingly toward knowledge and innovation policy (see Asheim and Gertler 2005 for a comparative study). This argument is reinforced in a recent study by Stimson, Stough, and Salazar (2005), where the authors demonstrate that leadership and institutional qualities have a great impact on regional welfare, in particular, when the role of leadership is linked with innovation and knowledge creation. To the same extent that innovative entrepreneurship is critical for long-term regional welfare growth, governance and leadership are essential for balanced regional development (Martin 1999). Leadership presupposes proactive behavior, visions for future development, awareness of institutional and behavioral processes, responses and bottlenecks, as well as acceptance by the population. Awareness of the importance of leadership and entrepreneurship lies with the recognition of creative actions and learning actors. Studies on regional leadership are rare, but can be found, among others, in Heenan and Bennis (1999), Hofstede (1997), Judd and Parkinson (1990), and Stimson, Stough, and Salazar

(2005). This is a promising and important new field of research, for both policy making and industrial organization.

Finally, in recent years, we have witnessed the emergence of a new strand of literature, coined the "new economic geography," in the vein of endogenous growth theory (see Brakman, Garretsen, and van Marrewijk 2001; Krugman 1991; Neary 2001). Although the term "new economic geography" is arguably not appropriate (most concepts can already be found in the regional economics and regional science literature since the 1950s), this seemingly new approach has attracted quite some attention within the neoclassical economics literature. It marries the increasing-returns monopolistic competition model (à la Dixit and Stiglitz 1997) with the micro foundations of spatial-economic behavior, including interregional trade (see Fujita, Krugman, and Venables 1999; Fujita and Thisse 2002; Krugman 1991; Naudé 2005; Redding and Venables 2004; Rivera-Batiz 1998; Romer 1986). This recent approach emphasizes the importance of agglomeration externalities (caused by increasing returns to scale) for regional welfare creation, in the context of global competitive forces where trade (between regions or countries) plays a critical role. Thus regions are part of a global competitive network system. Recent contributions within this literature have found that agglomeration can be a welfare-improving outcome for workers in both core and peripheral regions, for instance, if agglomeration raises the rate of innovation (see Fujita and Thisse 2003). This result provides theoretical support for regional development policies destined to support and enhance existing clusters of specialization, which may show a resemblance to Marshallian districts.

The Human Factor in Regional Development: Social Capital

Regional development is the outcome of socioeconomic processes and decisions, in particular the smart combination of various production factors and local resources that are decisive for the productivity-enhancing potential of various agents involved. Previous sections addressed locational decisions, factor mix decisions, and innovation and R&D decisions of firms as critical conditions for regional growth. Institutional support systems and leadership talents were also mentioned as flanking incentives that might spur economic development of regions or cities. Textbook economics has paid extensive attention to the conditions under which these factors might lead to accelerated growth, with sometimes significant variation among regions (for example, increasing returns to scale, product heterogeneity, and specialization). All these elements affect the welfare and productivity pattern of regional economic systems and may be a source of divergent economic achievements among various regions of the space economy. Nevertheless, the analysis of spatial-economic disparities often does not provide us with a complete picture of all relevant background factors. In other words, many models trying to explain regional growth and spatial differences are semantically insufficiently specified. In various cases, therefore, economists have resorted to the introduction of complementary explanatory factors, such as X-efficiency factors, which refer to often intangible factors (for example, personal devotion, altruistic behavior, concern about the future or nature, social engagement) and may offer additional explanations for the performance of various agents (for example, regions, administrations, entrepreneurs, employees).

The search for such new complementary explanatory frameworks has induced increasing interest in the contribution of "social capital" to regional development. Bourdieu (1986: 243) defines social capital as "an attribute of an individual in a social context. One can acquire social capital through purposeful actions and can transform social capital into conventional economic gains. The ability to do so, however, depends on the nature of the social obligations, connections, and networks available to you." Social capital can assume different forms such as social skills, charisma, cooperative nature, or care for others that may create various benefits for the individual or his or her social environment. They are essentially a form of social externalities, with positive revenues for all actors involved (see Baldwin 1999; Benhabib and Spiegel 1994; De la Fuente and Doménech 2006; Glaeser, Laibson, and Sacerdote 2000; Sobel 2002). Social capital is thus a productive resource at the interface of individual and collective interest (see Dasgupta and Serageldin 1999; Putnam 2000) and serves as an intangible (often hidden) source of well-being in an individualistic modern society.

Social capital is essentially based on the notion of trust (see Fukuyama 1995) and was introduced in the urban planning literature several decades ago by Jane Jacobs (1961). It has emerged in a new form as a productive factor that may stimulate regional (or urban) development. An interesting study from this perspective was undertaken by Westlund and Bolton (2003) and Westlund and Nilsson (2005). The authors argue that social capital has several manifestations:

- Capital in an economic sense (with a productivity-enhancing potential, with a blend of supporting factors, with accumulation and depreciation features, with a mix of private and public goods characteristics, and with various spatial and group levels)

- Generator of producer surplus (with a quality-generating potential, with an area-specific social benefit, and with a decline in transaction costs)

- Facilitator of entrepreneurship (with a combination of skills, risk-taking attitude, market insights, and goodwill trust).

Social capital clearly plays a prominent role in a networked society, where reliability, trust, standardization, and efficient interactor operations are the keys to success and competitive performance. Socioeconomic interaction in networks and confidence and trust among network actors are closely related phenomena (see also Dyer 2000).

A final remark is in order here. There has been a rapidly rising volume of studies on social capital and trust, from the side of both economists and sociologists (see also Chou 2006). Unfortunately, the number of applied studies that operationalize trust and social capital is disappointingly low. There is further scope for innovative empirical research on social capital, in particular in the context of regional development where local resources such as social capital play a prominent role. Applied research on the significance of social capital is once more warranted, as differences in social capital among regions may contribute to widening spatial disparities.

Spatial Disparities and Convergence

Regions and cities are not static socioeconomic entities, but always in a state of flux. Regions and nations in our world show complex patterns of development (Englemann and Walz 1995; Evans 1996; Grossman and Helpman 1990). Textbook economics would teach us that under conditions of free competition, homogeneity of preferences and technology parameters, and free mobility of production factors across all regions in the space economy, income per capita would tend to converge to the same growth rate. In neoclassical economic growth models, convergence between regions takes place through capital accumulation. Regions that are farther away from their states grow faster in the short run, but in the long run diminishing returns to capital set in, and the growth rate drops to the exogenous growth rate of technological progress. This tends toward a situation where the growth rate of GDP per capita falls and becomes constant (that is, it becomes equal to the exogenously determined technological growth rate). The neoclassical growth models therefore predict that in the long run countries and regions will converge in terms of per capita income levels, if one controls for the effects of differences in initial conditions. However, these theoretical-conceptual findings are often contradicted by empirical results.

A basic problem in this neoclassical explanation of the world is that technological progress is not exogenous "manna from heaven." It is part of the complex architecture of a regional economy and is determined by both internal and external R&D investments, on-the-job training, learning by doing, and spillovers from university research. Spillovers resulting from R&D expenditures and other activities generate increasing returns to scale for reproducible production factors (Lucas 1988; Romer 1990), the existence of which implies the possibility of long-run divergence in per capita income levels. Thus the use of new technologies may aggravate regional disparities.

The conflicting predictions of the neoclassical and endogenous growth models have generated intense scrutiny and a plethora of empirical studies, known collectively as the "convergence debate" (see Durlauf and Quah 1999; Islam 2003; Temple 1999). The literature has generally found that, while per capita income levels between the poorest countries (of Sub-Saharan Africa) and the richest countries (Europe and the United States) have diverged over the past few decades, there is convergence among countries that are similar in terms of initial conditions and policies, for instance, among the countries of the European Union or the fast-growing East Asian economies (a phenomenon known as "conditional convergence"). The evidence also suggests that per capita income levels among regions within countries have diverged markedly in recent years, particularly in large, diverse countries such as China and India. An increase in regional disparities in fast-growing regions such as China and India is not necessarily bad news, however. Improvements in living standards in vast countries such as these imply that global inequality as a whole may be decreasing (in tandem with improvement in living standards in these countries). Moreover, economic theory suggests that an increase in agglomeration forces may lead to further improvements in the long run, as knowledge spills over into other regions and sectors of the economy. The findings of the convergence literature therefore highlight the key role of regional development policies in promoting economic growth and human development. At the same time, they call for serious empirical work and comparative study.

Epilogue

Balanced development is a complex phenomenon in any policy attempt aimed at reducing spatial disparities. It calls for a through analysis of its driving forces. An important contributor to regional development is technological progress, an extensively studied topic in the recent economic growth literature. From a geographic (regional, urban, or local) perspective, much attention has been paid to the spatial conditions that induce technological progress (for example, entrepreneurial climate, availability of venture capital, and incubator facilities). Furthermore, the spatial diffusion of technology has received much attention, in particular in the geography literature. A particular case of knowledge and technology diffusion can be found in foreign direct investment (FDI). Several studies have demonstrated that FDI offers access to foreign production processes, so that interregional or multinational technology spillovers may occur (see, for example, Carr, Markusen, and Maskus 2001; Coe and Helpman 1995; Findlay 1973; Markussen 2002; Xu 2000). These studies demonstrate clearly that the region is a dynamic player in an intricate web of spatial-economic interactions that have an impact on spatial disparities.

With more regional dynamism and a trend toward an open world, regional disparities tend to increase, at least in the short and medium term. There is a clear reason for more solid, empirically based modeling work to identify the key drivers of disparities in regional development. Meta analysis—a systematic set of tools to identify key drivers from a quantitative angle—may be a fruitful tool with which to arrive at a better understanding of the causes of spatial disparities.

Any attempt to cope with undesirable spatial disparities has to recognize the complex force field within which regional development—and differences therein—is shaped. Regional development policy is not a simple, one-shot activity, but the result of endogenous forces in the space economy itself. It is based on the self-organizing potential of regions, with a multiplicity of actors and change agents involved. A fruitful way to analyze spatial disparities from a long-range strategic perspective may be to adopt an evolutionary economic perspective (see, for example, van den Bergh and others 2006), in which notions like spatial diversity, mutation, stability and resilience, path dependence, bounded rationality, and selection environment play a prominent role. Interesting recent contributions from an evolutionary viewpoint to the field of regional planning and development policy can be found in Bosschma and Lambooy (1999) and Cooke, Uranga, and Extebarria (1998), among others. Further development of evolutionary thoughts on differences in regional development need foremost solid and applied research work, making use of quantitative comparative analysis of the evolution of regions in a complex space economy.

References

Abreu, Maria. 2005. "Spatial Determinants of Economic Growth and Technology Diffusion." Ph.D. dissertation, Tinbergen Institute, Amsterdam.

Acs, Zoltan, Bo Carlsson, and Charlie Karlsson, eds. 1999. *Entrepreneurship, Small- and Medium-Sized Enterprises, and the Macroeconomy.* Cambridge, MA: Cambridge University Press.

Acs, Zoltan, Henri de Groot, and Peter Nijkamp, eds. 2002. *The Emergence of the Knowledge Economy.* Berlin: Springer-Verlag.

Aghion, Philippe, and Peter Howitt. 1998. *Endogenous Growth Theory.* Cambridge, MA: MIT Press.

Armstrong, Harvey W. 1995. "Convergence among the Regions of the European Union, 1950–1990." *Papers in Regional Science* 74 (2): 143–52.

Armstrong, Harvey W., and Jim Taylor. 2000. *Regional Economics and Policy.* Oxford: Blackwell.

Asheim, Bjørn. 1996. "Industrial Districts as 'Learning Regions.'" *European Planning Studies* 4 (4): 379–400.

Asheim, Bjørn, and Meric S. Gertler. 2005. "The Geography of Innovation: Regional Innovation Systems." In *The Oxford Handbook of Innovation,* ed. Jan Fagerberg, David C. Mowery, and Richard Nelson. Oxford: Oxford University Press.

Audretsch, David, A. Roy Thurik, Ingrid Verheul, and Sander Wennekers, eds. 2002. *Entrepreneurship: Determinants and Policy in a European-U.S. Comparison.* Dordrecht: Kluwer.

Baldwin, Richard. 1999. "Agglomeration and Endogenous Capital." *European Economic Review* 43 (2): 253–80.

Baldwin, Richard E., Rikard Forslid, Philippe Martin, Gianmarco I. P. Ottaviano, and Frederic Robert-Nicoud. 2003. *Economic Geography and Public Policy.* Princeton, NJ: Princeton University Press.

Barro, Robert J., and Xavier Sala-i-Martin. 1991. "Convergence across States and Regions." *Brookings Papers on Economic Activity* 1: 107–82.

———. 1992. "Convergence." *Journal of Political Economics* 100 (2): 223–51.

———. 1997. "Technology Diffusion, Convergence, and Growth." *Journal of Economic Growth* 2 (1): 1–27.

Baumol, William J. 1986. "Productivity Growth, Convergence, and Welfare: What the Long-Run Data Show." *American Economic Review* 76 (5): 1072–85.

Baumont, Catherine, Cem Ertur, and Julie LeGallo. 2003. "Spatial Convergence Clubs and the European Regional Growth Process, 1980–1995." In *European Regional Growth*, ed. Bernard Fingleton. Berlin: Springer-Verlag.

Benhabib, Jess, and Mark M. Spiegel. 1994. "The Role of Human Capital in Economic Development. Evidence from Aggregate Cross-Country Data." *Journal of Monetary Economics* 34 (2): 143–73.

Bernard, Andrew B., and Steven N. Durlauf. 1996. "Interpreting Tests of the Convergence Hypothesis." *Journal of Economics* 71 (1-2): 161–74.

Blakely, Edward J. 1994. *Planning Local Economic Development*. Thousand Oaks, CA: Sage Publications.

Blanchard, O. J. 1991. "Comments and Discussions on R. J. Barro and X. Sala-i-Martin, Convergence across States and Regions." *Brookings Papers on Economic Activity* 1: 159–74.

Boldrin, Michele, and Fabio Canova. 2001. "Europe's Regions, Income Disparities, and Regional Policy." *Economic Policy* 16: 207–53.

Bosschma, Ron, and J. G. Lambooy. 1999. "Evolutionary Economics and Economic Geography." *Journal of Evolutionary Economics* 9 (4): 411–29.

Bourdieu, Pierre. 1986. "Forms of Capital." In *Handbook of Theory and Research for the Sociology of Education*, ed. J. G. Richardson, 241–60. Westport, CT: Greenwood Press.

Brakman, Steven, Harry Garretsen, and Charles van Marrewijk. 2001. *An Introduction to Geographical Economics*. Cambridge, U.K.: Cambridge University Press.

Cameron, R. 2005. "Spatial Economic Analysis." *Journal of Development Perspective* 1 (1): 146–63.

Capello, Roberta. 2006. *Regional Economics*. London: Routledge.

Carr, David, James Markusen, and Keith Maskus. 2001. "Estimating the Knowledge-Capital Model of the Multinational Enterprise." *American Economic Review* 91 (3): 693–708.

Chatterji, Monojit. 1992. "Convergence Clubs and Endogenous Growth." *Oxford Review of Economic Policy* 8 (4): 57–69.

Chatterji, Monojit, and John H. L. Dewhurst. 1996. "Convergence Clubs and Relative Economic Performance in Great Britain: 1977–1991." *Regional Studies* 30 (1): 31–40.

Cheshire, P., and G. Carbonaro. 1995. "Convergence-Divergence in Regional Growth Rates: An Empty Black Box?" In *Convergence and Divergence among European Regions*, ed. H. W. Armstrong and R. W. Vickerman, 89–111. London: Pion.

Chou, Yuan K. 2006. "Three Simple Models of Social Capital and Economic Growth." *Journal of Socio-Economics* 35 (5): 889–912.

Coe, David T., and Elhanan Helpman. 1995. "International R&D Spillovers." *European Economic Review* 39 (5): 859–87.

Cooke, P., M. G. Uranga, and G. Extebarria. 1998. "Regional Innovation Systems: An Evolutionary Perspective." *Environment and Planning A* 30 (9): 1563–84.

Crozet, Matthieu. 2004. "Do Migrants Follow Market Potentials? An Estimation of a New Economic Geography Model." *Journal of Economic Geography* 4 (4): 439–58.

Dasgupta, Partha, and Ismail Serageldin, eds. 1999. *Social Capital*. Washington, DC: World Bank.

Davis, Donald, and David Weinstein. 1999. "Economic Geography and Regional Production Structure: An Empirical Investigation." *European Economic Review* 43 (2): 379–407.

De Groot, Henri L. F., Peter Nijkamp, and Roger Stough, eds. 2004. *Entrepreneurship and Regional Economic Development: A Spatial Perspective*. Cheltenham: Edward Elgar.

De la Fuente, Ángel, and Rafael Doménech. 2006. "Human Capital in Growth Regressions." *Journal of the European Economic Association* 4 (1): 1–36.

Dewhurst, John H. L., and Hernando Mutis-Gaitan. 1995. "Varying Speeds of Regional GDP per Capita Convergence in the European Union, 1981–91." In *Convergence and Divergence among European Regions,* ed. H. W. Armstrong and R. W. Vickerman, 22–39. London: Pion.

Dixit, Avinash, and Joseph Stiglitz. 1977. "Monopolistic Competition and Optimal Product Diversity." *American Economic Review* 67 (3): 297–308.

Döring, Thomas, and Jan Schnellenback. 2006. "What Do We Know about Geographical Knowledge Spillover and Economic Growth?" *Regional Studies* 40 (3): 375–95.

Durlauf, Steven N., and Danny Quah. 1999. "The New Empirics of Economic Growth." In *Handbook of Macroeconomics 1A,* ed. John B. Taylor and Michael Woodford. Amsterdam: North Holland.

Dyer, Jeffrey. 2000. *Collaborative Advantage.* New York: Oxford University Press.

Englemann, Frank C., and Uwe Walz. 1995. "Industrial Centers and Regional Growth in the Presence of Local Inputs." *Journal of Regional Science* 35 (1): 3–27.

Evans, Paul. 1996. "Using Cross-Country Variances to Evaluate Growth Theories." *Journal of Economic Dynamics and Control* 20 (6-7): 1027–49.

Fagerberg, Jan, and Bart Verspagen. 1996. "Heading for Convergence? Regional Growth in Europe Reconsidered." *Journal of Common Market Studies* 34 (3): 431–48.

Findlay, Ronald. 1973. *International Trade and Development Theory.* New York: Columbia University Press.

Fingleton, Bernard. 1999. "Estimates of Time to Economic Convergence: An Analysis of Regions of the European Union." *International Regional Science Review* 22 (1): 5–34.

Fingleton, Bernard, ed. 2003. *European Regional Growth.* Berlin: Springer-Verlag.

Fischer, Manfred, and Claudia Stirböck. 2006. "Pan-European Regional Income Growth and Club-Convergence." *Annals of Regional Science* 40 (4): 693–721.

Florida, Richard. 1995. "Toward the Learning Region." *Futures* 27 (5): 527–36.

Fujita, Masahisa, Paul Krugman, and Anthony J. Venables. 1999. *The Spatial Economy.* Cambridge, MA: MIT Press.

Fujita, Masahisa, and Jacques-François Thisse. 2002. *The Economics of Agglomeration.* Cambridge, U.K.: Cambridge University Press.

———. 2003. "Does Geographical Agglomeration Foster Economic Growth? And Who Gains and Looses from It?" *Japanese Economic Review* 54 (2): 121–45.

Fukuyama, Francis. 1995. *Trust: The Social Virtues and the Creation of Prosperity.* New York: Free Press.

Galor, Obed. 1996. "Convergence? Inferences from Theoretical Models." *Economic Journal* 106 (437): 1056–69.

Gilles, Saint-Paul. 1998. "The Political Consequence of Unemployment." Working Paper 343, Department of Economics and Business, Universitat Pompeu, Fabra.

Glaeser, Edward, David Laibson, and Bruce Sacerdote. 2000. "The Economic Approach to Social Capital." NBER Working Paper 7728, National Bureau of Economic Research, Washington, DC.

Grossman, Gene M., and Elhanan Helpman. 1990. "Comparative Advantage and Long-Run Growth." *American Economic Review* 80 (4): 796–815.

Hanson, Gordon. 1996. "Agglomeration, Dispersion, and the Pioneer Firm." *Journal of Urban Economics* 39 (3): 255–81.

Heenan, David, and Warren G. Bennis. 1999. *Co-leaders: The Power of Great Partnerships.* New York: John Wiley.

Hofstede, Geert, ed. 1997. *Cultures and Organizations.* New York: McGraw-Hill.

Islam, Nazrul. 2003. "What Have We Learnt from the Convergence Debate?" *Journal of Economic Surveys* 17 (3): 309–62.

Jacobs, Jane. 1961. *The Death and Life of Great American Cities.* New York: Random House.

Judd, Dennis, and Michael Parkinson, eds. 1990. *Leadership and Urban Regeneration*. Newbury Park, CA: Sage.

Keeble, David, and Frank Wilkinson. 1999. "Collective Learning and Knowledge Development in the Evolution of Regional Clusters of High-Technology SMEs in Europe." *Regional Studies* 33 (4): 295–303.

Kirchhoff, Bruce A. 1994. *Entrepreneurship and Dynamic Capitalism*. Westport, CT: Praeger.

Krugman, Paul. 1991. "Increasing Returns and Economic Geography." *Journal of Political Economy* 99 (3): 483–99.

López-Bazo, Enrique, Esther Vayá, Antonio Mora, and Jordi Suriñach. 1999. "Regional Economic Dynamics and Convergence in the European Union." *Annals of Regional Science* 33 (3): 343–70.

Lucas, Robert E. 1988. "On the Mechanics of Economic Development." *Journal of Monetary Economics* 22 (1): 3–42.

Magrini, Stefano. 2004. "(Di)Convergence." In *Handbook of Urban and Regional Economics*, ed. J. Vernon Henderson and Jacques-François Thisse, 741–96. Amsterdam: Elsevier.

Malecki, Edward. 2000. "Creating and Sustaining Competitiveness." In *Knowledge, Space, Economy*, ed. John R. Bryson, Peter W. Daniels, Nick Henry, and Jane Pollard, 103–19. London: Routledge.

Markusen, Ann. 1985. *Profit Cycles, Oligopoly, and Regional Development*. Cambridge, MA: MIT Press.

Markussen, John. 2002. *Multinational Firms and the Theory of International Trade*. Cambridge, MA: MIT Press.

Martin, Philippe. 1999. "Public Policies, Regional Inequalities, and Growth." *Journal of Public Economics* 73 (1): 85–105.

Martin, Philippe, and Gianmarco I. P. Ottaviano. 2001. "Growth and Agglomeration." *International Economic Review* 42 (4): 1003–26.

Naudé, Wim A. 2005. "Geographical Economics and Africa." *Journal of Development Perspectives* 1 (1): 1–4.

Neary, J. Peter 2001. "The New Economic Geography." *Journal of International Literature* 39 (2): 536–61.

Nijkamp, Peter. 2003. "Entrepreneurship in a Modern Network Economy." *Regional Studies* 37 (4): 395–405.

Okun, Arthur M. 1970. *The Political Economic of Prosperity*. Washington, DC: Brookings Institution.

Paldam, Martin. 1987. "How Much Does One percent of Growth Change the Unemployment Rate?" *European Economic Review* 31 (1-2): 306–13.

Patuelli, Roberto. 2007. *Regional Labour Markets in Germany*. PhD dissertation, Free University, Amsterdam.

Puga, Diego. 1999. "The Rise and Fall of Regional Inequalities." *European Economic Review* 43 (2): 303–34.

Putnam, Robert. 2000. *Bowling Alone: The Collapse and Revival of American Community*. New York: Simon and Schuster.

Quah, Danny T. 1996. "Empirics for Economic Growth and Convergence." *European Economic Review* 40 (6): 1353–75.

Redding, Stephen, and Anthony J. Venables. 2004. "Economic Geography and International Inequality." *Journal of International Economics* 62 (1): 53–82.

Rey, Sergio J., and Brett D. Montouri. 1999. "U.S. Regional Income Convergence: A Spatial Econometric Perspective." *Regional Studies* 33 (2): 143–56.

Rivera-Batiz, Francisco. 1988. "Increasing Returns, Monopolistic Competition, and Agglomeration Economies in Consumption and Production." *Regional Science and Urban Economics* 18 (1): 125–53.

Romer, Paul M. 1986. "Increasing Returns and Long-Run Growth." *Journal of Political Economy* 94 (5): 1002–37.

———. 1990. "Endogenous Technological Change." *Journal of Political Economy* 98 (2): 71–102.

Sala-i-Martin, Xavier. 1996. "The Classical Approach to Convergence Analysis." *Economic Journal* 106 (437): 343–70.

Serageldin, Ismail. 2006. *Science: The Culture of Living Change*. Alexandria: Bibliotheca Alexandrina.

Simmie, James, ed. 1997. *Innovation, Networks, and Learning Regions*. London: Jessica Kingsley.

Sobel, Joel. 2002. "Can We Trust Social Capital?" *Journal of Economic Literature* 40 (1): 139–54.

Stimson, Robert, Roger Stough, and Brian H. Roberts. 2006. *Regional Economic Development*. Berlin: Springer-Verlay.

Stimson, Robert, Roger Stough, and María Salazar. 2005. "Leadership and Institutional Factors in Endogenous Regional Economic Development." *Investigaciones Regionales* 7: 23–52.

Storey, D. J. 1994. *Understanding the Small Business Sector*. London: Routledge.

Temple, Jonathan. 1999. "The New Growth Evidence." *Journal of Economic Literature* 37 (1): 112–56.

van den Bergh, Jeroen C. J. M., Albert Faber, Annemarth M. Idenburg, and Frans H. Oosterhuis. 2006. *Evolutionary Economics and Environmental Policy*. Cheltenham, U.K.: Edward Elgar.

Westlund, Hans, and Roger Bolton. 2003. "Local Social Capital and Entrepreneurship." *Small Business Economics* 21 (2): 77–113.

Westlund, Hans, and Elin Nilsson. 2005. "Measuring Enterprises' Investments in Social Capital: A Pilot Study." *Regional Studies* 39 (8): 1079–94.

World Bank. 2006. *World Development Report 2006: Equity and Development*. New York: Oxford University Press.

Xu, Bin. 2000. "Multinational Enterprises, Technology Diffusion, and Host Country Productivity Growth." *Journal of Development Economics* 62 (2): 477–74.

Africans Need Not Miss Out on the Benefits of Globalization

FEDERICO BONAGLIA, NICOLAS PINAUD, AND LUCIA WEGNER

Globalization—the deepening of financial and trade integration associated with technological progress and multilateral liberalization—is creating unprecedented opportunities for developing countries to accelerate growth and lift millions of people out of poverty. African countries need to be among the beneficiaries. The rapid growth of the Asian emerging economies can offer this opportunity, as it is raising demand for Africa's commodities (oil, metals, and precious stones) and resulting in improved terms of trade. There are still risks and uncertainties, but they can be reduced by strengthening the internal capacities of African countries and nurturing the private sector.

Continuous Strong Performance

Africa grew 5.5 percent in 2006—well above the long-term trend and for the fourth consecutive year. Gross domestic product (GDP) per capita grew about 3.5 percent. Growth also appears set to accelerate somewhat on average in 2007 and to remain buoyant in 2008.

The challenge is to ensure that a large proportion of the proceeds from the minerals sector is invested in infrastructure and human capital development to support the medium- and long-term need for diversification. Temporary windfall gains make the reorientation of government budgets urgent. Enhancing transparency and combating corruption are keys to realizing this transformation and maintaining growth. The continuation of sound macroeconomic polices in most countries on the continent, for example, has increased business confidence, leading to a pickup in private investment generally.

Lucia Wegner is Senior Economist of the African Economic Outlook, at the OECD Development Centre, Organisation for Economic Cooperation and Development (OECD) in Paris.

Berlin Workshop Series 2009

Oil-importing countries will need to contain inflationary pressures, now running into double digits as a result of oil price increases, and to finance or contain increases in their current account deficits.

The economic gains of the oil producers are largely due to expanded oil production and sustained high prices. New producers (Chad, Equatorial Guinea, and Mauritania) and those opening up new fields (like Angola, which has more than doubled its production since 1990 to 1.4 million barrels a day in 2006) have been able to take advantage of the soaring world demand. The resulting windfall gains could set such countries firmly on the road to development.

The oil-importing countries have not been left behind. Metals producers also have profited from higher world prices and, to a lesser extent, higher export volumes. Mozambique, Namibia, South Africa, and Zambia all made up for the dearer oil with their aluminum, iron, copper, and platinum exports.

The price of agricultural exports has been falling, hurting countries dependent on them, but 2006 turned out not to be too bad. Rubber, coffee, and seafood exporters enjoyed good prices that strengthened trade balances. Some producers, despite weak world prices (of cotton, for example), managed to boost exports substantially, thanks to good weather, and some in Central and East Africa (Madagascar, Rwanda, and Tanzania) and West Africa (Benin, Burkina Faso, Ghana, and Mali) achieved high export growth as well. A number of diversified exporters also exhibited strong growth in the volume of exports (Arab Republic of Egypt, Mauritius, and Morocco).

High energy prices may be good for exporters of oil, but they can be bad for controlling inflation, and the continent as a whole saw inflation rise to 9.1 percent in 2006. This continental average masks important differences between net oil exporters and net oil importers, whose inflation rate rose from 8.4 percent in 2005 to 12 percent in 2006. Further increases, to 12.7 percent in 2007 and to 12.9 percent in 2008, are expected. Continuing high oil prices, which seem likely, are a major medium-term risk for the continent's net oil importers and may endanger their efforts to maintain macroeconomic stability if the financing of the larger current account deficits leads to a buildup of unsustainable debt levels once again. It also makes poverty reduction even harder by putting pressure on government budgets.

African countries need to husband their resources much more carefully to pay for the key goals of reducing poverty and raising the quality of life for their populations. This remains true for both oil-exporting and oil-importing countries. The temptation for the former is to waste resources through inefficiency and corruption, while for the latter, the challenge is to implement policies to sustain and diversify the economy in the face of variable world prices.

Does Africa Benefit from Globalization?

Africa has significantly increased its openness to international trade: merchandise trade as a share of GDP rose from 43 to 50 percent between 1980–95 and 1996–

2005. Foreign direct investment (FDI) inflows have surged, growing faster than in other developing regions and tripling their level between 2001 and 2005 (reaching US$30.6 billion).

Yet Africa's share in world trade remains minimal, at about 1.5 percent, and exports are concentrated in a narrow range of primary commodities. Albeit increasing in absolute terms, FDI heading for Africa accounts for less than 4 percent of the world total and is distributed unequally, with northern Africa, South Africa, and the largest Sub-Saharan oil producers being the main recipients by far. This reflects dependence on natural resources. The private sector is only marginally involved in international production networks, mainly in assembly at the bottom end of the value chain. The post–Multi Fiber Agreement closure of several foreign-owned clothing factories in southern and eastern Africa shows their vulnerability.

Is History Repeating Itself?

Commodity booms and busts have driven most of African postcolonial development, but a new landscape is emerging, and globalization is bringing new actors to Africa and opening up new markets, which could benefit the continent and prevent a rerun of the past. There are still risks and uncertainties, but they can be reduced by strengthening the internal capacities of African countries and nurturing the private sector better in order to realize fully the opportunities that globalization creates, while adequately coping with its risks.

The rapid growth of the Asian emerging economies is raising demand for Africa's commodities (oil, metals, and precious stones) and has resulted in improved terms of trade (exports to China reached around US$25 billion in 2006, twelvefold their level in 1995). The downside is that African exporters could be pushed further into specializing in exports of raw materials. Asian domination of labor-intensive industries, which are often considered potential avenues for the diversification of African economies, poses an additional challenge.

New Business Opportunities in a Changing World

In agriculture, despite high potential and market opportunities, sluggish productivity growth hinders the ability of Africa's producers both to feed its people adequately—42 countries are classified as net food importers—and to respond to the opportunities now available in global markets. Africa's share of global agricultural trade is less than 6 percent. With new investors, including Chinese, Indian, and southern and northern African operators, patterns of FDI have started to diversify into agriculture, manufacturing, construction, and services. Also, portfolio investors have started to regard Africa as a promising destination because of the higher potential yields on investment compared to traditional emerging markets.

The real story, however, remains in minerals, partly because poor governance and difficult business environments hamper FDI in sectors other than extraction.

From a Passive to an Active Player in Globalization

For African economies to realize the full benefits of globalization, conventional policy prescriptions, such as maintaining macroeconomic stability and improving the business environment, still hold. But equally important, external resources must be used more strategically. On one side, this implies capitalizing on oil and mineral windfall gains. On the other, it means exploring the potential of aid as a catalyst more systematically, especially as aid is expected to increase in the coming years (aid to Africa is expected to reach US$51 billion by 2010 from US$40 billion in 2006). "Aid for trade"[1] should be used more effectively as an instrument for strengthening productive capacities and promoting private sector development and trade-related infrastructure, thereby facilitating Africa's integration into the global economy. Funding for this has significantly expanded since the 2001 World Trade Organization (WTO) ministerial conference in Doha. In 2005 Africa was the largest recipient of trade-related technical assistance, receiving US$1.03 billion (about one-third of the world total), and the second largest recipient, after Asia, of aid to infrastructure, receiving US$3.8 billion. Aid for trade represented a fifth of global official development assistance in 2001–04, but it needs to be expanded further, and its effective implementation requires stronger actions by African governments in identifying priorities and better coordinating the efforts of donors. Supporting aid for trade initiatives in Africa is especially important, as the continent is in the final stage of negotiating with the European Union (EU) the critical Economic Partnership Agreements, which represent an important opportunity to integrate further efforts at promoting trade development and regional integration in Africa. At the same time, they also challenge African countries to tackle structural weaknesses in their economies.

Notes

1. Aid for trade refers to aid that is aimed at helping developing countries to benefit from trade liberalization at multilateral, regional, and unilateral levels. Its scope has been broadened by adding to the traditional categories of trade-related technical assistance (trade policy and regulations and trade development) four new categories: (1) trade-related infrastructure, (2) efforts to build productive capacity, (3) trade-related adjustment, and (4) other trade-related needs.

Part VIII: Wrap-Up Discussion and Closing Remarks

Implications for WDR 2009

INDERMIT GILL

Almost the entire team is here, and they have been listening to you. On behalf of them, I can say that we have learned a lot. This learning is going to continue to take place as we continue to discuss these issues. It would be hard to summarize what we have learned. In fact, it would be unfair to try to do it right now. I cannot think of a single lousy presentation other than perhaps the first one, which was mine.

I would like to thank all of you for giving so many of your ideas and so much of your time and for doing so cheerfully. As they say, no good deed ever goes unpunished, so we will be coming back to you for more ideas, more thoughts, and more help as we work on the report. For the next few months, at least, our motto will be, "Ask not what the *World Development Report* (WDR) will do for you; ask what you can do for the WDR." Once we are done with that, you should ask the question, "What can the WDR do for you?"

For now I will try to do two things: the first one is to share with you a few of the ideas that I took away: just a few; I am not offering a summary. In general, what I took away was that most of you did not mind the skeleton that we put forward for the overall structure of the report, but many of you had questions and also suggestions of how to put the flesh on that skeleton. And I think there were even some suggestions about making sure that we did not have a hand where a foot should be and so on. As we go back, we will look at the skeleton again, but we will also consider how to flesh out the body. We shared a lot of good ideas on all three sets of policy issues. For example, on the issue of urbanization, I do not know if Mantang Cai agrees with me, but I think that we might take away the idea that large and small cities should be seen as complements, not substitutes, and rural areas and large and small cities should also be seen as complements, not as substitutes. We are still trying to work through other issues, but the salient issue is to understand how the rural-urban transformation is related to the trans-

Indermit Gill is Director, World Development Report 2009. The World Bank, Washington D.C.

Berlin Workshop Series 2009
© 2009 The International Bank for Reconstruction and Development/The World Bank

formation that happens on the sectoral side. The sectoral transformation in the early stage of urbanization and the occupational transformation and specialization in the later stage are closely related to how cities evolve and what they do. Another issue of importance pertains to the delivery of social services, especially in areas where economic mass is not concentrating. On regional policy, Ángel de la Fuente Moreno made an interesting point. I do not know if I am paraphrasing this well or not, but one of the things that he said is that, even if the analysis shows that there are poor places and not just poor people, the policies that are designed to address poverty ought to focus on the welfare of the people, not the place. And if one keeps this in mind, it should be possible to come up with a set of principles that might help to clarify the debate that we had at the end. Policies ought to target the welfare of people. The case studies on Poland, South Africa, Brazil, China, Ireland, and others offer many good lessons.

I appreciate the discussion about what has been happening in the European Union (EU) with regard to regional integration. One insight that I took away from Philippe Martin, for example, is that Ireland has done well because it saw the regional structural funds as an opportunity to catch up internationally, not just as a way to address economic issues at the subnational level. My sense is that, in Europe, regional development policy has not worked that well, but regional integration has. This brings me to the regional integration part: we know how other regions of the world integrated—North America, Western Europe, and East Asia— but we do not know how these lessons help us to determine what will work in Sub-Saharan Africa (SSA). What we would like to do in the WDR is to build up to the problem of Africa by saying that there are problems that every region of the world faces, but Africa seems to have a multiplicity of them. One issue that I believe will find its way into the report is that one should not think of Sub-Saharan Africa as one neighborhood, but rather as several neighborhoods. Asia was not one neighborhood: not only was East Asia a neighborhood, but so were Northeast Asia and Southeast Asia. There is hardly any reason to expect, as Paul Collier pointed out, 50 countries to get together all at once. It is enough to get a few countries to work together and then allow the approach to spread.

I am immensely grateful to the organizers of this workshop. This is one of the most flawlessly organized workshops that I have ever attended, and I have been attending workshops in India and in East Asia, where things go very well indeed. This was superb. Thank you very very much.

The New World Bank Office in Berlin

CLAUDIA VON MONBART

The World Bank has dealt with spatial disparities only indirectly. I would like to address the Bank's presence and present distribution and density in Europe. We have been working out of Paris, where we have a small embassy for all of the European donor countries, for the Organisation for Economic Co-operation and Development (OECD), and for Europe. We also have a small presence in London, Brussels, and Geneva and a very small presence for the World Trade Organization (WTO) in Rome. It is no wonder that Berlin felt that the World Bank should be present here, and finally we are, as we have just opened a small office in Berlin. We understand our role as that of facilitator. We want to bring a larger World Bank presence here, but we also want to have more exchange of ideas and improve our mutual understanding. We want to seek political, intellectual, and financial support, of course, and to bring a little bit of what Michael Hoffmann yesterday called "continental European thinking" to the table.

I want to congratulate you as well. This workshop has been an excellent model and example for what we will strive to do in the future. Thank you very much.

Claudia von Monbart is Senior Counsellor, External Affairs, for The World Bank in Paris and Berlin.

Berlin Workshop Series 2009

Appendix 1: Program

International Policy Workshop

SPATIAL DISPARITIES AND DEVELOPMENT POLICY

in preparation for the

WORLD DEVELOPMENT REPORT 2009

convened by

the Development Policy Forum of
InWEnt - Capacity Building International, Germany
on behalf of the Federal Ministry for
Economic Cooperation and Development (BMZ) and in
cooperation with The World Bank

September 30–October 2, 2007 Berlin

Program

Sunday, September 30, 2007

INTRODUCTION

6.00 p.m.   Opening Addresses:

Opening Keynote:
Astrid Kuehl
Director
Development Policy Forum
InWEnt Capacity Building International
Germany

Boris Pleskovic
Research Manager
The World Bank
Washington D.C.

Indermit Gill
Director
World Development Report 2009
The World Bank
Washington D.C.

7.30 p.m.   *Dinner Buffet at the Grand Hyatt Hotel*

UNDERSTANDING SPATIAL TRENDS: PERSPECTIVES AND MODELS

9.00-10.30 a.m.   Session I:
"Macro-trends: Spatial Patterns of Economic Activity, Income and Poverty"
- Are there typical patterns of income disparities within countries and regions during similar stages of the development process?
- Where are the poor – urban, rural, large or small cities?
- How does all of this differ across regions, MICs, LDCs?

Chair: **Manfred Fischer**
Professor of Economic Geography
Vienna University Austria

Co-Chair: **Astrid Kuehl**
Director
Development Policy Forum

	InWEnt Capacity Building International

InWEnt Capacity Building International
Germany

Speakers: **Steve Haggblade**
Professor
International Development
Department of Agricultural Economics
Michigan State University
United States

Peter Lanjouw
Lead Economist
Development Research Group (DECRG)
The World Bank
Washington D.C.

10.30-11.00 a.m.   **Coffee break**

11.00 a.m.-1.00 p.m.   **Session II:**
*"New Economic Geography and the Dynamics of
Technological Change – Implications for LDCs"*
- State of the art in theoretical and empirical analysis
- How do these dynamics account for the patterns of
  urbanization and economic activity, intra and inter-
  countries?
- What do they suggest in terms of directions, constraints
  and pre-conditions for development policy in LDCs?

Chair: **Ludwig Schaetzl**
Professor of Economic Geography
Scientific Advisory Council Federal Ministry for Economic
Cooperation and Development (BMZ)
Germany

Co-Chair: **Astrid Kuehl**
Director
Development Policy Forum
InWEnt Capacity Building International
Germany

Speakers: **Eduardo Haddad**
Associate Professor
Faculty of Economics Administration and Accounting
University of São Paulo
Brazil

Diego Puga
Research Professor of Economics
Madrid Institute for Advanced Studies (IMDEA)
Universidad Carlos III de Madrid
Spain

Ingo Liefner
Professor of Economic Geography
University of Giessen
Germany

1.00-2.30 p.m. *Lunch*

2.30-4.00 p.m. **Session III:**
"Perspectives:
Rural-Urban Transformation: Leading, Lagging and
Interlinking Places"
• What are the pace and patterns of urbanization in LDCs?
• How does the organization of economic activity in the
countryside affect the pattern and outcomes of
urbanization?
• What are the challenges for lagging regions?

Chair: **Michael Hofmann**
Director General Global and Sectoral Policies – European
and Multilateral Development Policy Africa Middle East
Federal Ministry for Economic Cooperation and
Development (BMZ) Germany

Co-Chair: **Marisela Montoliu Muñoz**
Head Spatial and Local Development Team Sustainable
Development Network The World Bank Washington D.C.

Speakers: *"Rural Perspective"*
Mantang Cai
Deputy Director and Associate Professor Beijing
Development Institute Peking University People's Republic
of China

"Urbanization Perspective"
Frank van Oort
Professor of Urban Economics and Spatial Planning Utrecht
University The Netherlands

"Interlinkages and the Challenge of Lagging Regions"
Lee Boon Thong
Professor Department of Geography University of Malaya
Malaysia

4.00-4.30 p.m.	*Coffee break*

4.30-6.00 p.m.

Session IV:
"Spatial Disparity and Labor Mobility"
- The policy dilemma: People v.s. place prosperity
- Rural-Urban migration – motivations, pace, modalities and outcomes
- Human capital investments to promote regional convergence: Can they be effective?
- Labor assimilation in receiving regions: What's the evidence?
- The role of remittances in promoting growth in locations of origin

Chair:

Boris Pleskovic
Research Manager
The World Bank
Washington D.C.

Co-Chair:

Juergen Zattler
Head of Division
World Bank Group – IMF – Debt Relief – International
Financial Architecture
Federal Ministry for Economic Cooperation and
Development (BMZ)
Germany

Speakers:

Angel de la Fuente Moreno
Associate Professor
Universitat Autònoma de Barcelona
Spain

Adama Konseiga
Affiliate
African Population & Health Research Center (APHRC)
Kenya
Research Affiliate
GREDI (Research Group in Economics and International Development)
Faculty of Administration
University of Sherbrooke
Canada

Roman Mogilevsky
Executive Director
Center for Social and Economic Research (CASE)
Kyrgyzstan

6.45 p.m.	*Departure by bus and guided city tour*
7.30-10.00 p.m.	Dinner
Venue:	Restaurant h.h. mueller

Umspannwerk Kreuzberg
PaulLinckeUfer 20/21
10999 Berlin

Dinner Speech

"Megacities"
Frauke Kraas
Professor for Human Geography
Institute of Geography
University of Cologne
Germany

10.00 p.m.   *Return to the Hotel*

Tuesday, October 2, 2007

8.30-8.40 a.m.   Address:
Gudrun Kochendörfer-Lucius
Managing Director InWEnt – Capacity Building
International Germany

COUNTRY REALITIES AND POLICY OPTIONS

8.40-10.00 a.m.   **Session V:**
"Africa: Rethinking Growth and Regional Integration"
- Spatial development patterns in selected African countries (South Africa, Nigeria)
- Agglomeration without growth?
- Is it realistic to implement successful elements of economic development of East Asian countries in Sub-Saharan Africa?
- What are the fundamental socioeconomic and cultural differences between East Asian and African countries?
- Is export-orientated industrialization an appropriate strategy for Africa?
- How does China's engagement in Africa contribute to the development of African countries?

Chair: **Robert Kappel**
Professor
President
German Institute of Global and Area Studies
Germany

Co-Chair: **Aehyung Kim**
Consultant
The World Bank
Washington D.C.

Keynote: **Paul Collier**
Professor of Economics
Department of Economics
Oxford University
Director
Centre for the Study of African Economies
United Kingdom

Speakers: **Hassen Mohamed**
Chief Director
Planning, Policy Coordination and Advisory Unit
The Presidency
South Africa

Wim Naudé
Senior Research Fellow
UNUWIDER
Finland

10.00-10.15 p.m.   *Coffee break*

10.15-11.45 a.m.   **Session VI:**
"Learning from Europe's Efforts at Integration and Convergence"
- Lessons from the allocation and implementation of convergence funds: Preconditions for success, variations across countries
- Lessons and replicability in LDCs

Chair: **Tanja A. Boerzel**
Professor of Political Science
Chair
Centre for European Integration
Free University of Berlin
Germany

Co-Chair: **Boris Pleskovic**
Research Manager
The World Bank
Washington D.C.

Speakers: **Nicola de Michelis**
Head of Unit
Development of Cohesion Policy
European Commission
Brussels

Rolf J. Langhammer
Professor
VicePresident
Kiel Institute of World Economics
Germany

Philippe Martin
Paris School of Economics
Université Paris 1 Panthéon Sorbonne
France

11.45-12.00	*Coffee break*

12.00-1.30 p.m.   **Session VII:**
"Spatial Policy for Growth and Equity"
- When does it make sense to invest on convergence – Is there a workable typology?
- What policies and investment options have worked and what haven't and why?
- Are there clear regional distinctions?
- Impact of the political economy, institutions, ethnicity, conflict.
- Evaluation of experience and outcomes of different options:
  — connectivity to markets
  — development of local competitive advantages
  — longerterm investment in human capital
  — investments in labor assimilation in cities
  — subsidizing lagging regions' growth.
- What are the potentially fruitful areas for policy exploration?
- Infrastructure pre-conditions to national growth and multi-country corridors for regional integration.

Chair: **Indermit Gill**
Director
World Development Report 2009
The World Bank
Washington D.C.

Co-Chair: **Astrid Kuehl**
Director
Development Policy Forum
InWEnt Capacity Building International
Germany

Speakers: **Grzegorz Gorzelak**
Professor of Economics
Director
Centre for European Regional and Local Studies
Warsaw University
Poland

Peter Nijkamp
Professor
Department of Spatial Economies
Free University of Amsterdam
The Netherlands

Lucia Wegner
Senior Economist
African Economic Outlook
OECD Development Centre
Organisation for Economic Cooperation and
Development (OECD)
Paris

1.30-2.00 p.m.	*Wrap-up discussions and implications for WDR 2009*

Closing and Outlook: **Indermit Gill**
Director
World Development Report 2009
The World Bank
Washington D.C.

Closing Words: **Astrid Kuehl**
Director
Development Policy Forum
InWEnt - Capacity Building International
Germany

The New World **Claudia von Monbart**
Bank Office in Senior Counsellor
Berlin: External Affairs
The World Bank
Paris and Berlin

2.00 p.m. *Farewell Buffet*

Venue Hotel Grand Hyatt Berlin
Library
Marlene-Dietrich-Platz 2
10785 Berlin
Germany

T +49 30 2553 1234
F +49 30 2553 1235
berlin@hyatt.de

http://berlin.grand.hyatt.de

Appendix 1: Participants

Tanja Boerzel
Professor of Political Science
Chair
Centre for European Integration
Freie Universitaet Berlin (FU)
Ihnestrasse 22
14195 Berlin
Germany
fon: 0049 30 8385-4830
fax: 0049 30 8385-5049
e-mail: boerzel@zedat.fu-berlin.de

Mantang Cai
Deputy Director and Associate Professor
Beijing Development Institute
Peking University
5 Yiheyuan Lu
Haidan District
Beijing
People's Republic of China
fon: 0086 10 82529560
fax: 0086 10 82529538
e-mail: mtcai@pku.edu.cn

Paul Collier
Professor of Economics
University of Oxford
Director
Centre for the Study of African Economies
  (CSAE)
Professorial Fellows
St Anthony's College
Manor Road Building, Manor Road
OX1 3UQ Oxford
United Kingdom
fon: 0044 186527-1089
fax: 0044 186527-1094
e-mail: paul.collier@economics.ox.ac.uk

Angel de la Fuente Moreno
Associate Professor
Institute of Economic Analysis (IEA)
Higher Council of Scientific research (CSIC)
Universitat Autònoma de Barcelona (UAB)
08193 Bellaterra, Barcelona
Spain
fon: 0034 9 35806612
fax: 0034 9 35801452
e-mail: Angel.DeLaFuente@iae.sisc.es
Angel.DeLaFuente@uab.es

Nicola De Michelis
Head of Unit
Development of Cohesion Policy & Accession
  Negotiations
Directorate General (DG) for Regional Policy
European Commission
Avenue de Tervuren 41
1049 Brussels
Belgium
fon: 0032-2/2955230
fax: 0032-2/29 94684
    0032-2/29 63271
e-mail: Nicola.De-Michelis@ec.europa.eu

Manfred Fischer
Professor of Economic Geography
Institute for Economic Geography and
  GIScience
Vienna University of Economics and
  Business Administration
Nordbergstr. 15/4/Sector A
1090 Vienna
Austria
fon: 0043 1 313364836
fax: 0043 1 31336 703
e-mail: manfred.fischer@wu-wien.ac.at

Indermit Gill
Director World Development Report 2009
The World Bank
1818 H Street, NW
20433 Washington, D.C.
USA
fon: 001 202 4733449
fax: 001 202 5220308
e-mail: igill@worldbank.org

Grzegorz Gorzelak
Director
Centre for European Regional and Local
  Studies (EUROREG)
Professor of Economics
University of Warsaw
Krakowskie Przedmiescie 30
00-927 Warsaw
Poland
fon: 0048 22 82616-54
    0048 22 5520-106
fax: 0048 22 82621-68
e-mail: ggorzelak@uw.edu.pl
gorzelak@post.pl.

Eduardo Haddad
Associate Professor
Department of Economics
University of São Paulo
Av. Professor Luciano Gualberto, 908
05508-900 São Paulo
Brazil
fon: 0055 11 3818 1444
fax: 0055 11 3032 8334
e-mail: ehaddad@usp.br

Steven Haggblade
Professor of International Development
Department of Agricultural Economics
Michigan State University
202 Agriculture Hall
MI 48824-1039 East Lansing
USA
fon: 001 517 355-0257
fax: 001 517 432-1800
e-mail: blade@msu.edu

Michael Hofmann
Director-General
Global and Sectoral Tasks - European and
  Multilateral Development Policy - Africa -
  Middle East
Federal Ministry for Economic Cooperation
  and Development (BMZ)
Stresemannstrasse 94
10963 Berlin
Germany
fon: 0049 1888 535-2800
fax: 0049 1888 535-4800
e-mail: michael.hofmann@bmz.bund.de

Robert Kappel
Professor
President
GIGA German Institute of Global and Area
  Studies
Neuer Jungfernstieg 21
20354 Hamburg
Germany
fon: 0049 40 42825-501
fax: 0049 40 42825-547
e-mail: kappel@giga-hamburg.de

Aehyung Kim
Consultant
The World Bank
1818 H Street NW
20433 Washington, D.C.
USA
fon: 001 202 4588853
fax: 001 202 5220304
e-mail: akim3@worldbank.org

Gudrun Kochendörfer-Lucius
Managing Director
InWEnt – Capacity Building International
Friedrich-Ebert-Allee 40
53113 Bonn
Germany
fon: 0049 228-4460-1522/
     0049 30-43996-338
fax: 0049 228-4460-1529
e-mail: gudrun.kochendoerfer@inwent.org

Adama Konseiga
Lecturer
Research Afiliate
Economics Department
GREDI (Research Group in Economics and
  International Development)
Faculty of Administration
University of Sherbrooke
2500 Boulevard Université Sherbrooke
  (Quebec)
J1K 2R1 Quebec
Canada
fon: 001 819 821-7000/ -61940
     001 418 266 1223
fax: 001 819 5801342
     001 418 2661225
e-mail: akonseiga@aphrc.org
Adama.Konseiga@USherbrooke.ca
akonseiga@yahoo.com

Frauke Kraas
Professor for Human Geography
Chair for Urban and Cultural Geography
Department of Geography
University of Cologne
Albertus-Magnus-Platz
50923 Köln
Germany
fon: 0049 221 470-7050
fax: 0049 221 470-4917
e-mail: f.kraas@uni-koeln.de

Astrid Kuehl
Director
Development Policy Forum
InWEnt - Capacity Building International,
  Germany
Stresemannstr. 92
10963 Berlin
Germany
fon: 0049 30 43996-311
fax: 0049 30 43996-250
e-mail: astrid.kuehl@inwent.org

Rolf J. Langhammer
Professor
Vice-President
Kiel Institute for the World Economy
Duesternbrooker Weg 120
24105 Kiel
Germany
fon: 0049 431 8814203
fax: 0049 431 8814524
e-mail: rolf.langhammer@ifw-kiel.de

Peter Lanjouw
Lead Economist
Development Economics Research Group
  (DECRG)
The World Bank
1818 H Street NW
Washington, D.C.
USA
e-mail: planjouw@worldbank.org

Ingo Liefner
Professor
Department of Economic Geography
Institute of Geography
Justus Liebig University Giessen
Senckenbergstr. 1
35390 Giessen
Germany
fon: 0049 641 9936220
fax: 0049 641 9936209
e-mail: ingo.liefner@geogr.uni-giessen.de

Philippe Martin
Professor of Economics
Paris School of Economics
Maison des Sciences Economiques
Bureau 309
106-112, boulevard de l'Hôpital
75013 Paris
France
fon: 0033 1 44078265
e-mail: Philippe.Martin@univ-paris1.fr

Roman Mogilevsky
Executive Director
Center for Social and Economic Research
  (CASE)-Kyrgyzstan
Apt. 1, House 21
Microrayon 3
720064 Bishkek
Kyrgyz Republic
fon: 00996 312 492504
fax: 00996 312 595663
e-mail: rmogilevsky@hotmail.com

Hassen Mohamed
Chief Director
Planning, Policy Coordination and
  Advisory Unit
The Presidency
The Presidency Private Bag X 1000
0001 Pretoria
South Africa
fon: 0027 12 300-5455
fax: 0027 86 683-5455
e-mail: hassen@po.gov.za

Marisela Montoliu Muñoz
Senior Adviser and Head
Spatial and Local Development Unit
Sustainable Development Network (SDN)
The World Bank
1818 H Street NW
Washington, D.C.
USA
fon: 001 202 4737583
fax: 001 202 5223481
e-mail: Mmontoliumunoz@worldbank.org

Wim Naudé
Senior Research Fellow
UNU-WIDER
Katajanokanlaituri 6 B
00160 Helsinki
Finland
fon: 00358 9 61599-236
fax: 00358 9 61599-333
e-mail: Wim@wider.unu.edu

Peter Nijkamp
Professor in Regional Economics and
  Economic Geography
Department of Spatial Economics
Faculty of Economics and Business
  Administration
Free University of Amsterdam (VU)
De Boelelaan 1105
1081 HV Amsterdam
The Netherlands
fon: 0031 20 5986090
fax: 0031 20 5986004
e-mail: pnijkamp@feweb.vu.nl

Boris Pleskovic
Research Manager
The World Bank
1818 H Street NW
20433 Washington, D.C.
USA
fon: 001 202 4731062
fax: 001 202 522 0304
e-mail: bpleskovic@worldbank.org

Diego Puga
Research Professor of Economics
Madrid Institute for Advanced Studies
  (IMDEA)
Universidad Carlos III
Madrid 126
28903 Getafe
Spain
fon: 0034 93 542-2871
fax: 0034 93 542-1860
e-mail: diego.puga@imdea.org

Ludwig Schaetzl
Professor Emeritus of Economic Geography
Leibniz University of Hannover
Member of the Scientific Advisory Council
Ministry for Economic Cooperation and
  Development (BMZ)
Schneiderberg 50
30167 Hannover
Germany
fon: 0049 511 762 - 3536
                   - 4496
fax: 0049 511 7623051
e-mail: schaetzl@wigeo.uni-hannover.de

Lee Boon-Thong
Professor
Department of Geography
University of Malaya
50603 Kuala Lumpur
Malaysia
fon: 0060 3 79675605
fax: 0060 3 79675457
e-mail: leebt@um.edu.my

Frank van Oort
Professor of Urban Economics and
  Spatial Planning
Department of Economic Geography
Faculty of Geosciences
Utrecht University
P.O. Box 80115
3508-TC Utrecht
The Netherlands
fon: 0031 30 253 4437
mobile: 0031 654 998 5553
fax: 0031 30 254 0604
e-mail: f.vanoort@geo.uu.nl

Anthony Venables
Professor of Economics
University of Oxford
Chief Economist
Department for International Development
  (DFID)
1 Palace Street
SW1E 5HE London
United Kingdom
fon: 0044 20 70230522
fax: 0044 20 70230636
e-mail: A-Venables@dfid.gov.uk
tony.venables@economics.ox.ac.uk

Claudia von Monbart
Senior Counsellor
External Affairs
The World Bank
Paris and Berlin
66, avenue d'Iéna
75116 Paris
France
fon: 0033 1 40693014
fax: 0033 1 47237436
e-mail: cvonmonbart@worldbank.org

Lucia Wegner
Senior Economist
African Economic Outlook
OECD Development Centre
Organisation for Economic Co-operation and
 Development (OECD)
2, rue André Pascal
75775 Paris Cedex 16
France
fon: 0033 1 4524-9606
fax: 0033 1 44306150
e-mail: Lucia.Wegner@oecd.org

Juergen Zattler
Head of Division
World Bank Group - IMF - debt relief -
 international financial architecture
Federal Ministry for Economic Cooperation
 and Development (BMZ)
Stresemannstrasse 94
10963 Berlin
Germany
fon: 0049 1888 535-2709
fax: 0049 1888 535-2632
e-mail: zattler@bmz.bund.de

Observers:

Annette Baehring
Head of Unit
Regional and Local Governance,
 Decentralisation
Gesellschaft für Technische Zusammenarbeit
 (GTZ)
Dag-Hammarskjöld-Weg 1-5
65760 Eschborn
Germany
fon: 0049 6196 791660
fax: 0049 6196 79801660
e-mail: Annette.Baehring@gtz.de

Souleymane Coulibaly
Young Professional
DECWD
The World Bank
1818 H Street NW
20433 Washington, D.C.
USA
fon: 001 202 473 9845
fax: 001 202 640 8363
e-mail: scoulibaly2@worldbank.org

Uwe Deichmann
Senior Environmental Specialist
Development Research Group
Infrastructure and Environment
The World Bank
1818 H Street NW
20433 Washington, D.C.
USA
fon: 001 202 473-6400
fax: 001 202 522-0308
e-mail: udeichmann@worlbank.org

Paul Dorosh
Senior Economist
Rural and Spatial Development
Spatial and Local Development Team
The World Bank
1818 H Street NW
20433 Washington, D.C.
USA
fon: 001 202 458-4419
fax: 001 202 522-3481
e-mail: pdorosh@worldbank.org

Gerd Fleischer
Senior Policy Advisor
Division Agriculture, Fisheries and Food
Gesellschaft für Tecnische Zusammenarbeit
  (GTZ)
Dag-Hammarskjöld-Weg 1-5
65760 Eschborn
Germany
fon: 0049 6196 791432
fax: 0049 6196 797170
e-mail: gerd.fleischer@gtz.de

Maria Emilia Freire
Senior Adviser
Sustainable Development Network
The World Bank
1818 H Street NW
20433 Washington, D.C.
USA
fon: 001 202 473-9508
e-mail: mfreire@worldbank.org

Chorching Goh
Senior Economist
Develoment Report 2009
Development Economics
The World Bank
1818 H Street NW
20433 Washington, D.C.
USA
fon: 001 202 4580123
fax: 001 202 5220308
e-mail: cgoh@worldbank.org

Vivian Hon
Senior Economist
Spatial and Local Development Team
Sustainable Development Network
The World Bank
1818 H Street NW
20433 Washington, D.C.
USA
fon: 001 202 473-3429
fax: 001 202 522-3481
e-mail: vhon@worldbank.org

Andreas Kopp
Lead Transport Economist
ETWTR
The World Bank
1818 H Street NW
20433 Washington D.C.
USA
e-mail: akopp@worldbank.org

Somik Lall
Senior Economist
Spatial and Local Development
Sustainable Development Network
The World Bank
1818 H Street NW
20433 Washington, D.C.
USA
fon: 001 202 4585315
fax: 001 202 5223481
e-mail: slall1@worldbank.org

Khulekani Mathe
Senior Policy Analyst
The Presidency
Private Bag X 1000
0001 Pretoria
South Africa
fon: 0027 12 300-5383
fax: 0027 86 683-5383
e-mail: khulekani@po.gov.za

Nils-Henning Meyer
Principle Sector Economist
Agriculture and Environment
KfW Entwicklungsbank (KfW
  Development Bank)
Palmengartenstr. 5-9
60325 Frankfurt am Main
Germany
fon: 0049 69 7431-2364
fax: 0049 69 7431-3605
e-mail: nils.meyer@kfw.de

Ulrich Nitschke
Head of Division
Development Education Service Agency
  Communities in One World
InWEnt - Capacity Building International
Friedrich-Ebert-Allee 40
53113 Bonn
Germany
fon: 0049 228 4460-1634
    0049 228 4460-2634
fax: 0049 228 4460-1635
e-mail: ulrich.nitschke@inwent.org

Truman Packard
Senior Economist
Human Development Economics Europe and
  Central Asia
Regional Office
The World Bank
fon: 0044- 207-592-8406
Cell: 0044- 7814-600905
WB Tieline: 5783-8406
e-mail: tpackard@worldbank.org

Gerhard Ressel
Desk Officer
Division 301: World Bank Group; IMF; debt
  relief; international financial architecture
Federal Ministry for Economic Cooperation
  and Development (BMZ)
Stresemannstrasse 94
10963 Berlin
Germany
fon: 0049 30 18535-2786
fax: 0049 30 1810535-2786
e-mail: Gerhard.Ressel@bmz.bund.de

Guenther Taube
Director
Dep. 2: Intern. Regulatory Framework / Good
  Governance / Economic Policy
InWEnt – Capacity Building International
Friedrich-Ebert-Allee 40
53113 Bonn
Germany
fon: 0049 228 44601 – 800
    0049 30 43996 – 200
fax: 0049 228 44601 – 090
e-mail: guenther.taube@inwent.org

Hirotsugu Uchida
Assistant Professor
University of Rhode Island
Consultant
The World Bank
1818 H Street NW
20433 Wahington, D.C.
USA
fon: 001 202 458-1656
e-mail : huchida@worldbank.org

Themes for the

11TH ANNUAL BERLIN WORKSHOP SERIES

Berlin, Germany

"CLIMATE GOVERNANCE AND DEVELOPMENT"

September 28–30, 2008

Climate Change as a Development Priority

Energy and Development: Policies and Technologies

Natural Resource Governance for Adaptation, Migration, and Development

Development, Non-State Actors, and Climate Governance: Private Sector and NGOs

Financing Adaptation and Mitigation in an Unequal World

Changing Climate, Changing Institutions of Governance

www.ingramcontent.com/pod-product-compliance
Lightning Source LLC
Chambersburg PA
CBHW080228270326
41926CB00020B/4188